The Rural South in Crisis

Rural Studies Series

Published in cooperation with
the Southern Rural Development Center

The Rural South in Crisis
Challenges for the Future

edited by Lionel J. Beaulieu

Westview Press / Boulder and London

1988

Rural Studies Series, Sponsored by the Rural Sociological Society

This Westview softcover edition is printed on acid-free paper and bound in softcovers that carry the highest rating of the National Association of State Textbook Administrators, in consultation with the Association of American Publishers and the Book Manufacturers' Institute.

Published in 1988 in the United States of America by Westview Press, Inc.; Frederick A. Praeger, Publisher; 5500 Central Avenue, Boulder, Colorado 80301

Library of Congress Cataloging-in-Publication Data
The Rural South in crisis: challenges for the future/edited by
  Lionel J. Beaulieu.
    p. cm.—(Rural studies series)
  Includes index.
  ISBN 0-8133-7569-X
  1. Southern States—Rural conditions—Congresses. 2. Rural
development—Southern States—Congresses. 3. Agriculture—Economic
aspects—Southern States—Congresses. I. Beaulieu, Lionel J.
II. Series: Rural studies series of the Rural Sociological Society.
HN79.A13R87 1988
307.7′2′0973—dc19   87-35193
                                                                     CIP

Printed and bound in the United States of America

The paper used in this publication meets the requirements of the American National Standard for Permanence of Paper for Printed Library Materials Z39.48-1984.

6   5   4   3   2   1

Contents

Part II
CURRENT SOCIOECONOMIC ISSUES IN THE RURAL SOUTH

Part III
AGRICULTURE AND RURAL DEVELOPMENT POLICIES: PAST
REFLECTIONS, FUTURE DIRECTIONS

Part IV
OPPORTUNITIES FOR THE VITALIZATION OF THE RURAL SOUTH

Preface

To the casual observer, the South represents a truly vibrant and dynamic region of the United States. It is no easy task, therefore, to dedicate an entire volume to a subject that systematically reveals the serious flaws associated with this imagery. Despite the progress that has touched many Southerners in recent decades, a number of the region's rural residents remain mired in a state of economic and social deprivation.

In an effort to call attention to the plight of rural Southerners, the Southern Rural Development Center (SRDC), located at Mississippi State University, sponsored this volume dealing with the subject of "The Rural South in Crisis." I was fortunate to be awarded a faculty development grant with the SRDC to give leadership to this effort.

The present volume captures the views of people who are prominent students of rural America. Treatment is given to the serious state of affairs in rural areas of the South and to the possible strategies for stimulating long-term improvements in the well-being of rural Southerners. In the final analysis, if the volume spurs policymakers, leaders, and rural residents to redress the ills of the rural South, it will have been a most worthwhile effort.

Lionel J. Beaulieu

Acknowledgements

No product of this magnitude can be undertaken without the assistance and support of a number of individuals. Special thanks are extended to chapter authors for their untiring efforts to develop and refine their manuscripts, even under the most difficult timetables.

Sarah McLeod Knox, a publications editor in the Editorial Department, Institute of Food and Agricultural Sciences, provided technical editing for the volume, an effort she carried out in a most diligent, capable and professional manner.

Few words can capture the vital role that the staff of the Southern Rural Development Center, Mississippi State University, performed in bringing this edited book to fruition. Much of the financial support for this volume was provided by the Center. Dr. Doss Brodnax, Director of the SRDC, gave unselfishly of his time to facilitate completion of this product. Bonnie Teater shouldered much of the burden of producing the typeset version of this book. She is, without a doubt, the most talented and dedicated individual in a support staff position that I have had the good fortune of working with in my professional career. Moreover, I thank the entire SRDC staff for providing me with a most enriching experience during my one-year faculty development program leave with the Center.

To Dr. Susanne Fisher and Dr. John Woeste, administrators with the Institute of Food and Agricultural Sciences, University of Florida, I express my appreciation for their approval of my time to complete work on this volume.

The support of the Rural Sociological Society is sincerely appreciated, as is the guidance provided by Dr. Fred Buttel in his role as Chairman of the Society's Rural Studies Series Editorial Board. Finally, to my wife Barbara, and to my children, Brian and Andrea, I express my love and gratitude for their constant words of support during the countless months involved in the preparation of this volume.

L.J.B.

Contributors

DON E. ALBRECHT is Associate Professor in the Department of Rural Sociology at Texas A & M University. He is also research scientist with the Texas Real Estate Research Center at Texas A & M. Albrecht received his master's degree from Utah State University and his Ph.D. from Iowa State University. He currently is principal investigator for a project on farm failures in the United States.

EMERSON M. BABB is the Ben Hill Griffin, Jr. Professor at the University of Florida. He joined the Florida staff following 25 years as Professor at Purdue University. Babb has over 300 research publications in the areas of dairy marketing, regulatory activities, public policy and business management. He has a master's degree from Virginia Polytechnic Institute and State University and a Ph.D. from The Pennsylvania State University.

E. YVONNE BEAUFORD is Associate Professor in Sociology and a member of the research faculty at Fort Valley State College in Georgia. Her research interests and publications are in the areas of rural poverty, rural development policy, and the structure of agriculture, particularly as it relates to minority farm households.

LIONEL J. BEAULIEU is Associate Professor in the Institute of Food and Agricultural Sciences at the University of Florida. He received his master's degree and Ph.D. from Purdue University. His primary areas of research include community/agricultural linkages, adoption/diffusion of agricultural technology and rural development.

DWIGHT B. BILLINGS is Associate Professor in the Department of Sociology at the University of Kentucky. He has been with the University of Kentucky since 1974. His major teaching and research interests include social change, social stratification, social theory, and sociology of religion. He received his master's and doctoral degrees from the University of North Carolina at Chapel Hill.

JANET L. BOKEMEIER is Associate Professor of Sociology at the University of Kentucky. She received her Ph.D. in Rural Sociology from Iowa State University. Her research interests focus on gender, work, and family issues in American rural society.

ANNE S. DEATON received her master's degree from the University of Tennessee and her doctorate in adult and continuing education from the Virginia Polytechnic Institute and State University. Her research interests are focused on the productivity of older adults, and on aging issues in developing counties.

BRADY J. DEATON is Associate Director of the Office of International Development at Virginia Polytechnic Institute and State University. Deaton is also Professor and Extension Economist in the Department of Agricultural Economics at VPI. His master's degree in diplomacy and international commerce is from the University of Kentucky. His Ph.D. is from the University of Wisconsin.

ANN Z. DELLENBARGER is a Research Associate at Louisiana State University. She holds a master's degree in public administration from Harvard University. She is currently completing a Ph.D. degree in rural sociology at LSU. Dellenbarger's research areas of interest have included rural economic development and the sociology of agriculture.

FORREST A. DESERAN is Associate Professor with the Department of Sociology and Rural Sociology at Louisiana State University. Deseran received his master's degree and Ph.D. from Colorado State University. His primary work has dealt with community satisfaction and decisionmaking, social networks, sex roles, off-farm employment, and rural labor markets.

PATRICIA A. DUFFY is Assistant Professor of Agricultural Economics at Auburn University. She received a Ph.D. in Agricultural Economics from Texas A & M University in 1985. Duffy teaches and conducts research in the areas of agricultural policy and agricultural production economics.

LORRAINE E. GARKOVICH is Associate Professor in the Department of Sociology at the University of Kentucky. Her research focuses on two areas: patterns of family and work roles in farm households and consequences of population change in rural communities. Garkovich received her Ph.D. in sociology from the University of Missouri with a specialization in demography.

GARY P. GREEN is Assistant Professor in the Department of Sociology at the University of Georgia. From 1983-1985, Green served on the faculty at East Carolina University. His primary research interests are rural sociology, political economy and social organization. Green received his M.S. and Ph.D. degrees from the University of Missouri.

JUDITH C. HACKETT is Director of the Council of State Governments' Center for Agriculture and Rural Development. The center operates a national information clearinghouse, conducts policy research, and provides conferences and technical assistance for state policymakers. She joined the Council of State Governments in 1982 after eight years with the state of Kansas.

DAVID H. HARRINGTON is Deputy Director of the Agriculture and Rural Economics Division of Economic Research Service, U. S. Department of Agriculture. From 1980 to 1986, he was Chief of the Farm and Rural Economy Branch of ERS where he was responsible for research on the structure of agriculture and rural communities. Harrington has his master's degree from the University of New Hampshire and his Ph.D. from Purdue University.

MARK S. HENRY is Professor of Agricultural Economics at Clemson University. His primary research areas include regional economics, rural development policy, government finance and natural resources. Henry received his Ph.D. from Kansas State University.

RONALD D. KNUTSON is Professor and Extension Economist in agricultural policy and marketing at Texas A & M University. His research and extension program concentrates on the impact of alternative farm programs on agriculture. Knutson received his master's degree from The Pennsylvania State University and his Ph.D. from the University of Minnesota.

DANIEL T. LICHTER is Associate Professor of Sociology and faculty associate of the Population Issues Research Center, Institute for Policy Research and Evaluation, The Pennsylvania State University. He received his Ph.D. in sociology in 1981 from the University of Wisconsin - Madison. His current research focuses on underemployment and inequality in rural labor markets, patterns of nonmetropolitan population redistribution, and internal migration in the United States.

BURL F. LONG is Professor and undergraduate coordinator in the Food and Resource Economics Department at the University of Florida. Long received his M.S. degree from Oklahoma State University and his doctorate from The Pennsylvania State University. His primary research interests are in the area of rural economic development and natural resource policy.

THOMAS A. LYSON holds a teaching and research position at Cornell University in the Department of Sociology. He received his Ph.D. from Michigan State University in 1976 and has been on the faculty at Clemson University. He is co-author, with William W. Falk, of *Hi-Tech, Low-Tech, No Tech: Recent Occupational and Industrial Changes in the South* (SUNY-Albany Press, 1988).

DEBORAH M. MARKLEY is Adjunct Assistant Professor with the Department of Agriculture and Resource Economics at the University of Massachusetts. Her primary research experience involves the functioning of rural capital markets, agricultural lending of commercial banks and Farm Credit Service institutions, and shift-share analysis and the business cycle in rural counties. She received her Ph.D. from Virginia Polytechnic Institute and State University.

KEVIN T. McNAMARA is Assistant Professor and Rural Development Economist in the Department of Agricultural Economics and the Institute of Community and Area Development, University of Georgia. He received his Ph.D. from the Virginia Polytechnic Institute and State University. McNamara's research, extension, and teaching activities are in the area of rural economic development. His current research focus is on location decisions, and the relationship of human capital investment to economic growth.

MICHAEL K. MILLER is Director of the Center for Health Policy Research and Associate Professor in the Department of Medicine, University of Florida. He received his M.S. in sociology from Utah State University, and the Ph.D. in rural sociology from The Pennsylvania State University in 1975. Miller's research interests include health policy, policy and evaluation research and applied econometrics, community epidemiology, sociology of health and health service delivery systems in rural areas.

DAVID MULKEY is Associate Professor in the Food and Resource Economics Department, University of Florida. Prior to joining the staff of the University of Florida in 1977, Mulkey was with Clemson University. Mulkey received his master's degree in economics and his doctorate in agricultural economics from Clemson University.

STEVE H. MURDOCK is Professor and Head of the Department of Rural Sociology in the Texas Agricultural Experiment Station, Texas A & M University. He is the author or editor of six books and more than one hundred other publications. His published works are in the area of agriculture and natural resource use, including the socioeconomic dimensions and implications of the farm financial crisis on agricultural producers and rural areas. Murdock received his Ph.D. from the University of Kentucky.

MACK C. NELSON is Associate Professor of Agricultural Economics at Fort Valley State College. His research activities have focused on structure of agricultural issues (including the use of farm imputs and their effects on rural communities) and how farmers gather and use information in making farm production decisions. Nelson was awarded a Ph.D. degree in 1978 from the University of Illinois.

J. NORMAN REID is with the Economic Research Service, USDA, where he is Chief of the Rural Business and Government Branch, a group of economists and other social scientists conducting research on economic trends in rural communities and their governmental and policy implications. Before joining USDA in 1976, he was Assistant Director of the Illinois Commission on Intergovernmental Cooperation, a state legislative research agency. He received his Ph.D. in political science from the University of Illinois in 1975.

STUART A. ROSENFELD is Director of Research and Programs for the Southern Growth Policies Board and the Acting Director for the Southern Technology Council. Rosenfeld has written extensively on education, economic development, and technology policy issues. He received his doctorate in education planning, social policy, and administration from Harvard University.

LYLE P. SCHERTZ is Economist with the Economic Research Service at the U.S. Department of Agriculture. Since 1984, he has served as Editor of *Choices, The Magazine of Food, Farm and Resource Issues*. Schertz has served in various capacities at USDA including Deputy Administrator for Economic Research Service and Deputy Administrator for Foreign Economic Development Service. Schertz received his master's degree from the University of Illinois and his doctorate from the University of Minnesota.

JERRY R. SKEES is Associate Professor in the Department of Agricultural Economics at the University of Kentucky. Skees has been with the University of Kentucky since 1981. His master's degree is from the University of Kentucky and his Ph.D. is from Michigan State University. Skees' primary areas of concentration are agricultural policy, agricultural finance and risk analysis, systems science and simulation, and farm management.

LOUIS E. SWANSON is Associate Professor in the Department of Sociology at the University of Kentucky. The general focus of his research is on the socioeconomic organization and change of nonmetropolitan society. Swanson received his master's degree from North Carolina State University and his Ph.D. from The Pennsylvania State University.

KENNETH P. WILKINSON is Professor of Rural Sociology in the Department of Agricultural Economics and Rural Sociology at The Pennsylvania State University. During 1984-85, Wilkinson held the position of President of the Rural Sociological Society. He received his master's and doctoral degrees from Mississippi State University.

WILLIAM F. WINTER is former Governor of Mississippi. He is currently a senior partner in the law firm of Watkins Ludlam and Stennis in Jackson, Mississippi. Winter served as Chairman of the 1986 Commission on the Future of the South. He serves as Chairman of the Southern Region Education Board Commission on Quality in Education. Winter received his LL.B. from the University of Mississippi.

1

The Rural South in Crisis: An Introduction

Lionel J. Beaulieu

It is difficult to imagine that just a few short years ago, the overall health of rural America was believed to be showing signs of a major resurgence. Population growth was touching nearly all segments of the rural landscape (Beale, 1985; Brown, 1984; Lichter et al., 1985). The manufacturing, agriculture, mining, and energy-based sectors were expanding and adding strength to the economies of many rural communities (Beale and Fuguitt, 1986; Martinez, 1985; Pulver, 1986). Commonly used indices of well-being (such as per capita income and persons in poverty) were beginning to provide evidence that the welfare of rural citizens was slowly improving (Henry et al., 1986; Swanson and Skees, 1987; Winter, 1986). Surely, rural America had finally arrived.

But, the decade of the 1980s brought havoc to the rural countryside. A combination of international and domestic forces caused serious financial stress for many farm operators (Economic Research Service, 1985; 1986a; 1986b). While the Midwestern farm belt initially commanded much of the attention, it subsequently became all too clear that the "farm crisis" was more than a Midwest phenomenon, but a nationwide dilemma. Several reports put us on notice that farm-dependent communities were experiencing severe fiscal stress as a consequence of the troubled farm economy. Unfortunately, strains also were being evidenced by rural localities having little dependence on agriculture (Hite and Ulbrich, 1986; Lawson, 1986; Mueller, 1986; Petrulis et al., 1987; Reeder, 1987; U. S. Senate, 1986). Such stresses were being prompted, in large part, by a retrenchment or discontinuation in the activities of their manufacturing industries (Henry et al., 1986; Martinez, 1985; Wilkinson, 1986). Thus, by the mid-1980s, it became all too evident that the crisis enveloped many sectors of rural society beyond agriculture.

In many respects, the economic and social hardships that have made their presence felt across rural areas of the U.S. in recent years have forced rural development issues to be placed on the priority list of items being debated at the federal and state levels. The U.S. Senate report (1986) on *Governing the Heartland: Can Rural Communities Survive the Farm Crisis?*, the Joint Economic Committee/Congress of the United States study (1986) titled *New Dimensions in Rural Policy: Building Upon Our Heritage,* and the Economic Research Service's report (1987b) on *Rural Economic Development in the 1980s: Preparing for the Future* (a study commissioned by the U. S. Senate Appropriations Committee), are but simple reflections of the new wave of national interest that has surfaced regarding the hardships plaguing rural America.

WHY A FOCUS ON THE RURAL SOUTH?

As deliberations proceed on how best to respond to the problems of rural society in the U.S., it is critical that special attention be paid to the situation in the rural South. For one, demographics dictate the need to do so. The South has the highest proportion of any region in the U.S. of its residents living in nonmetropolitan areas (Rosenfeld et al., 1985). In addition, 93 percent of the blacks located in nonmetro areas of the U.S. reside in the South (Ghelfi, 1986). This region is home for nearly 40 percent of all the farms in the United States (Economic Research Service, 1986c) and, of all black-owned farm operations in the country, some 95 percent are located in the South (Hoppe et al., 1986).

But, the need to assess conditions in the rural South goes beyond simple demographics. The fact remains that on nearly all measures of well-being, the rural South emerges as the most ill-equipped region in the country. Consider the following facts:

1. The South is highest of any region in the country on: (a) the number of banks who discontinued financing on their farm loans; (b) the percentage of farmers who went out of business or who declared bankruptcy; (c) the percentage of farmers who were loaned up to their practical limit; and (d) the number of farmers with delinquent Farmers Home Administration loans (Economic Research Service, 1985; 1987a). Further, recent reports (see Economic Research Service, 1987a; King, 1987) suggest that while the Midwest has begun to turn the corner on financial stress, conditions have worsened in the South (due, in part, to the severe economic strains resulting from the drought of 1986).

2. Farmers in the South have the highest dependence on off-farm employment. In 1982, nearly 41 percent of the farm operators in the South worked 200 days or more off the farm; the U.S. figure was 34.4 percent (Beaulieu and Mulkey, 1986). Off-farm income is far more critical to Southern farm operators than to those in other regions of the country given that 82 percent of Southern farms are small in scale, with annual sales of less than $40,000. The national figure for farms in this sales category is 68 percent (U. S. Congress, 1986).

3. In contrast to other regions of the country, the rural South has the lowest median family income, the highest rates of unemployment/underemployment, the highest levels of poverty, and the highest rate of functional illiteracy (Lichter and Constanzo, 1986; MDC, Inc., 1986; Rosenfeld et al., 1985; Ross and Morrissey, 1987).

4. Dependence on nondurable manufacturing employment is highest in the rural South. The declining economic health of these traditional industries has placed severe hardships on Southern farm families who have been dependent on manufacturing for second incomes, and on rural residents who have little of the job skills needed to secure other employment (Hines and Petrulis, 1986; Lyson and Falk, 1986; Martinez, 1985).

Collectively, these factors provide the basis for asserting that the rural crisis now impacting our country is most prevalent in the rural areas of the South. What must be understood, however, is that the Southern version of the crisis is not simply a creature of the 1980s. Rather, it reflects a set of deeply-rooted conditions that have existed in the region for decades. Pertinent examples are worth outlining:

- **Low incomes persist in the rural South:** Of the 298 nonmetropolitan counties which ranked in the lowest per capita income quintile between 1950 and 1969, 231 remained in this persistent low income classification in 1979; better than 92 percent of these counties were located in the South (Hoppe, 1985).

- **Poverty continues to be highest in rural areas of the South:** When contrasted with other regions of the country, poverty levels were higher and median family incomes lower in the South both in 1970 and 1980. In fact, poverty levels in the rural South were still about 6 percent higher than in any other region of the country in 1980 (U. S. Congress, 1986). Present estimates show that 21 percent of the rural Southern population are now living in poverty, and the figure is moving upward (Johnson, 1986).

- **Educational attainment is lowest of any region in the country:** The proportion of college graduates in the rural South is 40 percent below the national average (MDC, Inc., 1986). Of the 489 counties in the U.S. having the lowest proportion of its adults with a high school education, nearly all are located in the South (Carlin and Ross, 1987). Further, functional illiteracy is much higher in the South than the rest of the nation. That is, approximately 25 percent of the adults in the South have less than an eighth grade education, a figure that is substantially higher than the 17 percent uncovered for the remainder of the United States (Southern Growth Policies Board, 1986).

- **Southern rural blacks continue to lag behind:** Even with the economic growth of the 1970s, the per capita income of rural black Southerners barely reached 30 percent of the U.S. average in 1980 (MDC, Inc., 1986). Most telling have been the poverty statistics for these individuals: more than 58 percent of black rural females were living in poverty in 1983; over three-fourths of rural black children under 18 years old living in a female-headed household were poor in 1983; and for rural black children under six years of age in a female-headed household, some 80 percent fell below the poverty threshold (Johnson, 1986). Exacerbating the situation has been a Southern industrial expansion that essentially has by-passed the bulk of rural areas having sizable minority populations (Ghelfi, 1986).

Thus, as attention is focused on strategies for addressing the needs of rural America, it is clear that the rural South offers the perfect laboratory for study given the complex set of social, economic and demographic forces at play in this region—forces that are unmatched by any other region of the United States. The collection of works contained in this volume is designed to provide a broader understanding of the nature and magnitude of the rural crisis in the Southern region. Moreover, it explores the mix of strategies that hold promise for introducing improvements in the quality of life of rural Southerners in particular, and rural Americans in general.

AN OVERVIEW OF THE VOLUME

The chapters contained in this volume represent the thoughts and views of leading scholars of rural society in the United States and the South. Collectively, they raise some disturbing issues regarding the South's poor educational performance, the region's fragile farm/nonfarm economy, the persistence of poverty, and the absence of strong visionary leaders at the local level. But, they do offer a glimmer of hope that with a renewed commitment to addressing the region's fundamental problems, the future can hold promise of a better life for those residing in rural communities of the South.

The purpose of *The Rural South in Crisis: Challenges for the Future* volume is fourfold:

- To articulate the dimensions of the agricultural/rural community crisis in the South;

- To examine current socioeconomic issues that are of critical importance to the well being of agriculture and rural communties in the region;

- To assess the impacts of past agriculture/rural development policies on the South and to delineate the directions that such policies might take in the future;

- To identify opportunities for vitalizing the rural South.

COMPONENTS OF THE CRISIS

Part I begins with a treatment of the historical forces that have helped shape the South. Billings notes that the Southern version of the crisis is intimately tied to the historical patterns of social, economic and political development in the region. He traces the evolution of three distinct subregions within the South—the Plantation South, the Upcountry, and the Applachian South. He argues that the different routes that each pursued to Southern modernity have left a mark that continues to influence their development today.

Consideration also is given in Part I to the various areas in which the crisis has manifested itself; in the agricultural and nonfarm areas of the region, in rural communities, and in the human sufferings of rural Southerners. Harrington suggests that the structure of Southern agriculture, with its preponderance of small-scale farmers who are heavily dependent on off-farm employment, has served to shelter many farm operators from the financial stresses evident in other regions of the country. However, problems areas do exist; for example, the percentage of farmers going out of business and the number of farm operators filing for bankruptcy are highest in the South.

Conditions that once proved favorable to economic development have now become the millstone around the neck of the rural South, exclaims Rosenfeld in his chapter. No longer are low taxes, low wages, limited-skilled employees, and a poorly developed community infrastructure attractive to the high growth industries of today. Presenting key social and economic data on the region, Rosenfeld paints a clear picture of the characteristics of the rural South's workforce that have severely limited the area's economic development potential.

Wilkinson states that the problems of the rural South reflect, to a great degree, a crisis *of* community. That crisis has at least four dimensions. Two of these—providing sufficient jobs/income and local services to meet the daily needs of people in the locality—are concerns that contribute to the problem of community. The remaining two dimensions, namely social inequality and poor social integration, cause rifts in the structure of local social life. The key to rural well-being in the South, claims Wilkinson, is community development—building the capacity for self-help and self-direction through community action.

The human distress experienced by countless people in the South is an integral part of the crisis in the rural South. Swanson describes the breath and characteristics of the human costs associated with the crisis in the region. In focusing on poverty, health care, employment, education, and racism, he presents a somber view of the human misery in the South, a condition that he states must no longer go unnoticed in rural policy deliberations.

KEY SOCIOECONOMIC ISSUES IN THE SOUTH

In moving beyond a discussion of those elements directly associated with the agricultural/rural community crisis, Part II gives treatment to a broader series of socioeconomic forces that influence the vitality of rural and agricultural communities in the region. Beauford and Nelson present a timely review of the status of black farm operators in the South. They note that in almost all Southern states, the number of black-operated farms has eroded, and the decline has been accompanied by a sizable reduction in the number of farmland acres owned by blacks. While most black-operated farms generate annual farm sales of less than $10,000, black farmers are often unable to supplement their meager farm income with off-farm work since many lack the basic skills needed to secure off-farm employment. But beyond this, most counties in which black farms are concentrated are among the poorest in the South and, as a result, are unable to capture any type of economic activity needed to stimulate jobs.

The critical role that farm women play in the childhood socialization process is the focus of the Garkovich and Bokemeier chapter. Employing data collected in a statewide mail study in Kentucky, they examine the relative importance of individual, household, and farm structure characteristics and attitudes toward farming on farm women's satisfaction. They suggest that the farm women's view of the quality of life associated with farming may affect the messages that they pass on to their children regarding farming as a vocation.

Skees and Swanson present an interesting piece on the relationship between farm structure and community well-being. Using 1970 and 1980 nonmetropolitan county-level data on 13 Southern states, the authors seek to retest and refine the Goldschmidt hypothesis which argues that rural community quality of life is associated with the structure of agriculture in the locality. Results of their study lend little support to the Goldschmidt hypothesis. Rather, Skees and Swanson demonstrate that many factors are needed to explain changes in community well-being.

Rural areas in the South will have to diversify their economic bases to weather the economic crises brought on by the farm financial problem and increased global competition, states Markley. But, the success of this initiative will be dependent on access to investment capital. With banks now operating in a deregulated environment, the question is whether they will agree to funnel resources to help stimulate rural economic growth. Markley provides an important and innovative framework for assessing the impacts of financial deregulation on rural capital availability.

The large cadre of Southern farmers who work off the farm is clear evidence of the close tie that exists between farming and the local labor market. Utilizing a unique set of data on local labor markets generated from commuting to work patterns of residents, Deseran and Dellenbarger explore the effects of industrial composition and location of local labor markets on part-time farm households in the South.

Employment experiences of blacks living in nonmetropolitan areas of the South is the central theme of the article prepared by Lichter. His focus is threefold: (1) to examine changes in the nature and extent of underemployment among rural blacks in the region over the 1970-85 period; (2) to assess underemployment conditions of rural blacks relative to Southern metropolitan-based blacks, Southern whites, and blacks residing outside the region; and (3) to identify determinants of black underemployment in the rural South. Lichter finds that race continues to be a key axis of social differentiation and inequality in the region.

Albrecht and Murdock give attention to the effects of the farm crisis on rural communities. Based on a study of three communties in Texas, the authors hypothesize that residents' perceptions of the impacts associated with the farm crisis are closely linked to the community's level of dependence on agriculture. Their findings provide important empirical support for this argument.

Consideration must be given to approaches that show sensitivity to the broader community context in which agriculture functions if we are to deal effectively with the financial crisis in agriculture, claim Beaulieu, Miller and Mulkey. Toward this end, the authors undertake a systematic assessment of the impacts that community changes have on the local farm sector. Specifically, they examine the impacts of socioeconomic and inputs factors on the structure of local farms. Utilizing secondary data on all counties in the South, the authors conclude that the strength of the relationship between the community and its farm sector is primarily a function of farm scale of operation. Consequently, community based strategies for assisting financially stressed farmers are likely to be successful when targeted to smaller scale farmers, but less so when directed to larger scale farm operators.

FARM AND RURAL DEVELOPMENT POLICY CONSIDERATIONS

The third thrust of this volume is on agriculture and rural development policies. Part III begins with a treatment of national farm policy initiatives. Duffy and Knutson provide an important synopsis of past and present federal farm programs and the impacts they have had on Southern agriculture. Moreover, they discuss future farm policy options, including continuation of the 1985 Farm Bill, reductions in target prices, and mandatory production controls. Duffy and Knutson delineate the key role that the South could play in formulating future farm policy given its long history of dominance of Senate and House agriculture and appropriations committees.

The major restructuring taking place in the rural South's economy provides the backdrop within which future development strategies for the rural South must be considered, claim Mulkey and Henry. The authors suggest that choices must be made between rural development policies that aspire to bring economic assistance to all rural areas, and rural transiton policies that seek to facilitate the movement of people and resources out of rural areas. Regardless of the policy option pursued, the long term viability of the rural South rests with a sustained commitment to improving the South's human capital.

Although interested in rural development policies, Lyson focuses his attention specifically on rural economic development strategies in the South. He notes that the current economic development programs across the South can be best characterized as de facto industrial policies—policies that fail to show any orderly planning for industrialization or attention to the types of jobs being created. It is these types of policies that have brought economic havoc to rural areas of the South. Lyson states that three policy alternatives exist for guiding future economic development activities in the region—continuation of the de facto industrial policy, a national industrial policy for rural areas, and a democratic economic planning initiative. He concludes that the time has come to replace the current de facto industrial program in the South with a more coordinated economic development effort.

Hackett discusses the increasing interest that states are giving to agriculture and rural development policies and programs. On the basis of a survey conducted in 1986 of governors, departments of agriculture, economic development, and community affairs, she reports on a large cadre of state-managed programs that have been instituted in states across the Southern region. These include agriculture development activities, transition tools, rural business assistance, and rural community assistance. Hackett argues for a new rural economic development strategy that embraces six key components: agriculture marketing, crop diversification, business expansion and retention, value-added business opportunities, recreational uses for land, and creation of commissions and task forces to advise state elected leaders on future policies and programs targeted to rural areas of the state.

AGRICULTURE/RURAL DEVELOPMENT STRATEGIES: SOME OPTIONS

Part IV explores opportunities for vitalizing the rural South. It includes discussions of program alternatives for strengthening this region of the country. Green and McNamara begin this section with a discussion of traditional industrial recruitment strategies and the types of rural locations where these approaches are most likely to be successful. Further, they outline five economic strategies that are designed to build upon the strengths of communities. Included are business expansion and retention programs, as well as approaches for more effectively capturing local dollars. Finally, alternative methods for generating economic development, involving nontraditional institutional arrangements, are presented. It is argued that communities must create new institutional arrangements if they are to lay the foundation for a strong economic development program in the future.

The critical building block for the vitalization of the rural South is educational reform, claim Deaton and Deaton. Four conditions which necessitate innovative responses are discussed by the authors: fiscal structure, illiteracy, linkages between schools and the community, and access to lifelong education. Deficits in these conditions, they argue, will limit human resource development and regional economic progress in the South. As a means of better understanding how these four conditions constrain development of the region, a supply-side perspective of institutional change is presented.

Is entrepreneurship a viable economic development strategy for the rural South? Reid reports that rural areas can indeed participate in economic growth through entrepreneurship. What is needed, however, is a commitment on the part of rural community organizations and leaders so that a climate supportive of entrepreneurial endeavors can be created. But, if the South is to realize any economic gain through entrepreneurship, it must overcome several important obstacles, of which the lack of a quality educational system is most prominent.

Babb and Long shift the focus of attention to Southern agriculture. Recognizing the financial strains impacting many farmers in the region, the authors explore the market potential for those alternative products and services being heralded as the salvation for Southern farmers. While obstacles to success in alternative enterprises are discussed, the roles that public and private organizations can play in reducing such obstacles are outlined.

A most insightful piece by a person who has been an active partner in the formulation of rural development policies in the South is reflected in the chapter by Governor Winter. He asserts that new approaches must be devised if the South is to break the chains of poverty, ignorance and neglect that continue to hold it in bondage. Those strategies must begin with education, especially a massive assault on adult illiteracy. Further, investments are needed in child care, family planning, job training and housing. New methods of job creation must be devised that will harness the entrepreneurial capacities of Southern communities in a way that will preserve them as viable economic entities. This, Winter claims, will require the emergence of the most creative leadership that the rural South has yet produced.

The final chapter, written by Schertz, provides a synthesis of *The Rural South in Crisis* volume. In carefully reviewing the collection of works contained in this book, Schertz detects the prominent place that education holds in many of the contributed chapters. There is an apparent consensus among authors, he notes, that educational opportunities are severely limited in the rural South and that substantive improvements in the region are likely to go unmet unless educational enhancements are realized. He suggests that the USDA/Land Grant System, as the lead federal agency in rural development, must consider placing education as the cornerstone of its rural development activities.

REFERENCES

Beale, Calvin L. 1985. "U.S. population trends break with past." *Rural Development Perspectives* (February):4-7.

Beale, Calvin L. and Glenn V. Fuguitt. 1986. "Metropolitan and nonmetropolitan population growth in the United States." Pp. 46-51 in *New Dimensions in Rural Policy: Building Upon Our Heritage.* Studies prepared for the use of the Subcommittee on Agriculture and Transportation of the Joint Economic Committee, Congress of the United States. Washington, D.C.: U.S. Government Printing Office (June 5).

Beaulieu, Lionel J. and W. David Mulkey. 1986. "An assessment of community forces and agricultural change." Pp. 267-299 in Joseph J. Molnar (ed.), *Agricultural Change: Consequences for Southern Farms and Rural Communities.* Boulder, Colorado: Westview Press.

Brown, David L. 1984. "Implications of population change in rural America." *Journal of the Community Development Society* 15 (2): 105-118.

Carlin, Thomas and Peggy Ross. 1987. "Investments in rural education can mean higher incomes, but in the cities." *Choices (Fourth Quarter):* 22-23.

Economic Research Service, U.S. Department of Agriculture. 1987a. *Agriculture Finance: Situation and Outlook Report.* AFO-27 (March).

——————. 1987b. *Rural Economic Development in the 1980s: Preparing for the Future.* Agriculture and Rural Economy Division, U.S. Department of Agriculture. ERS Staff Report No. AGES870724.

——————. 1986a. "The farm crisis in the 1980s." *Rural Development Perspectives* 2 (June): 8-9.

——————. 1986b. "The outlook for farmland values is still clouded." *Agricultural Outlook* AO-120 (June): 25-28.

——————. 1986c. *Financial Characteristics of U.S. Farms, January 1, 1986.* National Economics Division, U.S. Department of Agriculture. Agriculture Information Bulletin No. 500.

——————. 1985. *The Current Financial Condition of Farmers and Farm Lenders.* Economic Research Service, Agriculture Information Bulletin No. 490 (March).

Ghelfi, Linda M. 1986. *Poverty Among Black Families in the Nonmetro South.* Agriculture and Rural Economics Division, Economic Research Service, U.S. Department of Agriculture, Rural Development Research Report No. 62.

Henry, Mark, Mark Drabenstott, and Lynn Gibson. 1986. "A changing rural America." *Economic Review.* Federal Reserve Bank of Kansas (July/August): 23-41.

Hines, Fred and Mindy F. Petrulis. 1986. "An overview of the Southern nonmetro economy: An historical and current view with emphasis on Southern agriculture." *Proceedings of the Emerging Issues in the Rural Economy of the South Conference.* Mississippi State: Southern Rural Development Center (April).

Hite, James and Holley Ulbrich. 1986. "Fiscal stress in rural America: Some straws in the wind." *American Journal of Agricultural Economics* 68 (December): 1188-1193.

Hoppe, Robert A. 1985. *Economic Structure and Change in Persistently Low-Income Nonmetro Counties*. Agriculture and Rural Economics Division, Economic Research Service, U. S. Department of Agriculture. Rural Development Research Report No. 50.

Hoppe, Robert A., Herman Bluestone, and Virginia K. Getz. 1986. *Social and Economic Environment of Black Farmers*. Agriculture and Rural Economics Division, Economic Research Service, U.S. Department of Agriculture. Rural Development Research Report No. 61.

Johnson, Kenny. 1986. "The Southern stake in rural development." *Rural Flight/Urban Might: Economic Development Challenges for the 1980s*. The 1986 Commission on the Future of the South, Cross-Cutting Issue Report No. 3. Research Triangle Park, North Carolina: The Southern Growth Policies Board.

Joint Economic Committee. 1986. *New Dimensions in Rural Policy: Building Upon Our Heritage*. Studies prepared for the use of the Subcommittee on Agriculture and Transportation of the Joint Economic Committee, Congress of the United States. Washington, D.C.: U.S. Government Printing Office.

King, Juliana. 1987. "For farm finances: promising signs of a cooling crisis." *Farmline* (April): 6-7.

Lawson, Michael. 1986. "The impact of the farm recession on local governments." *Intergovernmental Perspective* (Summer): 17-23.

Lichter, Daniel T. and Janice A. Constanzo. 1986. "Underemployment in nonmetropolitan America, 1970 to 1982." Pp. 134-143 in *New Dimensions in Rural Policy: Building Upon Our Heritage*. Studies prepared for the use of the Subcommittee on Agriculture and Transportation of the Joint Economic Committee, Congress of the United States. Washington, D.C.: U.S. Government Printing Office (June 5).

Lichter, Daniel T., Glenn V. Fuguitt, and Tim B. Heaton. 1985. "Components of nonmetropolitan population change: the contribution of rural areas." *Rural Sociology* 50 (Spring): 88-98.

Lyson, Thomas A. and William W. Falk. 1986. "Two sides of the sunbelt: economic development in the rural and urban South." Pp. 158-165 in *New Dimensions in Rural Policy: Building Upon Our Heritage*. Studies prepared for the use of the Subcommittee on Agriculture and Transportation of the Joint Economic Committee, Congress of the United States. Washington, D.C.: U.S. Government Printing Office (June 5).

Martinez, Doug. 1985. "Will the rural South's job boom go bust?" *Farmline* (November): 12-14.

MDC. Inc. 1986. *Shadows in the Sunbelt: Developing the Rural South in an Era of Economic Change*. A report of the MDC Panel on Rural Economic Development (May).

Mueller, William. 1986. "Can we cope with farming's failures?" American Demographics 8 (May): 40-43.

Petrulis, Mindy, Bernal L. Green, Fred Hines, Richard Nolan, and Judith Sommer. 1987. *How is Farm Financial Stress Affecting Rural America?* Economic Research Service, U.S. Department of Agriculture. Agricultural Economic Report No. 568.

Pulver, Glen C. 1986. "Economic growth in rural America." Pp. 491-508 in *New Dimensions in Rural Policy: Building Upon Our Heritage*. Studies prepared for the use of the Subcommittee on Agriculture and Transportation of the Joint Economic Committee, Congress of the United States. Washington, D.C.: U.S. Government Printing Office (June 5).

Reeder, Richard J. 1987. "Facing new fiscal strains." *Choices* (Fourth Quarter): 26-27.

Rosenfeld, Stuart A., Edward Bergman, and Sarah Rubin. 1985. *After the Factories: Changing Employment Patterns in the Rural South*. Research Triangle Park, North Carolina: Southern Growth Policies Board (December).

Ross, Peggy J. and Elizabeth S. Morrissey. 1987. "Two types of rural poor need different kinds of help." *Rural Development Perspectives* 4 (October): 7-10.

Southern Growth Policies Board. 1986. *Halfway Home and a Long Way to Go*. The Report of the 1986 Commission on the Future of the South. Research Triangle Park, North Carolina.

Swanson, Louis E. and Jerry R. Skees. 1987. "Funding new ideas for old objectives: The current case for rural development programs." *Choices* (Fourth Quarter): 8-11.

U.S. Congress. 1986. "Impacts on Rural Communities." Pp. 221-249 in *Technology, Public Policy, and the Changing Structure of American Agriculture*. Office of Technology Assessment, OTA-F-285. Washington, D.C.: U.S. Government Printing Office (March).

U.S. Senate. 1986. *Governing the Heartland: Can Rural Communities Survive the Farm Crisis?* Report prepared by the Subcommittee on Intergovernmental Affairs (May).

Wilkinson, Kenneth P. 1986. "Community change in rural America: Challenges for community leadership development." *Proceedings of Resurgence in Rural America: Mandate for Community Leadership.* Extension Service, U.S. Department of Agriculture (September).

Winter, William F. 1986. "New choices for the rural South." *Proceedings of the Policy Forum: Diversification Strategies for New Southern Agriculture Conference.* Mississippi State: Southern Rural Development Center (October).

PART ONE

Dimensions of the Agriculture/Rural
Community Crisis in the South

2

The Rural South in Crisis:
A Historical Perspective

Dwight B. Billings

A decade ago, it would have seemed unlikely to many observers that circumstances in the late 1980s would prompt yet another focus on the economic and social ills of the South. After all, journalists had been busy proclaiming
the South—redubbed the "Sunbelt" to include the Southwest and to contrast
with the decay and decline in the "rustbelt" states of the North—to be "an
industrial and financial colossus" (Sale, 1977:165). Decades of steady industrial growth, educational investments, income improvements, and extensive
agricultural modernization appeared at last to be on the verge of matching
the region in reality with the "hype" promoters had used for nearly a century
to "sell the South" to outside investors (Cobb, 1982).

Significant regional progress had been made. White Southerners capitalized on the Congressional seniority their undemocratic politics guaranteed
in order to subsidize the reorganization of Southern agriculture with federal
tax dollars, as well as to win for the region a substantial share of military
and defense installations. The Carolinas became the nation's most highly industrialized region. Atlanta, Dallas, and Houston were boom cities. Poured
concrete and glass rose skyward to proclaim not only a "New South" but also
an urban South. Black Southerners led a massive crusade that brought a legal
end to the region's segregated public institutions in the 1960s and moved the
South closer to national norms. Politicians from Texas and Georgia came to
occupy the White House. Yet, beneath the surface of events—and inherent
in the way the South has "progressed"—farm crises, low wages, rural

unemployment and underemployment, and poverty persist. Simultaneously, declines in manufacturing and farming threaten rural communities throughout the region (MDC, Inc., 1986:4). In 1987, Mississippi, the nation's poorest state, had less than 50 percent of the annual per capita income of Connecticut, the nation's most prosperous. More than a third of all the poor families in the United States live in the South (Wood, 1986:1).

The problems of the rural South today include recent developments as well as patterns that trace back to earlier periods. If one looks to the past for a perspective on today's crisis, there is no better starting point than the ominous winter of 1607 in Jamestown. Many of the ragged adventurers who had traveled to Virginia were shocked by the hardships of the new world. Hard work, more than wealth and adventure, greeted them. Many refused the hard work and all grew hungry. Several starved. Captain John Smith exerted his authority, backed up with armed force, to proclaim that "He that will not worke shall not eat" (quoted in Breen, 1986:50). This was the first use of coercion and the first conflict in the region over the questions of *who works, who eats, and who prospers*—questions at the heart of the history of the South.

Looking briefly from Jamestown to the founding of Plymouth twenty-three years later in Massachusetts, the contrasts are striking. Before they left the Mayflower, John Winthrop and the other New England settlers made a covenant to be "knitt together in this worke as one man.../to/be willing to abridge /ourselves/ of /our/ superfluities, for the supply of others necessities" (quoted in Bellah, 1975:14). They were engaged in a utopian, communal experiment. The settlers built their homes nearby one another and farmed common fields together. When a new generation needed land, it was opened up collectively and distributed equally. Soon, of course, communal villages gave way to dispersed, private farms and a system of family labor, but not before a sense of community and the public good had taken root (Lockridge, 1970; Zukerman, 1970). A "moral economy" of reciprocity and exchange bound households and contributed to the beginnings of a healthy local and regional economy (Clark, 1979; Henretta, 1978; Merrill, 1977).

Virginia organized its economy and met its labor needs very differently. Rather than close-knit towns, reciprocity, and local exchange, Virginia moved in the direction of decentralized plantations, export-oriented agriculture, and forced labor. The latter resulted from the fact that landowners possessing vast estates in the Southern colonies found themselves unable to meet their labor needs as long as an unsettled "backcountry" beckoned to their laborers. After experimenting with indentured servitude, planters solved this problem by importing a workforce from Africa and keeping it permanently enslaved. Thus, they charted a course of institutional development vastly different from that followed in the Northern colonies.

The authors of a recent policy statement on the rural crisis in the South, *Shadows in the Sunbelt*, write that "to think of the rural Southern economy is to think of the family farm" (MDC, Inc., 1986:7). Remarkably, they over-look the one social institution which, more than any other aspect of the South's history, made the South what it is: *the slaveholding plantation*. Slavery set the South on a distinctive path of development that conditioned all aspects of its economic, political, and social life and set the region apart from the rest of the nation, even until the present.

As historian Carl Degler (1974) has pointed out, however, there are "other Souths" besides the plantation South. Outside the plantation zone, in the Up-country, in the piney woods, in parts of Cajun country, in the Ozarks, and in the Appalachians, non-slaveholding families struggled to make a living and to defend alternative ways of life. But even here, still beneath the "shadow of slavery"—as farmers, workers, or the owners of businesses—their lives were touched by the nearby presence of the plantations, as well as by distinct local conditions. In the remainder of this chapter, I will describe briefly the routes by which three Southern regions—the plantation South, the Upcoun-try, and the Appalachian South—entered the modern era.

In the past thirty years social scientists have learned a great deal about so-cial change by observing patterns of social, economic, and political develop-ment in the Third World. We know that rural modernization represents far more than attitudinal change. Just as farming systems—including crop types, ownership patterns, labor modes, political struggles, and the infrastructures they produce—help to shape development opportunities and constraints in developing countries (Moore, 1966), the same has been true of American regions. The "paths to modernity" followed, for instance, by the region of family farming in the Midwest, by the capital-intensive, state-dependent sys-tem of irrigated agriculture in the Southwest, and by the plantation South, have each been varied, to use but three examples (Kirby, 1987:1-22). Each route has left a legacy of institutions, organizations, and identity that con-tinue to distinguish American regions (Post, 1982).

Within regions, subregional variations, too, reflect the effects of geography as well as the historical legacies of how agriculture and industry have been or-ganized. In the following sections I will show that the Plantation South, the Up-country, and the Appalachian South represent not only distinct subregions of the South, but also distinct "routes" to southern modernity. At two extremes of dissimilarity—as distinct as were Jamestown and Plymouth—are Appalachia, characterized historically by subsistence-oriented family farming, and the Plantation South, its large-scale commercial farming based on forms of "forced labor," e.g., slavery and debt peonage. The Upcountry lies in between, ge-ographically as well as sociologically. Here, the *combination* of independent family farming and forced labor in the same vicinity posed unique constraints and opportunities and set the Southern Piedmont on its own path of social and economic development. Such an interpretation implies that the problems these rural regions face today should be looked at historically.

THE PLANTATION SOUTH

The growth of the plantation South influenced life chances in all the "other Souths." Understanding the logic of its development sheds light on the distinctiveness of other Southern subregions. By the plantation South, I refer to the 325 contiguous counties located east and north from Texas up to the Carolinas that were identified in the Census of 1910 as being farmed primarily by a plantation form of ownership and supervision (Wright, 1986:82). These were the counties where black farm laborers made up a majority of the population and cotton was the predominant crop. Slavery had set this portion of the South on a course of development that would make it a unique region within the United States, leaving a historical legacy of social problems that continue to confound rural developers and reformers to the present.

A vast literature summarizes the social patterns all plantation societies share (see Genovese, 1967; Beckford, 1972): economic, political, and social domination by a small upper class which allocates land, capital, and labor resources to export-oriented agriculture; labor repression and political conservatism; indifference or active opposition to industrialization; under-compensation for a majority of the population which exerts downward pressure on the wages of other rural workers; under-consumption for a majority of the population which limits local markets and business opportunities; dependent and undersized middle classes. During the antebellum period, these were interconnected facets of the economics of slaveholding.

Plantation culture profoundly shaped the South's rural life in other ways as well. Take the fixed costs of labor. Since planters owned slaves year round, they were more interested in keeping slaves involved in productive activities throughout the year than in maximizing productivity through labor saving techniques. This had several consequences for economic development. Mechanization, for instance, was minimized. The South failed to keep pace with the rest of the nation in the purchase and improvement of farm machinery—a market opportunity which gave significant impetus to urban and industrial growth elsewhere, especially in the Midwest (Mandle, 1978). The allocation of slave labor to the production of food items and to craft production and building, as well as to the cultivation of export staples, turned plantations into remarkably self-sufficient units (Wright, 1978). Intra-regional trade, town-building, and entrepreneurship suffered as a direct consequence. Plantations, not towns, became the region's meaningful social units. Public life and community institutions thus came to be less developed in the South than in other farm regions.

Plantation agriculture had a profound impact on Southern political development as well (Bartley, 1983; Billings, 1979). Planters monopolized wealth and power in the plantation counties and they dominated Southern legislatures. State policies supported the plantation system. Law, along with extra-legal force and terror, helped to secure social stability and labor control.   Racism permeated all institutional areas. Transportation investments, which were largely state sponsored in the antebellum South, linked plantation counties with outside markets. Upland and back country regions, however, were denied internal improvements and remained isolated and undeveloped. Planter control also limited public investments in human capital improvements such as education. This alone has had disastrous consequences for long-term regional development.

Historians and economists have debated the profitability of slaveholding as a farming system. Eugene Genovese (1967) argues that antebellum plantation agriculture yielded a low level of profits. The slaveholders, he contends, were more interested in maintaining class hegemony and privilege than in improving agriculture. But economists Fogel and Engerman (1974), who claim that southern plantations were 40 percent more efficient than Northern farms in 1860, reject the argument that slavery retarded Southern growth. They point out that between 1840 and 1860 the South's per capita income grew 30 percent more rapidly than did income in the North. Purchasing slaves was a rational investment which earned an average of 10 percent on the market price in the 1850s, a profit level that equalled or excelled nonagricultural alternatives. The decade of the 1850s, however, was the most profitable in the entire history of Southern cotton growing. Economist Gavin Wright (1976:304) best sums up the *long-term* detrimental effects of slaveholding on the Southern economy. "The slave South," he contends, "was typical of many economies in history based essentially on extractive resource-intensive exports, which expand rapidly during a period of rising external demand, but which do not lay the institutional foundations for sustained growth once this era has passed." The same may certainly be said of the sharecropping and tenancy system that replaced slavery after emancipation.

The years immediately following the Civil War were hard ones in the plantation South. Property in slaves, which had represented 60 percent of the total agricultural wealth in five Southern states, was eliminated (Wright, 1986:19). The region's infrastructure was in ruins but Southerners began a massive and successful recovery effort. Radical Reconstruction and its promise of land reform—a genuine opportunity for Southern modernization—were aborted. Former slaveholders retained their land and regained control of Southern politics (Billings, 1979; Wayne, 1983; Wiener, 1978). In the 1870s, they survived challenges to many of their class privileges by freed men and ascendant merchants. Freed men did succeed, however, in refusing to work as gang laborers on plantations for low wages. Consequently, planters were forced to subdivide their plantations into small, decentralized family-operated units farmed by sharecroppers and renters. But notorious crop lien laws guaranteed landowners the first claim on agricultural profits while debt, along with customary forms of violence and terror, kept nominally free black farmers subordinate and poor (Ransom and Sutch, 1977).

The shift from plantation supervision to sharecropping and tenancy arrangements represented a significant reorganization of agriculture, but in many other respects, rural life remained the same. Debt, fear, and poverty still plagued the black work force, as well as many white farmers who joined the ranks of tenancy as the nineteenth century drew to a close (Daniel, 1972). No longer bound to involuntary servitude, however, black sharecroppers moved about a great deal searching for better opportunities and fairer landlords. The Census of 1910 documented "remarkably high" levels of turnover among black farmers: 52 percent of all black sharecroppers and 40 percent of all black renters occupied the farms they were on in 1910 for only one year or less. Income, though low, improved. Under bad circumstances and despite racism, black farmers made "significant progress" economically. By 1920, one fifth of all farm owners in the South were black (Wright, 1986:81-123).

Landowners, too, experienced new opportunities and confronted old dilemmas. Economist Gavin Wright (1986:26) argues that with emancipation, "laborlords" became "landlords." Studies suggest that when their principal property, slaves, was movable, planters were geographically mobile, even "footloose." Consequently, they paid little attention to improving their localities, in some cases preferring to live a more refined life in coastal towns well removed from their farm lands for at least part of the year. But in the postbellum years, Wright argues, when their chief economic resource became land, planters shifted priorities and began to take more interest in improving the value of their land holdings through local improvements and entrepreneurialism. Town building and the economic activities associated with it were accelerated. This did not extend to "human capital" improvements, however. After having been threatened by a revolt of the Populists, planters achieved tighter political control and disfranchised black voters. With the passage of Jim Crow laws at the turn of the century, they waged a massively successful assault on black education, the effects of which today continue to retard regional development and to handicap black Americans (Kousser, 1974).

As an aspect of town-building, planters in the Deep South invested in businesses such as transportation, the cottonseed industry, and fertilizer plants that were complementary to cotton growing. Studies of planter politics in Mississippi and Alabama, however, document that black belt landlords were hostile to thoroughgoing industrialization. In Alabama, for instance, they threw up serious impediments to the business interests in northern Alabama that were trying to develop the state's iron and coal industries (Wiener, 1978). Planters opposed economic developments which would threaten their supply of low-wage rural labor. Cheap labor continued to mitigate against the mechanization and modernization of agriculture (Mandle, 1978).

For most of the Deep South, in good times and in bad, cotton retained a comparative advantage over alternative nonagricultural investments and over other crops (DeCanio, 1974). The market value of cotton was the most direct determinant of economic well being in the region. When prices were high, landlords prospered and Southern incomes improved. When prices fell, farmers suffered. Cotton prices rose dramatically after the Civil War and helped Southerners recoup wartime losses. But in the last quarter of the nineteenth century, as cotton production increased substantially, cotton prices fell drastically. They rebounded again from 1900 to 1920 and income rose, although the income gap between the South and the rest of the nation worsened.

Comparing Mississippi and Ohio, Wright (1986:66) shows that "the absolute difference, what one might call the 'cost of staying in the South,' widened over time from twenty cents per day around 1880 to fifty cents in 1902 and eighty cents in 1914." Soil erosion and the boil weevil seriously hurt some localities. Demand for Southern cotton began to decline again after World War I and by the end of the 1920s, with the depression and a shift in the comparative advantage of cotton growing to the mechanized farms of the Southwest, Southern cotton farming virtually collapsed (Kirby, 1987).

The agricultural policies of the New Deal modernized farming in the plantation South. Commodity price supports and payments to farmers to withhold land from cultivation provided large landlords with capital sufficient for mechanization. At the same time, meager relief payments enabled planters to sever obligations to farm laborers and their families, even though it is estimated that less than half of all black families received emergency federal assistance (Kirby, 1987:57). Mechanization raised both skill levels and incomes of farm workers but also displaced thousands of tenants and croppers from the agricultural system. Between 1935 and 1940, the number of farm operators for the South as a whole was reduced by 400,000, of which all but 30,000 were tenants and sharecroppers (Wood, 1986:71). Today more than half the labor used in cotton cultivation and harvesting is skilled. "By the early or mid-1960s, sharecropping as a form of labor control had passed into insignificance and so too had the Southern plantation economy" (Mandle, 1978:95). Rural poverty and unemployment, however, were left as harsh reminders of its prior existence.

A look at the inequities of the federal policies which helped to modernize the region is instructive. Agricultural experiment stations and the agricultural science research system of the land-grant universities in the South have, for the most part, been oriented to the interests of large farmers. Much of the leadership in the New Deal farm experimentation was provided by Southern planters and much of its federal implementation legislation was sponsored by Southern congressmen (Kirby, 1987:61). Although the Southern Tenant Farmers Union fought the U.S.D.A. on this, subsidies for land retraction went almost entirely to landowners. Croppers and tenants did not benefit (see Kirby, 1987:65) for citations to field studies documenting this). Reformers in the Farm Security Administration later spoke up for their interests but, in general, federal policy was not addressed to their long-term needs. Southern political leaders

were careful to insure that welfare benefits would be adjusted to state income levels so that labor costs would remain low in the South. They devised
welfare laws that would guarantee the presence of a large, low-income supply of reserve labor whose benefits could be cut off at planting and harvest
times (Piven and Cloward, 1971). Several hundred thousand farm laborers
and their families were forced to leave the South as economic refugees. Others
were left behind to live their lives in hidden desperation.

THE UPCOUNTRY

As we turn to examine the Upcountry or Piedmont South, more complex
patterns and events confront us. Now the heart of the South's urban and industrial development, the region was first homeland to both independent farmers (who were the majority) and to planters. Prior to the Civil War, many
areas of the Southern backcountry had been neglected by transportation
development and in these localities, such as the Georgia Upcountry, yeomen
lived semi-autonomously on small farms and engaged in semi-subsistence
agriculture. Here, before the war, the most important social unit was the *household,* not the plantation. "Relations of production," according to historian
Stephen Hahn (1986:181) "were mediated principally by ties of kinship rather
than by the market place." In Georgia, "these petty producers generally owned
basic productive resources or were related to those who did; they devoted
their energies principally to family subsistence, supplementing it through local exchanges of goods and labor; and the exchanges cast a net that brought
producers face-to-face in a market very much governed by local custom"
(Hahn, 1986:183; 1983).

In other Piedmont localities, such as in many North Carolina counties,
planters and yeomen lived in closer proximity. In the areas of mixed household and plantation production, planters dominated social life. According to
Genovese (1967:31), "the paternalism of planters toward their slaves was reinforced by the semipaternal relationships between planters and their neighbors."
Such relations were not, however, without conflict. Paul Escott has recently
documented the decades long struggle between North Carolina's "socially
conservative elite fearful of democracy" (Escott, 1985:110) and the state's huge
yeomen population which sought to defend what it could of an autonomous existence. Step by step, from 1850 to 1900, from the period of its mobilization
into an army raised to defend the planters' interest in slaveholding, to its ill-
timed abandonment of subsistence agriculture in favor of market oriented cotton cultivation, the yeomen population both surrendered its autonomy and organized to resist elite power. Diverse forms of popular opposition, beginning
with a massive peace movement during the Civil War and culminating in the
short-lived legislative accomplishments of a coalition of Populists and

Republicans in the 1890s, occurred throughout the last half of the nineteenth century in the Piedmont region of North Carolina. At the core of Upcountry history is the story of the yeomen's fall from independent, subsistence agriculture to dependence on commercial farming and, for many, to tenancy and/or low-wage factory employment.

Recent scholarship has investigated the causes for the southern farmers-'revolt (see Billings, 1981; Goodwyn, 1976; and Schwartz, 1976). Most stress the worsening of white farmers' economic position as cotton prices fell to all-time lows in the last decades of the nineteenth century and many formerly independent farmers fell into tenancy and sharecropping. In 1900, 41 percent of North Carolina's farmers were tenants and croppers and another 33 percent owned less than one hundred acres. A number of factors caused yeomen to shift from their traditional diversified, safety-first approach to agriculture to a more exclusive devotion to cotton growing. Hahn (1983) contends that in Georgia increasingly powerful merchants used their control over credit sources to force farmers to shift to cotton since this crop was the merchants' safest risk and surest return. Others point to the extensive postbellum expansion of railroads into the Upcountry which linked many isolated areas to outside markets for the first time and to the development of chemical fertilizers which expanded the geographical range of cotton (Weiman, 1983).

Whatever the pressures and motivations to commercialize, as cotton prices fell, farmers fell into debt and many lost their land. Perhaps even more than foreclosures and usurpation, however, demographic factors also contributed to the Upcountry crisis. Wright (1986:112) argues that the problem of farm ownership was less that of dispossession, although this was extensive, than of the "lack of room for the young farmers coming up," given the region's high level of fertility. "The heavy infusion of new entrants into farming," writes Gilbert Fite (1986:39), "created a surplus of agricultural labor and too many farms, which kept individuals and family incomes depressed." As the capital requirements for successful commercial farming rose, sharecropping and tenancy represented an entry point for many young farmers which few could escape (Fite, 1986:46; 1984).

At the same time that a rural crisis threatened to disrupt social patterns in the Piedmont, the Upland areas of the South presented favorable opportunities for industrial development. Research on the North Carolina textile industry reveals that Upcountry planters moved swiftly to take advantage of these opportunities (Billings, 1979; 1982). Although North Carolina is often been viewed as a state of small farmers, it was a state nonetheless dominated by planters. Seventy-two percent of all farmers who supervised croppers or rented to tenants in North Carolina controlled one such family production unit. However, the top 4 percent of all farmers who employed tenants—those who controlled five or more tenant-cropper operated farms each—supervised approximately 20 percent of all tenants and croppers and owned one-fifth of the total value of farm property in North Carolina. The fact that nearly half (48 percent) of the state's entire cotton crop in 1899 was produced by dependent labor reveals the wealth and power of this small group of planters.

North Carolina planters had invested in cotton mills before the Civil War and they had experimented in the use of slave labor in some of these factories. After the war, planters and their business associates expanded their industrial investments. The demand for cotton textile manufacturing had been a recurrent theme throughout the economic history in less remote areas of the Upcountry during the antebellum period. As long as investment in cotton growing held a comparative advantage, the industry received little attention, but, whenever agricultural prices dropped, the demand for manufacturing in the South was renewed. Social, economic, and technological factors after the Civil War rekindled interest in industrialization. The expansion of railroads and the development of water power aided in the expansion of internal and external markets. New developments in the technology of textile manufacturing, especially the perfection of the ring spindle and the automatic loom, permitted the use of unskilled labor. Surplus labor was an ever-present and potentially threatening element in the Upcountry agrarian social order. When cotton prices fell in North Carolina "from twenty-five cents a pound in 1868 to twelve cents in the 1870s, to nine cents in the 1880s, and to seven cents in the early nineties, finally reaching five cents a pound in 1894" (Lefler and Newsome, 1973:524), textile manufacturing, which brought returns as high as 22 percent per annum, seemed the answer to the region's economic problems.

In this respect, the Upcountry differed significantly from the plantation counties of the Deep South. Demographically, the Upcountry was the reverse of the Deep South with its small core of plantation counties and larger yeomen rim. The vast yeomen numbers represented a political threat to planter privilege but also a potential source of cheap, unskilled labor. Elsewhere (Billings, 1979:223), a positive correlation has been documented between long-run price elasticities for cotton growing—based on DeCanio's (1974) estimates for 1883 to 1914—and the per capita value added by manufacturing in ten Southern states. The more vulnerable was a state to drops in the price of cotton (as compared with other products), the greater its manufacturing activity. In contrast, the comparative advantage of cotton growing in Deep South states was so great that it was economically irrational for planters there to do anything other than to plant cotton. This factor, plus the labor needs of cotton production and the relatively small proportion of underemployed white farmers, disinclined planters in the Deep South from promoting industry as did their peers in the Upcountry.

Obviously, industrialization has benefited this portion of the South. Anthony Tang's (1958) study of economic development in the Piedmont demonstrates that industrial-urban development has helped to absorb underemployed farm labor. Farm incomes have been supplemented by off-farm work without reductions in output, while personal incomes per capita have risen dramatically in Piedmont counties (see Skees and Swanson, 1986) for a discussion of off-farm work and rural well-being in the South). In North Carolina, per capita personal income increased from 37 percent of the national average in 1880 to 81.4 percent in 1982 (Wood, 1986:18). On the other hand, the particular nature of rural industrialization has been, and continues to be, problematic.

In large measure the "success" of Southern industrialization has been dependent on cheap labor and rural poverty, legacies of the plantation economy. "By exploiting the region's cheap and abundant labor supply, its relatively undeveloped system of labor legislation, and by using cheap hydroelectric power and the most recently available automatic machinery, Southern manufacturers were able to achieve a significant reduction in production costs" (Wood, 1986:81). In a comparative study of the North Carolina and Massachusetts textile industries, Phillip Wood (1986) found that the Southern branch of the industry could produce identical cloth at 31 percent less cost than the North, the principal factor being the cost of labor. In 1900, industrial wages in the South were 40 percent lower than in New England and work days were 24 percent longer (Vance, 1935:291); since the 1950s, North Carolina industrial employers have maintained an average hourly wage rate below 75 percent of the U.S. average (Wood, 1986:19). This has been the key to Southern success. Wood estimates that from 1939 to 1979 Southern industry was 28 percent more profitable for investors than U.S. industry as a whole, largely because of its ability to keep down the costs of labor. It is no coincidence that the Carolinas rank first among states for their percentage of nonagricultural workers in industry and last both for their levels of wage earnings and unionization (Malizia, 1975).

Economists have argued that industrial wages have been repressed by the low wage levels of Southern agriculture. Gavin Wright puts it dramatically: "Mill owners were able to get white labor at a black wage" (Wright, 1986:13; also 124-55). The Piedmont's agricultural labor force has been an important source of labor power for new industry throughout the postwar period. For example, in 1978, 32 percent of North Carolina's rural farm families had total incomes less than 125 percent of the federally defined poverty level. Southern manufacturers have taken advantage of this, often locating in areas of high rural poverty. In North Carolina, "between 1960 and 1970 the percentage of manufacturing labor force classified as 'urban' fell from 43.6 percent to 29.5 percent, while those classified as 'rural nonfarm' increased from 47.9 percent to 55.3 percent" (Wood, 1986:180). It seems obvious that the poverty of the Piedmont's rural population has been attractive to industry employing low skilled workers. Recently, observers have noted a trend for the textile industry to move from the Southern Piedmont into poverty-stricken coastal counties to take advantage of cheap black labor (untouched by the urban civil rights activism) and the large number of tobacco farmers displaced by mechanization (Wood, 1986:195). But the real story is that the long term prospects for such localities are bleak. The Southeast has lost 95,000 jobs in textiles and 16,000 jobs in apparels since 1980 (MDC, Inc., 1986:6). Rural communities now find themselves competing with Third World countries for industrial expansion.

One should not attribute the low wage scales that have characterized the Southeast solely to the blind or mechanistic operation of rural Southern labor markets. Paternalism—the social relations of the plantation extended to the mill village (McLaurin, 1971), labor repression including the use of state police and national guard forces to block unionization efforts, right to work laws, and racial segregation each have contributed to employers' strategies to defend low wage rates in the rural South (Conway, 1979). Such a labor climate in rural counties has been offered as an inducement to outside capital. Covert actions on the part of business leaders and officials in many localities of the Piedmont to block the entry of high paying jobs has been frequently documented (Koeppel, 1976).

Speaking specifically of official economic development policy in North Carolina, Wood (1986:165) writes that the most important consequence of such policy has been the attraction of "primarily labor-intensive, low-wage industries seeking to escape unionization, labor market competition, and higher wages in other regions." Although Wood neglects important developments such as the growth in the research and development activities associated with the "Research Triangle" area, his general point is on target. As many rural communities in the South find themselves competing with Third World countries to offer high levels of unemployment and low wage rates for industrial expansion, the wisdom of such a strategy for development has been called into question (see MDC, Inc., 1986).

THE APPALACHIAN SOUTH

As we look, even more briefly, at the mountain South we encounter a subregion where the plantations had their least direct impact. But even here—whether in the form of neglect by planter governments or the low-wage conditions of the Southern labor market—slavery and tenancy had an indirect impact. While some mountain counties housed slaveholding farmers in their fertile valleys and river bottom areas, the predominant unit of agricultural production and social life in Appalachia was the family farm. Rugged terrain and a poorly developed transportation system isolated many sections of the mountain region. Consequently, the subsistence-oriented farming system described by Hahn (1986) as characterizing the antebellum Upcountry region of Georgia persisted far longer in the highlands.

The best account of this way of life has been provided by James S. Brown and his associates in a forty-year longitudinal study of the "Beech Creek" neighborhoods of rural East Kentucky. As late as the 1940s, 89 percent of all farm production in Beech Creek was consumed at home; only a small surplus (principally tobacco) was marketed commercially. Despite some part-time wage labor and the influx of government monies through pensions and farm subsidies, cash levels in the community were exceedingly low. Annual expenditures averaged an astonishingly low value of $84 per capita in 1942; family incomes averaged only $800 per household (Schwarzweller et al., 1971). Kinship relations, far more than economic markets, shaped social life in the rural mountains until the development of extractive industries began to open up the area to greater outside influence.

Industrialization in Appalachia, which began around 1900, was based on the region's rich natural resources, especially timber and coal. As in the rest of the South, however, low wages in comparison with other regions (such as the Northern coal fields of Pennsylvania, Ohio, and Illinois), provided additional incentives for development (Corbin, 1981). Whether measured in terms of environmental impacts or human costs, probably no other region in the South has borne a greater cost in terms of the suffering that has accompanied industrialization.

The key to understanding the region's development lies in its juxtaposition of subsistence agriculture and corporate power (Billings et al., 1986). Subsistence agriculture failed to generate sufficient local capital for indigenous entrepreneurs to undertake the huge costs of developing an industrial infrastructure in Appalachia. The capital costs for improving transportation alone in the mountainous sections were enormous. Thus, the impetus and resources for development came largely from outside. Railroad, timber, and mineral companies purchased huge tracts of land, opened up isolated areas, and built company towns devoted to the extraction of natural resources (Eller, 1982). Absentee owners accumulated vast amounts of land in the region. For example, two thirds of the surface land of West Virginia, and a vast majority of its underground mineral deposits, are presently owned by out-of-state corporations (Appalachian Landownership Task Force, 1983). It was this situation of an impoverished, indigenous population and its dependence upon powerful absentee corporations that were extracting vast wealth produced in the region and returning little in the way of taxes or lasting improvements in the quality of life, which led activists in the 1970s to label Appalachia a "colony" (see Lewis et al., 1978). While in some sense all of America has been "colonized" by corporations, Appalachia stands out as a symbol of corporate exploitation and neglect (Gaventa, 1980).

Low levels of economic accumulation in the farm sector, high levels of human fertility, soil depletion, and land shortages set limits on Appalachian agricultural capacity and capital accumulation. These same factors produced great strain in the subsistence system and contributed to the development of an underemployed labor pool that could be utilized cheaply. Corporate land acquisitions exacerbated land shortages by removing land from cultivation. For example, Harlan County, in the eastern Kentucky coal fields, experienced a decrease in average farm size from 260 to 74 acres between 1880 and 1930 and an increase in non-owner operated farms from 25 to 60 percent of total farms between 1880 and 1910. Total farm acreage in the county dropped from 220,000 acres in 1880 to just under 58,000 acres in 1930 (Banks, 1983). Throughout Appalachia, impoverished mountain farmers were available to work at low wages in the regions's mines and timber camps. Many others left to find work in mills and factories outside the mountains. When the timber resources were exhausted, and when mechanization and the competition with other fuels reduced employment in the mines by several hundred thousands of workers in the 1950s, displaced workers followed displaced farmers out of the hills and into industrial cities in the Midwest. Despite the migration of some three to eight million people from Southern Appalachia in the twentieth century (Billings and Walls, 1980), the region remains poor. A recent report estimates that more than one fifth of the people in the Central Appalachian portions of West Virginia, Kentucky, Virginia, North Carolina, and Tennessee continue to live below federally defined levels of poverty (Tickamyer and Tickamyer, 1987).

CONCLUSION

The current crises of agriculture, unemployment, low wages, and poverty in the rural South are not of recent origin. Inequality and poverty haunted the rural South for decades. Agricultural modernization was slow in coming and it did not benefit all members of the rural community equally. Manufacturing, while improving incomes and opportunities, has been predicated too often on low wages and high unemployment.

As we reflect today on new development strategies for the region, past experience—including the successes and failures of earlier reforms—can help to guide problem definition and planning. Obviously in a capitalist society, poor regions need money to affect change. In the South, however, capital investments have been made too frequently with inequitable results. The Agricultural Adjustment Act poured necessary money into the region that permitted farm mechanization, but it ignored croppers and tenants. The Tennessee Valley Authority contributed to the economic and industrial development of the Upper South, yet it displaced thousands of mountain farmers and, in the early 1960s, created the first market for strip-mined coal which had devastating environmental consequences. The Appalachian Regional Commission invested millions of dollars of public funds to improve mountain highways, but never confronted the tough issues of absentee ownership, taxation, and equity. The positive effects, as well as the severe limitations of such programs, offer instructive lessons for communities trying to respond to the challenge of today's rural problems. At a minimum, reflection on these programs may sensitize us to the need for viewing the impact of development strategies on all segments of the community. Change efforts always have their beneficiaries and their victims. As we face up to the issues of democratic social planning in the rural South, reflecting on the history of the region gives us an opportunity to deepen our commitment to what ethicist and theologian Mathew Lamb (1982) calls "solidarity with the victims" of poverty, injustice, and, often, modernization itself.

REFERENCES

Appalachian Landownership Task Force. 1983. *Who Owns Appalachia?* Lexington: University Press of Kentucky.

Banks, Alan. 1983-84. "Coal miners and firebrick workers: The structure of work relations in two eastern Kentucky communities." *Appalachian Journal* 11:1&2 (Autumn-Winter):85-102.

Bartley, Numan. 1983. *The Creation of Modern Georgia.* Athens: University of Georgia Press.

Beckford, George. 1972. *Persistent Poverty: Underdevelopment in Plantation Economies of the Third World.* New York: Oxford University Press.

Bellah, Robert N. 1975. *The Broken Covenant.* New York: Seabury Press.

Billings, Dwight B. 1979. *Planters and the Making of a "New South."* Chapel Hill: The University of North Carolina Press.

_____. 1981. "Class and class politics in the southern populist movement of the 1890s." *Sociological Spectrum* 1:259-292.

_____. 1982. "Class origins of the 'new South': planter persistence and industry in North Carolina." *American Journal of Sociology* 88 (Supplement):S52-85.

Billings, Dwight B., Kathleen Blee, and Louis Swanson. 1986. "Culture, family, and community in preindustrial Appalachia." *Appalachian Journal* 13:2 (Winter):154-70.

Billings, Dwight B., and David S. Walls. 1980. "Appalachians." Pp.125-128 in Stephen Thernstrom (ed.), *Harvard Encyclopedia of American Ethnic Groups.* Cambridge, MA: Havard University Press.

Breen, T. H. 1986. "Right man, wrong place." *The New York Review of Books* XXXIII:18 (November 20):48-50.

Clark, Christopher. 1979. "Household economy, market exchange and the rise of capitalism in the Connecticut Valley, 1800-1860." *Journal of Social History* 13:2 (Winter):169-90.

Cobb, James C. 1982. *The Selling of the South: The Southern Crusade for Industrial Development 1936-1980.* Baton Rouge: Louisiana State University Press.

Conway, Mimi. 1979. *Rise Gonna Rise.* Garden City, NY: Anchor Books.

Corbin, David Alan. 1981. *Life, Work and Rebellion in the Coal Fields: The Southern West Virginia Miners, 1880-1922.* Urbana: University of Illinois Press.

Daniel, Pete. 1972. *The Shadow of Slavery: Peonage in the South, 1901-1969.* Urbana: University of Illinois Press.

DeCanio, Stephen J. 1974. *Agriculture in the Postbellum South: The Economics of Production and Supply.* Cambridge: MIT Press.

Degler, Carl. 1974. *The Other South.* New York: Harper and Row.

Eller, Ronald. 1982. *Miners, Millhands and Mountaineers: The Industrialization of the Appalachian South, 1880-1930.* Knoxville: University of Tennessee Press.

Escott, Paul D. 1985. *Many Excellent People: Power and Privilege in North Carolina, 1850-1900.* Chapel Hill: University of North Carolina Press.

Fite, Gilbert. 1984. *Cotton Fields No More: Southern Agriculture, 1865-1980.* Lexington: University Press of Kentucky.

_____. 1986. "The agriculture trap in the South." *Agricultural History* 60(4):38-50.

Fogel, Robert and Stanley Engerman. 1974. *Time on the Cross*. New York: Little, Brown and Company.

Gaventa, John. 1980. *Power and Powerlessness: Quiescence and Rebellion in an Appalachian Valley*. Oxford: Clarendon Press.

Genovese, Eugene. 1967. *The Political Economy of Slavery*. New York: Vintage Books.

Goodwyn, Lawrence. 1976. *Democratic Promise: The Populist Moment in America*. New York: Oxford University Press.

Hahn, Steven. 1983. *The Roots of Southern Populism*. New York: Oxford University Press.

_____. 1986. "The 'unmaking' of the southern yeomenry." Pp. 179-197 in Stephen Han and Jonathan Prude (eds.), *The Countryside and Capitalist Transformation*. Chapel Hill: The University of North Carolina Press.

Henretta, James A. 1978. "Families and farms: *mentalite* in preindustrial America." *William and Mary Quarterly* 35:1 (3rd series, January) 2-32.

Kirby, Jack Temple. 1987. *Rural Worlds Lost: The American South 1920-1960*. Baton Rouge: Louisiana State University Press.

Koeppel, Barbara. 1976. "Something could be finer than to be in Carolina." *The Progressive* 40:2-23.

Kousser, J. Morgan. 1974. *The Shaping of Southern Politics*. New Haven: Yale University Press.

Lamb, Mathew. 1982. *Solidarity with Victims*. New York: Seabury Press.

Lefler, Hugh and Albert Newsome. 1973. *North Carolina: The History of a Southern State*. Chapel Hill: The University of North Carolina Press.

Lewis, Helen, Linda Johnson and Donald Askins. 1978. *Colonialism in Modern America: The Appalachian Case*. Boone, NC: The Appalachian Consortium Press.

Lockridge, Kenneth A. 1970. *A New England Town: The First Hundred Years - Dedham, Massachusetts, 1636-1736*. New York: W.W. Norton.

Malizia, Emile. 1975. "The earnings of North Carolina workers." *The University of North Carolina News Letter* 60:1-3.

Mandle, Jay. 1978. *The Roots of Black Poverty: The Southern Plantation Economy After the Civil War*. Durham: Duke University Press.

MDC, Inc. 1986. *Shadows in the Sunbelt: Developing the Rural South in an Era of Economic Change*. Research Triangle Park: MDC Panel on Rural Economic Development.

Merrill, Michael. 1977. "Cash is good to eat: self-sufficiency and exchange in the rural economy of the United States." *Radical History Review* (Winter):41-71.

McLaurin, Melton. 1971. *Paternalism and Protest*. Westport, CT: Greenwood Press.

Moore, Barrington. 1966. *Social Origins of Dictatorship and Democracy*. Boston: Beacon Press.

Piven, Frances Fox and Richard Cloward. 1971. *Regulating the Poor: The Functions of Public Welfare*. New York: Vintage Books.

Post, Charles. 1982. "The American road to capitalism." *New Left Review* 133 (May-June):30-51.

Ransom, Roger and Richard Sutch. 1977. *One Kind of Freedom: The Economic Consequences of Emancipation*. Cambridge: Cambridge University Press.

Sale, Kirkpatrick. 1977. "Six Pillars of the Southern Rim." Pp. 165-180 in Roger Alcaly and David Mermelsten (eds.), *The Fiscal Crisis of American Cities*. New York: Vintage Books.

Schwartz, Michael. 1976. *Radical Protest and Social Structure: The Southern Farmers' Alliance and Cotton Tenancy, 1880-1890*. New York: Academic Press.

Schwarzweller, Harry, James S. Brown, and J. J. Mangalam. 1971. *Mountain Families in Transition*. University Park: Pennsylvania State University Press.

Skees, Jerry and Louis E. Swanson. 1986. "Public policy for farm structure and rural well-being in the South." Research monograph published by the Office of Technology Assessment of the U.S. Congress (March).

Tang, Anthony M. 1958. *Economic Development in the Southern Piedmont 1860-1950*. Chapel Hill: The University of North Carolina Press.

Tickamyer, Ann and Cecil Tickamyer. 1987. *Poverty in Appalachia*. Lexington, KY: University of Kentucky, Appalachian Center Data Bank Report 5 (March).

Wayne, Michael. 1983. *The Reshaping of Plantation Society: The Natchez District 1860-1880*. Baton Rouge: Louisiana State University Press.

Weiman, David F. 1983. "Petty commodity production in the cotton South." Ph.D. dissertation, Stanford University.

Wiener, Jonathan M. 1978. *Social Origins of the New South: Alabama 1860-1885*. Baton Rouge: Louisiana State University Press.

_____. 1980. "Class structure and economic development in the American South." *American Historical Review* 84:970-1006.

Wood, Phillip J. 1986. *Southern Capitalism: The Political Economy of North Carolina 1880-1980.* Durham: Duke University Press.

Wright, Gavin. 1976. "Prosperity, progress, and American slavery." Pp. 302-336 in Paul David, Herbert Gutman, Richard Sutch, Peter Temin, and Gavin Wright (eds.), *Reckoning with Slavery.* New York: Oxford University Press.

_____. 1978. *The Political Economy of the Cotton South.* New York: W.W. Norton.

_____. 1986. *Old South, New South: Revolutions in the Southern Economy since the Civil War.* New York: Basic Books.

Zucherman, Michael. 1970. *Peaceable Kingdoms: New England Town in the Eighteenth Century.* New York: Knopf.

3

The Status of Southern Agriculture

David H. Harrington

The farm sector in the South has suffered the same economic reversals as the rest of the United States in the 1980s; but not with the same severity as the Upper Midwest. Land value declines have been later and less precipitous throughout most of the South. Financial stress among farm operators is less severe; but rates of exit from farming and rates of bankruptcy appear to be more severe.

This chapter examines each of these and shows why the structure and position of farming in the Southern rural economy make it less vulnerable to economic downturns than other regions. A second section examines the competitive position of the South in terms of enterprise costs of production. A final section presents some projections of the likely future of the structure of Southern agriculture.

This chapter will establish that, while the farm sector in the South has some remaining financial problems to work through, the diversity of rural economies in the South and the structure of Southern farming as predominantly small, diversified farms improves its prospect measurably.

SOUTHERN FINANCIAL CONDITIONS IN A NATIONAL CONTEXT

Land Price Changes

The mid-1930s to 1981 marked almost fifty years of near constant increases in farmland values in the United States (the 1960s to the present are shown in Figure 1). Only in 1954 did the average value of farmland fail to increase in nominal terms over the preceding year. Starting in 1981 and 1982, however, farmland values have declined each year—declining 35 percent nationally. Nominal prices of farmland are now back to levels that characterized the mid-1970s. In real terms—that is, corrected for inflation—land values have dropped to levels that characterized the early 1960s (Economic Research Service, 1987b).

The primary reasons for the drop in farmland values lie in the reversal of several factors that had been driving land values above their previous trends in the 1970s. These factors affected the expected future income flows to farming (expected returns to land) and how these flows are capitalized into land values (real interest rates).

Net returns to farmland were favorable in the 1970s because of generally favorable market conditions. Exports of farm products, for example, which had been increasing at rates of over 8 percent per year throughout the 1970s, abruptly started declining in 1981 (Harrington and Carlin, 1987). This decline was largely due to a rapid increase in the exchange value of the dollar, which made U.S. farm products more expensive to foreign customers. The trade-weighted value of the dollar had been declining throughout the 1970s, but abruptly increased to double its 1979 value in the first half of the 1980s (Harrington and Carlin, 1987). This doubling of the exchange value of the dollar was, in turn, partially the result of high real interest rates caused by tight monetary policies which rapidly brought the inflation of the late 1970s under control. Tight monetary policy, combined with deregulation of financial markets, rapidly raised real interest rates from their historic levels of 1 to 2 percent (and occasionally negative) in the 50s through 70s to unprecedented levels of 8 to 10 percent. As a result of all of these critical reversals, farmland values (which are strongly dependent on income growth expectations and real interest rates) suddenly reversed from growth to decline.

With recent declines in the exchange value of the dollar and in real interest rates, there are indications that the land market is strengthening. Moreover, the relationships of farmland values to current returns have returned to pre-1970s balances; and nominal land values are nearly back to the (apparently sustainable) trend line of the 1960s. Real land values have not returned to their pre-1970s trend line because the real interest rate remains above the rates that prevailed over that period, hence the plot of real land values has shifted downward, but may start paralleling the previous trend line in the near future.

On a state-by-state basis, Figure 2 shows that the change in land values from 1986 to 1987 (top number), and from 1982 to 1987 (bottom number). As is evident, the South as a whole has not suffered as severe declines in land value as the nation as a whole. Only Louisiana, Arkansas, and Oklahoma exceed the five year average decline for the nation; and in none of the states in the South do declines approach the severity of the Upper Midwest. Furthermore,

Figure 1
Real vs. Nominal Value Per Acre

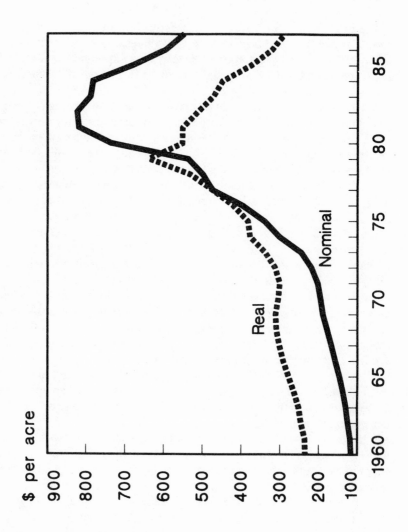

33

Figure 2

Percent Change in Land Value Per Acre February 1986–1987 and February 1982–1987

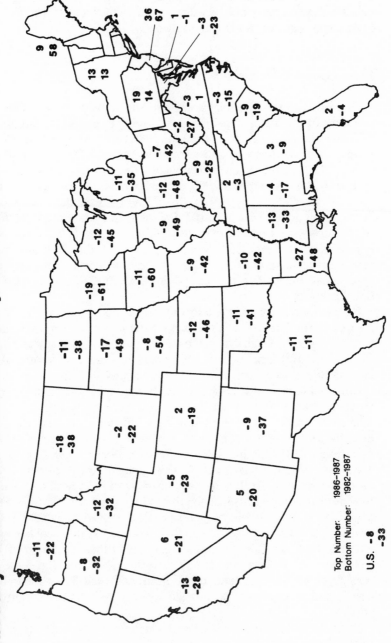

Top Number: 1986–1987
Bottom Number: 1982–1987

U.S. −8
     −33

all states in the South (except Louisiana) show evidence of bottoming out and possible slow recovery of land values, whereas they may still be falling rapidly in some states of the Upper Midwest.

Farm Operator Financial Stress

Turning now to the financial strength of Southern agriculture, Table 1 shows measures of the income position, asset and debt positions, and proportions of farms with financial stress from the 1985 Farm Costs and Returns Survey conducted by the Economic Research Service, U.S. Department of Agriculture (ERS). This survey quite accurately reflects the numbers and conditions of farms with sales of over $10,000, but undercounts the very small farms (Economic Research Service, 1986c). Specifically, it excludes the 300,000 or so farms which do not have at least $1,000 of sales of farm products in the year of the survey. From this survey data, the South has 550,000 farms or 35.5 percent of the United States total. Appalachian[1] and Delta farms are smaller than average in terms of total assets and net worth. Southeastern farms approximate the national average, while Southern Plains farms exceed the national average.

Income sources for average farms are clearly dominated by off-farm income sources rather than net farm income. Off-farm income is much more important to farms in the South than in the U.S. as a whole—especially in the Southern Plains, where off-farm income is 60 percent higher than the national average, and the Southeast where it is 25 percent higher than the national average.

Farms with financial stress are defined by most analysts as those farms which: (1) are unable to fully service their interest and principal payments and provide an allowance for family living from all sources of cash income—farm and off-farm, and (2) have high ratios of debts to owned assets (debt/asset ratios above 0.4) (Economic Research Service, 1986c). Such farms are termed as having current financial stress. A larger group of farms which have debt/asset ratios above 0.4, regardless of whether they can meet farm and family cash-flow needs, are termed as having potential financial stress, because they may not be able to fully discharge their cash-flow obligations in all years. A third possible measure of cash-flow status is not used in this analysis—all farms with negative cash flow positions regardless of their debt/asset ratios. This measure indicates farm and family cash-flow problems. But these may not stem from the debt positions of the farm, and such farms generally would have adequate net worth to provide security for additional borrowing, if necessary.

Farms in the South exhibit lower incidences of actual and potential farm financial stress than the nation as a whole. Only the Delta subregion shows a level of current financial stress that equals the U.S. average. The Appalachian

Table 1. Measures of Financial Strength, The South and Subregions of the South, 1985

Item	Appalachian	Southeast	The South* Delta	Southern Plains	All South	All U.S.
General						
Number of Farms (000)	222	87	69	173	551	1,551
Percent of Farms	14.3	5.6	4.4	11.2	35.5	100.0
Balance Sheet[1]						
Ave. Assets Per Farm ($)	181,981	317,250	280,157	420,480	290,480	325,087
Ave. Debts Per Farm ($)	24,424	54,340	60,516	61,702	45,372	73,124
Ave. Net Worth ($)	157,467	262,909	219,641	358,778	245,108	251,963
Debt/Asset Ratio	0.13	0.17	0.22	0.15	0.16	0.22
Income Statement[2]						
Ave. Net Cash Income ($)	2,600	3,214	7,643	-2,705	1,663	8,881
Ave. Off Farm Income ($)	21,481	28,408	24,241	36,370	27,594	22,757
Ave. Total Family Income ($)	24,081	31,622	31,884	33,665	29,258	31,638
Financial Stress						
Percent of Farm with Current Financial Stress[3]	5.7	7.9	11.3	8.0	7.5	11.2
Percent of Farms with Current or Potential Financial Stress[4]	9.3	15.8	16.5	15.2	11.2	21.3

Source: Calculated from *Financial Characteristics of U.S. Farms, January 1, 1986,* AIB 500, Economic Research Service, U.S. Department of Agriculture, August 1986.

[1]As of January 1, 1986.
[2]For calendar year 1985.
[3]Farms with high debt/asset ratios (over .4) and negative cash flow from all sources after payment of interest, principal and minimum family living needs.
[4]Farms with high debt/asset ratios with either positive or negative cash flow.
*Subregions of the South are defined as follows: Appalachian—VA, WV, KY, NC, TN; Southeast—SC, GA, AL, FL; Delta—MS, LA, AR; Southern Plains—TX, OK.

region has consistently shown the lowest level of financial stress in the nation, by both measures. The regions of the Upper Midwest—the Corn Belt, Lake States, and Northern Plains—show incidences of farm financial stress that are up to triple those experienced by the subregions of the South (Economic Research Service, 1986c).

Farms Going Out of Business

With lower rates of farm financial stress, one would expect fewer Southern farms to be going out of business than in the nation as a whole. This has not been the case. Data from the American Banking Association (see Table 2) show that higher proportions of farms go out of business for financial reasons or go through bankruptcy in the South than in any other region (Economic Research Service, 1987a). Farm exits from normal attrition appear to be the same as those nationwide; but, significantly higher proportions of farms exit for financial reasons in the South than in the nation as a whole. The patterns of increase—tripling since 1982—are the same for both the South and the nation.

Several characteristics of farming in the South may account for these differences—some are real, and some are purely statistical. First, a purely statistical difference; the American Banking Association data is based on an opinion survey of bankers who are asked "what percentage of farms went out of business (for various reasons) in your banking area in the last 12 months?" The respondents may have a mental image of larger commercial farms (over $40,000 in sales) in their minds, rather than all farms of all sizes, thus their estimates are probably based upon exit rates among the smaller number of nearly full-time farmers, and probably exclude the much larger numbers of farmers that have full-time off-farm employment. Such small farms are more common in the South than the rest of the country. And, rates of exit are higher for the larger commercial farms; hence, the bankers' estimates of rates of exit may be too high in relation to the rest of the nation. Other real differences in rates of exit may be that, with the diversified, smaller-farm economy of the South, farm operators with full-time off-farm employment may not be as willing to continuously subsidize their farm losses from off-farm income sources, and may voluntarily liquidate their operations earlier and more readily than in other regions. A further real reason is that farms with sales of more than $40,000 per year are, in fact, shown by the ERS survey data to have higher rates of financial stress than in the nation as a whole in the Delta, Southern Plains, and Southeast subregions.

Table 2. Farms Going Out of Business, The South and All United States, 1982-1986

Item	The South					All U.S.				
	1982[1]	1983	1984	1985	1986	1982[1]	1983	1984	1985	1986
	————————————————————Percent————————————————————									
Farms Going Out of Business										
All Reasons	3.9	3.1	4.4	5.6	8.9	2.2	2.3	3.6	4.8	6.2
Normal Attrition	NA	0.7	1.0	1.1	1.6	NA	0.9	1.1	1.3	1.8
Voluntary Liquidation	NA	1.0	1.8	2.5	4.5	NA	1.0	1.6	2.2	2.6
Legal Foreclosure	NA	0.8	1.4	1.9	2.5	NA	0.4	0.8	1.2	1.6
Other	NA	0.1	0.2	0.1	0.3	NA	—	0.1	0.1	0.2
Financially Related Reasons	NA	1.9	3.4	4.5	7.3	NA	1.4	2.5	3.5	4.4
Farms Going Through Bankruptcy	0.1	1.9	4.9	5.7	6.5	0.75	1.1	2.6	3.8	4.2

[1]Year ending in June of the stated year.
— = Less than 0.1 percent.
NA = Not available.
Source: American Banking Association. Reported in *Agricultural Financial Outlook*, AFO-27, Economic Research Service, U.S. Department of Agriculture, March 1987.

STRUCTURE OF FARMS AND RURAL ECONOMICS

Part of the explanation of why rates of farm financial stresss would be lower in the South than in regions like the Upper Midwest lie in three factors: (1) the dominant size structure of farms, (2) the dependence of farms on production of export crops, (3) the dependence of the rural economies on the farm sector. By each of these measures, most of the South comes out in a favored position with regard to farm financial stress. Only parts of the Delta, and some of the High Plains are in the unfavorable position of much of the Upper Midwest.

A Farm Size Classification of Counties

Most of the South is dominated by small farms (Carlin and Green, 1987). In the upper panel of Figure 3, counties which have 88 percent or more of their farms with sales of less than $40,000 are shaded in. Most of these small farm counties—over 75 percent of them—are in the South. Major concentrations of small farm counties are in the Appalachian subregion, the Eastern portions of Texas and Oklahoma, and in other scattered locations throughout the Southeast. By contrast (the lower panel of Figure 3) large farm counties, having less than 59 percent of their farms with sales of less than $40,000, characterize the Upper Midwest. Only in the Delta, the High Plains, Tidewater and Southwest Georgia do you find minor groups of large farm counties in the South. Only 17 percent of large farm counties are in the South.

What would one expect to find in the economy of a small farm county? Without ascribing cause or effect, one would expect to find:

- Diversified agriculture—many crops and livestock products being produced.

- Higher off-farm income sources—especially from full-time off-farm employment.

- More stable land values—neither as volatile on the upside nor as disastrous on the downside.

- Less vulnerability of the economy to agricultural market conditions.

In large farm counties, just the opposite would be expected. Both expectations are borne out to a large extent; but state-level reporting of statistics masks some of the land value relationships. The South comes out ahead on this measure, except for the Mississippi Delta counties, the High Plains, Tidewater, and Southwest Georgia.

Figure 3
Farm Size Classification of Counties
Small Farm Counties [1]

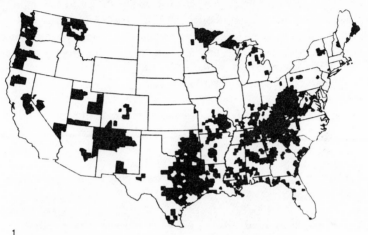

[1] 750 counties with more than 88 percent of farms with sales of less than $40,000 per year in 1982.

Large Farm Counties [2]

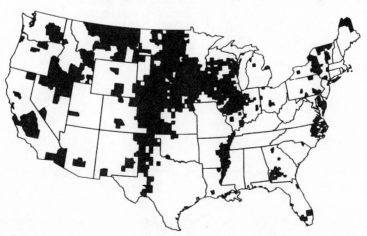

[2] 750 counties with less than 59 percent of farms with sales of less than $40,000 per year in 1982.

Dependence on Export Crops

We have measured farm dependence on export crops as the proportion of farm sales derived from five export crops—corn, wheat, soybeans, cotton, and rice (Hines and Sommer, 1987). Counties that are dependent upon these export crops for over 50 percent of farm sales are shown in the upper panel of Figure 4. These data are based on the *1982 Census of Agriculture,* the latest data available at the county level. Export dependent counties are concentrated in the Corn Belt, the Delta, and the Northern Plains along the Canadian border. What would one expect from export dependent counties? Again, without ascribing cause or effect, one would expect:

- Larger specialized farms, with crop farms dominant.

- More volatile net farm incomes.

- More dependence on levels and types of government commodity support policies.

- More volatile land values—both upward and downward.

- More vulnerability to financial stress and farm recession in the 1980s.

County Economic Dependence on Farming

In the lower panel of Figure 4 are plotted the counties that rely on farming for over 20 percent of labor and proprietor's income (Hines and Sommer, 1987). There are 702 farm-dependent counties, mostly in the Upper Midwest, but with scatterings throughout the South including minor concentrations in the High Plains, the Delta, and the Southeast. What does one expect from farm-dependent counties?

- Large farms.

- Fewer off-farm employment opportunities and lower off-farm incomes.

- Much more volatility of the total local economy to the financial conditions of agriculture.

- Generally, a predominant view that agriculture is the force that drives the whole economy.

Figure 4
Farm and Export Dependent Counties

Export Dependent Counties [1]

[1] 419 counties with more than 50 percent of 1982 gross farm sales from export-dependent crops--corn, wheat, soybeans, cotton, rice.

Both Farm and Export Dependent Counties [2]

[2] 173 counties meeting both definitions for export dependence and farm dependence.

Farm Dependent Counties [3]

[3] 702 counties with over 20 percent of labor and proprietor's income originating in farming in 1975 through 1979.

While these conditions appear to hold in the Upper Midwest, in the South they do not. Two reasons may account for this. First, in the South, farm counties are interspersed with counties that depend on manufacturing for most of their economic activity (Bender et al., 1985). This allows strong off-farm employment opportunities to be within easy commuting distance of farm dependent communities. Second, counties in the South have more diversified nonfarm economies, further weakening the connections between the farm economies and the nonfarm economies.

Combinations

The middle panel of Figure 4 shows those 173 counties that are both export dependent and farm-dependent. Four-fifths of these counties are also large farm counties; thus, they receive a "triple whammy"—all three factors have been unfavorable to them in the 1980s. In them you would expect:

- Extreme dependence of the local economy on farm conditions.

- Extreme dependence on the continuation of government commodity support payments, but vulnerability to their attendant acreage or supply reduction provisions and/or payment-in-kind (PIK) provisions.

- The largest adjustments in land prices and financial conditions to be made, and the least ability to make them without public sector assistance.

Few of these counties show up in the South, as they are fairly widely scattered from the Delta to the Northern Plains.

On financial stress indicators and on the farm and rural economy structure of the South, we find most areas to be relatively favored. This does not necessarily imply that these areas are wealthier, or have higher incomes—far from it. Instead, these measures show that Southern agriculture has more resilience and, because of less volatility of land values and net farm incomes, has smaller adjustments to make to restore normal profitability relationships.

The South did not fly as high in the 1970s, nor did it have as far to fall in the 1980s.

THE COMPETITIVE POSITION OF THE SOUTH

Another crucial set of variables concerns the competitive position of the South in major crop and livestock enterprises. These comparisons are based on the enterprise cost of production budgets maintained by ERS (1986a). Important relationships include:

- *Variable expenses per unit of output.* These are conditioned by the regional endowment of quality of land and climate factors as well as by the economic efficiency of production. They determine the lowest expected price at which it pays a farmer to continue production. Thus, they are crucial variables in determining the competitive position of farms and production regions.

- *Fixed cash expenses per unit of output.* These are conditioned by the scale of production and the structure of enterprises on the farms. These include general farm overhead, rents, taxes and insurance. These expenses cannot generally be avoided by cutting back on a particular enterprise, and are not properly part of the process of deciding what enterprises should be undertaken each year.

- *Capital replacement costs per unit of output.* These are costs of replacing capital used up in production, and generally do not have to be covered in any one year. However, they must be fully covered over a period of years or the capital base will not be replaced and production will be cut back or redirected.

- *Return to owned factors.* This is a residual return to the owner's land, labor, management, and risk-bearing. It can be positive or negative in any year, and generally reflects the return per unit that an average producer experienced in the production year. There will be wide variation in this return depending on an individual farmer's size of enterprise, management ability, and the conditions of market prices during the year.

The 1985 production cost budgets for crop enterprises are shown in Table 3, which compares the Southern subregions with the lowest cost region of the United States. The South contains the low cost production region only for the traditional Southern crops—cotton, rice, and peanuts. The total production cost advantage (regional differences between the sums of all cost components) of the Southeast in cotton is 2 to 3 cents per pound. For peanuts, the Southeast has about a 5 cents per pound cost advantage; and for rice, the Arkansas non-Delta region has about a 12 cent per hundredweight advantage over the Delta, and $1.83 per hundredweight advantage over the Gulf Coast.

For corn, the Southeast has a 37 cents per bushel disadvantage behind the Corn Belt. For soybeans, the Northern Plains has a 77 cents per bushel advantage over the Delta, and a $1.14 per bushel advantage over the Southeast.

Table 3. Production Costs for Selected Crops; Southern Regions Versus Low Cost Region, 1985

Item	Corn		Soybeans			Winter Wheat		
	Southeast	Low Cost Region (Corn Belt)	Southeast	Delta	Low Cost Region (No. Plains)	Southeast	Southern Plains	Low Cost Region (Central Plains)
Yield (Unit)	88.59 (bu)	122.21	24.67 (bu)	24.47	32.38	26.80 (bu)	23.80	34.34
Harvest Price Per Unit	2.37	2.20	5.04	5.01	4.68	3.12	2.85	2.62
Variable Expenses Per Unit	1.47	1.04	2.79	2.33	1.35	2.63	2.06	1.12
Cash Fixed Expenses Per Unit	.58	.65	1.24	1.22	1.73	.85	.81	1.21
Capital Replacement Per Unit	.28	.28	.82	.93	.63	.66	.70	.58
Total Cost Per Unit	2.34	1.97	4.85	4.48	3.71	4.14	3.57	2.91
Margin = Returns to Owned Factors	.03	.23	.19	.52	.96	-1.02	-.72	-.29

Item	Cotton			Rice			Peanuts		
	Southern Plains	Delta	Low Cost Region (Southeast)	Gulf Coast	Delta	Low Cost Region (ARK-Non-Delta)	Virg.-N. Car.	Southern Plains	Low Cost Region (Southeast)
Yield (Unit)	359.34 (lb)	671.10	712.22	47.93 (cwt)	49.84	52.01	2826 (lb)	1799	3125
Harvest Price Per Unit	.53	.54	.55	8.35	8.49	8.46	.24	.26	.21
Variable Expenses Per Unit	.39	.35	.38	5.66	4.52	4.32	.11	.11	.09
Cash Fixed Expenses Per Unit	.10	.14	.10	1.51	1.31	1.36	.06	.05	.03
Capital Replacement Per Unit	.09	.08	.08	1.20	.84	.86	.02	.03	.03
Total Cost Per Unit	.59	.57	.56	8.37	6.67	6.54	.19	.19	.13
Margin = Returns to Owned Factors	-.01	-.02	-.03[1]	-.02	1.83	1.91	.06	.08	.08

Source: Calculated from *Economic Indicators of Farm Sector: Costs of Production 1985*, ECIFS5-1, Econ. Res. Serv., U. S. Department of Agriculture, August 1986.

[1]Net margin earned considering both cotton lint and cotton seed sold.

For wheat, the Central Plains has a 66 cents per bushel advantage over the Southern Plains and a $1.23 per bushel advantage over the Southeast.

For livestock enterprises (Table 4), none of the Southern subregions have a total production cost advantage. Feeder pig production comes the closest, with a total cost disadvantage of only $1.49 cents per hundredweight in the Southeast. Hog finishing in the Southeast has a $4.22 per hundredweight disadvantage behind the Northern Plains; and Farrow-to-finish hog production has a $2.51 per hundredweight cost disadvantage behind the North Central region. Cow-calf production in the South has a $24.38 per hundredweight cost disadvantage behind the West—the largest absolute cost disadvantage. In dairy production, the Pacific region is lowest cost, with the Appalachian subregion having $1.51 per hundredweight cost disadvantage and the Southern Plains having a $1.63 per hundredweight cost disadvantage.

Regional differences in prices received in the various regions offset about half of the cost disadvantages for crop enterprises; but provide very little to the cost disadvantages for livestock enterprises. Accordingly, for crop farms in the South, per unit rates of return to owned factors are only slightly lower than those for the low cost production regions. But, for livestock enterprise, returns to owned factors are considerably lower in the South than in the lowest cost production regions. Thus, the South is nearly fully competitive in production of most major crops and has a cost advantage in the traditional Southern crops of cotton, rice, and peanuts.

SOME PROJECTIONS OF THE FUTURE STRUCTURE OF FARMING IN THE SOUTH

With the changes in profitability and increased exit of farms since 1982, the question naturally arises as to what the future numbers and size distributions of farms may be in the South. In this analysis, the changes in farm numbers and sizes from the 1978 to 1982 *Census of Agriculture* are corrected to the rates of change in farm numbers from 1982 to 1986 and projected forward to 1998. The method used is called Markov chains and employs a data base of actual farm size changes from the *Census of Agriculture*—a unique set of data currently available only to ERS and Census researchers. The uniqueness of these data are that actual changes in constant dollar sales classes of individual farms—growth, decline, entry and exit—can be tracked over the base period and projected into the future.[2] Former methods of projecting size distributions had to rely on *ex post* correction of ending size distributions of farms for changes in prices, and projecting them forward under the assumption that farms could only grow larger or exit farming—neither the former techniques nor their underlying assumptions were very defensible.

The methods employed in this analysis combine Census data on farm size changes and National Agricultural Statistics Service data on changes in

Table 4. Production Costs for Selected Livestock Enterprises; Southern Regions Versus Low Cost Region, 1985

Item	Feeder Pig[1]		Hog Finishing		Farrow to Finish[2]	
	Southeast	Low Cost Region (North Central)	Southeast	Low Cost Region (No. Plains)	Southeast	Low Cost Region (North Central)
Yield (cwt.)	1.0	1.0	1.0	1.0	1.0	1.0
Harvest Price Per cwt.	-	-	44.80	44.58	-	-
Variable Expenses Per cwt.	54.68	53.23	42.38	38.34	34.57	30.86
Cash Fixed Expenses per cwt.	14.87	14.73	8.97	9.0	8.75	8.88
Capital Replacement Per cwt.	11.80	11.90	3.10	2.89	4.68	5.75
Total Cost Per Unit	81.35	79.86	54.45	50.23	48.00	45.49
Margin = Return to Owned Factors	-6.50	-6.39	-9.65	-5.65	-3.50	-1.31

Item	Cow-Calf[3]		Dairy[4]		
	South	Low Cost Region (West)	Apppalachian	Southern Plains	Low Cost Region (Pacific)
Yield (cwt.)	4.048	4.894	1.0	1.0	1.0
Harvest Price Per cwt.	-	-	-	-	-
Variable Expenses Per cwt.	49.96	35.62	8.48	9.00	8.13
Cash Fixed Expenses Per cwt.	18.60	16.50	1.99	1.88	1.46
Capital Replacement Per cwt.	18.99	11.05	1.33	1.04	.70
Total Cost Per Unit	87.55	63.17	11.80	11.92	10.29
Margin = Returns to Owned Factors	-32.47	-9.50	2.57	2.70	2.79

[1]One hundred weight equivalent of feeder pigs and cull sows sold. [2]One hundred weight equivalent of market hogs and cull sows sold. [3]One brook cow equivalent of calves, yearlings, and cull cows sold. [4]One hundred weight of milk plus allocated proportions of calves, cull cows, and replacements sold. - = Not applicable, combination of products sold. Source: Caulcated from *Economic Indicators of the Farm Sector: Costs of Production 1985*, ECIFS-5-1, Econ. Res. Serv., U. S. Department of Agriculture, August 1986.

numbers of farms under the assumption that the forces acting on the farm sector in the base period (1978 to 1982 for size changes and 1978 to 1986 for farm number changes) will continue unchanged into future. While these assumptions may also be questioned, they are the most consistent and defensible assumptions available given current knowledge of how the sector is evolving.

Table 5 shows historical farm numbers and size distributions for 1978, 1982, and 1986 in constant dollar sales classes along with projections for 1998. Farm numbers in the South changed very little from 1978 to 1982, with the smallest and the two largest sales classes expanding somewhat. From 1982 to 1986, farm numbers declined 9.2 percent overall, with the steepest declines in the $40,000 to $99,999 sales class and the larger sales classes declining only slightly. In the 1986 to 1998 period, farm numbers are projected to decline another 9.4 percent, with the largest sales classes expanding slightly.

SUMMARY

In summary, several positive conclusions emerge from this analysis (see Table 6). First, the South is a very important agricultural area, comprising nearly 40 percent of all farms in the United States and nearly 37 percent of total sales of farm products in 1985. The structure of farms and rural economies in the South have made it more resilient and less vulnerable to economic downturns in farming than some other regions, notably the Upper Midwest. Farms are smaller, with over 83 percent having sales of less than $40,000; and a higher proportion of small farm operators have a non-farm primary occupation. Recall from Figure 3 that 75 percent of all small farm counties are in the South. Also, recall that county economic dependence on farming is only strong in selected areas of the South, such as the Delta and the High Plains. Thus, the South in general has been able to weather the 1980s quite well; what problems there are stem more from drought or weather conditions than from the National downturn of the sector.

Reflecting these tendencies are the facts that land values in the South have declined only about two-thirds as much as the average for the nation, and less than half as much as the Upper Midwest. The percent of farms with current financial stress is about two-thirds of the average for the nation, and again, is less than half of the rate of financial stress for the Upper Midwest. Only in the percentages of farms going out of business or through bankruptcy does the South exhibit higher levels of stress than the nation as a whole. But, as mentioned, these data may be suspect, or the willingness to leave farming in times of stress may be higher and the financial trauma of leaving farming may be less in the South because of the diversified rural economies.

All things considered, while it would have been better not to have to go through any economic downturn in agriculture, the South has so far come

Table 5. Farm Numbers and Sizes in the South: Historical and Projected to 1998

Number of Farms[1]	1978	Percent Change	1982	Percent Change	1986	Percent Change	Projected 1988
Less than $10,000[1]	511,826	+7.6	556,526	-9.0	506,481	-9.4	458,749
$10,000-39,999	202,870	-15.3	171,787	-9.9	154,736	-10.9	137,849
$40,000-99,999	84,007	-12.2	73,799	-13.8	63,605	-12.5	55,681
$100,000-249,999	51,254	-1.1	50,668	-6.6	47,345	-7.3	43,891
$250,000-499,999	15,689	+9.8	17,226	-1.7	16,925	+0.5	17,012
$500,000 - and over	7,101	+13.6	8,064	-0.5	8,021	+8.5	8,700
Total	878,147	-0.12	878,070	-9.2	797,112	-9.4	721,883

[1]In 1982 constant dollar sales classes.

Table 6. Summary—The Agricultural Sector in the South

Item	The South	United States
Size of Sector		
Number of Farms	878,000	2,214,000
Percent of U.S. Farms	39.7	100.0
Total Gross Sales	$52 billion	$142 billion
Percent of U.S. Gross		
Sales	36.6	100.0
Dependence on Farming		
Percent of Farms with		
Sales under $40,000	83.5	72.9
Percent of All U.S.		
Farms	41.8	100.0
Percent of Small Farmers		
with a Non-Farm		
Primary Occupation	63.1	59.0
Financial Stress		
Land Value Change Since		
1982	-21	-33
Percent of Farms with		
Financial Stress	7.5	11.2
Percent of Farms Going		
Out of Business for		
Financial Reasons	7.3	4.4
Percent of Farms in		
Bankruptcy	6.5	4.2

Source: Calculated from *Economic Indicators of Farm Sector: National Financial Summary* EC1FS–5-2, ERS-USDA, November 1986 and *1982 Census of Agriculture.*

out better than most regions. The Appalachian subregion has come out the lowest in the nation in the rate of financial stress; and the Southeast is second only to the Northeast in having the lowest rate of decline in land values. Only the Delta may have significant further adjustments to make to continued high levels of financial stress. For the rest of the South, the end of the adjustment is in sight, although recovery will likely be gradual.

The future structure of farms in the South also reflect these conditions. A small decline in the number of farms and very slight growth of farms in the largest sales class are expected from now to the turn of the century. The South will continue to be a diversified farming region with a high proportion of relatively small farms with strong off-farm income sources and opportunities in diverse rural economies.

NOTES

[1]See Table 1 for states included in each subregion of the South.
[2]See Smith et al. (1985) for a discussion of the methodology of Markov chains and a description of the Census of Agriculture longitudinal linkage databases.

REFERENCES

Bender, Lloyd D., Bernal L. Green, Thomas F. Hady, John A. Kuehn, Marlys K. Nelson, Leon B. Perkinson, and Peggy J. Ross. 1985 *The Diverse Social and Economic Structure of Nonmetropolitan America*, Economic Research Service, U.S. Department of Agriculture, RDRR No. 49.
Carlin, Thomas A., and Bernal L. Green. 1987. *Local Farm Structure and Community Ties*, Economic Research Service, U.S. Department of Agriculture.
Economic Research Service, 1987a. *Agricultural Finance Outlook*. U.S. Department of Agriculture. AFO-27.
_____. 1987b. *Agricultural Resources, and Values and Markets Situation and Outlook Report*. U.S. Department of Agriculture. AR-6.
_____. 1986a. *Economic Indicators of the Farm Sector, Cost of Production*, U.S. Department of Agriculture. ECIFS 5-1.
_____. 1986b. *Economic Indicators of the Farm Sector, National Financial Summary, 1985*. U. S. Department of Agriculture. ECIFS 5-2.
_____. 1986c. *Financial Characteristics of U.S. Farms, January 1, 1986*, U.S. Department of Agriculture. AIB-500.
Harrington, David H. and Thomas A. Carlin. 1987, *The U.S. Farm Sector, How is it Weathering the 1980's?* Economic Research Service, U.S. Department of Agriculture, AIB-506.
Hines, Fred K. and Judith Sommer. 1987, *Annual Report to Congress on the Status of Family Farms*. Unpublished Report, Economic Research Service, U.S. Department of Agriculture.
Smith, Matthew G., Clark Edwards, and R. Neal Peterson. 1985, "The changing distribution of farms by size: A Markov Analysis," *Agricultural Economic Research*, 37(4):1-16.

4

The Tale of Two Souths

Stuart A. Rosenfeld

The final chapter of *America II* begins, "A few hundred miles south of Philadelphia, down a winding country road, there is a green paradise, a place with the air of exile...." (Louv, 1983). That paradise, "the ultimate America II settlement," is the Research Triangle Park. It epitomizes the public's image of the "Sun Belt." But another conclusion to a different sort of book could begin, "A few hundred miles south of Cincinnati, down a highway of fading billboards, there is a milltown, once thriving but now with an air of despair...." That town also is in the "Sun Belt" and co-exists with the high-flying centers of technological growth.

Those two contrasting images illustrate the dilemma in which the South finds itself. On the one hand, many of the region's cities are prospering, attracting new capital, new residents, and new jobs. On the other hand, many of the South's rural communities, which took in low-wage manufacturing plants with the understanding that they would eventually be replaced by new industries with better jobs for local citizens, are faltering. The new, high-paying jobs have not arrived, and the branch plants that once flocked to the South for lower labor costs are now moving out for still cheaper labor overseas. As William Winter, former governor of Mississippi, told an audience of Southern officials and citizens at a conference in Birmingham, Alabama, in January 1985, "There remains that other South, largely rural, undereducated, underproductive and underpaid, that threatens to become a permanent shadow of distress and deprivation in a region that less than a decade ago had promised it better days" (Winter, 1986).

This situation seemed to catch Southern policymakers unawares in the early 1980s. But it should not have come as a surprise. Policymakers had been keeping dreams of prosperity for the South alive by building new roads, shopping centers, and industrial parks to attract branch plants. In 1971, a group of Southern governors created an organization charged with accelerating growth in the region and making sure that it is done in such a way that it improves the quality of life. Legend has it that the organization was conceived by Terry Sanford, then governor of North Carolina, when he found himself traveling through the northeastern industrial corridor seeking business expansion for his state. Observing the slums, polluted streams, and gray air that years of heavy industry had wrought, he realized that a mechanism was needed to preserve the South's environment and to, as he told a group of Southern leaders, "prevent Northern mistakes in Southern settings."

Thus, throughout the first decade of the Southern Growth Policies Board (SGPB), its principal concerns were urban growth and the Board's regional objectives (required in the interstate compact agreement of the Southern Growth Policies Board) focused on revitalizing and modernizing Southern urban economies. In 1986, however, when a Commission on the Future of the South was convened to draft another set of regional objectives, the political atmosphere was quite different. Governor Clinton opened his charge with the statement:

> For most of that 150 years we (Arkansas) have been like much of the South: rural, poor, and proud...always seeking elusive dreams and wanting something we knew we deserved and never had been quite able to achieve (Southern Growth Policies Board, 1986).

It took a substantial deterioration of economic conditions before the region's leaders were aware of what was happening, in part because the media were paying little attention to the plight of the rural South. Its problems were largely overshadowed by large-scale unemployment in the Northern industrial megalopolises, the declining value of the dollar, and trade and budget deficits. But eventually a critical mass of Southern rural plant closings, persistent double digit rural unemployment, and the stark contrast of the surging Southern cities, with population and job growth based on service and high-tech industries, dramatized the predicament the rural South found itself in. It had prepared for a manufacturing economy that was fading fast. With low educational levels, little wealth, and declining federal programs for revitalization, rural counties are ill-prepared for the future.

There are a number of unique characteristics of the rural South that should have provided early warning of poor economic performance. The first characteristic of the South that is important to understanding the crisis is the region's high level of industrialization. While the Midwest claims to be the nation's industrial heartland, the rural South is just as dependent on manufacturing.

About 27 percent of all nonagricultural workers in nonmetro counties are employed in manufacturing. About 30 percent of all Southern rural male and 23 percent of all Southern rural females (40 percent of all Southern rural blacks) identify themselves as "operators, assemblers, and fabricators." The comparable percentages for urban males and females are 22 and 10 percent, respectively. The map of nonmetro counties designated by the U.S. Department of Agriculture as "manufacturing-intensive" (at least 30 percent of the income in 1979 was derived from manufacturing), shows the high concentration in the South.

Second, unlike a decade earlier, unemployment is much higher in nonmetro than in metro counties. For SGPB's entire twelve-state region (Alabama, Arkansas, Florida, Georgia, Louisiana, Kentucky, Mississippi, North Carolina, Oklahoma, South Carolina, Tennessee, and Virginia), the nonmetro unemployment at the close of 1985 was considerably higher than the average rate for metro counties. Moreover, the disparities are becoming greater, not smaller. In ten of the twelve SGPB states, the ratio of nonmetro to metro unemployment rates were higher at the end of 1985 than at the end of 1984. In Virginia, for example, in 1984 the nonmetro rate was 62 percent higher but in 1985 it was 96 percent higher. In Tennessee at the end of 1984, the nonmetro unemployment rate was 60 percent higher than the metro rate; at the end of 1985, the nonmetro rate was 85 percent higher.

A third condition not generally known is that the South lagged far behind in the rural population turnabout in the 1970s, which captured the attention of policymakers everywhere. Southern cities continued to grow faster than Southern towns and villages—in population, jobs, and per capita income. Between 1970 and 1980, metro counties grew 23 percent faster than nonmetro counties; between 1980 and 1984, metro counties grew 70 percent faster than nonmetro counties. Both, however, grew faster than the national average.

Fourth, conditions that were once favorable to growth became a milestone around the neck of the rural South. Low taxes, low wages, an unregulated environment, and mediocre schools yielded high rankings on the Grant Thorton business climate index, but these same conditions do not produce high marks on the new indices of economic capacity being developed for the high growth industries. Today intelligence is replacing proximity to markets as a more important factor in plant location, and businesses are increasingly willing to trade higher taxes for better schools and services. These new attitudes, however, are offset by declining rural property values, diminishing federal support, and increased competition for state resources. If the new criteria for economic capacity—good schools, cultural amenities, a skilled work force—are necessary for growth, and if the federal and state governments do not help out, the prospects for the rural South are dim indeed.

Figure 1

Manufacturing-Dependent Counties

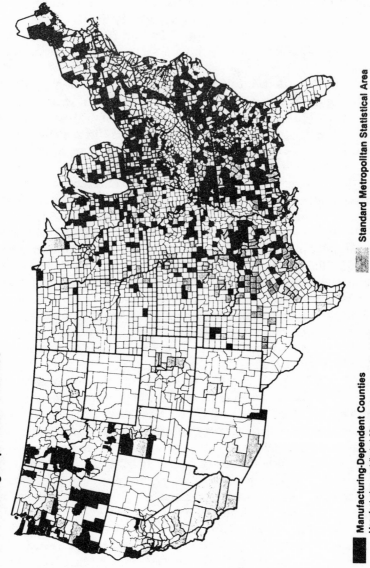

Manufacturing-Dependent Counties
Manufacturing contributed 30 percent or more of total labor and proprietor income in 1979.

Standard Metropolitan Statistical Area

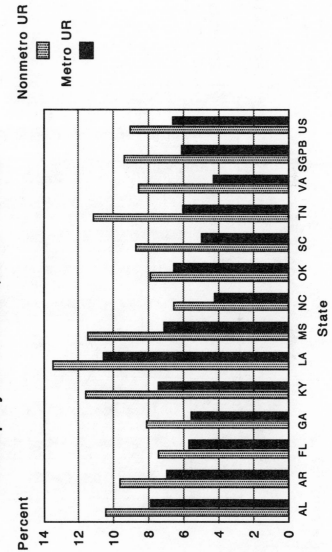

Figure 2
Unemployment Rates, End Of 1985

Figure 3

Ratio Of Nonmetro To Metro Unemployment Rates,
Dec 1984 And 1985

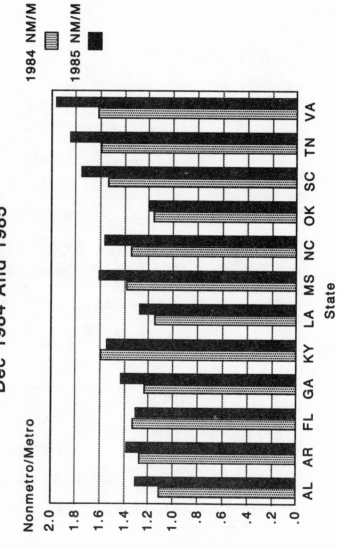

SOCIAL AND ECONOMIC CONDITIONS IN THE RURAL SOUTH

Despite the number of jobs created in the South in the period from 1950 to 1980, the quality of many of those jobs has been marginal. In terms of education, health, and wealth, rural areas lag far behind urban areas of the South (see Figure 4).

- Rates of functional illiteracy in 1980 in nonmetro areas, (i.e., percentage of the adult population with no more than eight years of education) were 71 percent higher than the rate in the urban South and 59 percent higher than the national average.

- The relative numbers of adults with high school diplomas and with college degrees were similarly lower. Nonmetro high school completion rates were only 76 percent of metro rates in the South and the percent of the adult population with college degrees was only 57 percent that of metro counties.

- The per capita income in the rural South in 1980 was $7,735; in the urban South it was $10,458, and for the nation as a whole it was $10,495. The per capita income of rural blacks in the South was $3,300.

- The number of physicians per capita in nonmetro counties was 42 percent of the number in metro counties.

Employment Patterns

In 1984, the Southern Growth Policies Board, which took early notice of the developing economic problems in the nonmetro South, began to analyze employment patterns. Using the five-year period from 1977 and 1982, a county file was created that included spatial, demographic, economic, and social conditions that might be associated with particular patterns of change. Each nonmetro county was assigned to one of five categories according to access to interstate highways and proximity to a metropolitan county. They ranged from *Remote*, which were not adjacent to a metro area and not near an interestate highway to *Adjacent/corridor*, which borders on a metro area and is dissected by an interstate highway with at least three interchanges or one within 20 miles of the center of the county (see Figure 5). County-level data on size and characteristics of population, composition of economy, and selected socioeconomic conditions were added to the file.

Changes in nonagricultural employment for each of the categories were compared. The results, published by the Southern Growth Policies Board in *After*

Figure 4

Selected Demographic and Economic Characteristics:
Averages For SGPB Nonmetro and Metro Areas, Total
SGPB Region, and United States

Characteristic	Nonmetro Average	Metro Average	Region Average	U. S. Average
Annual Pop. Growth Rate, 1970-80	1.65	2.03	1.87	1.02
Annual Pop. Growth Rate, 1980-84	1.35	2.29	1.90	1.04
Percent Rural, 1980	61.70	16.40	33.40	26.30
Percent Black, 1980	18.90	18.00	18.40	11.70
Percent Minority, 1980	21.00	21.70	21.40	16.60
Percent Completing 8th Grade	70.80	82.90	77.70	81.60
Percent High School Graduates, 1980	50.00	65.50	59.80	66.50
Percent College Graduates, 1980	10.00	17.40	14.60	16.20
Number of Physicians Per 100,000	76.90	181.80	142.40	173.70
Percent Self-employed, 1980	8.80	5.50	6.70	6.80
Per Capita Income, 1980	$7,735	$10,458	$9,436	$10,495
Unemployment Rate, 1985 (%)	9.40	6.20	7.50	--

Figure 5. County Location

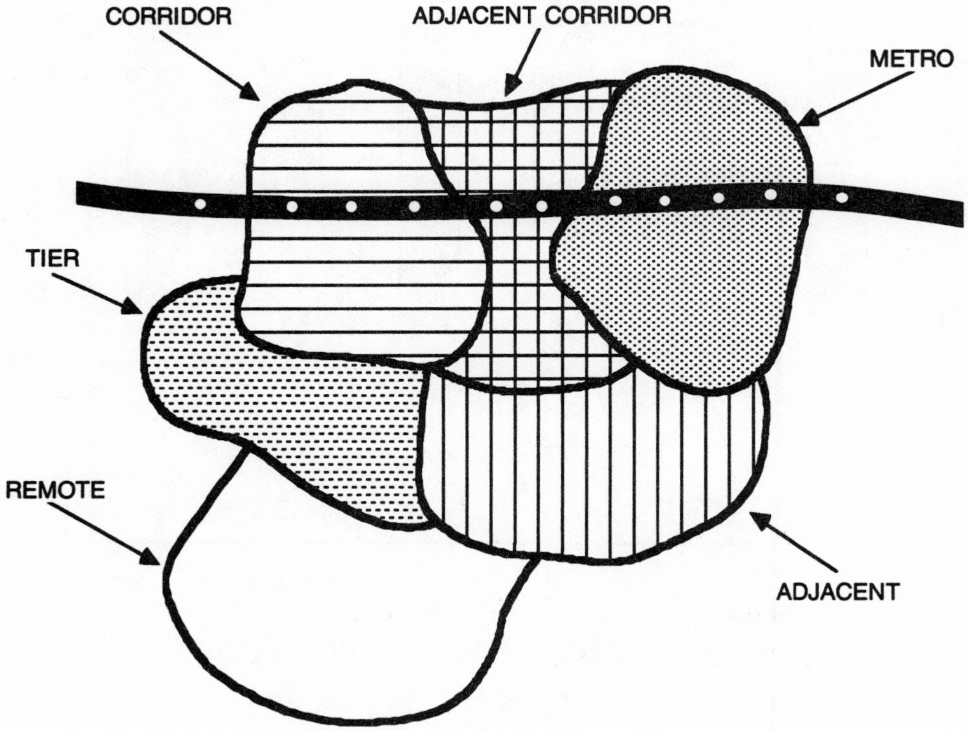

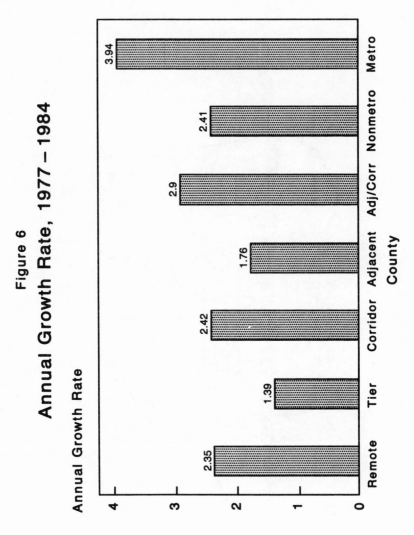

Figure 6
Annual Growth Rate, 1977 – 1984

the Factories: Changing Employment Patterns in the Rural South, (Rosenfeld et al., 1985) showed, for example, that (1) metro counties grew 65 percent more than nonmetro counties, (2) there was much more variation within spatial categories of nonmetro counties than among metro counties, (3) faster growth occurred in counties with better access to an interstate highway combined with adjacency to a metro county, and (4) faster growth was associated with greater concentration of employment in service industries (see Figure 6).

Although the patterns of employment change were consistent and strong, there was a great deal of debate over whether the patterns were primarily cyclical responses to a recession—since 1982 was a recession year—or marked permanent structural changes in the economy. If the changes were mostly cyclical, substantial recovery of jobs lost ought to be evidenced in post-recession years. If, however, the changes were structural, rural employment patterns would remain altered.

Subsequent analyses suggested that manufacturing in the South did recover substantially after 1982. Analyses of the Tennessee Valley Authority region by Robert Gilmer and Allan Pulsipher found that between 1982 and 1985 rural manufacturing regained most of the jobs lost during the earlier period (Gilman and Pulsipher, 1986). Further analysis by Thomas Till (1987) confirmed the recovery. Recovery, however, is not the same as growth. Although in the region selected and for the years selected, most of the jobs lost were regained, there was essentially no net gain and manufacturing continued to decline relative to total employment. Moreover, the jobs gained may not be located in the same communities so that labor dislocation remains a major problem. Between January 1979 and January 1984, 1.5 million Southerners were displaced, and more than half of those were in manufacturing.

The SGPB conducted a limited re-analysis of employment patterns for the years 1982 to 1984 to determine whether they changed significantly from the period 1977 to 1982. In the period from 1982 to 1984, employment in the metro counties in the South continued to grow about 65 percent faster than employment in nonmetro counties. Further, the impact of access to interstate highways became more pronounced.

Race, Education, Income, and Growth

The wide disparities among nonmetro counties suggest that it may be possible to identify characteristics that are associated with growth or decline in addition to highways and nearness to cities. For example, most political leaders now assume that better education is important for economic growth. This flies in the face of past policies that ignored education in order to keep taxes and wages low for employers. Civil rights leaders have claimed that state developers pay too little attention to counties with large proportions of minority residents. A charge lodged against state development agencies is that potential employers are not taken to counties that are more than one-third black—which is admitted, but attributed to the proclivity of black workers to organize, not to racism. Both of these assumptions were tested.

First, the nonmetro counties were ranked and placed in quintiles, with the first quintile containing the 20 percent of all nonmetro counties with the slowest annual growth rates, the second quintile with the 20 percent with the next lowest annual growth rates, up to the fifth quintile, which is the 20 percent of all nonmetro counties with the highest annual growth rates. Next, the rates of adult illiteracy, estimated as the percent of all adults over 25 in 1980 with no more than eight years of school, were calculated for each quintile. Adult illiteracy rates were highest in the slowest growing nonmetro counties and lowest in the fastest growing counties, as shown in Figure 7.

A similar analysis replacing rates of adult illiteracy with rates of high school completion shows similar results. The slowest growth is associated with the lowest concentration of high school graduates and the fastest growth is associated with the highest concentration of high school completers (see Figure 8).

Employment growth was also compared between counties with varying proportions of black residents (Figure 9). Counties where less than 20 percent of the population was black in 1980 grew an average of more than 2.6 percent per year. Counties where more than 50 percent of the population was black grew just over half as fast, or about 1.4 percent per year. Although the pattern shows a slight upturn when the percent rises above 60 percent, the impact is misleading. Those counties, while growing slightly faster than counties with fewer blacks, had an average per capita income of only $5,900 and had an average unemployment rate of 12.4 percent at the end of 1985.

Many of the factors that affect growth—education, race as well as income and other demographic factors—are correlated with one another. Identifying the unique contributions of any one would require further statistical analysis. But a very simple tabular analysis provides some preliminary insights. The annual growth rates for nonmetro counties were calculated (shown in Figure 10) for percentages of black residents, percentages of high school graduates, and per capita income at both above and below average for all nonmetro counties.

The growth rates indicate, for example, that in counties with low levels of education and at both low and high income, race has little effect (1.8 percent vs. 1.9 percent at low income and 1.6 percent vs. 1.8 percent for high income). In counties with high levels of education, however, race was a factor. At both lower-than-average per capita income and higher-than-average per capita income, counties with fewer-than-average numbers of blacks grew about 50 percent faster than counties with more-than-average concentrations of blacks. The tentative conclusion one might draw is that education is the most important factor, but race also influences growth in those counties with higher educational levels.

Figure 7

Adult Literacy And Employment Growth, 1977 – 1984

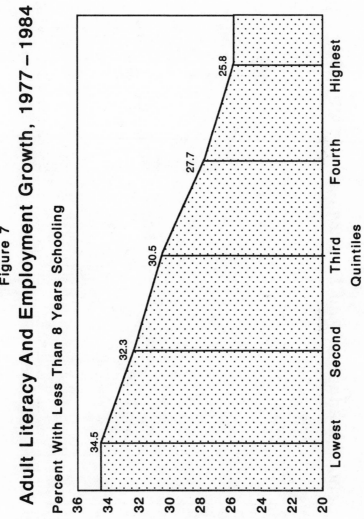

Percent With Less Than 8 Years Schooling

Figure 8

High School Graduation And Employment Growth, 1977 – 1984

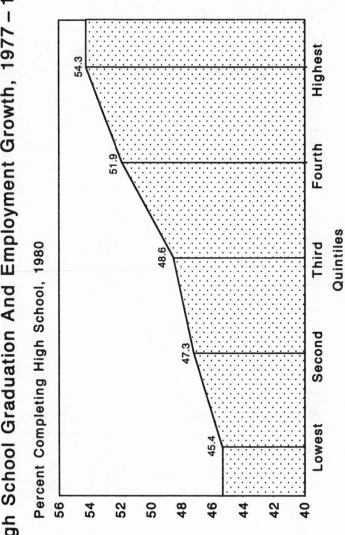

Percent Completing High School, 1980

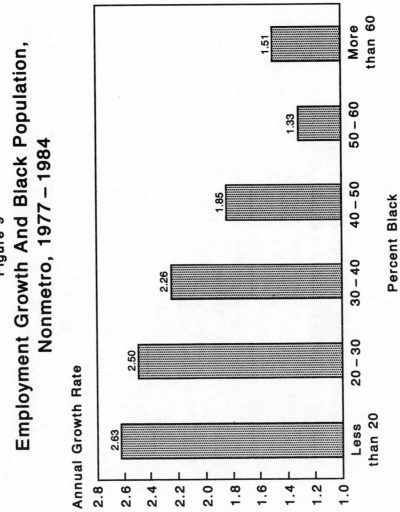

Figure 9

Employment Growth And Black Population,
Nonmetro, 1977–1984

Figure 10

ANNUAL EMPLOYMENT GROWTH RATE
SGPB NONMETRO COUNTIES
1977-1984

Percent Black	Percent High School Graduates		Per Capita Income	
			Low	High
High*	High		2.7 55**	3.0 100
	Low		1.8 99	1.6 56
Low	High		4.1 99	4.5 195
	Low		1.9 255	1.8 60

* High and low refer to above and below the average of all SGPB nonmetro counties.

** Number of counties

Employment Change and Economic Profile

The composition of employment in a county also influences growth. Loss of competitiveness in manufacturing was responsible for most of the economic ills of the rural South. The region's heavy concentration of low-skill, labor-intensive manufacturing made it exceedingly vulnerable to off-shore competition from counties where labor costs are even lower. Many firms shifted from labor to capital in order to improve productivity and remain competitive, but that reduced labor requirements and required workers with different skills and education.

Between 1977 and 1982, counties with the fastest growth in employment had the smallest proportion of their residents employed in manufacturing while those counties with the slowest growth had the largest proportion of their workers employed in manufacturing (as shown in Figure 11). This does not mean, however, that the region can simply shift to a service economy and growth. About one-fourth of all service jobs are directly linked to manufacturing, and the manufacturing sector, even if it employs fewer people, is vital to the health of the economy (Cohen and Zysman, 1987).

Small businesses created the majority of new jobs in rural America between 1976 and 1984 (56 percent), but the composition is counterintuitive. Perceptions of the economy of the rural South are large branch plants and small local retailers. Between 1976 and 1984, however, employment in small retail establishments grew 0.4 percent, in medium size businesses 39.4 percent, and in large businesses 71.6 percent. The Wal-Marts and K-Marts apparently are replacing the local dry goods stores and druggists. During the same period, the growth of small, medium, and large establishments in metro areas was 12.3, 24.4 and 21.3 percents, respectively. Employment growth in service shows the same pattern, though not as strong. Conversely, however, the growth from small manufacturing vastly outstripped large manufacturing on both nonmetro and metro areas. In nonmetro counties, employment in small manufacturing plants grew 21 percent, in medium-size plants 5.4 percent, and in large plants, 2.4 percent (Swain, 1987).

IS THE TALE OF TWO SOUTHS A "TALL TALE?"

Despite all of the indicators of rural decline, claiming that there are two Souths oversimplifies the situation. Southern economic development is not just the story of burgeoning, prospering cities and stagnant rural communities. The nonmetro annual employment growth rate, while far below the metro rate, *was* positive. The variation among nonmetro counties was much greater than among metro counties. Many rural areas performed quite well, even during the recession years. Although one in every five nonmetro counties

Figure 11

Percent Employed In Nonmetro Counties
Manufacturing And Services, 1977
By Quintle Of Employment Growth, 1977 – 1982

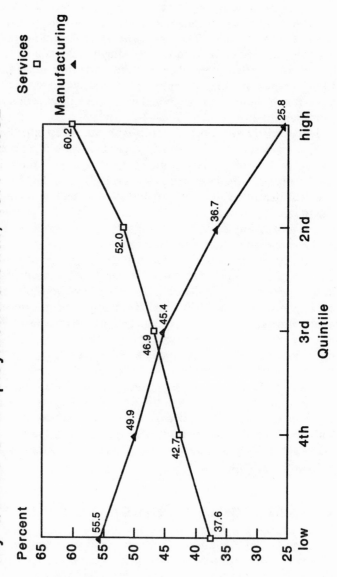

experienced a net loss in employment between 1977 and 1984, one in four actually grew faster than the average metro county and one in twenty more than doubled the average metro growth rate.

The term "two Souths" refers only to an overall pattern, which many rural counties do not fit. Information about the outliers—counties that vary greatly from the averages—may shed light on solutions for other rural areas. For example, those counties that have been designated by the USDA as retirement counties, where the net in-migration of people aged 60 and over was greater than 15 percent between 1970 and 1980, grew faster between 1977 and 1984 on average (4.7 percent per year) than the metro counties. Similarly, counties that were designated by USDA as "government" counties, where 20 percent of the population or more are employed in the public sector, grew at an average annual rate of 4.4 percent.

Other nonmetro counties with major tourist attractions, many of which are classified as *remote,* also did well. The combined nonmetro coastal counties in Virginia, North and South Carolina, and Georgia, for example, grew between 1977 and 1984 at an annual rate of 4.3 percent, nearly as fast as metro counties. Selected counties, however, boomed. Flagler, Citrus, and Hernando along the Florida coast and Dare in North Carolina grew more than 10 percent per year. Marion and Madison Counties, in the Ozarks region of northern Arkansas, also averaged more than 10 percent annual growth between 1977 and 1984.

HALFWAY HOME AND A LONG WAY TO GO: STATES' RESPONSES

Unfortunately, many of the conditions that hamper rural development cannot be easily rectified with a program here and there or even infusions of money. The six-year span set by the Southern Growth Policies Board to meet its regional objectives is not sufficient to alter structural conditions that have developed over decades or to change the average skill levels of the adult population, which had been educationally deprived early in life.

There must be a longer-term commitment—not just to increasing the *number* of jobs, but to improving the *quality* of the jobs. North Carolina is a case in point. Although the rural parts of the state have done better than many other parts of the South in terms of job growth, average wage rates remain the lowest in the nation. The state has appropriated about $2 million to establish a Rural Economic Development Center (Senate Bill 35, 1987) to find ways to promote growth and improve conditions in rural parts of the state.

Other states are also responding to calls of rural distress.

- The Georgia legislature enacted legislation known as the Rural Economic Development Law (Senate Bill 191, 1987) authorizing the Department of Community Affairs "to provide a program of rural economic development" to be targeted to rural counties where the per capita income is less than 70 percent of the national average or unemployment rate is more than 35 percent above the state average.

- Arkansas passed legislation this year (House Bill 2023) directing the state's industrial development commission to form advisory teams and coordinate rural development.

- The state of Mississippi passed a comprehensive economic development planning act (Senate Bill No. 2839, 1987) that specifies special programs "for rural areas of the state and those areas with the highest unemployment and lowest per capita income."

- The Advisory Committee on the Future of the Florida Legislature in 1987 recommended "a study committee of public and private sector members to develop strategies to assist rural Florida in providing short and long term economic development opportunities and needed infrastructure, including education and health facilities" appointed by the governor, the Speaker, and the President of the Senate. Proposed legislation is to be submitted to the Legislature by February 1988.

- The South Carolina Development Board has created a new position, Assistant to the Director of Rural Development. That person will be responsible for establishing a new state program to provide counsel, advice, and assistance to rural counties and communities to stimulate rural economic development.

There are no easy answers and some rural communities may not regain past levels of employment. Recent efforts are but first steps, but they are important steps. They show that state leaders understand the situation and are willing to work with local organizations to find ways to stimulate rural development. When the 1986 Commission on the Future of the South met one year after the report was released to measure progress, it was much easier to point to programs than to demonstrate results. The one aspect of rural recovery that was highlighted was leadership. Governor Bill Clinton and the Commission charged the Southern Growth Policies Board with developing a program to identify, support, and expand leadership in rural areas of the South. It is also evident that additional resources will be needed and that many rural counties lack the resources to take advantage of economic opportunities. Federal economic development programs, such as those carried out under the Appalachian Development Commission, the Tennessee Valley Authority, and the Economic Development Administration were instrumental in the past and they will be critical to future rural growth.

REFERENCES

Cohen, Stephen S., and John Zysman. 1987. *Manufacturing Matters: The Myth of the Post-Industrial Economy.* New York: Basic Books.

Gilmer, Robert W., and Allan G. Pulsipher. 1986. "Recent economic performance and the economic future of the rural South." *Forum for Applied Science and Public Policy,* 1 (Summer): 109-118.

Louv, Richard, 1983. *America II.* Boston: Houghton-Mifflin.

Rosenfeld, Stuart A., Edward Bergman, and Sara Rabin. 1985. *After the Factories: Changing Employment Patterns in the Rural South.* Research Triangle Park, NC: Southern Growth Policies Board.

Southern Growth Policies Board. 1986. *Halfway Home and a Long Way to Go.* Report of the Commission on the Future of the South. Research Triangle Park, NC.

Swain, Frank S. 1987. Chief Counsel for Advocacy, U. S. Small Business Administration statement before the Subcommittee on Rural Economy and Family Farming, Committee on Small Business, United States Senate, March 5.

Till, Thomas E. 1987. *The Shadows in the Sunbelt report: Has the wave of new factory jobs ended in the nonmetropolitan South?* Unpublished paper presented to the Southern Regional Science Association Conference, Atlanta, Georgia, March 26-28.

Winter, William F. 1986. "Prospects for economic development in the rural South." *Emerging Issues in the Rural Economy of the South.* Mississippi State: Southern Rural Development Center (April): 1-5.

5

The Community Crisis in the Rural South

Kenneth P. Wilkinson

A crisis is a turning point, a moment of instability when problems come to a head and decisive change—toward either improvement or deterioration—is at hand. Much evidence suggests that the rural South is in a state of crisis. Recent events, especially changes in farm economics, have brought longstanding problems of rural life in this region to the fore. The present crisis, however, involves much more than farming. What the rural South faces is a community crisis. It is a crisis that cuts across the whole of local social and economic life in the small towns and rural areas of this region. It involves jobs and income but also services and group life, and it affects the quality of social relationships among people who live together in rural settlements. The crisis in the rural South—a crucial turning point in the history and well-being of the region—is a crisis *in* communities, but also to no small degree it is a crisis *of* community.

Dimensions of this community crisis bear close investigation if ways are to be found to solve serious problems and promote social well-being in the rural South. This chapter reviews the background of the community crisis, identifies its main parameters, and suggests an approach that could be taken to turn the community crisis into a new era of community development in the rural South.

COMMUNITY, RURALITY AND THE SOUTH

Perspective for an analysis of the community crisis in this setting is gained by acknowledging that the rural South, for all its distinctiveness, shares a number of community and rural problems with other regions. In all of modern society, the community—an historically significant form of social organization—is at a critical juncture, and questions are being raised about the contribution of this form of social organization to social well being in the future. Likewise, in all societies, rural living tends to be associated with certain problems. To some extent, the community crisis in the rural South represents this larger crisis in community and rural life.

Still, the South is unique as a setting for the crisis, and the distinctive historical and contemporary attributes of the region obviously weigh heavily on how the crisis will work itself out. Essential to understanding the dimensions of the community crisis in the rural South, therefore, is an appreciation of the separate influences of three key factors that interact to structure the crisis, namely the community, rural life, and the South.

Community

Change is the keyword in the study of the modern community. Communities are changing and theories of the community are changing; and sometimes it is not clear which of these is changing more. Probably, as Drucker (1986:768) remarks about the economy, it is misleading to say the community is changing; in many ways it has *already* changed. Perhaps the community of the past was a static, self-contained organization for living, but not today. With modern contact technologies (e.g., automobiles, electronic communications and so on), "place-chains," as the ties to the local territory are called by some observers (e.g., Scherer, 1972), have lost their power. Individuals, groups, and organizations are connected to systems that extend beyond the local setting, and these connections are through such diverse and specialized channels that it is not accurate to speak of the community itself as an integrated whole or system. Instead, as some sociologists note (e.g., Warren, 1978:409-417), the local territory has become a stage or arena where various interest groups pursue their own agendas and where interactions and negotiations generate a turbulent process of action. The community is more of a field than a system: its dynamic and unpredictable qualities overshadow its systemic qualities.

If this is true, one must ask, why call it "community?" Usually, community implies closeness, harmony and wholeness. Is this image of the community only a myth in modern times, an ideal but not a reality?

One answer, suggested by research on interpersonal contacts of urban residents, is that a new kind of space-free community network has emerged to bind relatively footloose people into meaningful associations. Bender (1978) develops this thesis in an historical analysis of the community in America. Defining community as "a network of social relations marked by mutuality and emotional bonds" (1978:7), he observes that: "Territorially based inter-action represents only one pattern of community, a pattern that becomes less and less evident over the course of American history" (1978:6). Communi-ties, he says, occur not in particular places but in intimate networks wherever these might be found. Assisted by long-distance communications technologies and ease of travel, people can participate simultaneously in several commu-nities and these networks can extend over virtually unbounded spatial regions. The new community, from this perspective, is not to be found among people who live together so much as among people who are in contact with one another. Those who live together might be deeply embedded in numerous different communities and be only nominally connected to one another.

Quite a different perspective is taken by some students of the community, especially by those who insist that the term community be reserved specif-ically for relationships among people who share important aspects of a com-mon life (*Gemeinschaft*) on a common ground (*Gemeinde*)—the original meaning of community in Western language and thought. The major question about community from this perspective is how can it exist in the fluid, dy-namic setting of the modern local settlement; and basically this is an em-pirical question to be answered through research on community actions and interactions. Thus, community is seen either as a network that is independent of territory or as a territorially-based, locality-oriented action field.

Both of these are important social relationship structures, but only the latter—that is, only relationships among people who live together—meet all the criter-ia of being *community* relationships. Other networks can be community-like; but for community to exist, people must experience it *in their everyday lives*—in the relationships they have with the people they actually encounter face-to-face in going about the everyday business of meeting various needs and expressing various interests. For most people, these encounters occur mainly in the area of local residence. Outside involvements in intimate but space-free networks certainly are important to people, but they are less immediate and direct than contacts in the community. Immediate, face-to-face contacts are essential to human social well-being; and community development, therefore, specifical-ly within the local territory, can play a vital role in promoting social well-being.

Clearly, the community as a local network is in a state of crisis. Outside contacts and fragmentation of interest groups raise serious questions about the integrity of the community unit. Local boundaries are confused. The lo-cal society is comprised in large part of branches of outside organizations and special-interest groups. Private agendas dominate much of the local action stage. Whether the germ of "communityness" can persist in this milieu is in doubt.

Still, people live together in places, however fluid the boundaries of those places; they still encounter the larger society mainly through the direct contacts they have with one another in the local society; and, at crucial moments, they still might be able to act together to express and protect the interest they share in the locality (see Tilly, 1973). Thus, a potential exists as one always has for community to emerge and meet important needs of people who live together, even if this potential is suppressed somewhat by modern trends.

Rural Life

Considering the many social characteristics that typically accompany rural living, one that stands out dramatically as an influence on the community is the tendency for socioeconomic status (as indicated by family income, education, occupational prestige, housing quality, and so on) to vary inversely with the extent of ruralness of the locality. This tendency is found in more developed and less developed societies alike. Generally speaking, as rurality goes up, so do poverty and inequality. As a population urbanizes, its socioeconomic welfare tends to increase.

Why this is the case is subject to some debate. Explanations tend to follow three somewhat different lines. One is an ecological argument that emphasizes the function of urban agglomeration in economic development (see Hansen, 1973). Socioeconomic problems of communities tend to increase with distance from major centers of economic activity. A second argument is cultural, emphasizing the effects of depressed aspirations and limited world views of people in remote settings (e.g., Fitchen, 1981). A third argument is critical of ecological and cultural explanations and attributes rural socioeconomic problems to exploitative tendencies in capitalist development (Howes and Markusen, 1981). Whatever the causes, the result is a crisis of rural well-being—a crisis that is only partly explained by recent upheavals in agriculture and other traditionally rural economic enterprises. Rural areas and their residents are still being "left behind" in urban-industrial and post-industrial society (Warner, 1974; Wilkinson, 1986).

The rural crisis and the community crisis are related. Contrary to some observations about the past, the evidence for the present shows quite clearly that rural living entails problems for community development. Years ago, Galpin (1915) documented the tendency for residents of essentially rural areas to travel regularly to nearby urban centers for meeting many of their daily needs. He concluded that residents of Walworth County, Wisconsin lived in "rurban" communities rather than in rural or urban communities. With the further development of city-country contacts, the idea of a "rural community" has become even less plausible for most areas than it was in Galpin's time. Rural areas lack sufficient agglomeration of people to support the institutions that would be necessary to meet local needs on a daily basis. Thus as rurality increases, the probability decreases that the local society could be a more or less complete one and that residents, therefore, would be in daily contact with one another for meeting the full range of their common needs. As people travel elsewhere, the locality where they live becomes less and less of a community in fact, although it might continue to be thought of as a community. Moreover, the depressing socioeconomic effects of distance from urban resources can provoke cleavages in local social life, isolating social groupings from one another and setting them in opposition to one another on community issues (Kraenzel, 1980). The rural crisis, therefore, exacerbates the community crisis in rural areas.

The South

What is so special about the South? Other regions have community and rural problems, but in the South those problems take on the special qualities of the region. For one thing, the Southern census region contains a large share of the nation's rural population, including 43 percent of the nonmetro population in 1980 and 47 percent of the residents of open-country nonmetro areas. Thus, generalizations about rural America must be weighted heavily by observations about the rural South. The rural South also has striking community attributes—a pattern of small town-and-country settlements in contrast to the village pattern of the Northeast and the dispersed homestead pattern of the Midwest; and a long history of organized community development programs sponsored by churches, the Cooperative Extension Service and other organizations (see Kaufman et al., 1975). The economic history of the South is distinctive—a long period of reliance on primary industries with interregional dependency and, indeed, a war as part of its political-economic legacy; and more recently, the almost sudden growth of large metropolitan areas drawing resources from other parts of the nation but also increasing the gap dramatically between rural and urban portions of the region. The Southern pattern of stratification deserves attention—the lingering vestiges of a failed effort to establish a feudal system in the New World; the haunting specter of slavery and its aftermath; a pervasive lower class adaptation to turmoil and deprivation that some social scientists identify as a culture of lethal violence (Gastil, 1971); and a persisting pattern of sharp contrasts between the rich and the poor, rivaling in fact the gap between the rich and the poor in some developing nations. The effects of this historical context on everyday life in rural areas of the South continue, despite much change, to constrain the potential for cooperation among local population segments. Without belaboring the point, it is fair to say Southern culture and the structure of society in the South give a most distinctive twist to the community crisis in the rural areas of this region.

DIMENSIONS OF THE CRISIS

These three factors—a crisis of community in modern society, various problems associated generally with rural life, and the special setting of the South—converge to produce the community crisis in the rural South. It is clear that this crisis has at least four dimensions. Two of these are problems that occur in communities and contribute to the problem *of* community. These are the problems of providing sufficient jobs and income and sufficient services to meet the daily needs of people in the small towns and rural areas of the region. These deficits affect material well-being directly; and indirectly, they affect the social relationships among people that are essential to the formation and maintenance of a community. The other two dimensions of the crisis are cleavages in the structure of local social life. These include social inequality, which is perhaps the most wrenching problem of community in the rural South, and social fragmentation or isolation, which is the antithesis of community integration.

Jobs and Income

The economic dimension of this crisis has been well documented and need only be mentioned here. Stated plainly, the rural South is the nation's poorest area. Comparing rural and urban portions of the four census regions, the rural South stands out as lowest on almost all of the widely used indicators of socioeconomic well-being—even though the South as a whole has been experiencing considerable economic growth. The effects of the crisis in agriculture are well known. The effects of rapid metropolitan growth on the economic well-being of the communities left behind in the countryside also are well known (see Bergman, 1986). The results are described poignantly by Johnson (1986:13) as follows:

> *Almost seven million rural Southerners are poor—nearly twenty-one percent of the population in the rural South. Their numbers have grown dramatically since 1980, and are increasing. As a result of national trends that have reduced available benefits, curtailed investment in rural economic development, and feminized poverty, certain groups have suffered the most: the rural poor, the black poor, poor women, dependent children, the elderly poor, and the disabled poor. This is a national disgrace that could turn into a regional calamity; the South simply cannot afford to be constituted of so many people who are poorly paid, ill-housed, under-educated, and under-treated by the health care system.*

Thus, concludes Johnson, the South has a major stake in rural economic development. This state is especially important to development of community in the region. Without economic resources to meet the needs of people in the rural areas of the South, community development is blocked.

Services

Delivery of community services in the rural areas of the South is another dimension of the community crisis. In large part, rural service delivery is a problem because of two economic facts: a small population means high unit costs, and distance increases the cost of delivery (Coelen and Fox, 1981). These facts constrain the delivery of a wide range of rural services including health, education, recreation, transportation, safety, justice, water, wastewater treatment, solid waste disposal, energy, telecommunications, fire safety, and others. Consequently, many rural localities lack some if not all of the services people have come to rely upon for meeting their daily needs. In the rural area of the South, this has two severe effects. First, it means that rural community well-being is depressed by problems of access to vital resources; and, second, it means that the local area is not a complete community. Both of these play a role in the community crisis.

Inequality

Inequality has a number of more or less obvious effects on community well-being in the rural South. As in the other regions of the country, the South has two major forms of inequality, one based on economic differences and the other on ascribed characteristics such as race, age, and gender. In the rural South these two forms of inequality converge with staggering results. Reviewing data for 1983, Johnson (1986:18) reports that in the rural South more than 58 percent of black female-headed households were in poverty and, among black children under six in female-headed households, 80 percent were in poverty. Data on unemployment for 1984 also show a pattern of Southern inequality: the gap between the urban unemployment rate (6.7 percent) and the rural unemployment rate (9.5 percent) is greater than in any other census region (U.S. Department of Labor, Bureau of Labor Statistics, and U.S. Department of Agriculture, Statistical Reporting Service, 1986:152). Lyson and Falk (1986), commenting on the "two sides of the sunbelt," show evidence of sharp economic discrepancies in the South between predominantly white and predominantly black rural counties. Discussing recent economic development, they write (1986:162-163), "In stark contrast to the other county groups, the Black Belt counties in 1986 remain saddled with an economic base dominated almost entirely by slow growing, stagnating, and declining industries." In these counties, they note (1986:163), "most occupational opportunities are at the low wage, low skill end of the job ladder." Moreover, they report, blacks and women in these counties are concentrated in the least favorable positions.

Sociological research over many years in small towns and rural areas of the South show the effects of inequality on patterns of community mobilization, involvement and leadership (see Kaufman and Wilkinson, 1967). Inequality suppresses interaction among groupings of people whose lives and well-being are in fact tied together ecologically; and, without interaction, community—particularly a dynamic, interactional form of community—cannot exist. Moreover, when the inequality accompanies or is based upon ascribed characteristics such as race it tends to provoke not only separation and isolation of groupings from one another but also overt hostility between groupings—as shown clearly by Blau and Blau's (1982) research on urban violence. Gastil (1971), in fact, argues that the relatively high rate of lethal violence (that is, the high murder rate) in the South is partly a consequence of a stratification order based historically on the threat of violence. To be sure, Gastil's analysis refers to the region's overall rate of lethal violence and not explicitly to interracial or rural homicides. His argument, however, makes the point that a stratification structure based historically on the threat of violence can generate disruptive cleavages throughout a society.

Where such cleavages continue to exist, based on the combination of class and race, partial forms of community sometimes appear. Partial forms include class-specific or race-specific networks that might be cohesive within themselves, but are not linked to one another to form a community. Granovetter (1973), in a most perceptive essay, gives a conceptual framework for evaluating the overall consequences of such partial communities within a local setting. "Strong ties," he says, referring to intimate networks among people of the same ethnic or class grouping, serve important interpersonal needs in a pluralistic or differentiated society, but, for community to be maintained, these strong ties must be linked through "weak ties" to the larger community structure; otherwise, they become disruptive to the larger whole. Over the years, linkages no doubt have increased somewhat among the differentiated groupings in Southern communities, particularly in urban settings where formal mechanisms have developed to supply the "weak ties," (to use Granovetter's term) that are needed between, for example, black and white subcommunities. In less urban settings, however, old patterns tend to persist longer; and the old patterns can continue to block the emergence of community in the social life of the local settlement as a whole.

Does inequality represent more or less of a crisis in the rural South now than it did, say twenty years ago at the height of the civil rights movement? Opinions vary, although in some ways inequality obviously is as much of a crisis now as it was then. The crisis today tends to be concentrated in the remote reaches of a region that is urbanizing rapidly and becoming much like other regions in its social structure. Change is slower in the countryside, although change has occurred there also. The dimension of the crisis of community that is associated with inequality appears to be most evident today in the most rural portions of this region.

Social Integration

The fourth dimension of the community crisis in the rural South is fragmentation or isolation of local groupings from one another. In part, this is a consequence of the other dimensions of the crisis: poverty suppresses intergroup contacts; service deficits force people to look elsewhere for resources to meet vital needs; and inequality, especially that based on the combination of class and race, is a cleavage that holds people apart and can set them in direct and sometimes violent opposition to one another. In the rural South, these sources of fragmentation and isolation in community life interact with general societal trends which have wrought a community crisis in other regions as well as in this one.

In an earlier era, some sociologists (e.g. Sorokin and Zimmerman, 1929) observed that the effects of physical isolation in rural areas were offset, in many instances, by the effects of cohesion in rural family and community life. Today in the rural South, physical isolation is still a fact of life to some extent, even if less so than a half-century ago. For the very poor in rural areas, isolation is at least as much of a fact of life now as it was in the past. What about the offsetting effects of family and community life? Where is the cohesion that could counteract the effects of physical isolation in the past? The same trends that have changed family and community patterns in urban America have changed these patterns in the rural South. Physical isolation tends to mean social isolation today. Moreover, the rural South has the added problems of extreme concentrations of poverty, severe deficits in services, and persisting inequality. Consequently, isolation—physical and social—is a pervasive threat to community well-being in the rural South.

COMMUNITY DEVELOPMENT

The picture, of course, is not entirely one of gloom and doom. A crisis is a time of trouble but also of opportunity. The crisis of community, for example, could signal the emergence of a new form of community, one with fewer constraints on human well-being than some of the older forms. Perhaps, as Wellman (1979) argues, community is not "lost" as a result of modern trends but "saved" and even "liberated." The rural crisis also could be part of a transition to a new era. Perhaps as Blakely and Bradshaw (1985:4) argue: "Rural America is at the leading edge of the advanced industrial society." Moreover, the community crisis in the rural South could presignify a new era of community development. Perhaps by virtue of its history of adversity and the severity of some of its community problems, the rural South is where the pervasive human disposition toward community development will erupt to produce the new form of community that will fit society in the future.

Community development, of course, has about as many different meanings as one could extract from the nebulous root terms, community and development. For purposes of understanding and responding to the community crisis in rural areas of the South, the most useful definitions take the *process* of community action as the essential ingredient of community development. As a process, community development means capacity building—building (or at least trying to build) the capacity for self-help and self-direction through community action. Action is community action when people work together to solve the problems and express the interests they share in the local society. Community development occurs in community action when people try to improve their ability to work together.

With this definition, which emphasizes interaction processes and relationships among people, rather than material goals and other outcomes of programs, questions might well be raised about the other ends of development such as jobs and income, services, and equality. Are these neglected when the focus is on developing the community as an action capacity? If the local area were the setting where well-being on these other goals could be determined, there would be no question that community action capacity would be a key to achieving many other goals. But this hardly is the case in the rural areas of the South today. Instead, local well-being depends to a great extent on systems and actions in a much larger arena—in state, regional, national, and world systems. How can community action and the process of community development be expected to intercede in these larger systems on behalf of the wishes and needs of people in remote areas of the rural South? Why focus on community development if crucial issues require action at other levels?

There are at least two ways the process of community development can contribute to social well-being in the rural South, and in each of these the fact that a community crisis is in progress heightens the potential contribution. First, notwithstanding powerful forces in the larger society, community action, when it occurs, can make a difference in economic development, in development of local services, and in confronting and reducing inequalities. Recognizing that there are limits to what rural groups can achieve and recognizing the need for action and changes at other levels, one cannot rule out the possibility that local action will have important effects. Once the larger matrix is understood, specific opportunities for community action to be effective become apparent. Second, in addition to this instrumental contribution to well-being, community development can affect social well-being in a direct and intrinsic way. This is because people, as social beings, have a natural inclination to form community relationships with other people. This obviously is but one of many fundamental human dispositions, but it is a powerful one. People need and seek community in their daily contacts, although this need might be suppressed by external constraints. Community development, as a purposive effort to build community relationships, can help to liberate this natural human disposition from the barriers that suppress it—from barriers such as poverty, inadequate services, inequality, and isolation.

Clearly, however, community development in this setting faces some formidable barriers, and the people in rural areas of the South will need help if the potential for community development in the current crisis is to be cultivated and realized. Current trends give no indication that the small communities in the rural South will be able to effect their own development unless there are changes in larger regional and national systems which would create opportunities for local initiative to be effective. Policy intervention will be needed at state and national levels to address the economic and service problems of communities in the rural South and to confront again and again the debilitating problem of inequality. Help also is needed to cultivate and enhance the skills of local leaders in building the networks that can transform a settlement of isolated groups and families into a community. Grass-roots education for community development must accompany efforts at other levels to create opportunities for community action to occur and to influence the well-being of local residents in substantial ways. Concerted and studied action is needed at the policy level and in working directly with community residents to solve pressing problems and to take advantage of emerging opportunities for community development.

Such prescriptions, of course, are much easier to suggest in the abstract than to translate into specific suggestions for policy and education. An important step can be made toward formulating specific suggestions, however, by recognizing that what the present community crisis calls for and perhaps makes possible is community development. The idea that community development is what is needed is easily—and often—acknowledged but then ignored in programs that address particular problems, such as problems in agriculture, problems of retaining or expanding local employment, problems of service delivery, and even problems of inequality and injustice. These can be treated nominally as community problems, that is as problems that occur in communities, or they can be recognized as dimensions of an even more crucial problem—the problem of community. Recognizing these as dimensions of the problem of community gives a perspective that can guide policies and programs to respond specifically to the community crisis. Otherwise, policies and programs that address particular problems can run the risk inadvertently of contributing to the community crisis.

Two examples will illustrate this point. First, how should new contact technologies be deployed to promote community development in rural areas? Contact technologies include the products of what Dillman (1985) calls the "information society." These are almost certain to have far-reaching effects on community life in rural areas of the South. Computer linkages via fiber-optic cables, satellites and other communications breakthroughs carry the potential to reduce or even to remove entirely the drag effect of distance on access to information, and information has become a most important resource for economic and community development. Theoretically, in the "information society," human resources and data, rather than natural resources and location, determine competitive advantages (see Blakely and Bradshaw, 1985). Rural areas in general could benefit in obvious ways if location were to become irrelevant as an influence on access to vital resources. The new technologies, however, also carry the potential of furthering the present trends toward isolation among residents of rural localities; and there is the possibility, as Dillman (1985:22) remarks, that the rural-urban gap will increase if there is a rural lag in gaining access to the new technologies.

These potential problems take on special significance in the rural South. While electronic ties to the outside could isolate neighbors from one another in any setting, this effect could be particularly severe in the rural South where racial and class divisions have constrained intergroup cooperation in the past. As elite groupings gain first access to the new technologies, the result is likely to be further separation among neighbors. In remote settlements of the region where virtually all families are in or near poverty, widespread illiteracy limits the probability that the complex new technologies will be adopted quickly. Moreover, as Dillman (1985) also notes, rural areas literally are being "wired last" for the information age (e.g., urban telephone systems are first to receive special wiring and equipment for rapid long-distance communications).

What should be done? In the general case, with community development as the guide, two keys to a strategy for deploying the new technologies can be specified. First, obviously every effort should be made to secure the new technologies for use in rural areas. Given current trends in communications industries, which tend to be driven by the quest for profit, this will require much effort. Second, steps should be taken to establish the new information linkages through community auspices and facilities (e.g., a community library, a new community information center, etc.) rather through a proliferation of separate linkages among individuals and groups. In other words, the new technologies can be treated in policy and education as a community development resource. In the special case of the rural South, two problems must be confronted directly if the new technologies are to have beneficial effects on entire communities, namely the problem of racial and class separation and the problem of illiteracy.

Another example is community leadership education. What should be its focus in the rural South? Many programs of leadership development have little if anything to do with community development and some—even some that claim to be community leadership programs—actually undermine community development instead of encouraging it. The reason is that leadership education can do more for the individual or for some special-interest group than for the community unless the community's needs and capacities are the focus of the educational program. More often the focus is on interpersonal and analytical skills of the individual and/or on the details of specialized subject-matter problems (e.g., health care, solid waste, or economic development). The skills and knowledge of particular problems obviously are important components of leadership education; but, without a community concept to give perspective, these components do not necessarily lead to community development. In some instances, skilled leaders can manipulate community resources for their own gain. In many other instances, leaders intend to serve the community but fail to recognize the importance of a wholistic community perspective. Thus, some well-intentioned actions can actually work against *community* development. What is needed in the rural South certainly includes leadership education, but programs should give at least as much attention to the community as to the skills of individuals and details of specialized problems. In the rural South, this means in particular giving due attention to the problem of building working relationships across racial and class lines.

There are many other examples, but these suffice to illustrate the point that the community crisis in the rural South calls for renewed support for community development. In responding to particular problems and suggesting strategies to take advantage of opportunities for development, policy makers and other advocates for rural well being should keep in mind that the crisis is a community crisis and that the community, therefore, is where the emphasis should be put in development programs.

CONCLUSION

In summary, the community crisis in the rural South heralds a time of decision. The region is at a turning point, and the course of the future will emerge out of the turbulence of the present. This situation calls for careful study but also for decisive action. The crisis draws together two pervasive trends in modern society—a crisis of community and a crisis of rural living. The South, with its distinctive heritage, adds a special twist to the mix, and the result is a catalogue of problems confronting rural settlements in the region—problems of poverty and inadequate resources to meet material needs, problems of access to services, problems of inequality, and problems of social isolation. These are severe problems, but the crisis they produce also entails opportunities for change. This discussion in particular has emphasized opportunities for community development. As a turning point, the community crisis in the rural South is as exciting as it is troubling. The challenge is to cultivate opportunities for improvement that arise during this crisis. Community development, as a strategy for meeting the challenge, can enable people in rural areas to become effective participants in the process of improving their own well being.

REFERENCES

Bender, Thomas. 1978. *Community and Social Change in America*. New Brunswick, New Jersey: Rutgers University Press.

Bergman, Edward. 1986. "Urban and rural considerations in Southern development." In Commission on the Future of the South, *Rural Flight/Urban Might: Economic Development Challenges for the 1990s*. Research Triangle Park: Southern Growth Policies Board.

Blakely, Edward J., and Ted K. Bradshaw. 1985. "Rural America: the community development frontier." In Frank A. Fear and Harry K. Schwarzweller (editors), *Focus on Community*, Volume 2 of *Research in Rural Sociology and Development*. Greenwich, Connecticut: JAI Press.

Blau, Judith R., and Peter M. Blau. 1982. "The cost of inequality: metropolitan structure and violent crime." *American Sociological Review* 47:114-29.

Coelen, Stephen P., and William F. Fox. 1981. "The provision of community services." In Amos H. Hawley and Sara Mills Mazie (editors), *Nonmetropolitan America in Transition*. Chapel Hill: University of North Carolina Press.

Dillman, Don A. 1985. "The social impacts of information technologies in rural North America." *Rural Sociology* 50:1-26.

Drucker, Peter F. 1986. "The changed world economy." *Foreign Affairs* 64:768-91.

Fitchen, Janet. 1981. *Poverty in America: A Case Study*. Boulder, Colorado: Westview Press.

Galpin, Charles J. 1915. *The Social Anatomy of an Agricultural Community*. Madison, Wisconsin: University of Wisconsin Agricultural Experiment Station Bulletin 34.

Gastil, Raymond. 1971. "Homicide and a regional culture of violence." *American Sociological Review* 36:412-27.

Granovetter, Mark. 1973. "The strength of weak ties." *American Journal of Sociology* 78:1360-80.

Hansen, Niles M. 1973. *The Future of Nonmetropolitan America: Studies in the Reversal of Rural and Small Town Population Decline*. Lexington, Massachusetts: Lexington Books.

Howes, Candace, and Ann R. Marusen. 1981. "Poverty: a regional political economy perspective." In Amos H. Hawley and Sara Mills Mazie (editors). *Nonmetropolitan America in Transition*. Chapel Hill: University of North Carolina Press.

Johnson, Kenny. 1986. "The Southern stake in rural development." In Commission on the Future of the South, *Rural Flight/Urban Might: Economic Development Challenges in the 1990s*. Research Triangle Park: Southern Growth Policies Board.

Kaufman, Harold F., J. Kenneth Morland, and Herbert H. Fockler. 1975. *Group Identity in the South: Dialogue Between the Technological and Humanistic*. Mississippi State, Mississippi: Department of Sociology, Mississippi State University.

Kaufman, Harold F., and Kenneth P. Wilkinson. 1967. *Community Structure and Leadership: An Interactional Perspective in the Study of Community*. State College, Mississippi: Mississippi State University Social Science Research Center Bulletin 13.

Kraenzel, Carl F. 1980. *The Social Cost of Space in the Yonland*. Boseman, Montana: Big Sky Books.

Lyson, Thomas A., and William W. Falk. 1986. "Two sides of the sunbelt: economic development in the rural and urban South." In Joint Economic Committee (editors), *New Dimensions in Rural Policy: Building Upon Our Heritage*. Washington, D.C.: Congress of the United States.

Scherer, Jacqueline. 1972. *Contemporary Community: Sociological Illusion or Reality?* London: Tavistock.

Sorokin, Pitirim A., and Carle C. Zimmerman. 1929. *Principles of Rural-Urban Sociology*. New York: Henry Holt.

Tilly, Charles. 1973. "Do communities act?" *Sociological Inquiry* 43:209-40.

U.S. Department of Labor, Bureau of Labor Statistics, and U.S. Department of Agriculture, Statistical Reporting Service. 1986. "Employment in rural America in the mid-1980s." In Joint Economic Committee (editors), *New Dimensions in Rural Policy: Building Upon Our Heritage*. Washington, D.C.: Congress of the United States.

Warner, W. Keith. 1974. "Rural society in a post-industrial age." *Rural Sociology* 39:306-18.
Warren, Roland L. 1978. *The Community in America*. Third Edition. Chicago: Rand McNally.
Wellman, Barry. 1979. "The community question: the intimate networks of East Yorkers." *American Journal of Sociology* 84:1201-31.
Wilkinson, Kenneth P. 1986. "Communities left behind - again." In Joint Economic Committee (editors), *New Dimensions in Rural Policy: Building Upon Our Heritage*. Washington, D.C.: Congress of the United States.

6

The Human Dimension of the Rural South in Crisis

Louis E. Swanson

The current crisis in the rural South involves a considerable amount of human suffering. I do not use the term "suffering" lightly. Suffering here refers to material, health, and spiritual hardships that a middle class American would find unacceptable. While not all suffering is the product of poverty and illiteracy, the suffering described in this chapter does refer to the adverse circumstances of such conditions. Indeed, the historical character of this crisis means that current human suffering is not new, but generational.

In recent years it has not been politically popular to draw attention to the depth and variety of human suffering as a consequence of poverty and near poverty, unemployment and underemployment, or the shackles placed upon human potential by functional illiteracy and ignorance. However, ignoring the consequences of poverty and ignorance is not a panacea for its elimination. Consequently, the first hurdle in overcoming skepticism as to the meaning of this social crisis is to address such questions as "So there is a crisis . . . So what? Who is hurting, and isn't such hurt the 'natural order' of necessary social change? of progress? What is the degree of hurt? Isn't poverty the bane of all societies? Isn't ignorance always with us? Aren't the poor responsible for improving their lot?"

The purpose of this chapter is to briefly describe the breadth and characteristics of the human dimension of the rural South in crisis. An ancillary purpose is to make abstract statistics a meaningful dimension of human distress as a daily experience, and as a guide for policy formulation. The human dimensions of this crisis are multi-faceted, involving individuals and families, communities and industrial sectors (human resource needs), and institutional patterns such as manifested in racism.

Modernization, as Billings argues in another chapter in this text, is uneven in its benefits. Material progress is often accomplished at the expense of significant segments of the population. Nor is modernization an inevitable outcome. The phenomenal progress since World War II is now thought to be a permanent characteristic of the U.S. economy. We expect growth. However, the rural South has never been a full partner in this progress, especially for those, who like their ancestors now forgotten, have always known the fear and grind of rural poverty, whether in the Carolina coastal plain, the fertile black belt of the Deep South, or the isolated settlements of Appalachia. More recently, much of the rest of rural America has experienced a significant decline in its financial and social fortunes. These areas of our society can attest to the fact that progress is not a natural or even-handed phenomenon.

Much of rural America is mired in a crisis which has the potential for approaching and even surpassing the relative suffering of the Great Depression. Moreover, the rural South has always persisted on the periphery of U.S. society, is worse off than most other areas of rural America. Some of the empirical evidence of a national rural crisis will be presented in this chapter, and, when available, data for the rural South. It will be argued that the need for recognition of this crisis has long passed, that new ideas are needed, and that the moral basis for new activities rest upon a simple but ancient assumption, that a society should not be evaluated on the basis of how the very well-to-do live or its technological capacity, but rather on how the poorest members of a society subsist.

Central themes of this edited volume are to identify ways for weathering this crisis, to develop programs to ease the misery of poverty, and to explore new avenues for the *vitalization* of the rural South. Note, the book is *not* addressing the "*re*vitalization" of the rural South as might be the case if concerned with rural Iowa or Minnesota. The authors have a much more difficult and maybe even unachievable task given current socioeconomic conditions—they are seeking ways of making vital a portion of American society that by almost any measure has never been vital. Consequently, it is worth keeping in mind that the data that follow are for the most part an extension of the past. While many of the socioeconomic forces shaping the current situation are new and may not be directly comparable with the past, much of the human dimensions of the present situation in the rural South were familiar to earlier generations.

The human dimension is described from several vantage points. The first and most obvious is poverty. This discussion will be followed by some of the associated problems in health care, employment, education, racism and the consequences for the family.

POVERTY

The most available and general measure of social well-being is poverty, usually measured as a percentage of a population living at or below the poverty level. Given that neither political party benefits from a generous measure of poverty, the official definition tends to be quite conservative. Consequently, the poverty data that will follow represent a conservative estimate of the U.S. population who are unable to maintain minimal material, sustenance, and health standards in our advanced industrial society. And lest the obvious be missed, the majority of our poor and near-poor citizens work (see Morrissey, 1985). If a young woman works full time at a fast food outlet at the minimum wage for the entire year, her earnings would not be enough to escape poverty.

A common public perception is that poverty is a central city problem, since urban poverty apparently is more visible to a majority of the population. However, poverty is more prevalent and in some cases more severe in rural America. Since comparison aids description, if it does not necessarily establish truth, the following figures are useful. While there were 12.9 million poor living in the nation's central cities in 1983, the nation's rural poor numbered 13.5 million. The balance of the poor population lived in cities outside of the central cities, approximately 8.9 million people (Deavers et al., 1988). The rate of poverty for all metropolitan counties in 1985 was 12.7 percent, while in nonmetropolitan counties it was 18.3 percent (see Table 1).

Moreover, there has been an increase in both the rate and the number of rural people in poverty since 1978. In that year, the rate of poverty was 13.5 percent. Early estimates for 1986 suggest that the rate of rural poverty might be over 19 percent. Between 1978 and 1983, the number of rural people in poverty increased from 9.4 million people to 13.5 million, or an increase of 43.6 percent.

Rural poverty is heavily concentrated in the South (Deavers et al., 1988; Haas, 1986). Almost half of all the rural poor lived in the South in 1983. By contrast, less than one-third of the metro poor lived in the South at the same time. The 1983 poverty rate in the South was 20.7 percent compared with 16.3 percent in the rest of rural America (Deavers et al., 1988). In other words, using a conservative definition of poverty, it is estimated that at least one in five rural Southerners lived in poverty in 1983.

The case for the long-term nature of poverty in the rural South has been made by several USDA studies (Davis, 1979; Hoppe, 1986). Among nonmetropolitan counties nationally, some have remained severely depressed even during the 1970s. This trend was despite the economic growth and development that touched

Table 1. Persons by Poverty Status, Metro-Nonmetro Residence, 1968-1985 (numbers in thousands).

Year	Metro			Nonmetro		
	Total Population	Total Poverty	Percent Poverty	Total Population	Total Poverty	Percent Poverty
1968	128,710	12,871	10.0	69,544	12,518	18.0
1969	130,017	13,084	10.1	69,831	11,063	15.8
1970	130,907	13,317	10.2	71,580	12,103	16.9
1971	140,670	14,561	10.4	63,883	10,999	17.2
1972	141,129	14,508	10.3	64,875	9,952	15.3
1973	141,795	13,759	9.7	65,826	9,214	14.0
1974	142,297	13,851	9.7	67,065	9,519	14.2
1975	142,658	15,348	10.8	68,206	10,529	15.4
1976	142,931	15,229	10.7	69,372	9,746	14.0
1977	142,791	14,859	10.4	71,076	9,861	13.8
1978	145,730	15,090	10.4	69,926	9,407	13.5
1979	150,785	16,134	10.7	72,007	9,937	13.8
1980	151,993	18,157	11.9	73,034	11,483	15.7
1981*	153,612	19,347	12.6	73,545	12,475	17.0
1982	155,634	21,247	13.7	73,778	13,152	17.8
1983	157,615	21,750	13.8	73,997	13,516	18.3
1984*	--	--	--	--	--	--
1985	183,097	23,275	12.7	53,497	9,789	18.3

Source: Current Population Reports, Series P-60, Money Income and Poverty Status of Families and Persons in the United States, respective years.
*Beginning in 1981, differentials in the poverty threshold for sex of householder and farm-nonfarm residence were eliminated.

other sectors of rural America (Hoppe, 1985). In one study by Davis (1979), 298 nonmetropolitan counties were identified as ranking in the lowest per capita income quintile for 1950, 1959, and 1969. These were labeled as Persistently Low Income counties (PLIs). In 1979, of the original Persistently Low Income counties, 231 remained in the lower quartile. Of these counties, all except 18 were located in the South. In other words, 92 percent of the persistent low income rural counties nationally are located in the South. Four Southern states—Georgia, Kentucky, Mississippi, and Tennessee—each had more than twenty of these counties. Many of these persistent poverty counties are located where their populations contain a high percentage of racial minorities (Bender et al, 1985). A notable exception is southern Appalachia, where in 1980, 22.7 percent of the population lived in poverty (Tickamyer and Tickamyer, 1987).

A sad note on rural poverty nationally is that progress had been made in alleviating its most overt symptoms in the 1960s and early 1970s. The nonmetro poverty rate declined from 20.2 percent in 1967 to 13.5 percent in 1978. In recent years our nation has experienced economic decline. Henry et al. (1986) report that the per capita income gap between metro and nonmetro counties narrowed between 1965 and 1973, but has actually widened since then. The War on Poverty is once again being lost at a time when huge budget deficits and a sluggish economy militate against the reforms of the past, and demand new ideas for the future.

What are the costs of poverty? There are at least three identifiable costs associated with poverty: personal costs, program costs, and forgone output (Deavers et al., 1988). The personal costs include loss of self-esteem, increased family stress, chronic health problems, higher infant mortality, fear, and despair. The program costs, a popular political target in recent years, are insignificant when compared to national defense and Social Security. Unsurprisingly, as poverty has expanded without a corresponding increase in food aid, reports of growing hunger and malnutrition around the country have risen.

HUMAN HEALTH AND NUTRITION AMONG THE POOR

Perhaps the personal costs of poverty can best be described by the damage it does to the human body. There has been an increase in concern among the nation's leading health and nutrition scientists that once again America is backsliding with regard to nutritional status. Numerous studies, including those carried out by the Center for Disease Control, the National Center for Health Statistics, The Physicians Task Force on Hunger, and the Public Voice for Food and Health Policy, have consistently found that poverty is directly linked to malnutrition as well as a host of other health risks (see Hass, 1986:Chapter 1). A 1982 USDA study of low income household food consumption also linked poverty with the risks associated with an inadequate diet (USDA, 1982). The study by the Public Voice is particularly worth noting since it argued that the consequences of poverty for the rural poor are more severe than for the urban poor, and where data were available, the Southern rural poor fared the worst. Aggravating this situation are the inadequacies of health care services and delivery systems for other assistance programs, which have traditionally left rural populations underserved. Faced with fewer resources for maintaining or restoring health, the rural poor are particularly vulnerable (Haas, 1986).

Nor is health care a problem only for the rural poor. Most rural counties are at a locational disadvantage with regard to professional health care services, and among nonmetro regions, the rural South is considered to have the poorest access and infrastructure (Miller, 1982). Given the tendency for health care to be increasingly concentrated in fewer and larger towns, most rural residents have to travel to the services by their own means or do without (Miller, 1982). This is particularly true for the poorer residents.

The malnutrition and related problems among the poor are of societal concern not only because of the immediate human suffering they indicate, but also because they threaten the poor individual's health, and thereby exact an enormous direct and indirect toll on the individual, the family, and rural society. "Poor nutrition impairs learning, cognitive development, and the ability to concentrate and work productively . . . [as well as] reduces resistance to disease and increases the severity of disease" (Hass, 1986:12). One way of understanding the human dimension of poverty is by examining some of the conclusions of the Public Voice study (Hass, 1986).

The dietary intake portion of this study produced the following conclusions: The rural poor are over 65 percent more likely to consume diets which are inadequate for multiple essential nutrients. The rural poor were more than twice as likely as were the U.S. nonpoor to experience severe levels of dietary inadequacy (Hass, 1986).

Of the various regions, the Southern poor were consistently in the worst categories. For most of the nutrients studied, Southern rural poor consumed diets which were either the poorest quality or the second poorest quality. Their study of biochemical and hematological indicators of good health followed a similar pattern. The South was found to be the region in which the rural poor had the highest prevalence of biochemical deficiencies. This was true for two of the three indicators of iron status, and for vitamins A and C (Hass, 1986).

Their anthropometric measures were also disturbingly consistent. The rural poor were almost three times more likely to be growth-stunted as were children from nonpoor families. The South was considered to be the most affected region. Consistent with dietary and biochemical findings, the Southern rural poor exhibited the highest prevalence of low height-for-age. Not only was low height-for-age significantly more evident among rural poor children residing in the South, but the gap between the nonpoor and the rural poor was also larger in this region than in any of the other regions of the country. Furthermore, the rural nonwhite population tended to be worse off than the white population (Hass, 1986).

While all of these data paint a dismal picture of human health problems, the worst is saved for last—infant mortality and low birth weight. Among social scientists and epidemiologists, the infant mortality rate has been "regarded as a barometer of the adequacy of a population's overall nutrition and health, as well as a primary indicator of the effectiveness of a nation's or a community's health care system" (Hass, 1986:115). Further, low birth weight serves as a useful index of a population's health and nutrition status. The findings suggest that both infant mortality and low birth weight rates are considerably higher in rural poor counties than in the rest of the nation. While the national infant mortality has declined and then leveled off in recent years, the rate has actually increased in rural poor counties. Data for low birth weights points to a similar disparity. The gap between poor rural counties and the rest of the nation for these two health indicators has widened since 1981.

What about assistance programs to these people? The Public Voice report concluded that the "distribution of public assistance program benefits by both federal and state governments is grossly inequitable" (Hass, 1986:140). Less than 43 percent of the rural poor residents received Food Stamp benefits. Similar low participation was observed for the Free and Reduced Price School Lunch program, the Medicare program, and Aid to Families with Dependent Children. The combined effects of low participation and low benefit levels has had a synergistic effect in which the ability of the rural poor family to purchase adequate amounts of food becomes increasingly problematic. A characteristic of Southern rural poverty is hunger, malnutrition, and higher than average levels of infant mortality. This is one dimension of the human suffering that is part of the rural South in crisis.

EMPLOYMENT

The poverty of the Southern region is closely tied to local economies and the employment opportunities they offer. Here, too, we can see how unique characteristics of the rural South have contributed to a lack of economic and social vitalization.

The rural South has a highly segmented labor force, that is, one divided along clear social and economic lines, particularly by race and gender. Historically, this segmentation has shaped the restructuring of the rural Southern economy. This was especially clear in regard to the transition from agriculture and other extractive industries to manufacturing. Is it a coincidence that the partial success of the Great Civil Rights movement was accomplished at a time when the restructuring of Southern agriculture forced millions of black tenants off the land, only to be denied jobs in the factories because of Jim Crow laws? Is it a coincidence that the Civil Rights movement falters at about the same time as this once-excluded labor force of black men and women have been assimilated into the peripheral manufacturing enterprises, such as textiles, that dot the rural countryside? The demand for cheap rural labor and the existence of a massive cheap labor force that historically had been excluded from most rural manufacturing jobs, meant that the laws and customs that excluded this labor force had to be eliminated for Southern rural industrialization to proceed further.

This historical segmentation is again setting the parameters for the current restructuring of the rural economy. The characteristics of this restructuring have been discussed in number of excellent reports including *Shadows in the Sunbelt* (MDC, Inc., 1986), *Halfway Home and a Long Way to Go* (Southern Growth Policies Board, 1986), and *After the Factories* (Rosenfeld et al., 1985). Each paints a general picture of a fundamental, long-term restructuring of employment, both industrially and geographically. It is argued that traditional employment in manufacturing, such as furniture, food, textiles, and apparel, are being lost and that employment in service industries are emerging along with some new employment in the high tech industries, usually located near metropolitan areas. A common theme, though, is that the rural South's ability not to lose more ground is ". . . hampered by its lack of wealth and [by] underdeveloped human resources" (Rosenfeld et al., 1985:xi).

Evidence for this gloomy appraisal is readily available. In the Southeast, approximately 250,000 textile jobs were lost between 1975 and 1985. In 1985, 40 percent of all jobs lost in Georgia were in textiles (Rosenfeld et al., 1985). In order to comprehend the importance of textiles to this region, and thereby the loss of these jobs to the regional economy, it is worth noting that 58 percent of all textile jobs in the U.S. are located in North Carolina, South Carolina, and Georgia—most in rural areas.

The chances of a rural Southern community maintaining any semblance of economic autonomy is very much mediated by its past, its racial composition, its residents' level of skill, and its educational system. The report *After the Factories* (Rosenfeld et al., 1985) pointed out that the fastest growth counties in the region had the smallest percent minority populations and highest educational levels and per capita income. These counties also tended to be located near the major prosperous metropolitan areas. Moreover, the counties least likely to succeed were dominated by manufacturing—particularly traditional nondurable manufacturing. Farmers are facing the worst crisis since the Great Depression, and hired farm laborers in the region in 1985 averaged less than $5,200 in total annual income.

Perhaps the most salient characteristic of the rural labor force is that it is primarily composed of unskilled and semiskilled workers. The kinds of employment opportunities available to this type of labor are limited to low-wage and usually unorganized jobs, such as in textiles or in the service industries. "About 30 percent of rural [South's] workers are operators, assemblers, and fabricators, many of them in declining or departing industries" (Southern Growth Policies Board, 1986). The types of jobs that are evacuating the rural South are exactly the types of jobs needed to employ the great majority of the labor force.

If the future of the rural South is to be based on marginal manufacturing industries and low-wage service industries, then the future will certainly be an extension of the past. A recent study by the Congressional Office of Technology Assessment on the Rural South suggests that counties with a dependence on manufacturing during the 1970s may have had lower unemployment rates but they also tend to have lower levels of median family income. Counties with a dependence on service industries had higher levels of poverty and lower levels of median family income (see Office of Technology Assessment, 1986).

What does this mean for the Southern rural laborer? It means that he or she lives in the fear of losing the job they have, and even if they keep their job, it probably means living in or near the poverty level. Can you imagine what it would be like to find out that you have just lost the only decent job in town for your level of skill? What kind of pressure does that put on you and your family? What is happening to those workers who have lost their textile jobs? How many of these workers manage to return to the same or similar jobs? How many remain without jobs or eventually settle for different and usually lower paying jobs? Flaim and Sehgal (1985) of the U.S. Bureau of Labor Statistics examined the plight of displaced workers nationally for the five year period 1979–1983. They concluded that while some workers were able to find work after a relatively short period of time, the readjustment period for most was much more painful. A year following their displacement, most workers had found different jobs, but frequently at much lower wages than the jobs from which they had been displaced. About one-fourth were still unemployed and another 15 percent simply left the labor force. In other words, almost 40 percent did not find another job. These data were for the nation, not the rural South where there are fewer alternative employment opportunities.

EDUCATION

A key factor facilitating the persistence of a very large unskilled and semi-skilled labor force in the rural South has been the inability for public education systems to adequately train its disadvantaged citizens. This vast area of underdeveloped human resource is not only a millstone currently around the rural community's neck, but the inability to address the crisis of ignorance and illiteracy threatens individual development and dignity, undermines community well-being, and frustrates efforts to achieve regional social and economic viability. The South cannot take pride in perpetuating ignorance.

The average levels of education in the South are considerably lower than any other region. As the Southern Growth Policies Board (1985:15) has argued, some of this poor showing is due to the legacy of the past, particularly to the lack of access to educational opportunities for the black population and a general lack of attention to quality education. In 1980, only half of the population living in the rural South aged 25 years or more had finished four years of high school. In the nonmetro region of Central Appalachia, almost 60 percent of the adult population had not completed high school (Tickamyer and Tickamyer, 1987:14). Furthermore, adults in rural South are less likely to have "the financial means, educational qualifications, and aspirations to complete college" (Southern Growth Policies Board, 1986:16). Only 10 percent of the adult population had finished a four-year college in 1980.

Rosenfeld et al. (1985) report that in 1980, 820,000 people in North Carolina had no more than eight years of education. This substandard education may have cost the entire state more than a billion dollars in lost earnings.

A historical dilemma for rural areas is that much of the best educated youth migrate toward jobs in the urban areas, thus nullifying a significant portion of an important community investment in human resources for the future.

RACISM

An unsavory dimension of the rural South in crisis is the persistence of overt and subtle racism. Of course, racism has always been a part of the rural South's social fabric. The civil rights movement removed legal barriers to employment opportunities and thereby opened jobs once closed to black women and men. But, the majority of the jobs filled by blacks continue to be the most marginal. Moreover, while the civil rights movement healed some of the social fabric, recent events suggest that considerable racism persists. Examples would include the recent attack on civil rights marchers in Forsyth County, Georgia, and the Justice Department's expenditure of approximately $2 million to indict voting rights workers in west Alabama, yet obtaining only a single indictment[1]. The historical patterns of Southern apartheid continue to occur for those areas with a high proportion of black residents. As noted earlier, new industry, especially those with the most desirable jobs, generally locate in counties with the lowest proportion of blacks in their population. Southern rural development efforts that do not directly address the issues of black poverty will fail. Consequently, racism is still a formidable foe to the vitalization of the rural South and an important dimension of the current crisis.

FAMILY

What does the rural crisis in the South mean for rural families? How does a farm family broken by debt and drought cope with the loss of a farm homestead in the family for five or six generations? What does the feminization of poverty mean for the rural families and the rural social fabric?

In 1980, 35 percent of all nonmetro black families had incomes below the poverty level. Poverty among black families was most prevalent for those headed by women, 56 percent of whom had incomes below the poverty threshold (Ghelfi, 1986). In Appalachia, over 26 percent of the families were at or very near poverty (Tickamyer and Tickamyer, 1987). The largest source of income for these families was some type of employment, not government programs.

However, the increase in single head of household families headed by women should not be seen as the source of the problem, but a consequence of economic and social conditions, such as low wages, unemployment, and a lack of education, that mitigate against the formation and maintenance of a strong family structure. The deteriorating conditions of Southern rural families is not due to a culture of poverty, but the economics and politics of poverty. The concept of a culture of poverty blames the victims of poverty for their plight.

CONCLUDING REMARKS

The present crisis of the rural South is actually a historical condition. Consequently, the task before us is to counter forces shaping the history of our region. The sobering statistics presented here should provide some reference for the gravity of the crisis facing the region.

The historical persistence of this crisis, coupled with increasing evidence that the U.S. economy faces a period of contraction for the foreseeable future, suggests that the old ideas and programs will not be adequate. This region has not been a full partner in the economic progress following World War II. Laissez-faire development policies did not bring the rural South into the mainstream of U.S. prosperity during good times, which suggests that we cannot look in that direction for the bad times we now face. The dimension of human suffering is presently unacceptable and there are no signs of abatement. The history of the rural South has been characterized by a lot of pain and little gain. As the debate over policy emerges, we must never grow callous to the statistics of human misery. Rather, the plight of our rural citizens should help shape our policy options.

NOTES

[1]The Justice Department's intense investigation of voter fraud in Alabama only targeted rural counties controlled by black elected officials—Perry and Greene counties. The investigation, which journalists reported cost the taxpayers approximately $2 million, brought a total of 215 criminal charges against black voting rights activists. The results were one conviction on four counts and two plea bargains to misdemeanors. The effect was to harrass voting rights activists in these counties.

REFERENCES

Bender, L. D., B. L. Green, T. F. Kuehn, J. A. Nelson, M. K. Perkinson, and P. J. Ross. 1985. *The Diverse Social and Economic Structure of Nonmetropolitan America*. United States Department of Agriculture, Economic Research Service, Rural Development Report No. 49, Washington, D.C.

Davis, T. F. 1979. *Persistent Low-Income Counties in Nonmetro America*. United States Department of Agriculture, Economic Research Service, Rural Development Report No. 12, Washington, D.C.

Deavers, K. L., R. A. Hoppe, and P. J. Ross. 1988. "The rural poor: Policy issues for the 1980s." Paper that will appear in a book on rural poverty to be published by Greenwood Press.

Flaim, P. O. and E. Sehgal. 1985. "Displaced workers of 1979-83: How well have they fared?" *Monthly Labor Review* Vol. 108(6):3-16.

Ghelfi, L. M. 1986. *Poverty Among Black Families in the Nonmetro South*. United States Department of Agriculture, Economic Research Division, Rural Development Research Report No. 62, Washington, D.C.

Haas, E. 1986. *Rising poverty, declining health: The nutritional status of the rural poor.* Public Voice for Food and Health Policy, Washington, D.C.

Henry, M., M. Drabenstott, and L. Gibson. 1986. "A changing rural America." *Economic Review* July/August: 23-41.

Hoppe, R. A. 1985. *Economic structure and change in persistently low-income nonmetro counties.* United States Department of Agriculture, Economic Research Service, Rural Development Research Report No. 50, Washington, D.C.

MDC, Inc. 1986. *Shadows in the Sunbelt: Developing the Rural South in an Era of Economic Change.* A Report on Rural Economic Development (May).

Miller, M. K. 1982. "Health and medical care." In Don A. Dillman and Daryl J. Hobbs *Rural Society in the U.S.: Issues for the 1980s.* Boulder, Colorado: Westview Press.

Morrissey, E. S. 1985. *Characteristics of Poverty in Nonmetro Counties*. United States Department of Agriculture, Economic Research Service, Rural Development Research Report No. 52.

Rosenfeld, S. A., E. M. Bergman, S. Rubin. 1985 *After the Factories: Changing Employment Patterns in the Rural South*. Research Triangle Park, North Carolina: Southern Growth Policies Board.

Southern Growth Policies Board. 1986. *Halfway Home and a Long Way to Go: The Report of the Commission on the Future of the South*. Research Triangle Park, North Carolina.

Tickamyer, A. R., and C. Tickamyer. 1987. *Poverty in Appalachia*. Appalachian Center, University of Kentucky, Appalachian Data Bank Report No. 5, Lexington, Kentucky.

United States Department of Agriculture. 1982. *Food and Nutrient Intakes of Individuals in One Day: Low-Income Households*. Human Nutrition Information Center, Nationwide Food Consumption Survey, Preliminary Report No. 11.

PART TWO

Current Socioeconomic Issues in the Rural South

7

Social and Economic Conditions of Black Farm Households: Status and Prospects

E. Yvonne Beauford
Mack C. Nelson

Failures in the farm economy and the weakening of the nonfarm economy have severely threatened the financial well-being of many rural households. Since blacks have traditionally experienced a lower status on measures of economic well-being, the plight of rural black households becomes even more tenuous given the current crisis in rural America. Consistent with historical trends, blacks in the rural South continue to be plagued by lower levels of income and higher rates of poverty than the population in general. Almost without fail, problems of blacks in general are exacerbated within the black farm population. Black farmers, for example, have a higher rate of poverty than any population group (U. S. Department of Commerce, 1984b).

The lower level of economic well-being of black farmers, as measured by level of income and poverty rate, can be attributed to several factors related to characteristics of black farmers, their farms, their environment, and to historical patterns of racism and discrimination rooted in slavery and the plantation system. But long after slavery was officially ended, traditional patterns of behavior established during slavery pervaded many dimensions of the social and economic structure, restricting equality of access to opportunities for economic success. Legal constraints to education in particular, retarded the rate at which blacks could acquire the skills necessary for success. For black farmers,

discrimination in the purchase of land, restricted access to capital, and limited opportunities to gain experience with enterprises other than cotton and tobacco, help to account for the smaller size and lack of economic viability of the
majority of black-operated farms (USDA, 1983).

Most black-operated farms are small and generate low volumes of sales.
In 1982, their size was one-third that of all Southern farms, and most (79 percent) generated less than $10,000 in sales (U. S. Department of Commerce,
1984a). These salient characteristics are among the primary factors contributing to lower levels of economic well-being among black farmers. Typically,
their farms do not generate incomes sufficient to sustain nonpoverty levels
of income. Other factors which contribute to lower levels of well-being are
the advanced age of operators, inadequate human capital skills (particularly
education and appropriate training for off-farm employment), discrimination,
and the availability of opportunities for off-farm employment.

Black farmers seeking to supplement farm-generated income with income
from off-farm employment often find their opportunities to do so limited. Aside
from constraints imposed by advancing age or limited education and skills,
further barriers may be imposed by the communities in which they live. A
study by Hoppe et al. (1986) suggests that the nonfarm environment is potentially very important to the social and economic well-being of black farm families. But, most black farmers are concentrated in counties which are
slow-growing and which offer few opportunities for off-farm employment. Further, black farmers tend to be concentrated in areas having a large nonfarm
black population that suffers from high rates of poverty and limited education, and in areas having few amenities to attract industrial employers (Davis,
1979). Additional concern with the environments of black farmers is evidenced
by the fact that industrial growth and development in the rural South has by-
passed rural areas with large black populations and low levels of literacy (Hansen, 1973; Till, 1972).

Factors which contribute to diminished levels of economic well-being among
black farmers also have important implications for the future of blacks in production agriculture. The low level of well-being of many small farm households
has prompted many to discontinue farming. Young people in particular who
are better educated often pursue opportunities for enhanced levels of well-
being in the nonfarm environment. Young blacks are less likely than young
whites to choose farming as an occupation, further diminishing the black farm
population as older black farmers retire.

In this chapter, we examine selected factors which contribute to lower levels of economic well-being among black farm households and which threaten
the future of blacks in production agriculture. We focus on characteristics of
black farmers and their farms in the South, and on population characteristics
of five Southeastern states in which black farmers are found to be primarily concentrated (Alabama, Mississippi, Georgia, South Carolina and North Carolina).

Focus is given to indicators of well-being, namely, median household income and poverty rate, of blacks in these geographic areas. Attention also is given to the human capital characteristics of blacks in these five states.

PREVIOUS WORK

The economic well-being of black families in the rural South has been the focus of a number of recent studies (Banks, 1986; Hoppe, 1985; Hoppe et al., 1986; Ghelfi, 1986; Thompson, 1986). Consistently, these studies suggest that the difficult economic conditions in the rural South are exacerbated among blacks. Poverty, as an indicator of economic well-being, is more pervasive among farm populations and among blacks.

The historical trend of income inequalities between rural and urban populations persist and become more pronounced when race is considered. Farm families are more likely to be poor than nonfarm families. In 1982, 22.1 percent of farm families in the United States, compared to 14.8 percent of all nonfarm families, were below the poverty level. During this same time, poverty rates were significantly higher among the black farm population (51.4 percent) and nonfarm blacks (35.5 percent) than among the white farm population (21 percent) and nonfarm whites (11.7 percent). (U. S. Department of Commerce, 1984b).

The majority of poverty level farm households appear to share several characteristics: small farm size (as represented by volume of sales) and operators who are older and poorly educated (Crecink, 1986; Marshall and Thompson, 1976). Operators of farms that generate sales less than $20,000 are more likely to be poor than large volume producers, regardless of race. Unpublished Census data compiled by Crecink (1986) indicate that farm families generating less than $20,000 in sales are five times as likely as farms that generate more than $20,000 in sales to be poor. The same data suggest that blacks are almost twice as likely as whites to be low income farmers.

Low volume sales have prompted many small farm operators to supplement farm-generated income with income from off-farm employment. However, the extent to which farm households supplement farm income with income from off-farm employment varies with opportunities for off-farm employment. The smaller proportion of blacks consistently engaged in off-farm employment, in spite of greater need for supplemental income, may well reflect fewer opportunities because of discrimination, age, and education (Hoppe et al., 1986; Marshall and Thompson, 1976). This, in turn, affects labor force participation rates among blacks and contributes to higher unemployment and poverty rates (Hoppe et al., 1986).

The older age of black farmers has important implications for farm productivity, off-farm employment and the future of blacks in production agriculture.

Black farmers tend to be older (57 years in 1982) than the national average age of farmers (51 years old). Black farmers are also twice as likely as other farmers to be 65 years or older (Banks, 1986). Older age farmers tend to operate less productive farms, they invest less in their farming operations and are less likely to pursue aggressive expansion strategies, or to make changes which would enhance productivity or profitability (Hopkin et al., 1973). Older age and associated work-related disabilities may also serve as constraints to off-farm employment (Hoppe et al., 1986).

Prior to World War II, black farmers were typically younger than white farmers. But, because of problems experienced in acquiring the resources and expertise to make their operations profitable enough to sustain family well-being, and because of potential opportunities in urban areas, substantial numbers of young blacks left the farm (USDA, 1983).

On the average, black farmers complete fewer years of schooling than white farmers (USDA, 1983; Fratoe, 1979). The lower levels of educational achievement among blacks stems in part from historical patterns of discrimination, particularly in Southern educational systems. Inadequate educational preparation of blacks puts them at a "severe disadvantage in an industry that has come to rely heavily on information and technical training" (USDA, 1983). Lower educational levels also pose constraints to off-farm employment and earnings, restricting inadequately prepared blacks to diminished participation in the labor force, low-paying jobs and poverty (Perlman, 1976).

In summary, the literature implicitly suggests that factors which contribute to disparities in levels of economic well-being also threaten the existence of the black farm population. In the section which follows, a more detailed description of the conditions of black farmers and of other blacks in areas with concentrations of black farmers is presented. The intent is to describe the population and socioeconomic conditions of areas with high concentrations of black-operated farms, and the implications of such conditions for the economic enhancement and continued participation of blacks in production agriculture.

PROCEDURES

Because most black farmers are concentrated in the South, selected farm and operator characteristics for fourteen Southern states are analyzed. These states are: Alabama, Arkansas, Florida, Georgia, Kentucky, Louisiana, Maryland, Mississippi, Oklahoma, North Carolina, South Carolina, Tennessee, Texas, and Virginia.

In order to further derive implications for the economic well-being of black farmers, indicators of social and economic conditions of counties in five contiguous Southeastern states with high concentrations of black farmers also are examined. County selection was based on the existence of 20 or more black-operated farms. The states represented are Alabama, Georgia, Mississippi, North Carolina and South Carolina. These states were selected for several reasons: they contain approximately 50 percent of all black-operated farms and 47.6 percent of the persistently low-income counties in the South; they represent some of the most urbanized of the rural states and some of the most rural of the rural states; they represent the Southern states with the greatest and the least decrease in the number of black-operated farms between 1978 and 1982; and they have a high degree of homogeneity in the enterprise selections among black farmers (U.S. Department of Commerce, 1984a; Davis, 1979; Banks, 1986).

The designation of persistently low-income (PLI) counties provides a composite measure of the socioeconomic conditions within a county. PLI designation is based on analysis of population, employment and income characteristics of a county in relation to other counties in the United States. PLI counties are counties which ranked in the bottom quintile of a national ranking of nonmetropolitan counties, by per capita income, in 1950, 1959 and 1969. Counties which fell into the bottom quintile for all three years were designated PLI counties (Davis, 1979). Based upon these procedures, 298 counties across the United States were designated as PLI counties. The majority (273 or 91.6 percent) were located in the South, and 130 (43.6 percent) were located in the five contiguous Southeastern states that serve as the primary focus of this chapter. The state with the most PLI counties is Mississippi (47), followed by Georgia (37), Alabama (21), North Carolina (14) and South Carolina (11). Of the 130 PLI counties within the study states, 81 (62.3 percent) have 20 or more black-operated farms.

FINDINGS

The South: An Overview

Number of Farms and Land in Farms. Between 1978 and 1982, the historical decline in black-operated farms continued (Table 1). However, individual states within the South show varying rates of decline. Georgia and North Carolina experienced a decline in the number of black-operated farms approaching 25 percent. States with declines less than the regional average of -9.8 percent were Tennessee (-8.4 percent), Mississippi (-4.7 percent), Louisiana (-3.4 percent), and Maryland (-1.0 percent). Oklahoma and Texas were the only states with an increase in the number of farms operated by blacks and other minorities.

Decreases in the number of black-operated farms were accompanied by sizable reductions in the number of acres of farmland owned by blacks and other minorities. In all of the Southern states (except Arkansas, Georgia and North

Table 1. Selected Characteristics of Black-Owned Farms in the South: 1982 and 1978.

State	No. of Farms			Acres % Chg.	Occupation Farming			Occupation Other Than Farming		
	1982	%Chg.	1978	1978-1982	<$2500	$2500-$9999	≥$10000	<$2500	$2500-$9999	≥$10000
Alabama	2811	-12.4	3207	-18.1	474	309	218	1199	503	108
Arkansas	1368	-19.0	1688	-14.2	191	257	281	381	191	67
Florida	983	-15.9	1170	+12.4	110	130	176	271	173	123
Georgia	2097	-22.7	2714	-19.5	261	307	513	542	337	137
Kentucky	1006	-12.2	1146	-33.9	118	213	158	211	224	82
Louisiana	1949	-3.4	2017	-8.8	334	257	280	716	276	86
Maryland	601	-1.0	608	-34.0	58	130	112	136	125	40
Mississippi	4829	-4.7	5066	-10.7	958	599	400	2028	695	149
N. Carolina	5351	-23.2	6966	-17.2	599	945	1659	1035	800	313
Oklahoma	2745	+11.0	2472	-6.0	294	300	327	1046	600	178
S. Carolina	3170	-15.6	3799	-19.7	535	531	431	1016	484	173
Tennessee	1671	-8.4	1826	-20.0	208	293	221	479	375	95
Texas	5431	+10.0	4938	-17.7	766	582	498	2360	977	248
Virginia	2772	-12.2	3158	-12.5	386	542	560	667	467	150
REGION	36784	-9.8	40775	-14.6	5292	5395	5834	12087	6227	1949

Source: 1982 Census of Agriculture, U.S. Department of Commerce, Bureau of the Census.

Carolina), the percent decline in the number of farms was less than the proportional reduction in the number of farmland acres. Only one state, Florida, showed an increase in the number of acres of farmland owned by blacks and other minorities between 1978 and 1982. This trend may suggest that larger minority-owned farms are being lost, except in Florida. For example, Kentucky experienced a reduction in the number of farms of approximately 12 percent, but a net reduction in the number of acres of approximately 34 percent. Maryland lost only about one percent of its black-operated farms, but lost 34 percent of the acreage owned by blacks and other minorities. Similar but less extreme trends exist in most of the other Southern states.

Farm Size. Two measures of farm size, average size by number of acres and volume of sales, indicate that farms owned and operated by blacks in the South are small, compared to other farms. In general, black-operated farms are one-third to one-half the size of all farms in the South (Table 2). Black-operated farms are also concentrated in the lower sales categories with the majority (79 percent) generating less than $10,000 in annual sales (Table 1). The disparity between the percentage of black-operated and all farms with sales of $10,000 or more appears to be less in those states that benefit from the production of crops that have historically been subject to government regulations. Notable examples are peanuts and tobacco in Georgia, North Carolina, and Kentucky.

The discussion which follows focuses on characteristics of the population in selected areas with concentrations of black farmers (20 or more black- operated farms). We do so because an important focus of this chapter is on indicators of well-being (poverty rate and level of income) and human capital characteristics (educational level) of black farmers. Since farmer-specific data of these types are unavailable in published form, information on the broader population of which black farmers are part will be used as proxy measures for the black farm population. In general, characteristics of the black population are exacerbated in the black farm population. For example, black farmers tend to have fewer years of formal education, lower levels of income, and higher rates of poverty than other blacks (Banks, 1986; Fratoe, 1979; Marshall and Thompson, 1976). These indirect measures, in addition to the PLI designation, provide a basis for assessing conditions in areas where black farmers reside.

The Study Area

PLI Designations. As noted earlier, the five study states of interest contain 130 PLI counties of which 81 have 20 or more black-operated farms. Data reported in Tables 3 through 7 include the PLI (81) and non-PLI counties (135)

Table 2. Average Farm Size and Selected Sales Characteristics for all Southern Farms and Black-Owned Farms

State	Avg. Size All Farms	Avg. Size Black Farms	% All Farms with Sales ≥ $10,000	% Black Farms with Sales ≥ $10,000
	1982 1978	1982 1978	1982 1978	1982 1978
Alabama	211 220	107.5 112.3	31.3 33.2	11.4 10.1
Arkansas	291 291	127.5 115.8	41.2 42.9	24.7 20.9
Florida	353 360	106.8 126.0	40.6 43.9	26.8 29.0
Georgia	248 261	135.4 130.6	43.0 45.0	31.0 26.7
Kentucky	140 143	59.4 79.3	41.4 37.5	23.4 21.6
Louisiana	282 296	95.8 100.2	32.3 39.7	18.4 18.3
Maryland	158 168	49.3 70.6	50.1 51.5	25.6 25.2
Mississippi	292 300	99.1 105.4	32.2 32.7	11.3 9.0
N. Carolina	142 135	72.4 68.9	45.7 46.8	34.8 34.1
Oklahoma	446 467	157.6 168.5	40.1 42.6	12.2 10.7
S. Carolina	224 226	75.5 78.8	34.4 35.9	18.9 17.3
Tennessee	138 146	84.4 96.0	28.1 27.5	18.3 17.1
Texas	710 773	135.6 166.0	34.6 38.7	8.0 10.5
Virginia	182 189	94.5 93.3	34.5 35.0	25.6 24.9
REGION AVG.	329.9 340.0	99.2 104.8	42.9 45.3	22.9 22.4

Source: 1982 Census of Agriculture, U.S. Department of Commerce, Bureau of the Census.

in each of the five states with 20 or more black-operated farms. The number of PLI-designated counties in the study areas suggests that they are economically depressed and that residents suffer from relatively low levels of social and economic well-being. In many instances, median levels of education and income are lower, and poverty rates are higher in the PLI versus the non-PLI counties. The data also suggest that the benefits of economic growth appear to be unevenly distributed between blacks and whites in both PLI and non-PLI counties. Consistently, blacks have lower incomes and higher rates of poverty than whites.

Poverty levels. Throughout the study area, the counties in which black farms are concentrated are among the poorest in their respective states. These counties are characterized by persistent levels of poverty and poverty rates among blacks are consistently higher than those of whites. The percentage of blacks below the poverty level in the study area ranges from a high of 63.9 percent in Tunica County, Mississippi to a low of 12.5 percent in Chatham County, North Carolina (see Tables 3 through 7).

The PLI/non-PLI status of a county does not appear to correlate with the percentage of black families below the poverty level. There are numerous examples in Mississippi, Alabama and Georgia where more than 50 percent of the black families are below the poverty level but the county is not considered a PLI county. Because the classification is based on per capita income, a relatively few individuals or families with high incomes might influence the classification of a county even though poverty might be rampant. Extreme poverty is the fate of blacks where a large percentage of black farms are located. The predominance of low educational levels among blacks and a large number of single parent, female-headed households may account for some of the disparity in the poverty levels between blacks and whites.

Income. Across the study area, there is not one instance where the median income of blacks equals that of whites. There are numerous times, however, where the median incomes of whites is more than twice that of blacks. Generally, the median income of residents of PLI counties is lower than those of non-PLI counties. Of interest is the fact that the gap in median income levels between whites and blacks tend to widen in non-PLI designated counties.

Education. Median levels of education of residents of the study counties are markedly different when race is considered. Blacks lag considerably behind whites and are much less likely than whites to complete high school. Some of the greatest disparities are observed in Mississippi, where blacks have the lowest level of education achievement (9.4 years). In PLI counties in Mississippi, for example, the median level of education of whites ranges from a low of 11.4 years in Benton County to 14.1 years in Oktibbeha County.

Table 3. ALABAMA. Median Level of Education, Family Income and Percent of Families Below Poverty Level by Race and County: 1980.

County	White			Black		
	Educ.	Income	Poverty	Educ.	Income	Poverty
*Barbour	12.2	$13619	11.0	8.0	$6012	45.3
*Bullock	----	14008	9.1	8.7	6204	41.4
*Chilton	11.5	12372	13.1	10.0	----	----
*Choctaw	12.1	13212	17.5	8.7	----	----
*Conecuh	11.9	11205	13.9	----	----	----
*Crenshaw	10.5	10159	19.1	8.3	----	----
*Fayette	11.0	12250	14.0	11.2	9652	25.9
*Greene	12.5	14227	6.9	8.7	5879	47.0
*Hale	12.3	13192	8.6	8.0	5004	52.2
*Henry	12.1	13958	9.3	8.6	----	----
*Lawrence	10.9	12916	17.0	10.0	----	----
*Lowndes	----	15446	7.4	8.8	6355	50.5
*Marengo	----	18263	7.1	9.0	----	----
*Monroe	12.3	15199	8.8	9.4	7408	39.5
*Perry	12.2	----	----	9.0	5861	47.1
*Pickens	12.1	13069	9.7	8.8	6364	46.4
*Sumter	12.6	16482	6.3	9.0	6528	41.8
*Wilcox	12.4	----	----	8.3	5528	53.1
Autauga	12.4	20451	7.8	9.5	8952	39.1
Butler	12.0	15241	10.0	8.9	8056	41.2
Chambers	12.1	16877	7.3	9.2	----	----
Clarke	12.3	18635	9.2	9.6	9098	40.7
Coosa	11.8	13187	17.2	----	11222	29.9
Dallas	12.5	18881	6.3	10.1	7983	46.0
Elmore	12.3	19282	7.5	9.7	9200	40.8
Escambia	12.2	15957	11.4	10.0	9386	33.1
Houston	12.4	18249	8.2	9.7	9436	36.1
Jefferson	12.6	21759	5.5	12.0	11675	27.3
Lamar	10.8	15504	12.4	8.7	10824	31.2
Lauderdale	12.3	18344	9.5	10.6	10561	31.7
Lee	12.7	19967	8.0	9.4	10535	31.6
Limestone	12.1	16855	11.9	9.2	10893	30.2
Macon	12.3	17500	12.2	12.1	10423	31.8
Madison	12.7	20983	7.3	12.2	11663	28.1
Mobile	12.5	20016	7.6	11.6	10404	35.2
Montgomery	12.8	21951	5.2	11.4	10775	32.9
Pike	12.2	15896	10.0	8.5	7308	43.2
Randolph	11.2	13730	13.2	8.9	9359	38.6
Talladega	12.1	16472	10.6	10.6	9965	33.2
Tallapoosa	12.1	16789	8.2	9.2	10323	31.3
Tuscaloosa	12.5	19656	8.2	10.9	9711	34.3
Alabama	12.3	18153	9.9	10.8	10048	37.0

Source: Characteristics of the Population—General Social and Economic Characteristics. 1980 Census of Population, U.S. Department of Commerce. Bureau of the Census.

*Persistent low-income counties.

Table 4. GEORGIA. Median Level of Education, Family Income and Percent of Families Below Poverty Level by Race and County: 1980.

County	White			Black		
	Educ.	Income	Poverty	Educ.	Income	Poverty
*Baker	10.0	$15022	19.8	7.2	----	----
*Brooks	10.9	13927	20.6	7.2	$8278	46.5
*Burke	12.1	17907	11.3	6.8	9085	42.8
*Clay	12.1	----	----	7.6	6389	58.2
*Dodge	10.5	14437	19.2	7.6	8598	50.1
*Greene	10.5	15182	12.7	7.8	10765	38.9
*Jefferson	10.7	16426	13.5	7.2	8956	44.3
*Macon	10.6	16352	13.4	7.3	9413	47.4
*Screven	12.5	13889	18.9	7.4	8613	52.6
*Tatnall	10.8	12430	15.2	9.9	8069	47.1
Bulloch	12.4	17483	14.3	7.6	9701	40.8
Decatur	12.0	16087	13.1	9.1	10207	40.2
Dooly	10.6	15147	17.0	6.8	8608	51.1
Early	12.0	16993	14.1	6.4	----	53.5
Grady	10.7	14171	16.3	9.0	8878	45.9
Hart	10.4	15415	12.9	9.4	11307	39.8
Laurens	12.0	17533	11.3	9.2	10093	37.8
Lee	12.4	21494	7.8	7.5	8640	47.0
Lowndes	12.4	16859	11.2	10.0	9385	36.7
Meriwether	9.5	18294	11.0	7.9	10729	33.0
Mitchell	12.0	17386	14.8	7.8	9136	45.3
Morgan	12.0	17881	10.1	----	----	----
Peach	12.2	20546	9.7	10.1	9669	43.4
Pierce	11.0	14251	17.2	9.0	6397	57.4
Sumter	9.4	18339	12.0	7.4	10391	36.3
Telfair	10.6	13383	11.8	8.0	8494	46.8
Thomas	12.2	17318	10.9	9.4	10830	38.5
Toombs	10.8	14633	17.1	9.1	6755	52.6
Worth	10.7	17500	11.2	7.3	7984	47.9
Georgia	12.4	19655	10.2	10.2	11012	34.1

Source: Characteristics of the Population—General Social and Economic Characteristics. 1980 Census of Population, U. S. Department of Commerce. Bureau of the Census.

*Persistent low-income counties.

Table 5. MISSISSIPPI. Median Level of Education, Family Income and Percent of Families Below Poverty Level by Race and County: 1980.

County	White			Black		
	Educ.	Income	Poverty	Educ.	Income	Poverty
*Amite	12.3	$15365	13.4	8.3	$ ----	----
*Attala	12.1	14310	11.3	8.3	6827	51.9
*Benton	11.4	13669	13.1	8.3	12414	33.4
*Bolivar	12.6	17663	9.2	8.4	7084	50.7
*Carroll	12.0	15028	13.5	8.3	8093	43.6
*Chickasaw	12.1	14936	11.6	10.0	11143	31.3
*Choctaw	12.0	12221	17.9	8.5	----	----
*Claiborne	12.6	22146	8.7	9.6	9570	35.8
*Clarke	12.1	16250	12.7	----	11158	28.9
*Copiah	12.3	16791	8.2	9.3	8061	43.0
*Covington	12.0	13181	17.4	----	----	----
*Holmes	12.5	15873	9.2	8.4	6733	54.9
*Humphreys	----	----	----	7.7	6515	54.9
*Jasper	12.4	14601	10.9	9.4	----	----
*Jefferson	12.4	16414	17.4	8.8	8223	41.9
*Jefferson Davis	12.2	16136	12.7	9.6	9481	33.7
*Kemper	12.4	14725	12.6	8.5	7453	50.8
*Lafayette	12.7	17967	10.2	8.8	10556	29.3
*Leake	12.1	10406	16.9	9.2	6926	41.1
*Madison	12.9	21354	6.5	9.2	8251	43.4
*Marshall	12.1	16213	12.2	8.7	9350	40.8
*Montgomery	12.0	14231	13.8	----	7437	46.8
*Neshoba	12.1	14400	13.7	9.6	8495	39.3
*Newton	12.3	14433	13.4	9.1	9077	39.0
*Noxubee	12.4	16468	9.7	8.3	7034	47.1
*Oktibbeha	14.1	18571	9.9	9.3	8506	39.2
*Panola	12.2	14873	14.8	8.3	7809	46.1
*Pontotoc	11.8	13853	13.9	9.7	11034	29.4
*Quitman	12.0	14972	14.4	7.6	6943	50.1
*Tallahatchie	12.1	13019	20.0	7.5	7161	49.8
*Tate	12.4	17410	11.0	8.5	8834	41.8
*Tippah	11.5	12284	18.6	9.2	9650	33.4
*Tunica	----	----	----	7.1	6014	63.9
*Walthall	12.3	15585	14.9	8.9	8483	39.8
*Wayne	12.1	14590	15.9	8.8	----	----
*Wilkinson	----	----	----	8.4	8493	39.7
*Winston	12.2	15525	11.3	9.0	8932	37.2
*Yalobusha	12.1	14127	12.5	----	9837	35.1
Adams	12.6	20442	7.5	9.8	9385	42.3
Clay	12.3	18324	8.2	9.7	10785	33.0
Coahoma	12.5	19816	6.3	8.1	7789	50.3
Desoto	12.4	20498	7.0	7.8	7384	43.9
Grenada	12.4	15766	8.7	8.2	----	----
Hinds	13.1	19216	4.5	11.8	9764	29.4
Jones	12.3	14245	8.7	10.0	7716	34.7
Lauderdale	12.5	14959	8.2	10.2	6981	37.5
Lawrence	12.2	14586	10.2	----	----	----
Lee	12.4	14548	9.7	10.5	9815	27.5

Table 5. Continued

County	White			Black		
	Educ.	Income	Poverty	Educ.	Income	Poverty
Leflore	12.5	$14797	7.7	8.4	$6076	46.9
Lincoln	12.3	14040	10.4	10.1	7143	37.3
Lowndes	12.6	15423	7.6	9.1	7884	39.9
Marion	12.1	12373	12.5	9.6	6687	43.4
Monroe	12.0	13328	9.2	9.7	7338	38.8
Pike	12.4	12974	9.8	10.0	6904	41.1
Rankin	12.6	20178	9.8	8.9	9408	29.8
Scott	12.1	12430	13.5	9.0	7125	41.2
Simpson	12.2	12943	12.1	10.2	8943	32.6
Smith	12.1	11085	17.5	9.8	7581	36.6
Sunflower	12.4	15208	8.7	7.9	6679	49.1
Union	11.7	14181	14.0	9.2	9232	34.5
Warren	12.6	20765	4.3	9.5	7666	34.6
Washington	12.5	16284	10.5	8.9	6674	42.9
Yazoo	12.4	17570	7.8	8.3	6996	53.9
Mississippi	12.4	17264	10.5	9.4	9013	43.2

Source: Characteristics of the Population—General Social and Economic Characteristics.
1980 Census of Population, U.S. Department of Commerce. Bureau of the Census.

*Persistent low-income counties.

Table 6. NORTH CAROLINA. Median Level of Education, Family Income and Percent of Families Below Poverty Level by Race and County: 1980.

County	White			Black		
	Educ.	Income	Poverty	Educ.	Income	Poverty
*Bladen	11.8	$14699	12.4	10.3	$9173	37.2
*Northampton	12.0	16060	9.2	8.5	10040	32.9
*Pender	12.1	16960	9.0	10.6	10280	31.1
*Perquiman	11.8	14372	12.5	9.2	9474	37.9
*Warren	11.3	15697	9.8	9.7	9417	35.9
Alamance	12.2	16488	5.3	11.3	11782	17.6
Anson	12.1	14596	7.0	10.6	9968	22.0
Beaufort	12.2	13571	10.7	10.1	7813	35.1
Bertie	11.8	12641	10.0	9.7	7908	34.7
Brunswick	12.1	15751	14.0	11.5	11590	30.0
Caswell	11.4	16626	9.8	10.0	----	----
Chatham	12.1	18481	4.5	11.4	14899	12.5
Columbus	11.8	15072	14.6	10.1	8765	39.8
Craven	12.5	16890	9.7	10.6	9770	34.0
Cumberland	12.6	16890	8.6	12.3	10551	28.6
Duplin	11.7	14655	14.2	10.4	9913	34.5
Durham	12.8	22244	3.9	12.2	13248	20.4
Edgecombe	12.7	18440	6.8	10.2	11630	26.9
Franklin	12.5	14153	8.2	12.1	8286	31.4
Gates	12.1	18158	5.2	9.7	11626	29.9
Granville	11.9	18679	5.5	10.0	11952	26.1
Greene	12.0	16658	9.6	----	10385	35.3
Guolford	12.6	21211	4.6	12.2	13419	21.0
Halifax	12.1	16450	10.7	8.8	8426	44.6
Harnett	12.0	15242	9.9	10.1	9877	33.8
Hertford	12.3	17642	7.6	9.3	11086	31.9
Johnson	11.9	15814	11.2	10.2	9910	33.7
Jones	11.3	15192	10.1	----	----	----
Lenoir	12.3	18247	7.3	10.6	9984	32.0
Martin	12.1	17344	8.9	9.4	----	----
Moore	12.5	18153	7.1	10.7	11162	27.1
Nash	12.3	19053	7.3	9.0	9352	36.7
Onslow	12.4	14163	11.5	12.2	10154	30.4
Orange	15.2	20793	5.9	11.7	13788	18.7
Pasquotank	12.2	17154	8.4	10.4	10916	27.1
Person	11.8	17201	8.0	9.9	12106	28.4
Pitt	12.7	18942	9.0	9.7	9833	35.1
Robeson	12.1	16569	9.8	10.5	9715	36.4
Rockingham	11.5	17441	8.0	10.7	14516	20.2
Sampson	12.0	15315	10.4	10.2	9812	34.1
Union	12.2	19665	5.9	10.5	11932	22.8
Vance	12.0	16561	9.1	9.8	10363	31.7
Wake	13.2	20481	3.8	12.0	13280	20.3
Washington	12.2	19546	8.8	9.7	10733	34.2
Wilson	12.2	18604	7.0	9.7	10273	31.5
Wayne	12.4	16852	8.0	11.4	10339	30.2
North Carolina	12.6	18182	7.9	11.1	11388	28.8

Source: Characteristics of the Population—General Social and Economic Characteristics. 1980 Census of Population, U. S. Department of Commerce. Bureau of the Census.

*Persistent low-income counties.

Table 7. SOUTH CAROLINA. Median Level of Education, Family Income and Percent of Families Below Poverty Level by Race and County: 1980.

County	White			Black		
	Educ.	Income	Poverty	Educ.	Income	Poverty
*Allendale	12.3	$15203	6.2	8.6	$6905	42.4
*Bamberg	----	13967	11.0	9.5	----	----
*Calhoun	12.4	16121	6.1	9.4	8978	30.4
*Clarendon	12.1	14464	10.7	8.8	8067	38.1
*Dillon	11.4	13193	14.3	9.5	7794	41.2
*Jasper	12.2	17103	10.9	9.7	9903	39.0
*Lee	11.9	17462	9.4	9.0	10459	37.1
*Marion	12.1	16855	9.2	9.7	10063	33.9
*Marlboro	11.5	16245	10.4	9.5	10152	31.9
*Williamsburg	12.1	17386	8.3	10.0	13649	34.2
Abbeville	11.7	15291	6.3	9.4	10854	24.8
Aiken	12.3	17700	6.8	10.1	10634	24.2
Anderson	11.9	16277	7.5	10.1	10752	22.7
Barnwell	12.1	15452	9.0	9.9	9741	27.4
Beaufort	13.0	18484	5.2	11.0	8870	31.8
Berkeley	12.4	17760	7.8	10.8	10834	28.5
Charleston	12.7	17285	6.1	11.0	9540	32.2
Chesterfield	11.5	13734	9.9	9.3	9861	31.5
Colleton	12.0	14551	9.5	10.0	8271	37.6
Darlington	12.1	15492	9.5	10.1	9182	35.8
Dorchester	12.6	21141	6.1	10.2	11289	29.2
Edgefield	11.9	16972	15.3	9.6	12293	26.9
Fairfield	12.2	17959	7.4	9.3	----	----
Florence	12.3	18299	8.9	10.1	10331	35.1
Georgetown	12.3	20387	8.0	10.0	10622	33.9
Greenville	12.3	20077	6.2	10.9	12404	24.4
Greenwood	12.2	19761	5.7	10.1	12365	24.2
Hampton	12.1	17402	10.2	8.9	----	----
Harry	12.4	16338	9.6	10.4	9804	35.1
Kershaw	12.3	19341	7.2	9.5	11404	29.6
Lancaster	11.7	19181	5.4	10.9	13537	20.6
Laurens	11.3	18547	5.5	10.0	14143	18.4
Orangeburg	12.3	17709	8.5	10.3	9696	37.2
Richland	13.1	21832	5.2	12.1	12915	22.8
Saluda	11.7	15983	11.9	9.5	10563	32.2
Spartanburg	12.1	18681	7.2	10.3	11652	27.9
Sumpter	12.5	17525	6.6	10.2	9298	38.8
South Carolina	12.3	16635	7.3	10.4	9747	31.8

Source: Characteristics of the Population—General Social and Economic Characteristics. 1980 Census of Population, U.S. Department of Commerce. Bureau of the Census.

*Persistent low-income counties.

There are only three counties where the median is below 12 years. The range for blacks, however, in Mississippi PLI counties is from 7.1 years in Tunica County to 10 years in Chickasaw County. The median level of education of blacks is less than nine years in more than 55 percent of the PLI counties.

The educational levels of residents of PLI and non-PLI counties in North Carolina and Georgia show trends similar to those of Mississippi, except that in both North Carolina and Georgia the median levels of education tend to be higher, especially for blacks. In South Carolina and Alabama, the disparity in levels of educational achievement of blacks and whites parallel those outlined in the previously mentioned states.

DISCUSSION AND IMPLICATIONS

The persistently low levels of economic well-being of black farmers is inextricably linked to conditions of other blacks and to the communities in which they live. In this section we discuss the implications of some of these relationships by focusing on the following questions: Given the conditions which exist now, what are the prospects for significant reductions in poverty levels and thus, enhanced levels of economic well-being for blacks in selected areas of the rural South? What do current trends suggest for the sustained participation of blacks in production agriculture?

Reduction of Poverty (Enhanced Levels of Economic Well-Being)

The strategies for enhancing levels of economic well-being most often pursued by farmers include increasing farm-generated income and supplementing farm-generated income with income from off-farm employment. Traditional approaches to increasing farm-generated income have included expanding farm size and altering production strategies, particularly the selection of enterprises. Given their characteristics, it is not likely that these strategies will be successfully pursued by the majority of black farm operators.

Since most of the farm operators have a limited resource base, access to capital that might be needed to pursue aggressive strategies often is not available due to discriminatory practices of some lending agencies (U. S. Commission on Civil Rights, 1982). Further, there is a general reluctance among many black farmers to "experiment" with nontraditional enterprises. Among blacks, farming practices are often transmitted from one generation to the next. It is not uncommon for the off-spring of black farmers to produce the same combination of enterprises that their parents produced, because their parents produced them. Often there is a great deal of skepticism about trying something which is unfamiliar and which is "untried."

Traditionally, most black-operated farms have been and are still devoted primarily to livestock, cash grain crops and tobacco. These are enterprises with which blacks are historically most familiar and are considered relatively "safe" even though they may not be very profitable. Thus, the likelihood of substantial numbers of black farmers adopting enterprises with potential for high per acre returns but which require substantial additional investments, more sophisticated management practices and increased market and production risks, is remote.

In addition to the factors just mentioned, the age and educational levels of black farmers also pose constraints to significantly increasing levels of farm-generated income. As a group, black farmers are older and have fewer years of formal education than the general farm population. Older farmers typically follow the pattern suggested by the life cycle theory (Hopkin et al., 1973). The life cycle theory suggests that as farmers get older they will begin to show more caution, invest less in their farming operation, and are less likely to make significant changes in their operations. In essence, as farmers get older they begin to consolidate their operations and prepare for retirement or transfer of the farm. At this point, high rates of return to capital invested are less important than reducing the debt load. During this time, the probability of farmers adopting new enterprises requiring more sophisticated management skills is low, particularly given a low level of formal education.

Particularly because farm-generated income is often inadequate to sustain a household, many farmers seek off-farm employment to enhance economic well-being. But the communities in which most black farmers live are economically depressed and offer few opportunities for off-farm employment. When off-farm employment opportunities are available, black farmers are less likely to successfully compete for them because of lower skills levels, advancing age and other cumulative effects of past and present discrimination. Often, communities in which black farmers live also have high concentrations of other blacks who, like black farmers, have lower educational and skill levels. These communities may not successfully compete for industries which hold potential for community vitalization because population characteristics are important in the selection of industrial sites. Many industries are reluctant to locate in areas with large black populations and an unskilled labor pool (Hansen, 1973; Till, 1972). Thus, employment in communities which have large black and unskilled populations is likely to be in industries which are seasonal and unstable, low-paying and which offer limited opportunities for advancement.

That some opportunities and economic rewards are unequally distributed is evidenced by the racial disparities in poverty rates in communities with concentrations of blacks and black farmers. These disparities may well reflect expected outcomes from investments in human capital. The educational levels of blacks in the study communities are considerably lower than those of whites. Many better paying jobs require at least a high school education and blacks may be excluded because of their low educational levels. In instances where level of education is not a barrier to job entry, it is frequently an impediment to upward mobility and increased earnings.

The Future of Blacks in Production Agriculture

Many of the same factors which are constraints to enhanced levels of well-being also threaten the future of blacks in production agriculture. Difficulty in accessing resources and information, and in the transfer of farms and farmland to subsequent generations, contribute to decreases in the black farm population. But, the major threats stem from the older age of black farmers and the lack of economic viability of black-operated farms. The majority of black farmers are near retirement age and fewer young blacks than young whites choose to become farmers. Without a significant infusion of young blacks into production agriculture, the population of black farmers will continue to decrease and possibly diminish as a result of the normal process of attrition. The lack of economic viability or marginal economic situation of most black farms, in conjunction with the general social and economic conditions of communities in which black farms are concentrated, suggest that few young blacks will choose production agriculture as a career path.

Small farms with low sales provide few incentives and opportunities for farm children to enter farming. Children of farm families often have different goals and aspirations, as well as different attitudes toward rural life, than their parents. Increasingly, farm children are agreeing to "take over" the home farm only if it is large enough to provide incomes that are comparable to those earned in nonfarm employment. Thus, many young people migrate from rural areas generally and farms in particular because of difficulties incurred in achieving the "right" combination of quality of life and economic security (Durant and Knowlton, 1978). Many young blacks, especially, perceive farming as yielding a low return with regard to economic well-being. Thus, they seek the economic security provided by nonfarm employment.

The marginal economic condition of most black-operated farms also affects parental expectations and aspirations for their children. Black farm families have typically sought upward mobility for their children through education and migration to more economically active areas. Children who migrate are usually prevented by distance from actively sharing in the farm operation or taking over the farm business as the parent retires or reduces his level of activity in farming. Children who pursue upward mobility through increased levels of education do not normally return to the farm. The low level of demand for college-trained people in their communities prevents many young blacks from returning to share in the operation of the family farm.

Black farm children who express a preference for farming and rural life may, however, be constrained in their attempts to enter farming by several factors. First, the large investment required to enter farming, even on a small scale, may prevent young blacks from entering the occupation. Second, those who have an opportunity to enter farming through the avenue of their small family farms may be unwilling to accept the lower incomes from farming that their parents have. And finally, lenders may be unwilling to commit funds to these operations.

In some Southern states, slow rates of decrease and even small increases in the number of black-operated farms are not cause for optimism. Black farmers in states with the least decrease do not appear to be "traditional" black farmers. Their farms continue to be small, but most operators appear to have higher incomes, derived primarily from off-farm sources. In most instances, their commitment to farming is not as strong as that of traditional black farmers. These farmers often use agriculture as a tax shelter or hobby and have fewer constraints to movement out of agriculture if the economics of the situation so dictate.

In summary, current conditions which characterize black farmers, their farms and the communities in which black-operated farms are concentrated suggest that without changes in the problem areas identified, black farm households will continue to experience significantly lower levels of economic well-being and the participation of blacks in production agriculture will continue to decrease. Strategies which would appear to be most important in counteracting existing trends include enhancing the human capital skills, particularly through increased levels of education, and the vitalization of communities in which black farms are located. Education has long been viewed as the key to economic success. If current educational levels of black farmers and other blacks in areas with high concentrations of black farmers persist, then blacks will continue to experience low levels of economic well-being. If rural communities do not provide incentives and opportunities for enhanced levels of well-being, young people will continue to migrate to urban areas.

The anti-poverty programs of the 1960s assisted many of the long-term poor in escaping their poverty status. Present-day cuts in assistance to local communities, in education, in social programs and in affirmative action programs do not offer hope for the level of support needed by many communities to fund such programs and ameliorate poverty. Thus, prospects for significantly enhancing the economic well-being of black farm households is not bright. The key seems to be in getting individual communities to seek alternative solutions to problems. Foremost would appear to be the implementation of programs to enhance levels of educational achievement. Supplemental educational programs for black farmers might include instruction for potential heirs on the transfer of property and on intensive uses of land such as planted forest farms. Another option might include exploring ways management firms can provide for the operation of farms for absentee landlords. These programs could be implemented in conjunction with programs designed to increase the profitability of small farms, perhaps providing an incentive for young blacks to consider production agriculture as a career choice.

In addition to incentives which may be required to encourage young blacks to commit themselves to production agriculture, an equal challenge is that of encouraging young people to commit themselves to their rural communities. It is unrealistic to expect a complete reversal of the trends related to the economic well-being of black farmers or to reductions in the black farm population, but with aggressive and carefully planned strategies, perhaps conditions can be improved.

REFERENCES

Banks, Vera. 1986. *Black Farmers and Their Farms*. Rural Development Research Publication No. 59. Washington, D.C.: U.S. Department of Agriculture, Economic Research Service.

Crecink, John C. 1986. *Small Farms: Their Distribution, Characteristics and Households*. Agricultural Economics Research Report 161. Mississippi State, Mississippi: Mississippi Agricultural & Forestry Experiment Station.

Davis, Thomas F. 1979. *Persistent Low-Income Counties in Nonmetro America*. Rural Development Research Report No. 12. Washington, D.C.: U.S. Department of Agriculture, Economic Research Service.

Durant, Thomas, J. Jr. and Clark S. Knowlton. 1978. "Rural ethnic minorities: Adaptive responses to inequality." in Thomas R. Ford (editor), *Rural U.S.A.: Persistence and Change*. Ames, Iowa State University Press.

Fratoe, Frank A. 1979. *The Educational Level of Farm Residents and Workers*. Rural Development Research Report No. 8. Washington, D.C.: U.S. Department of Agriculture, Economics, Statistics, and Cooperatives Service.

Ghelfi, Linda M. 1986. *Poverty Among Black Families in the Nonmetro South*. Rural Development Research Report No. 2. Washington, D.C.: U.S. Department of Agriculture, Economic Research Service.

Hansen, Niles M. 1973. *The Future of Nonmetropolitan America*. Lexington, Massachusetts: D.C. Heath.

Hopkin, John A., Peter J. Barry and C. B. Baker. 1973. *Financial Management in Agriculture*. Danville, Illinois: Interstate Printers and Publishers, Inc.

Hoppe, Robert A. 1985. *Economic Structure and Change in Persistently Low-Income Nonmetro Counties*. Rural Development Research Report No. 50. Washington, D.C.: U.S. Department of Agriculture, Economic Research Service.

Hoppe, Robert A., Herman Bluestone and Virginia K. Getz. 1986. *Social and Economic Environment of Black Farmers*. Washington, D.C.: U.S. Department of Agriculture, Economic Research Service.

Marshall, Ray and Allen Thompson. 1976. *Status and Prospects of Small Farmers in the South*. Atlanta, Georgia: Southern Regional Council, Inc.

Perlman, Richard. 1976. *The Economics of Poverty*. New York: McGraw-Hill Book Company.

Thompson, Alton. 1986. "The isolation of poverty differentials in the rural South," in Jogindar S. Dhillon and Marguerite R. Howie (editors). *Dimensions of Poverty in the Rural South*. Tallahassee, Florida: Florida A&M University.

Till, Thomas E. 1972. *Rural Industrialization and Southern Rural Poverty in the 1960's.: Patterns of Labor Demand in Southern Nonmetropolitan Labor Markets and Their Impact on Rural Poverty*. Austin: University of Texas, Center for the Study of Human Resources.

U.S. Commission on Civil Rights. 1982. *The Decline of Black Farming in America*. Washington, D.C. U.S. Government Printing Office.

U.S. Department of Agriculture (USDA). 1983. *Report of the USDA Task Force on Black Farm Ownership*. Washington, D.C.: U.S. Government Printing Office.

U.S. Department of Commerce. Bureau of the Census. 1983a. *Farm Population of the United States: 1982*. Series P-27, No. 58.

_____. 1983b. *1980 Census of Population: General, Social and Economic Characteristics.*

_____. 1984a. *U.S. Census of Agriculture 1982. United States, Summary and State Data.* Vol. 1, Parts 1-51. Washington, D.C.: U.S. Government Printing Office.

_____. 1984b. *1980 Characteristics of the Population Below the Poverty Level: Current Population Report.* Consumer Income Series P-60, No. 144.

8

Factors Associated with Women's Attitudes Toward Farming[1]

Lorraine E. Garkovich
Janet L. Bokemeier

Research on farmer's satisfaction with farming and their subjective sense of well-being has two major shortcomings. First, it has proceeded along sex differentiated lines. That is, the conclusions are based almost exclusively on examinations of the attitudes of male farmers to the neglect of women's attitudes. Second, economic and farm structural factors are traditionally used to account for differences in farmers' satisfaction or subjective well-being to the neglect of lifestyles, family and household variables. These limitations are problematic. To a degree greater than in most other occupational paths, farming is a vocation passed from parent to child within the context of childhood socialization. Farm women's attitudes toward farming become critical in this process because their attitudes are a dynamic component of this socialization process. This chapter examines the influence of individual, household and farm structure characteristics and attitudes toward farming on farm women's satisfaction. The analysis will add to our substantive understanding of the factors that influence the satisfaction or subjective well-being of farm persons. Moreover, it will illustrate how the current farm crisis may affect socialization to the farming lifestyle through its effects on farm women's sense of the quality of life associated with farming as a vocation.

FARM CRISIS

The current crisis in agriculture is substantively different from prior ones for several reasons. Earlier farm crises have been precipitated by phenomena such as bad weather, mechanization or the introduction of new farming methods that tended to force out tenant farmers, those on small homesteads, the least educated or those most resistant to change (Mueller, 1986). The current farm crisis, on the other hand, has been precipitated by a unique complex of domestic and international fiscal and market trends that have threatened a very different group.

Many farmers in crisis today are the "Young Farmers of the Year," the graduates of our agricultural colleges. They eagerly adopted technological innovations that increased their productivity. Further, they assiduously followed the advice of national agricultural leaders and local financial leaders.

> *The farmers having the greatest financial difficulties are as good or, according to some research, better than the average farmer in production efficiency. But they were born at the wrong time to get into farming. The same management decisions that made a farmer rich in the 1950s are forcing farmers into bankruptcy in 1985"* (Campbell, 1985:33).

This comment underscores the role of the family socialization process in shaping not only aspirations and attitudes but also vocational behavior. Unfortunately, the farming practices of the parents, when enacted by their children as farmers in the 80s, have produced tragically different results due to a changed set of circumstances.

Recent studies highlight the effects of this crisis on the composition of the farm population. A 1986 statewide survey by the Iowa Farm Bureau of 1,906 farmers who had left farming found that "most were the youngest farmers with the smallest farms (250 acres or less) and they took nearly 1,000 children with them" (Mueller, 1986:56). A similar study of 482 "failed" farmers by Iowa State University found that while the average age of an Iowa farmer is 54, the average age of those forced out by financial difficulties was 42. This farm crisis, then, is thinning the ranks of those who had recently entered farming, those who had moved up from the ranks of renters into owner-operators, and those who had expanded their operations so as to move into the ranks of full-time operators. Hardest hit, in other words, have been the families of the next generation of farmers, especially the cash grain, crop and livestock producers.

THE FARM FAMILY HOUSEHOLD: REPRODUCING THE FUTURE

It is the younger farm families, who operate middle-sized farms that produce all or most of the family income, that bear a disproportionate burden of the current crisis. This should raise great concern, for these farmers are in the early to middle stages of the life cycle of a farm family. During these stages, the family farm is established, the economic base for its survival secured, and the next generation socialized into the aspirations, attitudes and behavioral practices of the family. The following describes this socialization process and the function of attitudes within the family.

In the family, parents and children interact to produce "mutually shared norms and expectations" (Peterson and Rollins, 1987:472). An important aspect of socialization is the transmission of attitudes and values across generations. Bengston and Kuypers (1971) argue that parents have a "developmental stake" or investment in transmitting their attitudes, values and expectations to their children. One reason for this developmental stake is the intergenerational transmission of social status or lifestyles. Lifestyles, in this usage, refer to the variations in tastes and preferences upon which consumption rests, and are "partly determined by economic factors, but they are also determined by factors such as education, experience, and collectively held values" (Schroeder et al., 1985:307). Zablocki and Kanter (1976) argue that certain features of occupations are salient to differentiation among lifestyles. Of particular importance here are "occupational cultures as socializers and teachers of values" wherein occupations are symbolic representations of deeply held values and attitudes that also influence family life, consumption patterns, work roles, and rewards (Zablocki and Kanter, 1976:276).

Research on farming as an occupation or vocation has noted differences with other occupational paths. For example, Schroeder et al. (1985:309) argue that "socialization in a farm setting influences the relative importance or prestige assigned to farming in relation to other occupations," thus increasing the likelihood that the social rewards of farming are at least as important as the monetary rewards. In other words, in the socialization process, farm parents justify their vocation—farming—in the context of its reflection of a lifestyle that encompasses preferred values and attitudes as well as work roles. Barlett's (1986) study of the life histories of armers in one Georgia county substantiates the importance of the lifestyle attributes of farming. The majority of part-time farmers consciously pursued sufficient education to acquire a full-time off-farm job, then pursued farming in order to attain a desired lifestyle. In this sense, we can conceptualize the intergenerational transmission of the farming lifestyle as a function of attitudes toward farming as a vehicle for achieving a desired quality of life.

ATTITUDES AND PERCEPTIONS OF FARM LIFE

Considerable research has been conducted on attitudes and their relationship to individuals' sense of subjective well-being with their quality of life (Andrews and McKennell, 1980; Andrews and Withey, 1976; Campbell, 1981; Campbell et al., 1976). This research has shown that satisfaction with various aspects of one's life functions as a valid and reliable measure of subjective quality of life (Andrews and Withey, 1976). Campbell et al. (1976) argue that satisfaction reflects not only the objective situation but also one's perceptions of that situation and the standards one employs to evaluate it.

Perceptions of a situation may be a function of values, aspirations, beliefs or expectations (Andrews and McKennell, 1980; Campbell et al., 1976). In other words, our perception of a situation is filtered by cognitive or "psychodynamic" processes that are formed through the socialization process described earlier. With respect to the evaluative standards applied to perceptions of objective conditions, Wilkening (1982) suggests that the evaluation is more closely tied to changes in conditions, rather than the objective conditions themselves. Hence, as Coughenour and Tweeten (1986:70) note:

> *the perceived gap between the present and the desired condition of life, i.e., self-oriented aspiration, is a better predictor of satisfaction than is the perceived gap between the present conditions of self and others, i.e., other-oriented aspiration.*

Previous research on farmers' perceptions of quality of life or satisfaction with farming has identified several factors that account for a portion of the variation. For example, farmers are more satisfied than most other occupational groups with the challenge in their work and the conditions of their work. The "entrepreneurial" aspects of farming, the opportunity to be one's own boss and to have control over the conditions of work, is a significant attraction of farming (Barlett, 1986). Yet, while farmers in general, "appear to value very highly the kind work they are doing. . . they see it as very poorly paid (Campbell, 1981:115-116). In a study of how Kentucky farmers rated farming on nine factors (e.g. freedom of decision, income, chance of success), Coughenour and Tweeten (1986) note that two dimensions—economic and noneconomic—underline these attitudes, but that neither is related to the scale of farming as measured by gross farm sales. Moreover, when these Kentucky farmers assessed the centrality or importance of these characteristics, they found that:

> *Although attachment to farming in this sense is directly related*
> *to education and inversely related to age, it is not related either*
> *to gross farm sales or to full-time or part-time farm operator sta-*
> *tus* (Coughenour and Tweeten, 1986:76).

Farm family income, however, has been found to be significantly related to subjective well-being and perceived quality of life (Molnar, 1985). In other words, while gross farm sales may not serve as an adequate predictor of satisfaction with farming, access to an adequate family income is significant. Total family income is a function of farm sales, whether one works off the farm, type of nonfarm employment, and age. Off-farm employment has been associated in some cases, with lower, and in other cases, higher satisfaction with farming.

Finally, satisfaction with farming has been associated with commitment or attachment to farming (Molnar, 1985). While commitment is not dependent upon full- or part-time status or the size of the farm, it is "directly related to education and inversely related to age" (Coughenour and Tweeten, 1986:76). It also is likely that attachment to farming reflects one's self-identification as a farmer or the centrality of this work role to the individual. Barlett's (1986) discussion of the reasons for part-time farming cited by Georgia farmers demonstrates that the commitment to farming encompasses both economic and noneconomic factors such as: a love of farming, being your own boss, the benefits to children of being raised in a farm environment, and, "the means of continuing a valued parental tradition" (Barlett, 1986:304).

Coughenour and Tweeten (1986:81) conclude their review of farmers' quality of life perceptions in this manner:

> *Although satisfaction with farming is not much influenced by the*
> *type of farm, the level of the farmer's satisfaction with life increases*
> *with family income and age and is depressed by minority group*
> *status. Type of farm is related to these factors. . .Family income*
> *is an important outcome of both farm size and off-farm occupa-*
> *tion. These personal characteristics, together with schooling, are*
> *important in developing a sense of personal competence and the*
> *ability to control the conditions of life, an important determinant*
> *of perceived well-being. The linkages between subjective well-*
> *being and the external, personal and structural conditions of life*
> *thus are more complex than those used in the analytical models*
> *heretofore.*

As noted earlier, the research on farmers' satisfaction with farming has two major shortcomings: it has proceeded along sex differentiated lines and, it has tended to neglect lifestyle, family and household variables. This research will expand the existing approaches by examining farm women's attitudes, by taking into account family and household factors, and by considering farm structure characteristics. Barlett's (1986) research demonstrates there often exist fundamental divergences in the attitudes toward farming of wives and husbands. The Georgia farm women rarely expressed the same positive feelings about farming as a lifestyle as their husbands did, and, "farming background does not correlate with these positive or negative attitudes" (Barlett, 1986:305). Barlett further notes that the farm women's lower level of involvement in farm work may account for their inability to appreciate, as their husbands' do, the lifestyle benefits of farming.

Theoretically, the traditional approaches to the study of satisfaction and subjective well-being note that these attitudes are formed in a social context. The social basis for the formation of attitudes provides a framework for understanding why particular factors have explanatory power. For example, age reflects generational differences in sociohistorical experiences that produce variations in basic values, expectations, and standards of evaluation. Studies of marital quality find that satisfaction is affected by family income, community involvement, family composition, and satisfaction with wife's working (Spanier and Lewis, 1980). In other words, the satisfaction or subjective sense of well-being of individual members is influenced by the structure and functioning of the family unit. The importance of the social context for the satisfaction of individuals is especially relevant for research on the well-being of farm families. The interpenetration of family, household and enterprise activities for farm persons is greater than for any other occupational group. In this sense, a change in any one aspect of these objective conditions is likely to affect the overall satisfaction of farmers more than others. A 1974 study of 500 Wisconsin farm couples illustrates this point. Bharadwaj and Wilkening (1974:739) found that the satisfaction of husbands and wives reflected "different perceptual frameworks which reflect the relative salience of farm and family roles in their lives." In other words, both farm and family aspirations and attainment influenced the satisfaction of husbands and wives.

We hypothesize that farm women who see a future in farming for their families will have a higher level of satisfaction with their farm life. This reflects the importance of a sense of control over one's life in shaping satisfaction. Farm women's optimism about farming and their satisfaction with farming will be influenced by both the structure of the farm enterprise and family and individual characteristics. Specifically, farm women with a high level of personal involvement in their farm enterprise, who live on farms that rely upon family labor and farm sales for their livelihood, will express higher levels of satisfaction with farming. With respect to family and individual characteristics associated with satisfaction with farm life, we hypothesize that older women, those with a personal identity as a farmer, and with higher family incomes, will express higher levels of farm life satisfaction.

PROCEDURES

Data were collected in the spring of 1984 by a statewide mail survey of Kentucky farm women.[2] A stratified random sample of 1,372 eligible respondents was developed and of these, 873 returned usable questionnaires for a response rate of 64 percent. Eligible respondents were women residing on farms currently operated by their families.

Dependent variables include women's attitudes about farming and participation in farm work. Women's optimism towards farming is represented by the statement: "I will be farming five years from now" and, responses ranged from (1) strongly disagree to (5) strongly agree. The second dependent variable, women's task performance score, is a scale measure of the women's actual involvement in 18 farm tasks.[3] Women were asked how often they personally performed a set of tasks and could respond (1) never, (2) occasionally, or (3) regular duty. The following procedures were used to handle missing values. If less than 50 percent of the items were missing, the mean values were used as substitutes. The reliability of the participation scale is Alpha=.903 with a mean of 33.15 (standard deviation=8.12). The third dependent variable is a scale of farm satisfaction composed of four items with a range of (1) very dissatisfied to (5) very satisfied. Items included the farm women's satisfaction with: farming as a way of life, farming as a way to make a living, the family's opportunities to continue farming, and her children's opportunities to farm. The reliability of the farm life satisfaction scale is Alpha=.772 with a mean of 11.84 (standard deviation 3.80).

Independent variables represent two types of factors that we hypothesize would influence farm women's attitudes. Individual and family characteristics include the following: women's age, women's education, and number of children living at home as reported by respondents. Whether the wife and the husband work off the farm are two additional individual factors and are measured as dummy variables with a positive value if the farm woman or man has off-farm employment.

Farm structure factors represent the immediate social context within which the farm family functions. Measures include: total number of acres in farm operation reported by respondent; type of farm operation (indicated by whether the operation is primarily crop, livestock or both); reliance on hired labor—a dummy variable with (1) coded for a positive response to whether they custom hire or contract over half the work on their farm); and dependence on farm income (respondent's report of the percentage of total family income derived from family farm income).

Another independent variable is the farm woman's perceived self-identity as measured by self-categorization. Respondents were asked:

> As a farm woman, do you see yourself as: (1) FARM HOMEMAK-ER: A woman whose main farm activities involve running errands and traditional homemaking chores; (2) AGRICULTURAL HELP-ER: A woman who participates in agricultural production mainly during busy times; (3) BUSINESS MANAGER: A woman whose main responsibilities are bookkeeping, information gathering, and financial decisionmaking, but her husband is the primary operator; (4) FULL AGRICULTURAL PARTNER: A woman who shares equal work, responsibilities, or decisionmaking on all aspects of farm operation with her husband; or (5) INDEPENDENT AGRICULTURAL PRODUCER: A woman who manages the farm largely by herself.

In our multivariate analyses, self-identity is recoded as a dummy variable and labeled as commitment to a farm work role, with women who indicate that they perceive themselves as full agriculture partners or as independent agriculture producers coded as (1).

The analysis is in two parts. The first, based on the bivariate analysis, describes farm women's attitudes toward and satisfaction with farming and identifies factors associated with these. In the second, we examine through path analysis relationships among individual, farm structure and attitudinal factors associated with farm women's satisfaction or subjective well-being.

RESULTS OF THE BIVARIATE ANALYSIS

The distribution of selected farm women's attitudes about farming and farm life are presented in Table 1. Most (6 out of 10) of these farm women consider farming as strictly a business, emphasizing its economic rather than its lifestyle aspects. Women's optimism about their future in farming is like a glass half filled with water. While over half the women are optimistic and believe that they will still be farming in five years, from the other viewpoint, over 40 percent are clearly uncertain of or discouraged regarding their future in farming.

This discouragement with farming is reflected in women's high dissatisfaction with "farming as a way to make a living," "farm income," and "prices received for farm products." In addition to their discouraged attitudes regarding farm economic factors, farm women are pessimistic about their children's future in farming, with only 20 percent reporting satisfaction with their

Table 1. Farm Women's Attitudes on Farming and Farm Life

Approach to:	Strongly Disagree	Disagree	Unsure	Agree	Strongly Agree
For me, farming is strictly a business (Farm Entrepreneur)	7.0%	28.3%	6.9%	39.5%	18.4%
I will be farming five years from now (Farm Optimism)	3.3	5.5	36.4	38.5	16.3

Farm Lifestyle Satisfaction

How satisfied are you with:	Very Dissatisfied	Dissatisfied	Unsure	Satisfied	Very Satisfied
Farming as a way of life	7.8%	20.6%	4.9%	42.4%	24.4%
Farming as a way to make a living	23.9	25.2	13.3	26.6	10.9
Family's opportunity to continue to farm	12.9	18.8	32.3	26.7	9.3
Children's opportunity to farm	25.9	21.9	32.3	14.5	5.4

Farm Economic and Work Role Satisfaction

How satisfied are you with:	Very Dissatisfied	Dissatisfied	Unsure	Satisfied	Very Satisfied
My opportunities to work off-farm	6.2	13.9	20.6	37.7	21.6
My role in farm decision-making	4.6	13.1	19.1	45.8	17.3
Prices received for farm products	43.9	34.3	5.8	14.4	1.6
Our farm income	36.4	33.3	4.6	23.3	2.3

children's opportunities to farm. Of course, a significant group of the older women have already experienced children struggling with the decision of whether to enter farming. On the other hand, women are very positive about their farm lifestyle, with two-thirds indicating satisfaction with "farming as a way of life." In addition, the majority of these farm women report satisfaction with opportunities for off-farm employment and their role in farm decisionmaking. Hence, like farm men, most farm women consider farming as a business and are dissatisfied with the economics of farming, but they remain fairly satisfied with farming as a way of life.

Table 2 presents the results of the bivariate analysis of individual and family factors associated with farm women's attitudes. Women with higher educational attainment, who are younger and who have larger families report higher optimism about their farm future. One might expect age to be inversely related to believing one will still be farming in five years. Older women may expect to retire soon, are more likely to be widowed, and have lower educational attainment and family incomes (Bokemeier and Garkovich, 1987). Although older farm operators are more likely to own the land they farm and tend to have lower debts, their farms tend to be smaller. Interestingly, employment off the farm by either the husband or the wife is not significantly

Table 2. Individual and Family Factors Associated with Farm Women's Farm Attitudes

	Will be farming in 5 years			Farming is a business		
	Disagree	Unsure	Agree	Disagree	Unsure	Agree
Age						
Under 35	3.0%**	33.5%	63.5%	48.9%**	6.5%	44.7%
36-45	7.9	26.4	65.7	39.2	6.4	54.3
46-64	8.6	39.4	52.0	30.5	7.1	63.1
65 years or older	19.6	49.5	31.0	18.9	8.7	71.8
Educational Attainment						
3-11 years	13.2**	43.2	43.6	29.2	9.6	61.1
12 years	7.0	35.3	57.7	35.7	5.9	58.3
13 or more years	7.7	31.2	61.1	40.7	5.8	53.5
Wife Works off Farm						
Yes	7.4	32.5	60.1	39.7	5.4	54.9
No	10.1	38.1	51.9	32.1	8.0	60.0
Husband Works off Farm						
Yes	6.2	36.9	56.8**	43.9**	9.4	46.8
No	10.1	34.1	55.8	30.3	4.3	65.4
Farm Women's Self Identity						
Homemaker	11.1**	40.3	48.6	32.3	7.3	60.4
Agricultural helper	5.3	35.6	59.2	40.0	7.6	52.4
Business manager	2.3	29.5	68.2	35.4	1.5	63.2
Agricultural partner/Independent producer	12.2	32.8	55.0	35.4	6.9	57.7
No. of Children at Home						
0	13.1**	41.1	45.8	29.9*	5.6	64.5
1-2	5.5	33.9	60.5	38.3	7.0	54.7
3 or more	8.2	31.9	60.0	39.8	9.6	50.8

*Significant at p ≤ .05
**Significant at p ≤ .01
N = 844

related to optimism about farming. However, women who perceive themselves as farm business managers are more optimistic about their farm future.

Older women, those with no children at home, and those whose husbands are full-time farmers (i.e., their husbands do not work off the farm) are most likely to see farming as a business. Barlett (1986) argues that a significant proportion of farm people with off-farm employment are or have always been committed to a career off the farm. These farmers are less dependent on farm income and thus more likely to value farming as a lifestyle rather than a business. Moreover, women who self-identify as business managers for the farm operation are also most likely to believe they will still be farming in five years.

Table 3 presents the results of the bivariate analysis of farm factors associated with farm women's attitudes. It is clear from this analysis that farm characteristics influence women's sense of their future in farming. Women on the largest farm enterprises (in total acreage), those who do not rely on hired custom or contract labor (with dependence on family labor inputs), and those in mixed crop and livestock operations are most likely to see themselves still farming in five years. With respect to the relationship between farm characteristics and women's attitudes toward farming as a business, we find that women who reside on middle-sized farms (200 to 499 acres) are most likely to see farming as a business. No other farm characteristics seem to differentiate statistically farm women's attitudes on this issue.

Recent analyses of trends in agricultural production have suggested a tendency toward a disappearance of middle range farm operations (Bartlett, 1986).

Table 3. Farm Factors Associated with Farm Women's Farm Attitudes

	Will be farming in 5 years			Farming is a business		
	Disagree	Unsure	Agree	Disagree	Unsure	Agree
Total Acres						
1-49 acres	13.1%**	43.8%	43.0%	44.1%**	10.7%	45.2%
50-199	8.7	37.5	53.8	33.9	6.1	60.0
200-499	4.3	29.0	66.7	25.9	2.9	71.1
500-3800	4.3	18.8	76.8	32.3	5.9	61.8
Custom Hire Labor						
Yes	13.6**	44.2	42.2	35.3	8.7	56.0
No	6.3	33.4	60.2	36.2	6.1	57.7
Type of Farm Operation						
Crop	10.1*	38.0	51.8	39.6	8.9	51.5
Livestock	11.7	36.4	52.0	35.0	5.0	60.0
Both	4.7	33.8	61.4	32.2	4.7	63.1

*p ≤ .05
**p ≤ .01

In contrast, we find that women on this type of farm are more likely than other farm women to have a "farming as a business" model of farming and to report a more optimistic future in farming.

Thus, the bivariate analyses indicate that farm structure factors are key determinants of farm women's attitudes toward their families' future in farming. This suggests that the immediate social context within which the family functions has a powerful effect on the development of women's attitudes, especially their attitudes about farming and its future. The final aspect of the bivariate analysis examines the factors associated with farm women's satisfaction with farm life. Table 4 presents Pearson correlation coefficients of variables for the multivariate analysis, as well as the means and standard deviations. All the relationships

Table 4. Correlations, Means, and Standard Deviations

	Age	Education	Employed Off-Farm	Farm Work Role	Dependent Farm Income	Total Acres	Hired Custom Labor	Farm Task Performance	Farm Optimism
Age	1.00								
Education	-.239**	1.00							
Employed Off-Farm	-.217**	.301**	1.00						
Farm Work Role	.031	-.087**	-.073*	1.00					
Dependent Farm Income	-.077*	-.027	-.217**	-.016	1.00				
Total Acres	-.042	.175**	-.022	-.075*	.270**	1.00			
Hired Custom Labor	.187**	.037	.036	.037	-.206**	-.101**	1.00		
Farm Task Performance	.053	-.049	-.108**	.277**	.107**	-.015	-.122**	1.00	
Farm Optimism	-.243**	.090**	.073*	-.031	.207**	.158**	-.158**	.139**	1.00
Farm Life Satisfaction	.080**	-.066*	-.130**	-.031	.196**	.093**	-.070*	.142**	.286**
Mean	46.39	12.20	0.43	0.17	32.29	205.64	1.24	33.52	3.66
Std. Dev.	12.91	2.56	0.50	0.37	32.19	300.68	0.43	7.97	0.89

**p ≤ .01
*p ≤ .05

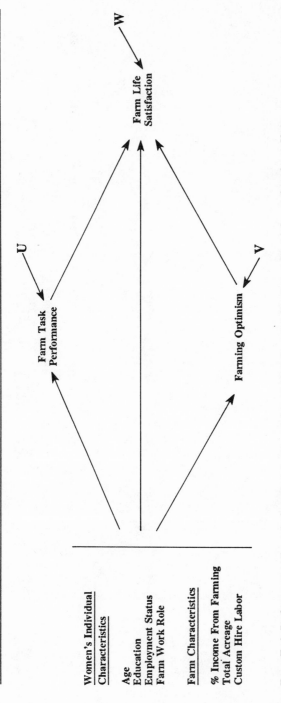

Figure 1. Causal Model of the Influences on Farm Life Satisfaction

Farm Task Performance = b_0 + b_1 income + b_2 acres + b_3 custom + b_4 age + b_5 educ. + b_6 employ. + b_7 role. + U

Farming Optimism = c_0 + c_1 income + c_2 acres + c_3 custom + c_4 age + c_5 educ. + c_6 employ. + c_7 role. + V

Farm Life Satisfaction = d_0 + d_1 income + d_2 acres + d_3 custom + d_4 age + d_5 educ. + d_6 employ. + d_7 role. + d_8 perform. + d_9 optimism + W with farm life satisfaction (except for commitment to farm work role) are statistically significant. In examining individual and family factors, we find that these factors are differentially related to farm life satisfaction and farm optimism. Younger women are more likely to believe that they will be farming in five years but report less satisfaction. Likewise, women who have more education and those who are employed off-farm are more optimistic about farming, but report lower farm life satisfaction. In contrast, farm characteristics are similarly related to farm optimism and satisfaction. Women on larger farms that have higher dependence on farm income and lower reliance on hired labor are more optimistic about farming and have high farm life satisfaction. Women who believe that they will be farming in five years report higher farm life satisfaction. Regular participation in farm tasks also is positively related to farm women's farm life satisfaction.

STRUCTURE OF THE PATH ANALYSIS

The next step is to explore these causal relationships with path analysis. The causal model is developed to explain the way in which individual and farm characteristics, as well as farm task participation and farming optimism account for farm life satisfaction. Farm task participation and farming optimism (i.e., will be farming in five years) act as intervening variables between individual and farm characteristics and farm life satisfaction. Farm women's age, education, employment status, and identity with farming as a work role are the main individual characteristics. The farm characteristics include dependence on farm income, farm size and reliance on hired labor. Farm women's personal and farm characteristics influence farm life satisfaction directly and indirectly through women's participation in farm tasks and their optimism about farming. These exogenous variables also influence farm task performance and farming optimism directly.

Results of the Path Analysis

The parameters of the model are estimated using ordinary least squares regression analysis. Table 5 presents the standardized and unstandardized coefficients of the variables for reduced form and structural equations for all endogenous variables. Also included are multiple and adjusted R^2 and F ratios for each equation. The first two reduced form equations presented in Table 5 provide estimates of the direct effects of the exogenous variables on the intervening variables. Each of these equations explains slightly more than 10 percent of the variance. The third reduced form equation estimates the total effects of the exogenous variables on the final dependent variable, farm women's farm life satisfaction, and explains approximately 5 percent of the variance.[5]

Table 5. Reduced Form and Structural Equations for Farm Life Satisfaction

Predetermined Variables	Farm Task Performance		Farm Optimism		Farm Life Satisfaction		Farm Life Satisfaction	
	b	beta	b	beta	b	beta	b	beta
Age	.046	.075*	-.014	-.203**	.018	.060	.030	.103**
Education	.011	.004	.013	.037	-.011	-.007	-.031	-.021
Employed	-1.034	-.065	.068	.038	-.437	-.057	-.440	-.057
Farm Work Role	6.030	.280**	.043	.018	-.310	-.030	-.602	-.059
Depend on Farm Income	.012	.048	.004	.152**	.021	.176**	.016	.136**
Total Acres	.0001	.002	.0002	.075*	.001	.040	.0002	.018
Hired Custom Labor	-2.399	-.130**	-.151	-.072*	-.248	-.028	.137	.015
Farm Performance	—	—	—	—	—	—	.047	.098**
Farm Optimism	—	—	—	—	—	—	1.222	.286**
Constant	33.278**		4.124**		10.883**		4.267**	
F	12.767**		11.683**		5.664**		12.629**	
R²	.110		.104		.052		.140	
Adj R²	.101		.096		.043		.129	

*p ≤ .05
**p ≤ .01
N = 709

Dependent Variables

The final structural equation provides estimates of the direct effects of the predetermined variables on farm life satisfaction. The inclusion of the intervening variables in the structural equation significantly increases the explained variance from 5 to 14 percent. Each of the reduced form equations and the structural equation are statistically significant at or below the .01 level.

Table 6 shows the decomposition of effects into their component parts, including total, direct, and indirect effects, using standardized coefficients only.

Table 6. Decomposition of Effects for Farm Life Satisfaction (Standardized Betas Only)

Dependent Variable	Predetermined Variable	Total Effect	Indirect Effects via Task Performance	Indirect Effects via Farm Optimism	Direct Effects
Farm Task Performance	Age	.075*	--	--	.075*
	Education	.004	--	--	.004
	Employ Off-farm	-.065	--	--	-.065
	Farm Work Role	.280**	--	--	.280**
	Depend/Farm Income	.048	--	--	.048
	Total Acres	.002	--	--	.002
	Hired Custom Labor	-.130**	--	--	-.138**
Farm Optimism	Age	-.203**	--	--	-.203**
	Education	.037	--	--	.037
	Employ Off-Farm	.038	--	--	.038
	Farm Work Role	.018	--	--	.018
	Depend/Farm Income	.152**	--	--	.152**
	Total Acres	.075*	--	--	.075*
	Hired Custom Labor	-.072*	--	--	.072*
Farm Life Satisfaction	Age	.060	.007	-.058	.103**
	Education	-.007	.001	.011	-.021
	Employ Off-Farm	-.056	-.006	.011	-.057
	Farm Work Role	-.030	.027	.005	-.059
	Depend/Farm Income	.176**	.005	.043	.136**
	Total Acres	.040	.001	.021	.018
	Hired Custom Labor	-.028	-.013	-.021	.015
	Task Performance	.098**	--	--	.098**
	Farm Optimism	.285**	--	--	.286**

*p ≤ .05
**p ≤ .01

Examining Table 6 in conjunction with Table 5, we can see a number of interesting results. Focusing on the direct effects of the exogenous variables on women's task participation, the individual characteristics of age and farm work role identity have statistically significant positive effects on women's farm participation. The farm characteristic of reliance on hired labor has a negative effect on farm task participation. In regard to the influence of the exogenous variable on farming optimism, we see that age has a strong negative association. Also, all three farm characteristics are significant determinants, with dependency on farm income and acreage positively related and reliance on hired labor negatively related to farming optimism. Thus, as hypothesized, the intervening variables are directly influenced by individual and farm characteristics.

In examining farm life satisfaction, we see that both intervening variables have significant direct positive effects on farm life satisfaction. As hypothesized, women who participate more in farm tasks and who expect to be farming in five years are more likely to be satisfied with farming as a way of life.

Although correlation analysis found significant bivariate relationships between exogenous variables and farm life satisfaction, in multivariate analysis, dependence on farm income is the only statistically significant determinant in the reduced form equation. Women who derive a greater percentage of their income from farming are more likely to be satisfied with farm life. Dependence on farm income also has a weak indirect influence on farm life satisfaction through farm task performance. Women who depend more on farm income are likely to perform a greater number of farm tasks. This high performance, in turn, has a positive influence on farm life satisfaction.

Dependence on farm income has a larger indirect influence through farming optimism. Those who depend more on income from farming are more likely to expect to be farming in five years which in turn, has a positive influence on farm life satisfaction. Thus, the positive direct effect of dependence on farm income on farm life satisfaction, in conjunction with the positive indirect effects, results in a significant total positive effect of dependence on farm income on farm life satisfaction. The majority of this total effect is direct rather than indirect.

Several interesting results are found in terms of women's age. Age has a direct influence on satisfaction with farm life. Women who are older are significantly more satisfied with farm life. Age also has an indirect influence through farm task participation. Older women participate more in farm tasks and those who participate more report more satisfaction with farm life. Age also has a much larger indirect effect through farming optimism. Older women are less likely to expect to be farming in five years. However, farming optimism has a positive influence on farm life satisfaction. The negative influence of age on farming optimism creates an overall negative indirect effect of age on satisfaction through farming optimism. The fact that older women are less likely to expect to be farming in five years creates a negative indirect effect on farm life satisfaction through farming optimism.

The majority of the effect of age on satisfaction is direct. Older women are more satisfied with farm life. This positive influence is reinforced slightly by the small positive indirect effect of age through task performance. However, the substantial negative indirect effect of age on satisfaction through farming optimism undermines the positive influence of age on satisfaction, creating a much smaller total positive effect.

Thus, the use of causal modeling proves informative as to the process by which age influences satisfaction, though the total effect may appear insignificant. Although these effects are not statistically significant, the indirect effects of farm work role and farm characteristics on satisfaction, through task performance and optimism, are interesting. The influence of farm characteristics tend to be indirect through farm optimism.

SUMMARY AND CONCLUSIONS

While farm women place a high value on farming as a way of life, they are fairly dissatisfied with the opportunities that farming offers as a way to make a living. Although the farm crisis had not yet seriously affected the Kentucky farm economy when these data were collected in 1984, Kentucky farm women could see what was happening in the Midwest and could recognize that they were at risk too. What is remarkable is that despite the fact that two-thirds to three-quarters of the farm women expressed dissatisfaction with the economics of farm life, over half still felt they would be farming in five years. This finding substantiates the importance of the lifestyle dimension of farming (Schroeder et al., 1985) and suggests that families may attribute greater social value to the status enhancement opportunities of farming than to its economic rewards.

The path analysis demonstrates that farm task performance and farming optimism are intervening variables between individual and farm characteristics and farm life satisfaction. Both farm task involvement and optimism about the family's future in farming have significant direct effects on farm life satisfaction. Women who are actively engaged in the farm enterprise experience psychological rewards from the "process of accumulating 'family' property and equity" that increases the likelihood of "passing the farm enterprise on to their children."

But the effect of these intervening variables on farm life satisfaction is influenced by individual and farm structure characteristics. Specifically, age has an indirect influence on farm life satisfaction through both performance and farming optimism. Dependence on farm income has a direct effect on farm satisfaction, as well as an indirect effect through farm task performance and the woman's attitude toward the family future in farming.

The relationship of farm attitudes and off-farm employment deserves additional comment, even though these relationships often do not achieve statistical significance when other factors are held constant. Off farm employment yields more stable sources of income, and those with off farm employment rely less on farm income to support the family. Not surprisingly, women in these farm families are less likely to perceive farming as a business. Differences in optimism regarding their current farm operation were not found among those who are full-time farmers and those who work off-farm. An interesting research question for future consideration is whether off-farm employment, as it leads to a greater focus on farming as a lifestyle, is related to farm families' desire to maintain family lands and to transfer farms intergenerationally.

Another general pattern that emerges is that with off-farm employment, farm women participate less in farm tasks and decisions and express less satisfaction with farm life. Note that this scale of satisfaction with farm life emphasizes opportunity and economics, as well as farming as a way of life. The current trend toward more off-farm employment may lead to more general dissatisfaction with farm life. One's assessment of lifestyle is related to one's expectations.

The multilevel analytic approach utilized in this study highlights the importance of the farm household as the unit of analysis. The fact that individual, family and farm characteristics all influenced women's attitudes toward and satisfaction with farming indicates that the household is an appropriate context within which to consider the dynamics of the farm family. For example, the importance of the husband's employment off the farm and the level of the woman's involvement in farm tasks on the nature of women's attitudes, demonstrates that these attitudes do not emerge independent of significant others or her role performance. Rather, women's attitudes are grounded in both the social context and their behavior. Moreover, the analyses demonstrate that there is considerable variation in farm women's attitudes that reflects the variety of individual and structural conditions confronting farm families.

Finally, we must consider the possible consequences of women's attitudes for the socialization of the next generation. A substantial proportion of the farm women are uncertain or discouraged regarding their future in farming. The farm women express a high level of dissatisfaction with farming as an economically viable occupation capable of supporting their families or one offering opportunities for their children. Yet, this is tempered by a high level of satisfaction with farming as a way of life. This suggests that farm women may be communicating a mixed message to their children about their options for the future, a message that may reduce the "status value" of farming in the eyes of the children. In other words, the current crisis in farming may be "devaluing" the intrinsic rewards associated with farming, rewards that have, in the past, compensated for the financial uncertainties associated with this vocation. This is only speculative, but does suggest that there is a need to expand our research on the current farm crisis to consider its effects on the socialization of the next generation of farmers.

NOTES

[1]This chapter is based on data collected under a cooperative agreement with the Agricultural Cooperative Service (USDA) and the College of Agriculture, University of Kentucky agreement number 58-31C7-2-1007 and in part in connection with projects of the Agricultural Experiment Station, Nos. 824, 829 and 840. The authors gratefully acknowledge the contributions of Connie Hardesty in the development of this chapter.

[2]Dillman's (1978) total design method was used to gather data and involved three separate mailings. Potential respondents were women living on farms currently in family operation. The sampling frame included a list of all households of patrons of Southern States (which represents 89 percent of all farm supply cooperative membership in Kentucky) and a stratified list of farm landowners provided by the Agricultural Stabilization and Crop Service of USDA in Kentucky. Multiple lists were compiled because no single reliable list of Kentucky farm operators was available.

[3]Farm tasks included in the performance scale are: make major purchases of farm supplies and equipment, check market prices, haul goods or animals to market, pay farm bills, do farm bookkeeping, prepare farm income tax forms, order farm supplies, attend meetings of farmer organizations, gather production outlook information, gather information on new products or technologies, mow or bush hog fields, run errands to town, keep equipment and tools organized, bale hay, set tobacco beds, top tobacco, strip tobacco.

[4]In order to depict the model, the arrows representing all the paths are not drawn. Each of the exogenous variables are correlated with one another and each directly affects endogenous variables. The model is recursive with all arrows pointing in the same direction. The variables used in the path analysis have been described previously. The individual characteristics refer to women only. The attitude regarding whether or not farming is strictly a business proved insignificant in preliminary multivariate analysis and was therefore not included in the path analysis.

[5]Typically, analyses of satisfaction/subjective well-being explain relatively less variance. In establishing structural effects on satisfaction, the amount of explained variance is probably a poor criterion for theoretical importance. Rather, we would argue, it is more important to identify how alternative factors operate.

REFERENCES

Andrews, F. M. and A. C. McKennell, 1980. "Measures of self-reported well-being: Their affective, cognitive and other components."*Social Indicators Research* 8(June):127-156.

Andrews, F. M. and S. B. Withey, 1976. *Social Inidcators of Well-Being: American's Perceptions of Life Quality.* New York: Plenum.

Barlett, Peggy F., 1986. "Part time farming: saving the farm or saving the life-style?" *Rural Sociology,* 51(3):289-313.

Bengston, V. L. and J. A. Kuypers, 1971. "Generational differences and the developmental stake." *Aging and Human Development,* Vol. 2:249-260.

Bharadwaj, L. and E. A. Wilkening, 1974. "Occupational satisfaction of farm husbands and wives." *Human Relations,* 27(8):739-753.

Bokemeier, J. and L. Garkovich, 1987. "Assessing the influence of farm women's self-identity on task allocation and decision making." *Rural Sociology,* 52(1):13-36.

Campbell, A., 1981. *The Sense of Well-Being in America.* New York: McGraw-Hill.

Campbell, A., P. E. Converse and W. L. Rogers, 1976. *The Quality of American Life.* New York: Russell Sage.

Campbell, R. R., 1985. "Crisis on the farm." *American Demographics,* 7(10):30-33.

Coughenour, C. M., 1978. "Farm structure, social class and farmers' policy perspectives." Pp. 67-86 in D. E. Brewster, W. E. Rasmussen and G. Youngberg (editors), *Farms in Transition.* Ames, IA: Iowa State University Press.

Coughenour, C. M. and L. Tweeten, 1986. "Quality of Life Perceptions and Farm Structure." Pp. 61-87 in J. J. Molnar (editor), *Agricultural Change: Consequences for Southern Farms and Rural Communities*. Boulder, CO: Westview Press.

Dillman, D. A., 1978. *Mail and Telephone Surveys: The Total Design Method*. New York: John Wiley and Sons.

Molnar, J. J., 1985. "Determinants of subjective well-being among farm operators: characteristics of the individual and the farm." *Rural Sociology*, 50(2):141-162.

Mueller, W., 1986. "Can we cope with farming's failures?" *American Demographics*, 9(4):40-43:56.

Peterson, G. W. and B. C. Rollins, 1987. "Parent-child socialization." Pp. 471-507 in M. B. Sussman and S. K. Steinmetz (editors), *Handbook of Marriage and the Family*. New York: Plenum Press.

Schroeder, E. H., F. C. Fliegel and J. C. van Es, 1985. "Measurement of the lifestyle dimensions of farming for small-scale farmers." *Rural Sociology*, 50(3):305-322.

Wilkening, E. A., 1982. "Subjective indicators and the quality of life." Pp. 429-441 in R. M. Hauser, D. Mechanic, A. O. Haller, and T. S. Hauser (editors), *Social Structure and Behavior: Essays in Honor of William Hamilton Sewell*. New York: Academic Press.

Zablocki, B. D. and R. M. Kanter, 1976. "The differentiation of lifestyles." *Annual Review of Sociology*, Vol. 2:269-98.

9

Farm Structure and Local Society Well-Being in the South

Jerry R. Skees
Louis E. Swanson

A common assumption is that the twin processes of concentration, the decline of farm numbers and the increase in average farm size, will adversely affect the well-being of rural counties and communities. This assumption is based upon the widely held belief that rural community well-being is, in large part, a function of farm well-being. Hence, if there is a farm crisis in the South, then there must be a crisis in community well-being as well. This raises a question as to the degree to which a rural community crisis is a function of the farm crisis as opposed to nonfarm factors that might help explain such a crisis in the rural South.

This chapter seeks to assess the association between farm structure and community well-being in order to understand the varied dimensions of the Southern rural crisis. Assuming that social historians, such as Billings in this book, are correct in their statements that the rural South has been enduring a historical crisis in well-being, then empirically examining the period 1970 to 1980 should provide some insight into this crisis, and, more importantly, into the relationship between farm and community well-being.

The prevailing hypothesis in the literature on farm and community change has been that farm well-being and structural change will influence rural community well-being. The converse of this assumption, that socioeconomic factors associated with rural well-being might influence farm well-being, has only recently received attention. The former unicausal assumption that farm structure shapes rural community well-being is grounded in the ideology of the Populist political tradition, which generally asserts various forms of agrarian fundamentalism and the primacy of the family farm. The validity of this hypothesis is said to be empirically verified by the work of Walter Goldschmidt (1978) and his 1940s California case studies of the communities of Arvin and Dinuba.

Goldschmidt's hypothesis now is well known to researchers, but a brief summary may be useful. The primary assumption is that large-scale farms that are characterized by industrial production will vary inversely with community quality of life. On the other hand, it is assumed that viable family farm operations will vary positively with community quality of life. The Goldschmidt study has been loosely replicated in recent years. Petterson (1977) reports that the major differences between Arvin and Dinuba continue to persist. Fujimoto (1977) expanded Goldschmidt's study to an ecological analysis of 130 places among eight counties within the San Joaquin Valley. Again, Goldschmidt's findings were confirmed. During the past four decades, the enduring Goldschmidt hypothesis has guided most discourse on farm and community change. Its powerful influence over both academic and public analysis of farm and community change rested upon a dominant American value that small producers are both virtuous and the backbone of the American economy—overwhelming evidence to the contrary notwithstanding.

In the last decade, rural sociologists have raised questions associated with Goldschmidt's regional controls as well as aspects of history and farm structure (Buttel, 1983; Flora et al., 1979; Goss, 1979, Swanson, 1982). Furthermore, while follow-up studies (Fujimoto, 1977; Petterson, 1977) propose no substantive changes in Goldschmidt's original hypothesis, empirical studies outside of California suggest substantial modifications and serve to limit its generalizablity (Harris and Gilbert, 1982; Flora et al., 1979; Swanson, 1982). Recently, agricultural economists also have critiqued Goldschmidt's regional controls (Hayes and Olmstead, 1984). Swanson (1982) argued that as rural economies transferred their economic dependency from farming to nonfarm enterprises, the influence of farm structural changes declined. Swanson concluded that to the extent that the dependence of smaller farms was a function of off-farm income, then the viability of the nonfarm economy not only influenced nonfarm rural well-being but also farm structure.

Most recently, the Office of Technology Assessment (OTA, 1986:Chapter 11) completed a national study in which the nation's rural areas were divided into five regions to assess the association between changes in farm structure and rural community well-being. All five studies tested the Goldschmidt hypothesis with very mixed results. The study concluded that the influence of farm structure on rural well-being varies greatly by region. In several regions, little or no association was found between farm change and community change. However, for four states identified as having an industrial farm structure (California, Arizona, Texas, and Florida), the Goldschmidt hypothesis was strongly confirmed, suggesting that the intra-regional vagaries of Goldschmidt's original study were not a major limitation as suggested by Hayes and Olmstead (1984). This chapter is an extension of the OTA report for the South (Skees and Swanson, 1988). The overall conclusion of the OTA report was that variation of farm structure and variation in the nonfarm economies of regions in the U.S. make the Goldschmidt hypothesis conditional. Reif's (1986) national study tends to confirm these conclusions.

These recent studies collectively suggest important qualifications when employing the Goldschmidt hypothesis. First, the relationship between farm scale and community well-being may not be a linear one. Second, the regional economy may be of great importance in mediating the influence of farm change upon community well-being. Third, as the regional economy expands, the well-being of a community may become more dependent upon the nonfarm economy than upon the farming hinterland. Fourth, regional characteristics may influence the changes in farm characteristics. For example, the increase in part-time farming may be due in part to the expansion of rural nonfarm employment opportunities. Fifth, the Goldschmidt hypothesis was not a test of small family farms versus corporate farms, as is often incorrectly assumed by persons employing the Goldschmidt study, but a comparison of very large family farms, and larger-than-family farms (see Skees and Swanson, 1988).

This study assumes that the Goldschmidt hypothesis is overly simplistic. It is our belief that the way in which farm structure is likely to be associated with community well-being depends upon a complex assortment of factors, including the relative dependency of the local economy upon farming, the array of farm structures and agricultural commodities produced within the immediate hinterland, the mix of nonfarm enterprises, and the relative position of the community within its regional hierarchy of places. At national and international levels, both farm structure and community well-being are shaped by national fiscal and financial policy and by international market conditions. The late 1970s and 1980s provide ample examples of these types of influences. The financial policy of controlling inflation contributed to the sharp decapitalization of all farm assets while the expanding national debt and huge international trade deficit, coupled with a high dollar, made U.S. manufactured products (such as textiles) less competitive in international markets. These local and macro factors certainly do not exhaust the list of factors. Moreover, we believe that community characteristics may have as much or more influence upon farm structure than farm structure has on community well-being under certain circumstances. For example, the availability of off-farm employment may present opportunities for part-time farming, and thereby enable the persistence of marginal farms that were not present several decades ago.

THE PRESENT STUDY

The purpose of this study is to assess the association of selected farm structure indicators with county well-being, while controlling for potential nonfarm economic influences. This is a test of the Goldschmidt hypothesis since indicators of farm structure are included in three different models of county well-being. Three quality-of-life dependent variables are examined: (1) level of unemployment, (2) median family income, and (3) percent of families below poverty. These dependent variables are the same as those examined in the five OTA communities studied (Office of Technology Assessment, 1986).

Two cross-sectional analyses are used to determine how the independent variables were associated with the dependent variables in 1970 and 1980. This analysis will provide evidence of the relationship among the farm structure variables and the three measures of county well-being. The cross-sectional analysis is accompanied by an examination of how change among the independent variables are associated with change among the three dependent variables between 1970 and 1980. The change analysis followed the suggestions of Kessler and Greenberg (1981) for panel analysis for two points in time. Following their reasoning, the first point in time for the dependent variable was controlled.

This research design not only tests the Goldschmidt hypothesis at two points in time, but also permits the analysis of how change in farm structure is associated with change in county well-being, controlling for several nonfarm economic variables. Goldschmidt did not empirically examine how farm change influences community well-being over time.

The cross-sectional analysis is comprised of four indicators of farm structure: (1) average farm scale measured in gross farm sales (all monetary values are adjusted to 1982 dollars using the GNP implicit price deflator), (2) concentration of smaller farms measured as the proportion of farms with less than 180 total acres, (3) the percent of farm operators working 100 or more days off the farm, and (4) the percent of the farm population as a proportion of the county's rural population (see Office of Technology Assessment, 1986; Swanson, 1988). This latter measure is an indirect indicator of the rural economy's dependency upon farming. These same variables were used for the change analysis as well. In addition, the analysis of change between 1970 and 1980 included a fifth farm indicator, change in farm numbers. (Farm number was not used in the cross-sectional analysis since it is a function of a county's geographical size.)

An important limitation of our model is the absence of a control for business cycles. With two points in time, as opposed to a time-series analysis, it is difficult to account for this market phenomenon. However, a study conducted for a similar period of time by Henry et al. (1986), that examined per capita income differentials for metro and nonmetro counties, reported that the business cycle was not significantly important. Since the present study uses family income and related data, we assume that business cycles were not important, though we cannot empirically vouch for this assumption.

If the Goldschmidt hypothesis is correct for both cross-sectional analyses, average farm size will be positively associated with the level of unemployment and the level of poverty, but negatively associated with median family income. However, the opposite association will be expected for the indicators of small farm concentration and the rural population's dependency on farming. For the change models, the Goldschmidt hypothesis predicts that change in farm numbers should be positively associated with change in the median family income and negatively associated with change in the level of unemployment and poverty.

Goldschmidt does not directly address the phenomenon of part-time farming. However, Swanson's (1982) study, as well as the work of Bonanno (1985), suggest that part-time farming may be a function of nonfarm employment opportunities. Bonanno argues that part-time farming can represent a type of "welfare" function for rural areas and a labor pool for nonfarm industries. Swanson's work suggests that entry into part-time farming may limit the severity of the transition to a highly concentrated farm structure. Therefore, part-time farming is included for reasons other than the Goldschmidt hypothesis.

Five control variables are used: (1) the percent of the county's workforce employed in manufacturing and (2) in service industries, (3) the county's proximity to metropolitan areas, (4) education and (5) the size of a county's black population. Both manufacturing and service industries, which were measured directly according to Census of Population definitions, represent the most likely arenas for nonmetropolitan employment (see Reif, 1986; Skees and Swanson, 1988; Swanson, 1982). The third variable assesses the influence of proximity to a metropolitan employment structure. Those counties that are the farthest away are assumed to be the least likely to experience the immediate benefits of favorable economic change but the first to experience downturns in the regional economy. The proximity variable was the same as the work of Hines et al. (1975) (also see Fuguitt and Johanson, 1973; Fuguitt and Thomas, 1966).

The final two control variables attempt to account for the employment potential of the population, sometimes referred to in terms of human capital, and the degree to which past patterns of racial discrimination influence community well-being. The former is measured in terms of the adult population's completion of high school. Elsewhere in this book education is considered to be a necessary but not a sufficient condition for social and economic development (see Schertz, Chapter 24). This variable helps assess the degree to which this assumption is relevant. The latter variable is measured directly as the percent of the county's population that is black (Ghelfi, 1986). It is reasoned that this measure will indirectly assess the degree to which historical patterns of discrimination have and continue to impede a county's social and economic development.

This study goes beyond the Goldschmidt hypothesis by including indicators of regional economic conditions. By including four indicators of farm structure, we expect to give the Goldschmidt hypothesis a fair chance to be associated with one of several dimensions of farm structure. However, we make no claim to having a fully specified model. But we do believe that the three models of quality of life for two points in time, as well as for change between the two points in time, provide at least an indirect test of the Goldschmidt hypothesis.

This study includes the universe of nonmetropolitan counties in 13 Southern and border states with an aggregate of 778 counties. (For this study, the South includes: Alabama, Kansas, Delaware, Georgia, Kentucky, Louisiana, Maryland, Mississippi, North Carolina, South Carolina, Tennessee, Virginia and West Virginia). However, the use of the county as the unit of analysis is potentially an important divergence from the Goldschmidt study. The counties in this study are likely to contain numerous towns and places that are dissimilar. The trade-off, though, is that a much more generalized picture of farm and county well-being can be assessed.

Furthermore, this study uses data from three reliable and well-documented sources: the Census of Population, the Census of Agriculture, and the *County City Data Book*. Consequently, this analysis examines a total population rather than utilizing a random sample. This presents some unique opportunities for interpretation of the results since all relationships are real, given measurement error. The timing of the data collection was not consistent. The agricultural data were collected in 1969 and 1978 respectively, while the population data were collected in 1970 and 1980. We do not feel that these different points in time present a serious methodological problem. The reader should be cautioned to recall that the national economy at these two points in time was dissimilar. While the farm economy was relatively comparable, the overall economy in 1970 was rather robust compared with the stagnant economy of 1980 that was poised on a major recession.

INTERPRETATION OF MODEL RESULTS

Since the models presented below are for all of the nonmetropolitan counties in the South and therefore, constitute a complete population, the focus is on the degree to which each dependent variable (measuring three dimensions of community well-being) is associated with each independent variable. Results of the multiple regression models will be summarized by using point elasticities. A point elasticity provides for focus on percentage changes at the mean values for all other variables. In a simple linear model where:

Table 1. Reference for Model Variables

Percent of pop. unemployed	This variable is the official measure of unemployment in 1970 and 1980.
Percent of families below poverty	This is measured directly by the census of population and refers to all families who reported incomes below the poverty level in 1970 and 1980.
Median family income	This variable is measured directly as the family whose income has half of all families below and half of all families above it in terms of family income.
Farm number	Farm number was measured directly as the number of farms in the 1969 and 1978 Censuses of Agriculture.
Average farm size sales	Farm size was measured directly as the average gross sales per fam. This was computed by dividing a county's total agricultural sales by the county's total number of farms.
Percent part-time farms	Part-time farming was measured indirectly as those farm operators who stated that they worked over 99 days a year off of the farm. This number was then divided by the total number of farms in a county.
Concentration of small farms	This is an indirect measure that uses the principle of a Gina coefficient. It is the proportion of farms with less than 180 acres.
Percent farm of rural pop.	This variable is measured directly as the total number of the farm population divided by the total rural population in a county.
Percent in manufacturing	This variable is measured directly using the industry code in the census of population. The total number of people employed in manufacturing is divided by the county's entire labor force.
Percent in service industries	This variable is measured directly using the industry code in the census of population. The total number of people employed in service industries is divided by the county's entire labor force.
Proximity to SMSA	This ordinal scale measure is based upon a county's geographical position relative to metropolitan areas of different population sizes. The measure was developed by Calvin Beale.
Percent black	This variable is the percent of total population who are black within each county in 1970 and 1980.
Percent with high school education	Percent of adult population with 12 years or more of education.

$y = a + bx$,

the percentage change in y with respect to x is calculated by taking the partial derivative of y with respect to x and multiplying by the ratio of the mean values:

$\delta y/\delta x = b$, or

the point elasticity $= b * x/y$.

The point elasticity represents the percentage response in the dependent variable as the explanatory variable is increased by one percent. All other variables are maintained at their mean values. Thus, larger point elasticities represent stronger relationships between the dependent and independent variables.

Table 2 presents mean values for all variables. The findings from the three models are presented using point elasticities in Tables 3 through 5. It is possible to calculate the coefficients from this information. Variables that are statistically different than zero at the 10 percent level or below are starred. Concern for statistical significance is mitigated considerably given the complete universe of nonmetropolitan counties. However, measurement error is still present in the data. The 10 percent level will be used for identifying the substantive elasticities.

THE INFLUENCE OF FARM STRUCTURE ON UNEMPLOYMENT, POVERTY AND INCOME

Unemployment

Of the three well-being variables, unemployment has the greatest measurement difficulties due to the exclusion of a significant portion of the labor force. People who have not actively searched for employment in the previous six weeks are excluded and dismissed as "discouraged workers." This is particularly important in nonmetropolitan areas where employment opportunities may be limited and people may be more quickly categorized as discouraged.

A quadratic function was used to assess the MacCannell and Dolber-Smith hypothesis (1985) of "U"-shaped relationship between farm scale and community well-being for the unemployment models. The standard quadratic was formed by using the farm scale variable and farm scale squared. The nadir of the curve was calculated following standard calculus procedures (Netter and Wasserman, 1974: 291). Using 1982 dollars, the nadir in 1970 was $52,500 and in 1980 $115,950. This indicates that as farm size goes down, unemployment also goes down until these points are reached and then unemployment increases as average farm size (measured in gross sales) in the counties increases. The curvilinear relationship between unemployment and farm size corresponds well with the MacCannell and Dolber-Smith hypothesis. Counties with medium sized farms are most likely to be associated with low levels of

Table 2. Mean values for model variables—nonmetropolitan counties in the South

Dependent Variables (well-being measures)

	1970	1980	Change
Unemployment	4.93%	7.79%	2.86%
Median Income	$14055	$18112	4057
Poverty	26.68%	17.57%	-9.11%

Explanatory Variables

	1970	1980	Change
Farm Numbers	849	624	-225
Farm Size	$24675	46112	21437
Small Farms	71.1	67.2	-3.8
Part-time Farms	44.2	47.4	3.1
Farm/Rural Pop	17.5	9.0	-8.5
Manufacturing	30.3	29.3	-1.1
Service	7.7	16.8	9.1
Black	22.6	21.3	-1.3
Education	30.9	45.8	14.9

Table 3. Explaining unemployment in nonmetropolitan counties in the South

	1970	1980	Change
Farm Numbers	na	na	+.02
Farm Size[1]	nr*	nr*	-.10*
Small Farms	-.24*	+.17*	+.02
Part Time Farms	-.21*	+.03	-.04*
Farm/Rural Pop	-.05*	+.009	-.18*
Manufacturing	-.32*	-.25*	-.007
Service	-.04	+.12*	+.09*
Proximity to SMSA	+.01	+.06	+.55*
Black	+.02	-.02	+.05*
Education	-.28*	-.69*	-.31*
Unemployment in 70	na	na	-.62*
Adjusted R-Square	.211	.275	.192

Values are the percentage response in unemployment as the explanatory variable is increased by 1 percent—all other variables are at the mean values reported in Table 2.

[1]Farm size is a quadratic for the 1970 and 1980 models. Therefore, point elasticities are not reported. Both components of the quadratic are highly significant. The nadir of the quadratic is $52,750 in 1970 and $115,950 in 1980.

nr = not reported
na = not applicable
*p ≤ .01

unemployment. Counties with either small-scale or very large-scale farm averages are most likely to be associated with relatively higher levels of unemployment. To the extent that the hinterland of Dinuba was comprised of medium sized farms as opposed to very small farms, this finding supports the Goldschmidt hypothesis. However, if Goldschmidt's hypothesis is considered to be linear such that a community's well-being is best with the smallest farm scale, then the hypothesis is rejected.

It should be noted that the nadir for each of the curves is substantially different for the two points in time. This suggests that what was a medium sized farm in 1970 may be a sub-medium sized farm by 1980, due to increased farm concentration and higher thresholds of economies of scale. For this model, there was an increase of approximately $63,000 for the region as a whole during the decade. (This finding also indicates the limitations of using constant dollar gross sales as a measure of viable farms.)

The association between unemployment and percent of small farms undergoes a change in direction between 1970 and 1980. The negative association in 1970 has become positive by 1980. Apparently in 1970, counties with a larger concentration of small farms had lower unemployment rates, but by 1980 such counties tended to have higher unemployment. This seemingly anomalous finding is actually consistent with the earlier observation of a curvilinear relationship between farm gross sales and unemployment. In this case, the measure of scale is acres. Consequently, this measure also suggests that what was a viable farm scale in 1970 was sub-viable in 1980. In other words, while the concentration of small farms was beneficial for unemployment in 1970, by 1980 it was likely to have adverse effects.

In 1970, there was a strong negative relationship between part-time farms and unemployment. A one percent increase in the rate of part-time farming within a county (above the mean value) was associated with a .21 percent decline in the rate of unemployment. By 1980, this association is no longer present. This contrast is most likely due to the change in the general employment opportunities. In 1970, farmers could depend on off-farm jobs more than in 1980.

POVERTY AND MEDIAN FAMILY INCOME

Farm structure variables were relatively noninfluential with county poverty (see Table 4). In 1970, a one percent increase in farm size was associated with a .06 percent decline in the rate of poverty. This finding, though weakly associated, is contrary to the Goldschmidt hypothesis. The remaining farm structure variables were insignificant or only slightly associated with poverty. An examination of Table 5 suggests the same is true for the association between farm structure variables and median family income. Among the significant relationships, an increase in farm size between 1970 and 1980 was negatively

Table 4. Explaining poverty in nonmetropolitan counties in the South

	1970	1980	Change
Farm Numbers	na	na	+.04*
Farm Size	-.06*	+.01	+.05*
Small Farms	+.04	-.05	-.01
Part Time Farms	+.02	-.03	-.02*
Farm/Rural Pop	+.07*	+.07*	-.08*
Manufacturing	-.26*	-.13*	+.004
Service	+.03	+.20*	+.01*
Unemployment	+.21*	+.37*	+.05*
Proximity to SMSA	+.26	+.17	-.12*
Black	+.17*	+.17*	+.02*
Education	-.60*	-.93*	-.33*
Poverty in 70	na	na	-1.26*
Adjusted R-Square	.695	.694	.699

Values are the percentage response in unemployment as the explanatory variable is increased by 1 percent—all other variables are at the mean values reported in Table 2.

Table 5. Explaining median family income in nonmetropolitan counties in the South

	1970	1980	Change
Farm Numbers	na	na	+.03
Farm Size	+.04*	-.005	-.04*
Small Farms	-.01	+.006	-.04*
Part Time Farms	-.004	+.04	+.03*
Farm/Rural Pop	-.07*	-.04*	+.06*
Manufacturing	+.11*	-.05*	+.0005
Service	-.05*	-.14*	+.02
Unemployment	-.13*	-.17*	-.06*
Proximity to SMSA	-.26*	-.19*	-.21*
Black	-.05*	-.03*	-.05*
Education	+.33*	+.41*	+.36*
Median Income in 70	na	na	-.49*
Adjusted R-Square	.669	.569	.218

Values are the percentage response in unemployment as the explanatory variable is increased by 1 percent—all other variables are at the mean values reported in Table 2.

associated with median income. Although this result lends support to Gold-schmidt hypothesis, such support is weak. None of the remaining independent variables were supportive of the Goldschmidt hypothesis.

In general, the farm structure variables were not associated with the three measures of local society well-being used in this study. With the notable exception of unemployment, these variables offered little explanatory power. In the case of unemployment, the quadratic relationship between farm size and unemployment supports the MacCannell and Dolber-Smith contention that these relationships are not simply linear. There is only very limited support for the Goldschmidt hypothesis. In fact, results provide evidence that is contrary to the idea that communities suffer when farm concentration occurs.

THE INFLUENCE OF NON-FARM VARIABLES ON UNEMPLOY-MENT, POVERTY AND INCOME

Unemployment

A number of non-farm variables were highly associated with the three well-being measures. Education, distance from metropolitan areas, and rates of employment in manufacturing and service industries consistently explained more than farm structure variables.

As might be expected, the percent employed in manufacturing was negatively associated with unemployment (see Table 3). In 1970, a one percent increase in those employed in manufacturing could be expected to reduce the unemployment rate by .32 percent. In 1980, the reduction was .25 percent. Conversely, the percent employed in service industries was positively associated with unemployment in 1980. A one percent increase in service sector employment was associated with a .12 percent increase in unemployment. The change model also suggest that where there was an increase in service sector employment, there was a corresponding increase in the level of unemployment.

The distance from metropolitan centers was not associated with unemployment in the cross sectional models. However, changes in unemployment were positively associated with the proximity to an SMSA variable in the change model. This might demonstrate how an economic recession could adversely affect isolated nonmetropolitan communities relatively more than those closer to metropolitan areas.

The influence of education on unemployment was greater in 1980 than in 1970. In 1970, a one percent increase in adults with 12 years or more of education was associated with a .28 percent reduction in the unemployment rate—this compares to a .69 percent reduction in 1980. A one percent increase in the level of unemployment in 1970 suggests that the rate of change in unemployment between 1970 and 1980 declined .62 percent. This means that those counties with the highest levels of unemployment in 1970 experienced a lower rate of increase in the unemployment rate between 1970 and 1980.

Poverty

The models explaining poverty (Table 4) had similar relationships to those explaining unemployment. Manufacturing employment reduced the rate of poverty. However, once again, the service sector employment was adversely associated with a well-being measure. In 1980, a one percent increase in service employment was associated with a .2 percent increase in the rate of poverty. The measure for distance from metropolitan areas demonstrated that the higher levels of poverty occurred in the most remote areas. But, the negative value in the change model suggests that the most remote areas were also the most successful in reducing poverty between 1970 and 1980. The percent of black population was positively associated with poverty in 1970 and 1980, such that one percent increase in black population was associated with a .17 percent increase in the rate of poverty.

Education was even more highly associated with poverty than unemployment. Moreover, the same increase in importance was apparent from the beginning to the end of the decade. In 1980, a one percent increase in the percent of population with 12 years or more of education was associated with a .93 percent decline in the rate of poverty. Once again, the change model for poverty suggest that those counties with the worst conditions (i.e., the highest level of poverty in 1970) could be expected to be the most successful in reducing poverty between 1970 and 1980. A one percent increase in the 1970 poverty rate was associated with a 1.26 percent decline in the rate of poverty between 1970 and 1980.

Median Family Income

Models explaining median family income (Table 5) were also consistent with those for poverty and unemployment. However, there is one disturbing exception. While manufacturing employment was positively associated with median family income in 1970, by 1980 it was negatively associated. In 1980, a one percent increase in manufacturing employment was associated with a .05 percent reduction in median family income. Once again the service industry sector was adversely associated with this well-being measure in 1980.

Counties closer to metropolitan centers tended to have higher median family incomes than those further away. Also, the higher the black population, the more likely a county would have a relatively low median family income.

Education continued to be an important variable in explaining well-being in nonmetropolitan areas. A one percent increase in the education measure was associated with a .33 and .41 percent increase in income in 1970 and 1980, respectively. The increase in education levels between 1970 and 1980 was also positively associated with gains in income.

Finally, those counties which had the highest levels of income in 1970 could be expected to have a lower rate of gain between 1970 and 1980, as is demonstrated by the -.49 value on the change relationships

SUMMARY

There were two distinct dimensions to these findings. First, indicators of farm structure and the process of farm concentration were, with an important exception, not particularly associated with rural county well-being. Second, indicators of the nonfarm economy and of social infrastructure were highly associated with rural county well-being, but not always in the expected direction.

A primary aim of this study was a test of the Goldschmidt hypothesis for the South. The results suggest that with the exception of unemployment, indicators of farm concentration were not substantively associated with county well-being. Moreover, the association with unemployment indicates an important modification of the linear assumption of the Goldschmidt hypothesis. The Goldschmidt hypothesis is often interpreted to mean that as average scale of farms increases from the very small to the very large, community well-being will be adversely affected (see Vogeler, 1981). However, this study supports the MacCannell and Dolber-Smith (1985) argument of a curvilinear relationship. Our interpretation of this relationship is that one cannot assume that a small farm sector, such as found in the South, will be automatically associated with desirable indicators of community well-being.

While farm structure was found to be less important than would be expected from the Goldschmidt hypothesis, the nonfarm and social infrastructure variables were highly associated with rural well-being. Both measures of rural employment, manufacturing and service industries, were associated with well-being, but not necessarily favorably. A type of Faustian dilemma was found for manufacturing. While a high level of manufacturing employment was found to be associated with lower levels of unemployment and poverty, in 1980 it was also associated with lower levels of family income. Service employment was generally unfavorably associated with the indicators of well-being. The higher the level of service employment, the more likely a county would have higher unemployment, higher levels of poverty, and lower levels of family income

The measures of social infrastructure, education and distance from a metropolitan area, deserve special attention given their consistent strength of association. For both points in time, the higher the proportion of a rural county's population having finished high school, the lower the unemployment rate, the lower the level of poverty, and the higher the level of family income. Similarly, the further away a county was from a metropolitan area the more likely it would have high levels of unemployment and poverty and lower family income. The third social indicator, the percent of the population that was black, was a less consistent indicator of well-being. This variable was not associated with unemployment, but was associated with higher levels of poverty and lower levels of family income.

POLICY IMPLICATIONS

Several policy conclusions can be drawn from these results. First, farm policy that stabilizes the trend toward concentration will probably not have a great influence upon rural county and community well-being. This indicates that those who argue in favor of a farm policy to slow the trend toward larger and fewer farms in order to improve the well-being of rural communities are simply wrong. Further, it raises serious questions as to whether farm policy can be considered a surrogate for rural development policy.

Second, a simple strategy of encouraging any manufacturing and service industry to locate in a rural county cannot be assumed to be automatically beneficial for the county or community. This is particularly true for the service sector, which is often called the cutting edge of post-industrial employment and job expansion. While this study cannot infer the causal relationship, what is minimally clear is that the introduction of service employment will very likely not improve local socioeconomic conditions.

Third, social infrastructure appears to be the most important determinant of a county or community's social well-being. What is encouraging is that these factors can be directly addressed. This is particularly true for education, which was consistently the most highly associated factor with all three indicators of well-being. Simply stated, as long as rural areas continue to have substandard public education systems, so too will they have high unemployment and poverty and low levels of family income. These findings suggest that while the substantive improvement of education may not be a sufficient condition for rural development, it is a necessary condition. This is also true for other sectors of social infrastructure as measured by the degree of isolation of a rural county. However, these results also indicate that racism is still a problem in the South. Percent of the population that is black has a negative influence on well-being independent of education and geographic isolation. In order for Southern rural development to occur, de facto racism must be addressed, both legally and in state and county planning.

In summary, these findings suggest the need for a rural development policy that is independent of farm policy for vitalizing the rural South. Furthermore, such a policy must at a minimum include (1) an aggressive program to upgrade education at all levels, including adult education, (2) a program that improves social and physical infrastructure, requiring outside funding, and (3) directly addresses the past patterns of covert racism. The vitalization of the rural South will require a dynamic partnership among the federal, state, and local governments, as well as private sector cooperation. This development effort cannot be accomplished without considerable outside funding, but such capital transfers must be accompanied by increased local participation by all segments of the local rural society—by an increase in community cooperation.

REFERENCES

Bonnano, Alassandro. 1985. "The persistence of small farms in marginal areas of advanced Western societies." Ph.D. dissertation, University of Kentucky, Lexington, Kentucky.

Buttel, Frederick H. 1983."Farm structure and the quality of life in agricultural communities: A review of literature and a look toward the future." pp. 150-173 in *Agricultural Communities: The Interrelationships of Agriculture, Business, Industry, and Government in the Rural Economy.* Committee Print prepared by the Congressional Research Service, Library of Congress, for the Committee on Agriculture, U.S. House of Representatives, 98th Congress, 1st Session. Washington, D.C.: U.S. Government Printing Office, 1983.

Flora, Jan, Ivan Brown, and J. L. Conboy. 1979. "Impact of agriculture on class structure and social well-being in the Great Plains." Paper presented at the Annual Meeting of the Rural Sociological Society, Madison, Wisconsin.

Fujimoto, Isao. 1977. "The communities of the San Joaquin Valley," in U.S. Congress, Senate, Priorities in Agricultural Research of the U.S. Department of Agriculture—Appendix. Subcommittee on the Judiciary, 95th Congress, 2nd Session, Part 2, pp. 1374-1396.

Fuguitt, G., and D. Thomas. 1966. "Small town growth in the United States: An analysis by size, class, and by place." *Rural Sociology* 30 (3):513-527.

Fuguitt, G., and J. E. Johanson. 1973. "Changing retail activity in Wisconsin villages: 1939-1954-1977." *Rural Sociology* 38 (2):207-218.

Ghelfi, L. M. 1986. *Poverty Among Black Families in the Nonmetro South.* United States Department of Agriculture, Economic Research Division, Rural Development Research Report No. 62, Washington, D.C.

Goldschmidt, Walter. 1978. *As You Sow.* New York: Harcourt, Brace.

Goss, Kevin F. 1979. "Three studies in the social consequences of agribusiness." *Rural Sociology* 44 (4):802-805.

Harris, G. K., and J. Gilbert. 1982. "Large-scale farming, rural income, and Goldschmidt's agrarian thesis." *Rural Sociology* 47 (3):494-458.

Hayes, Michael N. and Alan L. Olmstead. 1984. "Farm size and community quality: Arvin and Dinuba revisited." *American Journal of Agricultural Economics* 66 (4):430-436.

Henry, M., M. Drabenstott, and L. Gibson. 1986. "A changing rural America." *Economic Review* July/August: 23-41.

Hines, F. K., D. L. Brown, and J. M. Zimmer. 1975. *Social and Economic Characteristics in Metropolitan and Non-metropolitan Counties in 1970.* Washington D.C., United States Department of Agriculture Economics Research Service, AER Report 272.

Kessler, Ronald C. and David F. Greenberg. 1981. *Linear Panel Analysis: Models of Quantitative Change.* New York: Academic Press.

MacCannell, Dean, and Edward Dolber-Smith. 1985. "Report on the structure of agriculture and impacts of new technologies on rural communities in Arizona, California, Florida and Texas." Paper prepared for the Office of Technology Assessment, U.S. Congress.

Netter, John and William Wasserman. 1974. *Applied Linear Statistical Models: Regression, Analysis of Variance and Experimental Designs.* Homewood, Illinois: Richard D. Erwin, Inc.

Petterson, Steve. 1977. "The family farm." In *California Small Farm Visibility Project*. Technology Task Force Report, Appendix A, November.

Reif, L. 1986. "Farm structure, industry structure and socioeconomic conditions: A longitudinal study in economy and society." Unpublished doctoral dissertation, Department of Sociology and Anthropology, North Carolina State University, Raleigh.

Rosenfeld, S. A., E. M. Bergman, S. Rubin. 1985. *After the Factories: Changing Employment Patterns in the Rural South*. Research Triangle Park, North Carolina: Southern Growth Policies Board.

Skees, J. R., and L. E. Swanson. 1988. "Public policy for farm structure and rural well-being in the South." In Louis E. Swanson, (ed.), *Agricultural and Community Change in the U.S.: The Congressional Community Studies*. Boulder, Colorado: Westview Press.

Southern Growth Policies Board. 1986. *Halfway Home and a Long Way to Go: The Report of the Commission on the Future of the South*. Research Triangle Park, North Carolina.

Swanson, Louis E. 1982. "Farm and trade center transition in an industrial society: Pennsylvania, 1930-1960." Ph.D. dissertation University Park: Pennsylvania State University.

Swanson, Louis E. 1988. *Agricultural and Community Change in the U.S.: The Congressional Community Studies* (forthcoming). Boulder, Colorado: Westview Press.

Vogeler, I. 1981. *The Myth of the Family Farm: Agribusiness Dominance of U.S. Agriculture*. Boulder, Colorado: Westview Press.

10

Changing Financial Markets and the Impact on Rural Communities: An Alternative Research Approach

Deborah M. Markley

The early 1980s marked a time of major change in U. S. financial markets. Beginning in 1980 with the Depository Institutions Deregulation and Monetary Control Act (DIDMCA), and continuing in 1982 with the Garn-St. Germain Act, the nation's financial markets were stripped of the regulatory framework that had constrained their operation since the 1930s. Interest rates were deregulated, allowing banks to compete on a more equal basis with money market funds. Thrift institutions were given expanded powers to offer a product line including many of the services previously reserved for commercial banks. In addition, geographical limits on bank expansion were weakened by regional banking agreements, originating in New England and more recently spreading to the Southeast. As a result, competition has increased in the nation's financial markets, bringing with it increased pressure on banks to improve asset liability management, find new niches in the financial service marketplace, and compete more aggressively for new customers.

These changes have not been restricted to metropolitan areas, but have spread to rural areas of the country as well. The impact of increased competition and geographical deregulation is perhaps felt most severely in rural areas where small, country banks were relatively insulated by past regulation from national financial markets and the competitive pressures of large financial institutions. Problems in the nation's agricultural sector and increased global competition, combined with deregulation in the banking industry, have created additional problems for rural and agricultural banks during this period. In the past few years, bank failures have increased from seven in 1981 to 143 in 1986, reaching post-Depression highs. The number of agricultural bank failures during this period has been quite large, accounting for 40 to 60 percent of the failures in the past three years (Melichar, 1987).

There is little question that deregulation of the financial services industry will have some effect on rural capital availability. In some rural areas, financial deregulation will bring benefits. In Louisiana, rural banks hurt by the concurrent downturns in agriculture, energy, and commercial real estate activity will be able to diversify their asset and liability bases as a result of new statewide branching and interstate banking laws (Kahley and Uceda, 1986). Similar benefits are likely in other rural areas of the South. However, rural banks face a changing market situation that makes it more difficult for them to accept the higher level of risk and uncertainty that is typically associated with new ventures in rural areas. As a result of increased competition from institutions outside the local area and greater scrutiny by bank regulators and stockholders, community bankers are forced to pay greater attention to returns on assets and equity to the possible exclusion of goals such as community growth.

In addition, increased consolidation of banking activities within states and regions—as large bank holding companies continue their geographical expansion by acquiring weaker institutions—may lead to a reduction in local control over bank investment decisions, greater concern with bank profitability, more frequent changes in bank leadership as branch managers rotate out of small rural affiliate banks, and potential transfers of funds from slowly growing rural areas to more rapidly growing rural or urban areas. The full range of benefits and costs to rural areas from banking deregulation has yet to be determined.

The purpose of this chapter is not to provide answers regarding deregulation's impact on rural capital markets. Rather, this chapter lays out an alternative research approach that can provide the data necessary to analyze the empirical evidence on this issue. As background, past research efforts directed toward evaluating banking deregulation and structural change in the banking industry are categorized in the following section. Then, an alternative approach is described and its benefits and costs evaluated. Finally, some recommendations for future research are discussed.

PAST RESEARCH APPROACHES

Since deregulation was not completed until 1984, most past research on financial deregulation was based on assumptions about the expected impact of deregulation on the structure of the banking industry. In general, it was assumed that the role of multibank holding companies would increase with more mergers and acquisitions and that such consolidation would generate increased efficiency in the marketplace. To evaluate the potential impact of this structural change on local markets, several general research approaches have been used. First, research has been directed toward evaluating the potential for increased efficiency in a deregulated financial services industry as weaker institutions are forced out by greater competition. This research also has considered the potential for increased concentration in financial markets as a result of deregulation, with particular attention to the behavior and performance of multibank holding companies and the banks they acquire. Second, efforts have been made to evaluate the benefits and costs associated with different types of banking organizations, i.e., unit banks vs. branch or multibank holding company affiliates, and with different size banks. Third, some research has focused specifically on rural banking institutions and their relationship to the process of economic growth.

Before discussing an alternative research approach, it is useful to summarize the results of past research on the impact of banking deregulation. This discussion is not designed to provide an exhaustive review of studies on financial deregulation, but rather to highlight various research approaches. The application of the results of these studies to rural areas, in some cases, is constrained by the research design. In those cases, an alternative approach may enable more useful information to be obtained and used to guide policy decisions in the future.

Observations from Past Research

Although economic theory suggests that a freely functioning market should produce an optimal allocation of goods and services, evidence from a number of studies is quite mixed. There appears to be no clear consensus about the impact of deregulation on capital markets, either at the national or local level. Work by Rhoades (1980) suggested that geographical deregulation would not have pro-competitive effects since statewide concentration actually increased in New York and Virginia following liberalization of branching laws. At the local level, results based on the New York and Virginia experiences were mixed with some markets experiencing increased competition while others experienced decreased competition.

On the other hand, Kohn (1964) found that the expansion of New York City banks into the upstate New York market resulted in public benefits as services were expanded and costs were reduced. These results were substantiated in a study of multibank holding company operation (Lawrence and Talley, 1976). The latter study found that bank holding company entry was pro-competitive if performed de novo and that bank holding companies tended to be more aggressive lenders. The result was greater benefit to the community through increased quantity and quality of services. Based on the results of these latter two studies, deregulation and expanded multibank holding company activity is expected to bring benefits to local financial markets through increased competition and efficiency.

While no consensus has been reached in terms of deregulation's effect on market efficiency at the local level, there is rather clear evidence that banks organized as holding company affiliates behave differently than banks organized as independents. Barkley et al. (1984) found a number of important differences between Arizona branch banks and Colorado independent banks. The branch banks made proportionately more loans than the independent banks because of their more diversified deposit base and, consequently, greater ability to assume risk. There was evidence that branch banks were more responsive to differences in loan demand among local markets in the state. In particular, they found an intrarural reallocation of funds, moving from more slowly growing rural areas to more rapidly growing rural areas. Based on these results, deregulation and the expansion of multibank holding companies are unlikely to have a negative impact on all rural areas, but will likely mean less capital available in slowly growing or declining rural communities.

Similar results were seen in Texas in a study of nonmetropolitan banking markets (Duncan and Woods, 1987). Multibank holding company institutions were more aggressive lenders than rural independent banks, primarily due to the lower liquidity levels they maintained. This less conservative behavior also resulted in lower levels of government security holdings and, thus, less money exported from the local community. As a result, the authors suggested that "contrary to prevailing opinion, nonindependent banking may in fact increase availability of funds in rural financial markets" (Duncan and Woods, 1987:14).

Similar work has been done to consider differences in behavior by the size of banking institution. The argument is that deregulation will result in greater control of financial resources at all levels by large banking institutions. However, according to a study by Dunham (1986), replacing small banks with larger institutions does not necessarily mean that capital will flow out of the communities served by those banks. Dunham's research shows that all banks, regardless of size, shift funds to nonlocal investment. By comparing local uses of funds to local sources of funds, Dunham found that small banks had a much higher proportion of funds generated locally than returned to the community through local investment. Dunham estimated that 40 percent of a small bank's predominantly local funds were invested nonlocally. Large banks, on the other hand, achieved parity in their local sources and uses of funds. They returned about 100 percent of their locally generated funds to the community. These results are in line with those from the Texas study.

Finally, limited research has been done to evaluate the role of banks in the economic growth process, particularly in rural areas. An early study by Dreese (1974) in Appalachia found no causal relationship between banks and economic growth. Rather, there was some interrelation between lending and growth, but bank lending did not appear to cause economic growth in either growing or lagging rural counties in the region. More recently, Barkley and Helander (1984) also found no causal link between banking activity and economic growth. They concluded that "the passive investment behavior of Arizona's nonmetropolitan branch banks has prevented these banks from assuming a catalytic role in the development process" (Barkley and Helander, 1984:8).

Limitations of Past Research

The studies reviewed above and the research approaches they represent are typical of past research on financial deregulation, in general, and rural capital markets, in particular. The results of these studies taken together suggest that deregulation's impact on market concentration in a rural community is unclear and will likely depend substantially on the type of banking institutions present prior to deregulation. In addition, holding company banks may bring a greater range of services to the community, along with more loans and lower prices for services. However, there is some evidence that affiliate banks have less operating flexibility due to more centralized decision making (Markley, 1984). Lower flexibility may make it difficult to respond to rapid changes in the rural economy as experienced recently.

However, the studies have a number of limitations for evaluating the impact of deregulation on rural areas. First, in most cases, data are aggregated at the national or the state level. In some cases, strictly rural or nonmetropolitan capital markets are analyzed and their results provide useful information for considering the impact of deregulation. However, it is clear when a number of studies are compiled that results will differ depending on the type of rural area analyzed, i.e., growing vs. lagging, single industry vs. diversified, and the present structure of banking markets. Clearly the impact of deregulation, with its consequent expansion across product and geographic boundaries, will be greater in rural areas of those states that maintained more restrictive banking laws into the early 1980s. Rural communities in these states will be faced with increased competition from a number of sources and will have to rely, in some cases, on very limited management expertise to address the new issues that deregulation raises. As a result, studies that predict local level impacts using data from the state or national level may be limited.

Second, most of the studies were based strictly on the analysis of aggregate data provided by the Federal Reserve Board. Aggregate data have a number of limitations from the perspective of analyzing rural capital markets. For example, it is impossible to determine the geographical distribution of loans, the types of commercial or industrial firms receiving loans, the various classes of loans made by the bank, particularly commercial loan types, the collateral requirements for lending, the attitude of management toward lending, and the role of the bank in stimulating local economic growth. These types of information can be obtained only when primary data are collected from rural banking institutions. While expensive, the detail obtained through such primary data collection is critical to the analysis of the impact of deregulation on rural capital markets. Collection of such data would allow additional questions about rural capital availability in a deregulated market to be addressed.

Third, there is no explicit consideration of the demand side of rural capital markets in these studies. The importance of demand is alluded to in some of the studies, such as Barkley et al., (1984). Their results suggest that branch banks are more responsive than independent banks to differences in loan demand among rural areas. It is important to design research about rural capital markets that can consider the demand for loanable funds. By examining lending patterns of rural financial institutions, as some studies have done, one can conclude that a low level of lending is the result of either an insufficient supply of loanable funds (a problem with the responsiveness of financial institutions to community needs or with a more conservative form of banking organization) or an insufficient demand for loanable funds (a problem with the community's effective demand for credit, as perceived by the bankers). To determine which explanation applies, it is necessary to consider both the supply and demand sides of the financial market.

AN ALTERNATIVE RESEARCH APPROACH

While this alternative approach has an advantage over most past studies in that it is designed to be applied to post-deregulation financial markets, this fact is not its most significant departure from past research approaches. Rather, the approach focuses directly on how deregulation affects rural capital availability, rather than a strict focus on structural change within the industry itself. To determine how deregulation will affect rural capital availability and, consequently, economic growth, several questions must be addressed. How has the structure of the rural financial market changed with financial deregulation? How do commercial banks of various types support the economic growth process via their lending activities, e.g., types of loans made, particularly commercial loans; collateral requirements; lending to businesses and households within the community vs. outside? How conservatively managed is the bank? What differences exist between independent bank behavior and that of affiliates of an in-state or out-of-state holding company? What do bankers see as their role in the economic growth process of their community? What demand exists for bank loans? What constraints do small businesses see in terms of obtaining loans from banks? What credit needs are not being met by the commercial banking institutions in their community?

The focus of attention is the rural community, rather than some aggregate like the state or the nation. Aggregate data cannot provide the level of detail necessary to determine how funds are allocated by rural financial institutions and to whom those funds flow. Differences in institutions, either in terms of size or organizational structure, may not be apparent when only aggregate statistics are analyzed. A realistic picture of the impact of financial deregulation cannot be obtained without identifying the demand prospects or constraints which the banking institution faces. Without evaluating the demand side of the rural capital market, it is difficult to distinguish between what the commercial bank can do to help foster economic growth and what new types of institutional arrangements must be created or supported in order to provide the required stimulus to growth.

Components of Research Approach

The alternative research approach proposed here has four components:

1. aggregate analysis of secondary data on rural banks and the structure of rural financial markets;
2. micro level analysis of primary data collected via interviews with bankers in rural areas;
3. micro level analysis of primary data collected via interviews of business enterprises operating in rural areas;
4. policy analysis of both primary and secondary data.

This approach does not abandon the use of secondary data. Rather, aggregate data are used to describe the structure of rural financial markets and the changes that have taken place in them in the post-deregulation period. Only by using secondary data can a time series of accurate information be obtained to permit an initial evaluation of changing rural capital markets. However, this research approach goes beyond the analysis of aggregate data.

The use of micro level analysis represents an important departure from past banking research studies. With a few exceptions (Dreese, 1974; Markley, 1984), banking research has not been conducted on the level of the individual bank.

The expense of primary data collection as well as the limitations of using a case-study approach likely have contributed to the trend toward strict aggregate analysis. However, primary data collection and analysis, particularly in a deregulated financial services industry, can provide important information for understanding the functioning of rural capital markets as well as for informing bank regulatory policy in the future.

The greatest advantage of using primary data collection for the study of rural capital markets is the level of detail that can be acquired. It is important to understand how the flow of funds in rural communities is affected by deregulation and this can be done only by determining where loans are made. In addition, to link bank lending behavior and local economic growth, it is important to identify to whom banks lend money, i.e., what types of borrowers, and to what extent bankers are willing to sacrifice profits in order to make an investment to stimulate community growth. This information can be obtained only through interviews with bankers, either mailed or personal, since the Federal Reserve Board does not require any accounting of the geographical distribution of loans, with the exception of mortgage lending requirements under the Community Reinvestment Act.

Another area that can be explored through primary data collection is the question of decisionmaking in different types of banking institutions. Interviews with bankers can provide information on how lending decisions are made, the degree of centralization of decisionmaking within a holding company, what bank goals are and how community economic growth ranks among those goals, and the amount of flexibility in decisionmaking. Such information can only be implied from aggregate data, not determined directly.

Micro level analysis is also applied to the demand side of a rural banking market. Unlike other research studies, this approach directly considers the demand for loanable funds within rural areas. However, it would be prohibitively expensive to evaluate all aspects of credit demand in a rural market, i.e., housing, consumer, agricultural, commercial and industrial. Therefore, this approach focuses on the commercial sector, since increases in credit demand from this sector would more nearly reflect increased economic activity in the community. The primary objective of evaluating credit demand is to determine the extent to which viable investment opportunities exist in rural areas relative to other areas of the state or nation. By determining what type of demand exists for commercial bank loans and any problems experienced in tapping those loan funds, it is possible to provide a more accurate picture of the performance of commercial banks in a rural capital market. The loan-to-deposit ratio, a frequently used measure of bank lending performance, has greater meaning when coupled with information about the effective demand for loans within a particular rural area. For example, a very low bank loan-to-deposit ratio in a rural area where businesses express unmet credit needs might suggest that the bank is being very conservative or is unable to interpret or identify credit demand. On the other hand, such a situation may indicate the need for alternative institutions that can provide credit to those businesses if commercial banks are unable to meet that demand, e.g., demand for equity capital, for whatever reason.

The final step in this research approach is policy analysis of the primary and secondary data collected. The research is designed to include an advisory board of bank experts (policymakers, researchers, community advocates, bankers) to review the results of the project and make a series of recommendations based on those results. The recommendations can be directed to the state, regional, or national level. The need for such policy analysis arises from the dynamic nature of the deregulatory process. Banking deregulation is proceeding rapidly at the state and regional level, with Congress responding much more slowly to the important issues of deregulation, such as interstate banking. As a result, research to evaluate the impact of deregulation on rural capital markets is timely and could have an influence on the ultimate shape of banking regulations at the state or regional level, as well as nationally. The results of banking research, such as that described above, can be used to inform the policymaking process and research projects can be designed to facilitate that contribution.

Benefits and Limitations of Research Approach

There are two primary benefits associated with this research approach. First, it is designed to evaluate the impact of a macroeconomic change, financial deregulation, on rural areas directly, rather than applying national level impacts to rural areas. In the case of financial markets, past regulation created distinct and relatively isolated rural markets that were protected from competition. The removal of such protection, while likely contributing to increased financial market efficiency on a national scale, could be expected to have a different impact in rural areas. To evaluate what that impact is requires a research approach that focuses on rural capital markets and explores banking issues beyond those associated with bank performance, e.g., demand for capital, bank decisionmaking, bank role in pursuing local economic growth. The research approach presented here addresses these issues. Second, this approach connects research and policymaking in a direct way by making evaluation of results by policymakers part of the research design. By using an advisory board to review research results and make policy recommendations, a mechanism for getting results translated into policy is established. While it is recognized that providing such a mechanism does not insure that research results are used to guide policymaking, this research design could facilitate this process by bringing the results to the attention of policymakers in a relatively quick and direct manner.

Despite the benefits that can be achieved from using this approach, some limitations must be recognized. First, the approach is necessarily more capital- and labor-intensive. More research time must be devoted to the development and implementation of suitable survey instruments and more money must be allocated for data collection and analysis. Second, there is a trade-off between the benefits of analysis based on aggregate data with its relatively large sample size and the more in depth analysis that can be obtained through primary data collection. The results of the approach described here will be limited to the extent that the sample of banks and businesses interviewed is limited. However, these limitations may be overcome by utilizing this approach in a number of states and comparing the results obtained. This comparison will be possible in the near future as such research is ongoing in West Virginia and Wisconsin and is soon planned for four New England states.

Potential Applications of Research Approach

While there are certainly limits to the use of the approach presented here, there are a number of important issues involved with financial deregulation in the rural South that can be analyzed using this approach. For example, the failure of Congress to rule on nationwide interstate banking has resulted in numerous states and regions taking the lead in establishing some form of interstate banking. The New England region has the longest history of interstate legislation, but most states in the Southeast have adopted some form of regional interstate banking legislation in the past few years. This movement toward interstate banking, particularly in the South, is occurring rapidly and with limited investigation of the impact such change may have on rural communities. By applying this research approach to states in the Southeast, it would be possible to evaluate what the impact of interstate movement will be on rural areas in the region. By identifying differences in lending patterns, decisionmaking, and the attitude toward stimulating economic growth among different types of banks, particularly in-state vs. out-of-state holding companies, prospects for rural capital availability in an environment of interstate banking can be identified. These results would provide an evaluation of interstate banking in relation to rural areas in the South that would be useful in future considerations of nationwide interstate banking.

While interstate banking is an important issue in many state legislatures at the present time, other changes in financial markets will have an impact on rural areas. The expansion of nonbank banks predominantly in the South, and the involvement of nonbank institutions, such as Sears, in traditional banking activities will likely alter the availability of credit in many rural areas. In addition, thrift institutions may assume greater importance in rural capital markets if small banks have difficulty competing with the larger holding companies that are expected to proliferate in a deregulated financial market. Whether these changes result in a positive or negative impact on capital availability could be evaluated by expanding this analysis to include consideration of other types of financial institutions, not simply commercial banks. In turn, the results of such an analysis would provide useful information to members of Congress engaged in discussing issues of further financial market regulation and deregulation.

As stated previously, this research approach is beginning to be applied in a number of areas. Research in West Virginia is focusing on the commercial lending activities of banks in different types of counties, i.e., growing vs. lagging, by interviewing bankers in the state. This study does not explicitly consider demand by the business sector, but does address the issue of quality of loan applications to the bankers. Work in Wisconsin has focused in the past on business demand for credit through interviews with commercial establishments. The focus of more recent research is to combine bank level analysis with demand analysis. Finally, the proposed project in New England will evaluate interstate banking and its impact on rural capital availability by utilizing the research approach described in this chapter. To the extent that these separate research projects yield similar results regarding deregulation's impact on rural areas, the potential for input to policymaking at the national level will be strengthened.

CONCLUSIONS

The South, as well as other regions in the country, faces a rural crisis. A number of macroeconomic forces, including financial deregulation, combine to place stress on rural areas. The key to survival is diversification of the rural economy so that change in one sector does not spell disaster for all sectors. However, this diversification process requires access to financial capital to make requisite investments for the future.

Capital availability to rural areas in the future will be affected by the changes taking place in the nation's financial markets. However, information about the impact of these changes on rural areas is lacking. Past attempts to identify such impacts are limited by reliance on the analysis of aggregate data and, in some cases, using the state or region as the unit of analysis rather than the rural capital market itself. To help provide more useful information for analyzing rural capital availability, an alternative research approach is suggested. This approach relies on micro level analysis combined with aggregate information. There is explicit consideration of both the supply and demand sides of the rural capital market so that a more accurate picture can be obtained. And, the approach incorporates a policy component by building into the analysis the review of results by banking experts and the development of policy recommendations to inform the regulatory debate ongoing at the state and national levels.

While limitations in this approach are recognized, it has value in focusing research attention on how financial deregulation affects rural capital availability rather than on the impacts on financial market structure itself. While structural change will certainly have an impact on rural markets, there is a need to go beyond this type of analysis to a more in depth focus on the functioning of the rural capital market itself. To do so requires primary data collection from both the suppliers and demanders of credit so that a complete picture of capital availability can be obtained. Such an approach can provide useful information for determining the impact of deregulation on rural capital markets and, consequently, for guiding regulatory policy making in the future.

REFERENCES

Barkley, David L. and Peter Helander. 1984. "Commercial bank loans and economic activity in non-metropolitan Arizona: A question of causality." Paper presented at the Annual Meetings of the American Agricultural Economics Association, Ithaca, New York.

Barkley, David L., Cindy Mellon, and Glenn T. Potts. 1984. "Effects of banking structure on the allocation of credit to nonmetropolitan communities." *Western Journal of Agricultural Economics* 9:283-292.

Dreese, G. Richard. 1974. "Banks and regional economic development." *Southern Economic Journal* 40(April):647-656.

Duncan, Douglas G. and Mike D. Woods. 1987. "Commercial bank characteristics in metropolitan Texas counties: Implications for rural funds availability." Paper presented at the Annual Meetings of the Southern Agricultural Economics Association, Nashville, Tennessee.

Dunham, Constance R. 1986. "Interstate banking and the outflow of local funds." *New England Economic Review* (March/April):7-19.

Kahley, William J. and Gustavo A. Uceda. 1986. "Louisiana: The worst may be over." *Economic Review,* Federal Reserve Bank of Atlanta 71 (November-December):47-60.

Kohn, Ernest. 1964. *Branch banking, bank mergers and the public interest.* New York: New York State Banking Department.

Lawrence, Robert J. and Samuel H. Talley. 1976. "An assessment of bank holding companies." *Federal Reserve Bulletin* 62(January):15-21.

Markley, Deborah Morentz. 1984. "The impact of institutional change in the financial services industry on capital markets in rural Virginia." *American Journal of Agricultural Economics* 66(December):686-693.

Melichar, Emanuel. 1987. "Financial condition of agricultural banks." *Agricultural Finance Review* 47:23-39.

Rhoades, Stephen A. 1980. "The competitive effects of interstate banking." *Federal Reserve Bulletin* 66(January):1-8.

11

Local Labor Markets in Agricultural Policy Dependent Areas of the South

Forrest A. Deseran
Ann Z. Dellenbarger

There can be little argument that the social and economic prominence of agricultural production in the South has steadily diminished over the last few decades. The family farm, which remains the principal unit of agricultural production, has been steadily dropping in numbers since the 1940s. This decline has occurred at a time of significant rural diversification, precipitating a rural South that is far from homogeneous either economically or socially. A notable facet of the changing structure of agriculture has been the sharp rise in part-time farming. As off-farm employment increasingly has become a factor in farm operations, farming as a way of life and as a family-centered economic activity is becoming more and more intertwined with the composition and character of local labor markets.

Although little research examines labor market conditions in agricultural areas, Falk and Lyson's (1987) analysis of the "industrial transformation" of the South during the 1970s employs an urban/rural distinction that is informative for our purposes. In general, the authors demonstrate that the much publicized economic success of the sunbelt during the 1970s was not necessarily a boon for all residents—for the most part, the good times were restricted to the larger urban centers while other areas remained in the economic backwaters. Unlike the tremendous expansion of high tech and service related industries enjoyed by major urban centers, the rural economy for much of the South remained heavily dependent upon manufacturing industries, especially those producing nondurable goods (e.g., textiles). These rural regions are especially vulnerable to plant relocations precipitated by foreign competition and a general decline in the manufacturing industry.

Also during this period, a growing interdependence between the nonfarm local economy and agricultural production was accelerated by a sharp increase in off-farm employment by farm family members, especially women. Indeed, off-farm earnings now exceed farm income for a majority of U.S. farm families (Deseran et al., 1984). It is clear that the availability of off-farm employment has become a requisite for many families to remain in farming.

The implications of the changing industrial structure of the rural South for the farm family in particular and the agricultural industry in general remain open to question. In an attempt to address this issue, Falk and Lyson (1987) investigate the relationship between the nonfarm economy and off-farm employment in the South by correlating the proportion of farms that are part-time with the proportion of workers employed in selected industries and occupations. Finding a strong positive correlation between the percentage of the work force employed in manufacturing and the proportion of part-time farms, they conclude that nonfarm employment opportunities in *manufacturing* industries are required to support a large part-time farming sector. These findings suggest that the apparent deterioration of the manufacturing industry in the rural South should have a distinct and negative impact on the farm population.

Our purpose in this chapter is to explore the effects of industrial composition and location of local labor markets on part-time farm households in the South. Our research goes beyond previous efforts in several respects: (1) we employ a unique data set of local labor markets derived from commuting-to-work patterns of residents, (2) our analysis encompasses the family (in this case, the married couple), and (3) we compare farm with nonfarm members of the labor force.

THE LOCAL LABOR MARKET

Local labor markets (LMAs) are basic units of economic and social organization defined by the relationship between place-of-work and place-of-residence. The LMAs used in this research were determined from journey-to-work data from the 1980 "Place of Residence by Place of Work" file prepared for the Bureau of Labor Statistics by the Census Bureau. From these data, commuting flow measures were used to group counties into areas of at least 100,000 inhabitants (this population restriction meets the Census Bureau's requirement for survey confidentiality).[1] As geographical areas where employment is sought and job decisions are made based upon the ability to commute to and from work, LMAs are particularly appropriate for our purposes here. Also, because they do not necessarily contain metropolitan centers, they allow researchers to examine nonmetro labor markets.[2]

Our findings are from a unique version of the 1980 Census that incorporates the LMA geographic structure outlined above—Public Use Microdata Sample D (PUMS-D). This data file was produced by the Census Bureau in consultation with researchers from the S-184 Regional Project and the USDA Economic Research Service. The PUMS-D is a powerful research tool which contains detailed individual and household level data by LMA, offering much greater analytical flexibility for studying labor market experiences than is possible using aggregate level data.

Agricultural LMAs

To insure that our analysis includes labor markets that are salient for the farm population, we restricted our sample to LMAs containing counties designated as "agricultural policy dependent." This classification scheme, developed by Ross and Green (1985), identifies those counties with 20 percent or more of total earnings from agriculture. We limited our sample further by excluding those labor market areas where less than fifteen percent of the total labor force resides in agricultural dependent counties. Although an arbitrary cutting-off point, we felt it focused analysis on LMAs with sizable proportions of their total labor force residing in agriculturally dependent counties.

Proximity to Metropolitan Centers

As mentioned above, major metropolitan centers defined the sunbelt's economic boom while rural areas remained depressed and relatively anonymous. The economic advantage urban centers enjoy over most rural areas has been explained in terms of industrial base (Parcel, 1979; Thompson, 1965). Thompson (1965), for example, argues that an urban area is like a small industrially-oriented nation which must export products to survive economically. High wages in the predominant export sectors indirectly increase the wages of other jobs in the local service sector through competition within the labor market area.

To examine the effects of metropolitan influence on *agriculturally* dependent labor markets, we grouped the LMAs into three categories depending on proximity to metropolitan statistical areas (MSAs)—*isolated, adjacent,* and *metropolitan.* The procedures outlined here yielded a total of twenty-three LMAs located in ten states in the South. Twelve of the LMAs were identified as isolated from and five as adjacent to LMAs with metropolitan centers. Six included metropolitan areas within their boundaries.[3]

The Family as a Focus

Because the family remains the major unit of production and decision-making in agriculture, and because the earnings from off-farm employment of *both* the husband and wife have become a major source of income to support this way of life, we focus on married workers. More specifically, we look at patterns of nonfarm employment and earnings by industrial categories for married farm men and women, comparing their patterns to those of nonfarm couples residing in the same LMAs. Those couples for whom either spouse reported farm self-employment earnings are treated as farm couples.[4]

FINDINGS

The Prevalence of Off-Farm Employment

The degree to which farm couples are involved in off-farm employment is summarized in Figure 1. Particularly noteworthy is that one-third of the couples in our sample represent what might be considered the traditional organization of farm family work roles, i.e., neither spouse works off the farm. Over half of the farm men and about 45 percent of the farm women report earnings

Figure 1   OFF—FARM EMPLOYMENT

Percent working off farm by spouse

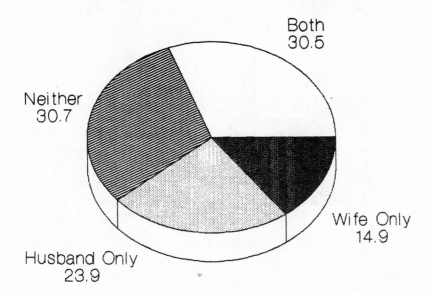

Both
30.5

Neither
30.7

Wife Only
14.9

Husband Only
23.9

from nonfarm work. In fact, we see about as many dual off-farm job-holding couples as "traditional" farm couples.[5] These figures for off-farm employment are very similar to what has been found at the national level (Deseran et al., 1984), suggesting that this is not merely a regional pattern.

The financial significance of off-farm employment is obvious when we examine the earnings of part-time farm families in our sample (Figure 2). On the average, farm self-employment income constitutes less than half of the couples' reported earnings. Although husbands contribute most to family earnings, wives augment family incomes by about twenty percent. Additionally, it is apparent from Figure 2 that part-time farm families in metropolitan LMAs enjoy substantially greater nonfarm (and farm) economic returns from their labor than do their counterparts outside metropolitan areas.

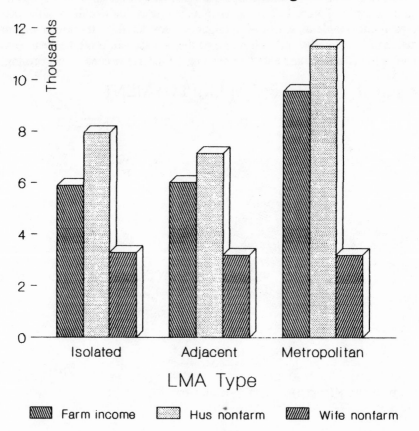

Figure 2   MEAN EARNINGS OF FARM COUPLES
Farm self-employment, husband's off-farm and wife's off-farm earnings

The Industrial Composition of LMAs

Pursuing the question of the importance of *manufacturing* industries for part-time farming, we now examine the types of jobs that comprise the three types of local labor markets in our sample. To more fully depict employment opportunities within the LMAs, we consider the distribution of nonfarm jobs of *farm* and *nonfarm* husbands and wives (Figure 3).[6]

Husbands' off-farm employment. It is evident that durable and nondurable manufacturing industries provide a relatively small proportion of part-time farmers with employment regardless of LMA location.[7] Though a slightly higher proportion of the *nonfarm* husbands in the sample are employed in manufacturing industries (especially in isolated LMAs), manufacturing industries only contribute less than a fourth of the total employment. Also noteworthy is the small proportion of jobs provided by agriculture. It is clear that off-farm employment opportunities for men (and women) are not to be found in durable or nondurable manufacturing or in agriculturally related industries.

The sales/finance industry is the largest single employer of farm husbands; predictably, jobs in this sector are more plentiful in metro than in outlying LMAs. Service industries account for the second largest proportion of husbands' nonfarm jobs and are also more widespread in the metro LMAs. Together, these two categories account for close to half of all nonfarm jobs for farm *and* nonfarm husbands.

Wives' off-farm employment. The findings shown in Figure 3 reveal that farm wives are much more likely than their husbands to be employed in sales/finance and service industries. Over 65 percent of the working farm wives hold jobs in these types of industries. As we saw for husbands, farm wives in metropolitan LMAs are even more likely to be employed in one of these two industries than are farm women residing in nonmetropolitan LMAs. Nondurable manufacturing, often considered to be pivotal to the Southern rural economy, fails to show up as a major component of the labor markets in our sample.

Off-Farm Earnings and Industry of Employment

The above findings suggest that the much-discussed shift to a service sector economy (i.e., postindustrial society) was in clear evidence by 1980 in the LMAs in our sample. A theme underlying much of the speculation about the consequences of this expanding service sector is that jobs in this segment of the economy are characterized by low pay and poor benefits, especially in nonmetropolitan areas. In other words, good jobs are being replaced by less

176

Figure 3
EMPLOYMENT IN SELECTED INDUSTRIES

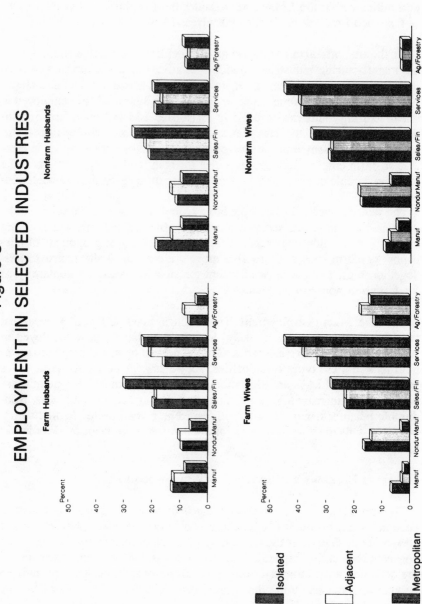

Farm Husbands

Nonfarm Husbands

Farm Wives

Nonfarm Wives

Isolated

Adjacent

Metropolitan

desirable ones. In this vein, our concern with rural labor markets in the South raises several questions. To what extent (if any) is employment in service and sales kinds of industries an economic disadvantage compared to other types of off-farm employment? Does proximity to metropolitan centers make a difference in this regard? Are there major variations between the earnings of farm and nonfarm workers in the nonfarm sector?

Husbands' earnings. Our findings for off-farm earnings (Figure 4) suggest that income from employment in the service and sales/finance industries may not be as much of an economic handicap as commonly thought. Looking first at husbands' earnings, these two categories each yield more in average earnings than do either durable or nondurable manufacturing industries. Taking into consideration that the service and sales/finance industries employ nearly half of the husbands in our sample, our findings seem to question the contention that manufacturing jobs are necessary to support part-time farming.

Looking at differences across LMA types, farmers in metropolitan labor market areas fare better in their off-farm earnings than do farm men outside of these labor market areas. Although this is most noticeable for the sales/finance category (where the mean earnings in the metropolitan LMAs are nearly double those of the isolated LMAs), the pattern remains distinct across all industries and is reflected, although somewhat less, in the earnings of nonfarm men. These findings, among other things, suggest that part-time farm husbands in metro LMAs occupy a comparatively elite niche in their local labor markets.

Wives' Earnings. The earnings of wives shown in Figure 4 reveal some interesting patterns compared to what we saw for husbands. Most conspicuous, of course, is the very large discrepancy from the earnings of men. Women's earnings remain well below men's regardless of industrial category.[8]

Unlike what we found for husbands' earnings, industry of employment has little effect on the earnings of wives. In fact, the relative *absence* of differences in earnings across industries or geographical location is more noticeable. Also, although the earnings of farm wives tend to be higher than the earnings of nonfarm wives in the two high employment categories (services and sales/finance), the differences are not as great as those found between farm and nonfarm husbands.[9]

These findings for wives reconfirm the pervasiveness of gender stratification found throughout the economy. Structural factors (such as proximity to metropolitan places and kinds of industry) which were found to have a marked impact on the earnings of men, have little comparable effect on women's earnings. The labor market confronting rural women is definitely a different labor market than the one rural men experience.

Figure 4

MEAN EARNINGS FOR SELECTED INDUSTRIES

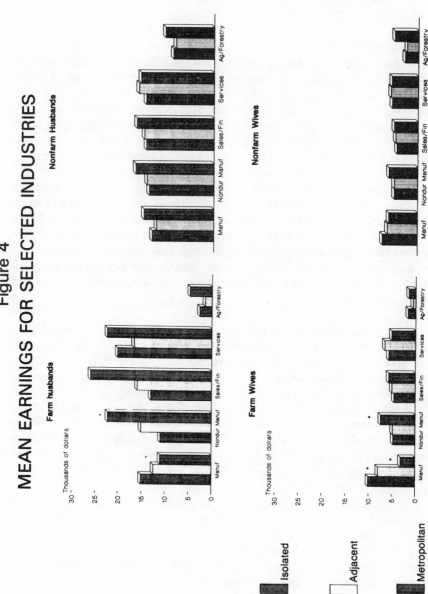

CONCLUSIONS

In this chapter we focused primarily on the impact of the current rural crisis for farm families in agriculturally dependent labor market areas. We found that off-farm employment has become an integral part of Southern farming. As we noted earlier, only 31 percent of Southern farm families report no off-farm employment. In other words, for most Southern farm families their ability to remain on the land is tightly bound up with their ability to find suitable off-farm jobs for either or both spouses.

The importance of non-farm income to the structure of Southern agriculture was brought home when we saw that the husband's non-farm income was greater than the family's farm earnings regardless of labor market location, and that the nonfarm earnings of wives added about 20 percent to total family earnings. Obviously, without sources of off-farm income for both husband and wife, the current number of Southern farm households would decline dramatically.

Southern farm families in general, and those in the more remote labor market areas in particular, face a precarious future. Looking to the years ahead, we believe that farm families living in the more urban labor market areas of the region will probably fare better than those living in more rural and isolated environs. Job opportunities for both husbands and wives are more plentiful in and around the cities of the South. Isolated rural labor market areas, on the other hand, offer a more restricted range of employment alternatives.

In recent years many rural places have seen unemployment levels rise as the local manufacturing enterprises have succumbed to Third World competition. Our findings that a relatively small proportion of jobs are in manufacturing industries, and that these jobs actually paid less than the more numerous service and sales/finance jobs, suggest that the prospects for off-farm employment *in these particular areas* may not be as vulnerable to the changing industrial structure of the rural South as has been supposed. At the same time, there can be little doubt that women's earnings will continue to lag well behind their male counterparts regardless of labor market location or composition.

In any case, our findings are best interpreted in light of the national trend toward increasing size, concentration, and specialization among agricultural producers. Those farm families that cannot compete as full-time producers may find, as our analysis seems to indicate, that their ability to remain in farming is less dependent upon the amount of sales they generate on the farm than upon their ability to find adequate sources of off-farm income to supplement their farm earnings.

NOTES

[1]The LMA designation to be used here was developed as part of a larger research effort by Southern Regional Project S-184 ("Labor Markets and Labor Market Differentiation in Nonmetropolitan Areas") in collaboration with the Agricultural and Rural Economics Division, Economic Research Service, U.S. Department of Agriculture. The procedures used to identify 382 labor market areas in the United States are discussed in detail elsewhere (Tolbert and Killian, 1987).

[2]As Tolbert and Killian (1987) point out, the nonmetro research potential of these LMA designations is a definite advantage over other strategies to represent labor markets, including state planning districts, Metropolitan Statistical Areas, and the Bureau of Economic Analysis' economic areas.

[3]It should be noted that the selection criteria used in this research restricted the sample to relatively small MSAs (e.g., Lubbock, Texas; Ocala, Florida; Monroe, Louisiana), none of which approach the proportions of an Atlanta or Dallas.

[4]Because farm earnings do not necessarily reflect the scope of a farm operation, we do not specify the dollar amount of farm self-employment earnings in our operationalization of farm families. Although this criterion may introduce a bias toward small or "hobby" farms, the proporation of part-time farmers found in our sample is consistent with what has been found elsewhere.

[5]These figures for off-farm employment are very close to what has been found elsewhere for farm families in the U.S. (e.g., Deseran et al., 1984), suggesting that, as in other parts of the country, off-farm employment is a factor of everyday life for most farm families and is an important link between agricultural production and the local economy.

[6]It should be kept in mind that our off-farm employment findings are for farm self-employment income recipients who report their occupation as other than farming. Although this reduces the number of cases used in the analysis and possibly introduces some bias, when considered in conjunction with findings for nonfarm couples, we can construct a rough profile of the industrial makeup of these labor markets. Additionally, although our analysis initially considered all major census-defined industrial categories, we have confined our discussion to industrial categories which are most relevant to the objectives of this chapter.

[7]Construction, which we treat as separate from nondurable manufacturing, is an exeption in isolated LMAs where it accounts for about 18 percent of husbands' off-farm employment.

[8]A higher rate of part-time employment among women accounts for some of the sex-specific discrepancy shown in the tables; however, even when we control for part-time employment status, women's earnings remain significantly lower than men's.

[9]Income attainment obviously is influenced by more than industry of employment and location. Certain attributes individuals bring to the labor market (i.e., human capital variables) consistently have been shown to have a bearing on earnings. In multiple regression analyses not reported here, we included three of the more important of these factors as predictors of earnings—education, race, and age. Education was the best predictor of both husbands' and wives' earnings, and, because educational attainment levels were much higher in metro than other LMA types, it accounts for much of the inflated earnings found in these LMAs. However, the partial regression coefficients for location and industry of occupation remained significant for husbands. On the other hand, location and industry had no appreciable effect on wives' earnings.

REFERENCES

Deseran, Forrest A., William W. Falk, and Pamela Jenkins. 1984. "Determinants of earnings of farm families in the U.S.," *Rural Sociology* 49: 210-229.

Falk, William W. and Thomas A. Lyson. 1987. *High-Tech, Low-Tech, No-Tech: Recent Occupational and Industrial Changes in the South*. Albany, NY:SUNY-Albany Press.

Parcel, Toby L. 1979. "Race, regional labor markets and earnings," *American Sociological Review* 44 (April):262-279.

Ross, Peggy J. and Bernal Green. 1985. *Procedure for Developing a Policy-Oriented Classification of Nonmetropolitan Counties*. Report No.AGES850308. Washington: USDA,ERS.

Thompson, W. R. 1965. *A Preface to Urban Economics*. Baltimore: Johns Hopkins University Press.

Tolbert, Charles and Molly Killian. 1987. *Labor Markets in the United States*. Technical report submitted to the Agricultural and Rural Economics Division, Economic Research Service, U.S.D.A.

12

Race and Underemployment: Black Employment Hardship in the Rural South

Daniel T. Lichter

The changing status of black Americans continues to capture the general interest of the social scientific community (see Jaynes and Williams, 1987).[1] To date, much of this concern has concentrated on national trends in racial differences in unemployment, earnings, occupational status, and the like (Farley 1984; Smith and Welch, 1986), or has focused on metropolitan central cities where a disproportionate share of U.S. blacks live and work (Kasarda, 1985; Lichter, 1988; Tienda and Lii, 1987). Surprisingly little attention has been paid to the comparative socioeconomic status or work experiences of blacks and whites living outside central cities, especially those in rural areas (for exceptions, see Marshall and Christian, 1978; Walker, 1977). This is surprising on two counts: (1) the black population historically was a decidedly rural population located overwhelmingly in the Southern United States (Sly, 1981); and (2) postbellum Southern rural blacks have long represented one of the poorest segments in American society, with poverty rates well above those of whites and those of blacks living elsewhere (Moland, 1981). Given the historic significance of race in the South (Lichter and Heaton, 1986), few areas of the United States provide a better context for reevaluating recent economic and employment gains of blacks.

Consequently, using the labor utilization framework of Clogg and Sullivan (1983), this chapter presents several indicators of black underemployment in the nonmetropolitan South.[2] As a labor force concept, underemployment refers broadly to inadequacies in employment, and is represented not only by the jobless but by those unable to find full-time work or a job that provides adequate earnings. In this chapter, three questions are addressed regarding changing racial differences in rural employment hardship. First, how have employment problems of Southern rural blacks, as measured by several indicators of underemployment, changed over the 1970–85 period? Second, how have the employment circumstances of rural blacks compared with Southern metropolitan blacks, Northern blacks, and Southern rural whites over the recent past? Third, and finally, what are some of the factors that have contributed to black underemployment in the rural South, and to the persistence of black/white differentials in labor force marginality? These questions are especially relevant today as economic and demographic change continues apace in the American South.

CHANGING EMPLOYMENT CONDITIONS OF SOUTHERN BLACKS

The economic fortunes of rural blacks have been traced historically to the slave and Southern plantation economy that ended only a century ago (Mandle, 1978; Fligstein, 1981). After the emancipation, well over 90 percent of U.S. blacks resided in the South, with the vast majority living in rural areas (Moland, 1981). Most rural blacks eked out a minimal living from subsistence agriculture, usually as tenant farmers or sharecroppers. Living standards were extremely low and poverty was widespread. Except for menial and low-paying jobs, black employment opportunities outside of agriculture were limited, as industrialization in the South lagged far behind the North. A rigidly structured system of stratification, based largely on race, also excluded blacks from good jobs. Unfortunately, migration to the North before World War I provided little escape. The burgeoning industrial centers of the North were flooded with an influx of European immigrants favored over blacks by prospective employers (Mandle, 1978). Mired in the economically depressed rural South, blacks represented the poorest of the poor in the poorest region of the country.

Not until after World War I, when immigration was substantially reduced through legislation, did the massive exodus of blacks from the rural South begin in earnest (Johnson and Campbell, 1982; Sly, 1981). To be sure, the surplus of black labor in the rural South, encouraged by the mechanization of agricultural production, provided an ample supply of potential outmigrants to the North (Fligstein, 1981). The massive redistribution of blacks to the North also reflected a simple economic reality. Differences in employment opportunities and per capita income were substantial between the South and the rest of the nation. The South, particularly the rural South, was a backwater region according to virtually every

economic indicator. Most blacks employed outside of agriculture found themselves in a "secondary" labor market, usually segregated by race, with jobs
whose defining "characteristic often was that the pay was so low that they
were shunned by white workers" (Mandle, 1978:99). By 1950, only a small
percentage of blacks were employed in professional or other white-collar occupations. A large disproportionate share of black men continued to be classified
as laborers and nearly half of employed black women were private household
workers (i.e., largely domestic servants) (Marshall and Christian, 1978).

How have the economic and employment circumstances of rural blacks
changed in recent decades? There are reasons for both optimism and pessi-
mism. For example, the return of Northern blacks to the South, beginning
in the 1970s, is cause for optimism; it implies that the employment conditions
of Southern blacks improved compared with those working in other regions
(Johnson and Campbell, 1982). During the 1965-70 period, the South experienced a net loss of over 200,000 blacks to other regions. By the 1980-85
period, the Southern black population *gained* through net inmigration about
87,000 people (Robinson, 1986). Not surprisingly, much of the inmigration
occurred in metropolitan and urban areas (Dahmann, 1986). But recent evidence
suggests that the inter-regional exchange of black population also favored the
nonmetropolitan South at the expense of the non-South (Dahmann, 1986; cal-
culations based on his Table 3). If we accept the traditional economic assumption that the flow of labor responds largely to spatial differences in economic
opportunity, then recent migration patterns of blacks suggest relative
improvements in employment opportunities not only in the South but in its
rural areas as well.

This movement of population, both of whites and blacks, has been attributed in part to an economic reawakening of the South (Kasarda et al., 1986).
Indeed, there is substantial evidence that the South is converging economically with the rest of the nation (Poston and Weller, 1981). For example, the
ratio of per capita income in the South to that of the United States increased
substantially during this century (Singelmann, 1981). Between 1940 and 1970
alone, this ratio increased from .69 to .86 in the South Altantic states. In East
South Central states the ratio increased from .55 to .74, and the West South
Central increased from .70 to .85 during this period (Singelmann, 1981).
Moreover, the industrial structure of the South has converged with the rest of
the nation. Singelmann (1981) has compared the industrial structure (a 6-category
classification) of the South with the rest of the nation using the index of dissimilarity. This index provides the percentage of the Southern labor force that
would have to be reclassified in order to have the same industrial distribution
as the nation as a whole. As evidence of convergence, Singelmann (1981) showed
that the index declined substantially in the South from 20.55 to 2.35 between
1920 and 1970. This was due in large part to the shift away from agriculture and
other extractive industries in the South during this period.

The resurgence of the South holds economic promise for blacks as well as whites. Some suggest that economic gains in the South have trickled down even to those on the bottom rungs of the economic ladder, including rural blacks (for discussion, see Walker, 1977). Other indicators, however, fail to reveal appreciable economic progress among Southern blacks, especially for those living in rural areas. For example, the South is a heterogeneous region, a characteristic that has apparently become more pronounced over the past decade. The large metropolitan areas have experienced an unprecedented demographic and economic revival, yet the rural areas have lagged behind (Lyson and Falk, 1986). Marshall (1978:16) suggests that surplus labor in rural areas remains a persistent problem, primarily because "many who work have been displaced by innovations, are underemployed, or have very low productivity because their agricultural work experiences and rural educations have not prepared them for high-wage nonfarm work." Unfortunately, growth in nonagricultural employment in Southern rural areas appeared to have slowed in the early 1980s, as international foreign competition accelerated and firms bypassed or left rural areas for Third World countries where labor is cheap (Deaton, 1986).

Employment marginality appears to be especially problematic in the so-called Black Belt extending from the Mississippi Delta to the Carolina coast. According to Lyson and Falk (1986:162), the economic base of Black Belt counties is largely dominated by slow growing, stagnating, and declining industries. As a result, Southern blacks have not shared equitably in the expansion of nonmetropolitan employment since 1970 (Walker, 1977). Black counties continue to lose population (O'Hare and Engels, 1986) and firms are reluctant to relocate there (Walker, 1977). Moreover, the spatial segregation of blacks has often been found to have adverse effects on labor market outcomes, a relationship most demonstrable among blacks in decaying inner-city neighbors (Tienda and Lii, 1987). But the apparent adverse effects of racial segregation may be no less true for blacks working in largely black rural counties in the South. Indeed, it may be significant that the 1970s revealed increases in the spatial segregation of blacks and whites across Southern counties (Lichter, 1988). This may have contributed to increasing racial inequality in Southern employment conditions since 1970. It may also help to explain why black migration to the South slowed in the early 1980s compared with that of the mid-1970s (Robinson, 1986).

The period since 1970 thus provides an interesting era in which to examine the comparative employment circumstances of rural blacks and whites in the South. Not only is the status of blacks interesting from a historical perspective, but recent economic and demographic changes in the South are cause for both optimism and continuing discouragement about the integration of blacks—particularly rural blacks—into the economic mainstream of American society.

DATA AND MEASUREMENT

The data used in this analysis are from the 1970, 1975, 1980, and 1985 annual demographic files of the March *Current Population Survey* (U.S. Bureau of the Census, 1985). Each yearly sample contains approximately 60,000 households and each is representative of the noninstitutionalized population of the United States. The analysis here is restricted to men, and includes the traditional labor force aged 18–64. These sample restrictions keep the focus squarely on racial differences, while avoiding the confounding issues of sex inequality and youth unemployment.

This focus on underemployment is appropriate for several reasons. Many studies of racial inequality, for example, deal with earnings or occupational attainment (Smith and Welch, 1986), but restrict their analyses to the currently employed or to full-time, full-year workers. Such sample restrictions ignore long-standing racial differences in employment status (Kasarda, 1985). To be sure, racial convergence in earnings, say, may occur at the same time that unemployment rates are diverging by race. Unfortunately, the alternative focus on unemployment status is also potentially problematic. As an indicator of labor force performance, the unemployment rate is the target of increasing criticism (Tweeten, 1986; Korsching and Lasley, 1986; Lichter, 1988). Such concerns seem especially relevant for the black labor force. According to Moland (1981:484-485),

> *Unemployment rates are imperfect indicators of black labor market disadvantage because they reflect only those who are able to work and are actively seeking employment. Not included are those underemployed, those working part time who would like full-time jobs, those working but not earning enough to raise themselves above the poverty levels, or those who have become discouraged and stopped looking for jobs altogether.*

As described below, underemployment represents a useful conceptual tool with which to reevaluate labor force marginality of rural blacks since 1970.

Several forms of underemployment are measured here using the *Labor Utilization Framework* (LUF) of Clogg (1979) and Sullivan (1978). The LUF provides a comprehensive measurement scheme for assessing the extent of labor force marginality in rural areas (Lichter, 1988; Lichter and Costanzo, 1986). The categories of underemployment include the following: First, the *sub-unemployed*, or discouraged worker category, includes those no longer looking for work because they believe none is available. Second, the *unemployed* are identified following traditional practices of the Bureau of Labor Statistics. It includes those currently out of work but who have actively looked for work during the last four weeks. The third underemployment category is the *underemployed by low hours*, or the involuntary part-time employed.

This includes individuals who are working part-time as defined by the Bureau of Labor Statistics (i.e., less than 35 hours a week), but who desire a full-time job. Fourth, the *underemployed by low income* includes those whose labor market earnings are less than 1.25 times the individual poverty threshold, as defined by the Social Security Administration. This is a measure of earnings inadequacy, and identifies full-time workers whose jobs fail to provide earnings significantly above poverty levels. The LUF is a hierarchical measurement scheme in which underemployment categories are ordered by "hardship," with workers evaluated sequentially from most (i.e., sub-unemployment) to least hardship (i.e., underemployment by low income). Workers are thus included in only one underemployment category or they are not considered to be underemployed. For more detailed discussion of measurement procedures, see Clogg and Sullivan (1983) and Lichter and Costanzo (1986).

The analysis begins in the next section by providing the distributions of underemployment for nonmetropolitan areas of the South for 1970, 1975, 1980, and 1985.[3] To assess how nonmetropolitan blacks fared over this period compared with Southern nonmetropolitan whites and Southern metropolitan and Northern blacks, underemployment ratios between the Southern nonmetropolitan blacks and these population subgroups are presented. Ratios that gravitate over time toward 1.0 suggest a pattern of increasing racial convergence in employment hardship, or convergence between rural blacks and blacks residing elsewhere.

Finally, several logit models are presented which reveal the effects of race, human capital, and employment characteristics on Southern nonmetropolitan underemployment in 1985 (Hanushek and Jackson, 1977). The dependent variable in this analysis is dichotomous; it distinguishes whether or not workers experience any of the economic underemployment forms in the LUF. The logit model can be written as:

$$\log(P/(1-P)) = B_o + B_1 R + \sum_j B_{2j} E_j + \sum_k B_{3k} A_k + \sum_m B_{4m} I_m + \sum_n B_{5n} O_n$$

P refers to the probability of being underemployed. R denotes the variable for race, where R=1 for blacks and 0 otherwise.[4] E_j refers to the *j*th level of education, where E_1=1 for those with less than 12 years of completed schooling and 0 otherwise; E_2=1 for those with 12 years of schooling and 0 otherwise; and E_3=1 for those with 13–15 years of schooling and 0 otherwise (with 16 or more years of schooling representing the reference category). A_k indicates the *k*th level of age, where A_1=1 for those aged 18–29 and 0 otherwise; and A_2=1 for those 30–49 and 0 otherwise (with ages 50–64 providing the reference category). While not disaggregating their analysis by race, Clogg and Sullivan (1983) have shown that education and age (as a proxy for experience) were strongly related to total U.S underemployment for the 1969-80 period, a finding replicated by Lichter (1988) for central city blacks. I_m refers to the mth industry category of current or longest employment (if unemployed). The two industrial categories used here are taken from Hodson's (1983) six-category industrial sector classification scheme. $I_1=1$ denotes workers in **periphery** industries and 0 otherwise; and $I_2=1$ for those working in the **trades** sector and 0 otherwise.[5] (All other industries represent the reference category). As shown by Hodson (1983), workers in periphery and trades industry sectors have much lower mean earnings than those in other categories. Finally, O_n identifies the nth occupation category, where $O_1=1$ for managerial and professional specialities and 0 otherwise; and $O_2=1$ for technical, sales, and administrative support and 0 otherwise (with other occupations representing the reference category). Results from this analysis provide a basis for drawing inferences about the effects of race vis-a-vis human capital and job characteristics on underemployment, and identifies some of the key mechanisms underlying persistent black underemployment in rural areas of the American South.

FINDINGS

Changing rural black underemployment

Table 1 provides the distribution of underemployment categories for Southern nonmetropolitan black men. These data indicate that nonmetropolitan Southern blacks have experienced substantial levels of underemployment since 1970. Regardless of year, about one-third to two-fifths of rural blacks faced some form of economic underemployment. It also is clear from these data that a sizable proportion of blacks experienced labor market hardship in forms other than unemployment. Indeed, unemployment represented only about 14 percent of overall underemployment in 1970. Such a finding reinforces the criticism of Moland (1981) that the unemployment rate seriously underestimates the extent of labor force problems experienced by rural blacks.

Table 1 also provides little evidence that overall underemployment levels are either increasing or decreasing systematically over this period. Rather, black male underemployment has fluctuated largely in response to national or cyclical shifts in the economy. Black underemployment, especially in the form of unemployment, was greatest in the economic bad times of 1975 (at about the time of the recession) and 1985 (at about the time of the farm crisis and when declines in manufacturing and oil industries were most likely to be felt in rural labor markets). It is significant to note, however, that unemployment was three times higher in 1985 than in 1970, but that underemployment by low income declined somewhat over this period. These data suggest a cyclical trade-off between period unemployment rates and the prevalence of the low income underemployed.

Table 1. Underemployment Rates Among Black Men in the Nonmetropolitan South, 1970-1985.

| Year | Categories[a] | | | | |
	SU	UN	LH	LI	Total
1970	2.1%	5.1%	9.1%	19.6%	36.0%
1975	2.4	15.7	8.5	14.2	40.9
1980	1.4	12.3	6.7	13.0	33.4
1985	2.7	15.5	9.2	13.5	40.9

[a]SU=Sub-Unemployed; UN=Unemployed; LH=Underemployed by low hours; LI=Underemployed by low income; Total=sum of SU, UN, LH, and LI.

Table 2. Ratios of Southern Nonmetro Black Underemployment to Southern Metro and Northern Black Underemployment.

| Residence and Year | Categories[a] | | | | |
	SU	UN	LH	LI	Total
Southern Metro:					
1970	1.6	.9	2.7	2.8	2.1
1975	1.8	1.3	1.3	2.0	1.5
1980	1.4	1.5	1.8	1.4	1.4
1985	1.4	1.2	1.1	1.6	1.3
Northern:					
1970	1.8	.7	2.9	4.0	2.1
1975	1.0	.8	1.9	4.2	1.4
1980	.8	.9	1.8	2.6	1.1
1985	.6	.8	1.3	1.3	1.0

[a]SU=Sub-Unemployed; UN=Unemployed; LH=Underemployed by low hours; LI=Underemployed by low income; Total=sum of SU, UN, LH, and LI.

How have Southern blacks compared with blacks living elsewhere? To what extent have the employment circumstances of Southern rural blacks converged with blacks living in the metropolitan South and in the North? Answers are contained in Table 2, which provides underemployment ratios of Southern rural blacks to Southern metropolitan and Northern blacks.

These data provide several interesting contrasts. Not suprisingly, Southern nonmetropolitan blacks generally experienced greater levels of employment hardship than either their metropolitan counterparts or blacks working in the North during this period. More interesting is that there is striking evidence of spatial convergence in black underemployment. The ratios of Southern non-metropolitan black underemployment to both Southern metropolitan and Northern black underemployment declined significantly over time. Whereas Southern nonmetropolitan black underemployment was 2.1 times greater than that of Southern metropolitan blacks in 1970, it was only 1.3 times greater in 1985. Convergence with Northern blacks was even more pronounced. In 1970, Southern nonmetropolitan blacks experienced underemployment levels that were over twice those of Northern blacks. By 1985, virtual parity had been achieved. Indeed, in the 1980s, joblessness among Southern nonmetropolitan black men was less than that of Northern blacks. And the declines in regional differences in underemploymnet by low hours and low income were dramatic. In 1970, for example, Southern nonmetropolitan blacks experienced levels of underemployment by low income that were quadruple those of Northern blacks. By 1985, Southern nonmetropolitan black underemployment was only 1.3 times that of Northern blacks.

It would be easy to paint a favorable portrait of changing employment conditions for blacks in the rural South. But as shown previously in Table 1, there is little evidence of significant improvement over time in black underemployment levels in nonmetropolitan areas of the South. The spatial convergence in black underemployment levels reflects a simple but hard fact: the employment circumstances of blacks in metropolitan areas and in the North deteriorated over the 15-year period since 1970. Black employment conditions in Southern rural areas have not been elevated to the generally more favorable conditions found elsewhere. Rather, black employment conditions elsewhere have become increasingly like the depressed employment conditions historically found in the rural South (see Lichter, 1988).

Changing Racial Inequality in the Rural South

As described above, black underemployment in the rural South, although substantial, appears to have converged somewhat with that of blacks living elsewhere. But how have rural blacks compared with rural whites? Has racial inequality declined since 1970? The black/white underemployment ratios provided in Table 3 address this question.

These data indicate that substantial racial differences in underemployment persisted throughout the 1970–85 period. Black underemployment was substantially higher than white underemployment, regardless of form. Indeed, overall underemployment among nonmetropolitan blacks in the South was over twice that of whites (last column).

Table 3 also provides little evidence of racial convergence in overall underemployment during this period. This is attributable to off-setting patterns of convergence and divergence among the various components of underemployment. Racial differences in joblessness, either in the form of "discouraged workers" or unemployment, became more pronounced over the 1970–85 period. The black/white ratio in subunemployment was higher in the 1980s than in the 1970s, and the ratio for unemployment increased monotonically over the 1970–85 period. Despite divergence in joblessness, however, there seems to be a pattern of convergence in the other forms of underemployment, but especially for the low income category. For the low income category, the ratio declined from 2.5 in 1970 to 1.7 in 1985. Again, this finding can be viewed with either optimism or skepticism. On the optimistic side, these results clearly indicate that, among those blacks with jobs, they have become more like their white counterparts in the nonmetropolitan South. On the other hand, a less optimistic view is that increases in black joblessness have preyed largely on those with marginal jobs (i.e., the underemployed by low hours or low income), leaving behind a higher percentage of employed blacks with adequate employment.

Table 3. Ratios of Southern Nonmetro Black Underemployment to Southern Nonmetro White Underemployment.

	Categories[a]				
Year	SU	UN	LH	LI	Total
1970	3.5	1.6	3.5	2.5	2.5
1975	3.0	2.2	2.1	2.2	2.2
1980	7.0	2.4	2.3	1.9	2.2
1985	4.5	2.5	2.1	1.7	2.2

[a]SU=Sub-Unemployed; UN=Unemployed; LH=Underemployed by low hours; LI=Underemployed by low income; Total=sum of SU, UN, LH, and LI.

Determinants of Rural Underemployment

Clearly, the persistence of racial inequality in employment circumstances has many possible sources. Black/white differences may be attributable in part to racial differences in human capital or other job circumstances, such as employment in unfavorable industrial sectors or occupational categories. Consequently, Table 4 provides several logit models that evaluate the effects of race, net of education, age, industry, and occupation.

As shown in model 1, the logit coefficient of .552 for race suggests that the odds of underemployment among rural black men are about 1.74 (i.e., $e^{.552}$) times those of rural white men.[6] Moreover, the race coefficient is not substantially reduced in model 2, which includes the human capital variables of education and age. The odds of black underemployment are still 1.57 ($e^{.454}$) times those of whites. Finally, the inclusion of occupation and industry in model 3 has virtually no additional effect on black/white differences in overall

underemployment in Southern rural areas. As these results suggest, racial inequality in employment conditions in the rural South cannot be explained by
racial differences in human capital attributes or differences in the location
of blacks and whites across industrial and occupational sectors of the labor
force.[7] Although it would be a mistake to discount the effects of other characteristics excluded from this analysis (e.g., quality of schooling, job tenure,
etc.), the persistence of racial inequality reported here undoubtedly reflects
in part the continuing effects of racial discrimination in employment
opportunities found historically in the rural South.

Table 4. Logit Models of Underemployment in the Nonmetropolitan South,
1985.

	1		2		3	
	B	SE	B	SE	B	SE
Constant	-.892	.039	-1.192	.052	-1.336	.063
Race (Black=1)	.552	.039	.454	.041	.453	.042
Education:						
LT 12			.862	.058	.686	.064
12			-.028	.058	-.104	.061
13-15			-.204	.082	-.192	.084
Age:						
18-29			.478	.048	.446	.049
30-49			.234	.047	-.227	.048
Industry:						
Periphery					.395	.049
Trades					.004	.050
Occupation:						
Managerial and Professional					-.426	.095
Tech., Sales, Administrative Support					.068	.083
Likelihood Ratio x^2	530.86		236.19		124.73	
df	214		209		205	

As expected, the logit coefficients in model 3 clearly reveal the importance
of education, age, industry, and occupation in the allocation of workers into

the underemployment categories of the LUF. The likelihood of underemployment is greatest for those with less than 12 years of completed schooling (B = .686, or $e^{.686}$ = 1.99); the odds of underemployment among the less educated are twice those of other education groups. This effect exceeds that of age, with the odds of underemployment among those aged less than 30 being about one and one-half times the odds for other age groups ($e^{.446}$ = 1.56). Similarly, workers in the periphery sector are significantly more likely to be underemployed than are those working in other industrial sectors. Finally, and not surprisingly, those in managerial and professional speciality occupations are least likely to experience any of the forms of underemployment in the LUF, while the odds of underemployment among those working in nonwhite-collar positions (i.e., the reference category) are the greatest ($e^{-(-.426 + .068)}$ = 1.43).

Because the effects of human capital and job characteristics on labor market outcomes have been shown in the past to vary by race, Table 5 presents logit models separately for Southern rural blacks and whites. These results suggest several observations. First, it is clear that education is less strongly related to underemployment among blacks than among whites. For example, among the least educated, the odds of under employment are 1.8 times greater for blacks ($e^{.584}$ = 1.79), but over two times greater for whites ($e^{.719}$ = 2.05). This does not mean that poorly educated blacks are less disadvantaged than poorly educated whites (as previously shown in Table 4). Indeed, the implied logit coefficients for education further suggest that 16 or more years of schooling reduces the odds of underemployment to a greater extent among whites (B = -.419) than among blacks (B =-.226). "Returns" to education, in the form of reduced underemployment (or adequate employment), are clearly less in evidence for rural black men than they are for whites.

Although the effect of education on underemployment is stronger for whites than blacks, age effects are stronger for blacks. Among blacks, being young has a particularly strong positive effect on the likelihood of being underemployed (B = .630). Indeed, the odds of underemployment among young blacks is nearly twice ($e^{.630}$ = 1.89) those of blacks in other age categories, while the odds of underemployment are increased about one and one-half times among young whites ($e^{.393}$ = 1.48). Finally, the results indicate that industry and occupation are not strongly related to black underemployment. Unlike for whites, the experience of underemployment among black men has less to do with the structure of their employment—as indicated by their location across occupation and industry categories—than with their human capital attributes.

Table 5. Logit Models of Black and White Underemployment in the Non-metropolitan South, 1985.

	Blacks		Whites	
	B	SE	B	SE
Constant	-.105	.163	-1.796	.062
Education:				
LT 12	.584	.142	.719	.072
12	-.246	.144	-.075	.068
13-15	-.112	.194	-.225	.095
Age:				
18-29	.630	.108	.393	.056
30-49	-.177	.108	-.232	.054
Industry:				
Periphery	.156	.111	.462	.055
Trades	-.023	.109	.012	.057
Occupation:				
Managerial and Professional	-.209	.256	-.472	.104
Tech., Sales, Administrative Support	.264	.271	.120	.088
Likelihood Ratio x^2	28.29		104.42	
df	98		98	

DISCUSSION AND CONCLUSION

Despite the historic significance of race in the rural South, there have been surprisingly few attempts to document the changing labor market circumstances of Southern rural blacks. Past studies have had a decidedly urban bias, which is understandable given that a disproportionate share of blacks live in the nation's central cities. Past research has contributed greatly to renewed concerns about the urban black underclass and continuing racial inequality in U.S. cities (e.g., Wilson 1980). Unfortunately, rural blacks are less visible, more spatially dispersed, and easier to forget or simply ignore.

As shown in this chapter, studies of national or metropolitan trends in black underemployment and racial inequality do not adequately portray employment conditions experienced by blacks working in rural areas. The legacy of black employment hardship continues to be felt in rural areas of the South, where fully two out of every five black men are without jobs, cannot find a full-time job, or cannot earn enough to raise themselves much above poverty thresholds. Furthermore, there is little evidence that overall employment conditions of rural blacks have improved significantly since 1970.

Perhaps most surprising is that the work experiences of Southern rural blacks have converged with those of blacks living elsewhere, particularly with those in the North. This suggests that blacks may now be participating in the general narrowing of regional differences in standards of living and income which has characterized the overall population since at least mid-century (Poston and Weller, 1981). There is, however, at least one important distinction. Whereas overall regional convergence reflects relative gains made in Southern working conditions, the black regional convergence apparently reflects a relative deterioration in conditions for blacks working in the North. In fact, the recent shift of black population to the South, even to its nonmetropolitan parts, may have little to do with the pull of improved employment opportunities in Southern rural labor markets. Rather, the economic push of blacks from Northern metropolitan labor markets has apparently gained strength during the past decade or so.

Results presented here also reinforce claims that race continues to be an important axis of social differentiation and inequality in the South. Race remains a significant determinant of underemployment in Southern rural areas, and there is little indication that its significance will decline in the foreseeable future given the persistence of racial differences observed since 1970. Moreover, the continuing significance of race cannot be attributed to racial differences in human capital or to differences in the distribution of blacks and whites across occupational or industrial sectors. Racial differences in underemployment extend broadly across population subgroups, which suggests that investments in black human capital alone are not likely to eliminate inequality entirely. There is little basis here for discounting claims of continuing employment discrimination against blacks in the rural South (Walker, 1977).

Finally, the Southern economic optimism so widely evident in the 1970s— and even in the early 1980s—should be tempered by evidence of continuing racial inequality in rural areas. The post-1970 economic and employment boom in many Sunbelt states has not had tangible effects on those rural blacks on the bottom rungs of the socioeconomic ladder. Indeed, past concerns about the economically disadvantaged rural black population, which some regard as a continuing legacy of the Southern slave and plantation economy, remain as salient today as ever.

NOTES

[1]As described by Jaynes and Williams (1987), in the mid-1980s the National Research Council formed a Committee on the Status of Black Americans, which was charged with assessing recent social and economic gains of U.S. blacks. Five Committee panels, each comprised of eminent social scientists, are expected to soon release status reports on the following topics: (1) education, (2) employment, income, and occupations, (3) health status and demography of black Americans, (4) political participation and administration of justice; and (5) social and cultural change and continuity.

[2]For purposes of exposition, nonmetropolitan and rural are terms used interchangeably throughout this chapter.

[3]A common problem with analyzing CPS data over several years is the inability to adjust for changing designations of metropolitan and nonmetropolitan over time. Any evidence here of spatial convergence in employment hardship, however, is not likely to be an artifact of changing definitions. Instead, changes from nonmetropolitan to metropolitan are likely to have the effect of exacerbating metro-nonmetro differences in underemployment, if it is assumed that areas "growing up" to metropolitan status are likely to be more economically vital than those left behind. Changing definitions are likely to accentuate rather than reduce metro-nonmetro differences in underemployment. Indeed, as later shown, the employment circumstances of blacks in Southern nonmetropolitan areas appear to have improved relative to recent changes in metropolitan areas. Despite this reassuring finding, some caution nevertheless should be exercised in interpreting changes in underemployment since 1970.

[4]Here we refer to nonblacks as whites. Not only does this aid the discussion, but the vast majority of nonblacks in the nonmetropolitan South are white.

[5]Hodson's (1983) original classification scheme included 16 industrial sectors. For purposes of analysis, however, Hodson collapsed the 16 categories into six sectors. Periphery industries represents one of these sectors and includes those classified as periphery, small shop, and real estate from his 16-category scheme. Trades, as defined by Hodson, includes local monopoly, education and nonprofit, and agriculture industries. For specific detailed industry codes describing these categories, see Hodson (1983: Table 4.4, pp. 73-77).

[6]To aid interpretation, multiplicative effects on the odds of underemployment can be calculated by taking the natural antilogarithms of the logit coefficients (i.e., exponentiating the logit coefficients). Values exceeding 1.0 indicate an increased odds of underemployment, while values less than 1.0 indicate a decreased odds of underemployment.

The logit coefficients also can be used to estimate the probability of underemployment for any given labor force profile. Consider the following logit equation: $\log[P_i/(1-P_i)] = \Sigma B_k X_{ik} = Z_i$. Any probability, P_i, can be computed as $P_i = \exp(Z_i)/(1+\exp(Z_i))$. From Table 4 (model 1), $Z = -.892 + .552 = -.340$ for blacks. Hence, the probability of black underemployment is $e^{-.34}/(1 + e^{-.34})$ or .416. (Note that this is consistent with the 40.9 percent reported in Table 1 for rural blacks). Similarly, from Table 4 (model 2), the probability of being underemployed among young blacks with less than 12 years of education can be similarly calculated. That is, $Z = -1.192 + .452 + .862 + .478 = .148$, with the probability of underemployment calculated as $e^{.148}/(1 + e^{.148})$ or .537. This result, of course, provides striking evidence of the seriousness of underemployment for this population subgroup. Similar computations may be made for other profiles that are of special interest to the reader.

[7]In some additional analyses, the effects of regional location within the census-defined South were evaluated by distinguishing between the "Old South" and the rest of the South. Using the definition of Sly (1981), the Old South is comprised of seven states: Alabama, Mississippi, Georgia, Kentucky, Tennessee, South Carolina, and North Carolina. About 75 percent of all blacks lived in these seven states at the time of the emancipation. About 15 percent of all blacks lived in other Southern states. The inclusion of this residence variable in a logit model, along with the other variables in model 3 (Table 4), did not greatly effect the size of the logit coefficient for race. This suggests that black-white differentials in underemployment cannot be explained by the disproportionate concentration of nonmetropolitan blacks in Southern areas where blacks faced the greatest employment hardship historically.

REFERENCES

Clogg, Clifford C. 1979. *Measuring Underemployment: Demographic Indicators for the United States*. New York: Academic Press.

Clogg, Clifford C., and Teresa A. Sullivan. 1983. "Labor force composition and underemployment trends, 1969-1980." *Social Indicators Research* 12:117-152.

Dahmann, Donald C. 1986. *Geographic Mobility: March 1983 to March 1984*. Population Characteristics, Series P-20, No. 407. Washington, D.C.: U.S. Government Printing Office.

Deaton, Brady. 1986."Rural labor market linkages with metro, national, and international economies: Toward a research agenda." In Molly S. Killian, Leonard E. Bloomquist, Shelley Pendleton, and David A. McGranahan (editors), *Symposium on Rural Labor Markets Research Issues*. Washington, D.C.: U.S. Department of Agriculture.

Farley, Reynolds. 1984. *Blacks and Whites: Narrowing the Gap?* Cambridge, Massachusetts: Harvard University Press.

Fligstein, Neil. 1981. *Going North: Migration of Blacks and Whites From the South, 1900-1950*. New York: Academic Press.

Hanushek, Eric A., and John E. Jackson. 1977. *Statistical Methods for Social Scientists*. New York: Academic Press.

Hodson, Randy. 1983. *Workers' Earnings and Corporate Economic Structure*. New York: Academic Press.

Jaynes, Gerald D., and Robin M. Williams Jr. 1987. "Challenges and opportunities." *Society* 24(January/February):3-18.

Johnson, Daniel M., and Rex Campbell. 1981. *Black Migration in America*. Durham, North Carolina: Duke University Press.

Kasarda, John D. 1985. "Urban change and minority opportunities." In Paul E. Peterson (editor), *The New Urban Reality*. Washington, D.C.: The Brookings Institute.

Kasarda, John D., Michael D. Irwin, and Holly L. Hughes. 1986. "The South is still rising." *American Demographics* 8(December):32-39,70.

Korsching, Peter K., and Paul Lasley. 1986. "Problems in identifying rural unemployment." *The Rural Sociologist* 6:171-80.

Lichter, Daniel T. 1988. "Racial differences in underemployment in American cities." *American Journal of Sociology* 93(January):.

_____. 1987. "Measuring rural underemployment." *Rural Development Perspectives* 3:11-14.

_____. 1985. "Racial concentration and segregation across U.S. counties, 1950-1980." *Demography* 22:603-9.

Lichter, Daniel T., and Janice A. Costanzo. 1986. "Underemployment in nonmetropolitan areas, 1970 to 1982." In Joint Economic Committee of U.S. Congress (editor), *New Dimensions in Rural Policy: Building Upon Our Heritage*. Washington, D.C.: U.S. Government Printing Office.

_____. 1987. "Nonmetropolitan underemployment and labor force composition." *Rural Sociology* 52(Fall): 329-44.

Lichter, Daniel T., and Tim B. Heaton. 1986. "Black composition and change in the nonmetropolitan South." *Rural Sociology* 51:343-53.

Lyson, Thomas A., and William W. Falk. 1986. "Two sides of the Sunbelt: Economic development in the rural and urban South." In Joint Economic Committee of U.S. Congress (editor), *New Dimensions in Rural Policy: Building Upon Our Heritage*. Washington, D.C.: U.S. Government Printing Office.

Mandle, Jay R. 1978. *The Roots of Black Poverty*. Durham, North Carolina: Duke University Press.

Marshall, Ray. 1978. "The old South and the new." In Ray Marshall and Virgil L. Christian, Jr. (editors), *Employment of Blacks in the South*. Austin, Texas: University of Texas Press.

Marshall, Ray, and Virgil L. Christian, Jr. 1978. "South and non-South comparisons." In Ray Marshall and Virgin L. Christian, Jr. (editors), *Employment of Blacks in the South*. Austin, Texas: University of Texas Press.

Moland, John. 1981. "The Black population." In Amos H. Hawley and Sara Mills Mazie (editors), *Nonmetropolitan America in Transition*. Chapel Hill, North Carolina: University of North Carolina Press.

O'Hare, William, and Richard Engels. 1986. "Rural renaissance in the black belt." Paper presented at the annual meetings of the South Regional Demographic Group, Baltimore, Maryland.

Poston, Dudley L. Jr., and Robert H. Weller. 1981. *The Population of the South*. Austin, Texas: University of Texas Press.

Robinson, Isaac. 1986. "Blacks move back to the South." *American Demographics* 8(December):40-43.

Singelmann, Joachim. 1981. "Southern industrialization." In Dudley L. Poston Jr. and Robert H. Weller (editors), *The Population of the South*. Austin, Texas: University of Texas Press.

Sly, David F. 1981. "Migration." In Dudley L. Poston Jr. and Robert H. Weller (editors), *The Population of the South*. Austin, Texas: University of Texas Press.

Smith, James P., and Finis R. Welch. 1986. *Closing the Gap: Forty Years of Economic Progress for Blacks*. R-3330-DOL. Santa Monica, California: The Rand Corporation.

Sullivan, Teresa A. 1978. *Marginal Workers, Marginal Jobs*. Austin, Texas: University of Texas Press.

Tienda, Marta, and Ding-Tzann Lii. 1987. "Minority concentration and earnings inequality: Blacks, Hispanics, and Asians compared." *American Journal of Sociology* 93:141-65.

Tweeten, Luther. 1986. "Rural labor market performance." In Molly S. Killian, Leonard E. Bloomquist, Shelley Pendleton, and David A. McGranahan (editors), *Symposium on Rural Labor Markets Research Issues*. Washington, D.C.: U.S. Department of Agriculture.

U.S. Bureau of the Census. 1985. *Current Population Survey: March 1985 Demographic File*. Washington, D.C.: U.S. Bureau of the Census.

Walker, James L. 1977. *Economic Development and Black Employment in the Nonmetropolitan South*. Austin, Texas: Center for the Study of Human Resources, The University of Texas.

Wilson, William Julius. 1980. *The Declining Significance of Race (2nd edition)*. Chicago: University of Chicago Press.

13

The Effects of the Farm Crisis on Rural Communities and Community Residents

Don E. Albrecht
Steve H. Murdock

During the 1980s, three major events have occurred in agriculture that have resulted in the emergence of a severe farm financial crisis (U.S. Department of Agriculture, 1985). The first of these is falling land values. Until 1981, farmers had experienced four decades of virtually uninterrupted increases in farmland values. Based on the speculation that such trends would continue, land values had been bid to levels far above what their productive potential would warrant. Since 1981 when farmland prices peaked, land values have steadily dropped. By early 1986, land prices had declined by an average of 29 percent nationwide, and by as much as 59 percent in some Corn Belt states such as Iowa and Nebraska (Brooks et al., 1986). As a result of these eroding land values, the debt levels that some farmers had assumed during the 1970s were no longer sustainable, especially for those farmers whose financial solvency depended on continuously rising land values or who had pursued an aggressive expansion strategy (U.S. Department of Agriculture, 1985).

A second factor leading to the current farm crisis is the record high interest rates that were prevalent during the early 1980s (Ginder et al., 1985). Throughout the 1970s, farmers had responded to accelerating inflation by borrowing heavily to invest in new capital equipment, to adopt new production technologies, and to purchase increasingly expensive farmland. The much higher real interest rates of the 1980s made it increasingly difficult for farmers to repay such loans (Walden, 1982).

The last major factor leading to the farm crisis is the relatively low commodity prices that have been prevalent during the past few years. Declining export markets and increased farm production have resulted in much lower real commodity prices than those of the 1970s, consequently, farmers' incomes have declined considerably (Goodwin and Jones, 1986).

As a result of these factors, the financial condition of many farm operators in the United States has deteriorated significantly, and it appears that farmers are experiencing their worst financial crisis since the Great Depression (Bultena et al., 1986; Murdock et al., 1986). This farm crisis is having major effects on rural America, and is the focus of a growing body of research. To date, much of the farm crisis research has focused on the farm operators and has been concerned with determining the characteristics of farmers most and least likely to experience financial stress (Albrecht et al., 1987a; Bultena et al., 1986; Campbell et al, 1984; Jolly, 1984; Leholm et al., 1985; Murdock et al., 1985; 1986; Schotsch, 1985). A few studies also have examined the consequences of the farm crisis on the personal lives of farm operators and their families (Albrecht et al., 1987b; Blundall, 1985; Hargrove, 1986; Heffernan and Heffernan, 1986; Rossman and Joslin, 1985). These studies have generally concluded that because of the farm crisis, many farm operators will be forced to leave agriculture, many of those remaining will experience severe financial stress which will affect the way the farm is managed and the family's level of living, and many farm people will experience major problems with psychological and family stress that may have lasting effects.

It has also been assumed by many writers, especially those of the popular press, that the farm crisis will have major implications for the residents and businesses in agriculturally-based rural communities. There are several reasons that such community impacts are expected. First, the farm crisis is likely to result in a reduction of the farm population, and fewer people mean a reduced clientele for local businesses. Although the farmland that was operated by persons leaving agriculture will be farmed by other individuals, most likely there will be fewer persons farming. A second factor is that many remaining farmers have reduced buying power that will result in their postponing capital purchases and in reducing their families' living expenses. This reduced spending will negatively effect community businesses. Third, the events described above will have a negative multiplier effect on the economies of rural communities.

While there is reason to expect that extensive community effects will occur in agriculturally-based rural communities as a result of the farm crisis, there is little empirical research to verify the actual presence of such hypothesized effects (Korsching and Gildner, 1986; Leistritz and Ekstrom, 1986). Actual empirical research is limited and only a few studies of the impacts of the farm crisis in rural communities have been completed (Doeksen, 1987; Ginder et al., 1985; Murdock et al., 1987; Heffernan and Heffernan, 1986). Those that have been completed have tended to be analyses of either a very small number of respondents (Heffernan and Heffernan, 1986), or a single community (Doeksen, 1987; Murdock et al., 1987). Studies of the effects of the crisis on respondents from multiple communities simply have not been completed.

A further problem in determining the effects of the farm crisis on rural communities is that the historical base of evidence linking agricultural structure and changes therein to transformations in rural communities is far from conclusive (Leistritz and Ekstrom, 1986). Much of the research on agriculture and community interdependence is based on Goldschmidt's study of the towns of Arvin and Dinuba in California (Goldschmidt, 1946; 1978). From his analysis, Goldschmidt concluded that a structure of agriculture in which smaller sized farms predominated was best for the preservation of the quality of life in a rural community, while larger production units had less positive effects. Over the years, numerous studies have attempted to test Goldschmidt's basic premise (Eberts, 1979; Flora et al., 1977; Gilles et al., 1984; Green, 1985; Harris and Gilbert, 1982; Heffernan, 1972; Heffernan and Lasley, 1978; La Rose, 1973; LeVeen, 1979; Poole, 1981; Small Farm Viability Project, 1977; Sonka, 1979), with some generally supporting it (e.g., Heffernan and Lasley, 1978; LeVeen, 1979; Poole, 1981), and others finding results that contradict those of Goldschmidt (e.g., Flora et al., 1977; Green, 1985; Harris and Gilbert, 1982; Heffernan, 1972).

One likely reason for the inconsistencies of past research on the relationship between agriculture and the community is the tendency to simplify a very complex relationship. Most researchers have failed to consider some of the numerous factors that could influence the relationship between farm size and community viability. For example, there are several agricultural factors in addition to farm size that have important influences on nearby rural communities, but which seldom have been considered. Some of these include the presence or absence of corporate farms, the tenure structure of farms, and extent of off-farm employment. Further, researchers have failed to account for the potential implications of the type of commodities being produced in an area.

Another critical factor that has not been considered in the past is the extent to which the community is economically dependent on agriculture. In some rural areas, agriculture employs only a small proportion of the total workforce, and changes that occur in agriculture in such areas may be of little consequence for the community. In contrast, changes in agriculture may have profound effects in communities that are economically dependent on agriculture.

In sum, past research on the relationship between agriculture and the rural community has not examined many critical factors. Thus, relationships that have been found may actually be a result of other factors not considered. Consequently, this literature provides little theoretical basis or empirical results to help us understand the potential impact of the farm crisis on rural communities. Equally problematic is the fact that much of the current and historical literature has examined only a limited number of dimensions of the community that are likely to be affected by changes in agriculture. For example, few available studies have assessed the effects of changes in farm structure on the personal lives of nonfarm community residents who are dependent on the rural community for their livelihood.

In this chapter, we attempt to address both the lack of multi-community studies of the impacts of the farm crisis (and agricultural change in general) on rural community residents, and the paucity of information on residents' perceptions of the impacts of the farm crisis on their communities and their personal lives. This is done by reporting the results of an analysis of such impacts in three agriculturally-dependent communities in North and West Texas. Results from 300 respondents (100 in each of the three communities) are examined in relation to respondents' perceived impacts of the farm crisis on their communities and their personal lives.

In the analysis we describe the range and magnitude of effects perceived to have occurred by residents in these three communities. This provides an empirical evaluation of the effects which have often been assumed to be occurring as a result of the farm crisis, but have seldom been empirically examined. In addition, because these communities have different levels of economic dependence on agriculture, we attempt to improve our understanding of the relationship between agriculture and the community by comparing the effects of the farm crisis under these varying conditions. Specifically, we test the hypothesis that community residents' perceptions of the severity of the effects of the crisis (both in terms of community and personal effects) will be directly related to the dependence of the respondents' community of residence on agriculture. This is assessed both by crosstabular analysis and by the use of multiple regression analysis.

METHODS

Selection of Communities

To examine the implications of the farm crisis on rural communities, three rural communities in North and West Texas were selected for analysis. These communities were selected because they are about the same size (between 2,200 and 3,400 residents in 1980), and are located in rural, agriculturally-based counties. However, the communities differ in the type of agricultural enterprises that are located nearby and in the extent to which they are dependent on agriculture.

Table 1 presents information on the three study communities and the counties within which the three communities are located from the 1980 Census of Population and the 1982 Census of Agriculture. For this table, community level data are used when available. However, the county is the smallest geographic unit for which Census of Agriculture data are available. This table shows that the percent of the labor force employed in agriculture is greatest in Community A (32.1 percent) and least in Community C (16.4 percent), with Community B being intermediate (24.9 percent). The median family income and the median family income of the farm population were substantially higher in Community B when compared with the other two communities, while the percent in poverty in Community B was substantially lower. On each of these income variables, Community A was in worse condition than Community C.

In examining some of the characteristics of agriculture in the counties that the three communities are located, differences are again apparent. Gross farm sales in Community B are substantially greater than in the other communities. An extensive amount of these farm sales in Community B are from several large cattle feedlots that are located near the community. Consequently, less than 14 percent of the total farm sales in Community B are from crops. In contrast, most (86.8 percent) of the farm sales in Community A are from crops, while farm sales are almost evenly divided between crop and livestock sources in Community C. Most of the farmland in Community A is devoted to cotton production. Table 1 also shows that a relatively large proportion of the farm operators in Community C (44.6 percent) have off-farm employment. In contrast, few farmers in Community A (18 percent) have off-farm employment, while the proportion in Community B is intermediate (27.8 percent). Community C is the location of a relatively large manufacturing firm that provides employment to many community residents and some farm operators. Community A is located about 40 miles from the nearest urban center (Lubbock), Community B is located about 100 miles from one (Amarillo), and Community C is located about 50 miles from the nearest urban center (Abilene).

Based on these community and farm characteristics, it is expected that while the farm crisis will have important consequences for all three study communities, the impacts will have the most severe effects in Community A. Of the three communities, Community A is the most economically dependent on agriculture as is evident by the larger proportion of their labor force that is employed in agriculture. In addition, many residents of the county where Community A is located were in unstable economic conditions prior to the farm crisis. This is shown by the fact that their median incomes are low and many had incomes below the poverty level. Further, the farmers in Community A are primarily dependent on crop production. Previous farm crisis research has shown that farmers producing crops have tended to be affected more negatively by the farm crisis than have livestock producers (Murdock et al, 1986). Also, few Community A farmers have off-farm employment that could serve to cushion them from the financial crisis in agriculture. Further, there are few opportunities for them to obtain off-farm employment within the county.

Community C is expected to be the least affected by the farm crisis because the county is less economically dependent on agriculture a high proportion

Table 1
Comparison of the Social, Economic, and Farm Characteristics
of the Three Study Communities (1980-1982)

Characteristic	Community A	Community B	Community C
County Population	8,859	6,209	11,872
Community Population	2,289	3,413	3,061
Percent employed in agriculture	32.1%	24.9%	16.4%
Median family income	$13,071	$21,124	$14,737
Median family income of farm population	$12,193	$26,429	$15,528
Percent below poverty level	28.5%	10.7%	19.9%
Gross farm sales ($1,000)	$25,549	$194,651	$31,104
Percent from crops	86.8%	13.6%	45.3%
Percent of farm operators with 100 or more days of off-farm employment	18.0%	27.8%	44.6%

of the farmers in the county have off-farm employment to shield them from the impacts of the farm crisis. The impacts of the farm crisis should be inter- mediate on Community B. Community B is between Community A and Com- munity C on the extent to which its residents are economically dependent on agriculture, and also on the proportion of its farm operators with off-farm employment. In addition, Community B residents and farmers were relatively well off financially in 1980, which should provide an economic cushion for them as they deal with the farm crisis. Further, most of the farmers are livestock producers which should mean that they will not be impacted as severely by the farm crisis as crop producers.

Selection of Respondents

A total of 100 randomly selected community residents were interviewed by telephone in each of the three study communities during the March to June 1987 time period. The names of potential respondents were drawn randomly from the local telephone directory. The bias from this approach should be limited because nearly every household in each community has a telephone, and in rural areas there are few unlisted telephone numbers. Persons selected for the study were interviewed only if they were not operating a farm or ranch at the time of the interview, if they were less than 65 years of age, and if they were residing within the boundaries of the town or city. Over 80 percent of those contacted who were eligible for the study completed the interview in each community.

Data Analysis

To compare the consequences of the farm crisis as perceived by residents in these communities, crosstabulations were run and the chi-square statistic was utilized to determine if the differences between the communities were statistically significant. Comparisons were made initially on the extent to which residents perceived their community as having been affected by the farm crisis, and on what some of these community effects had been. Following this, comparisons were made of the personal effects of the farm crisis on residents of the three communities and on their immediate families.

In addition to the crosstabular analysis, multiple regression analysis was completed to examine the extent to which respondents' perceptions of the impacts of the crisis were a product of individual factors rather than structural and other conditions likely to have resulted from the structure of agriculture surrounding the community. In this analysis, individual demographic and socioeconomic characteristics (age, education, and income), and dummy variables indicating the city of residence are used to examine the relative effects of various factors on perceptions. It is possible that differences found between the communities may be due to variations in these demographic and socioeconomic characteristics. Thus, the intent of this analysis is to more completely test the effects of alternative factors on respondents' perceptions.

FINDINGS

Perceptions of Community Effects

In Table 2, data are presented in which residents of the three communities are compared on the extent to which they perceive that their community has been affected by the farm crisis. Respondents were initially asked whether their community had been affected a great deal, some, or not at all by the farm crisis. Survey results revealed that a majority of the residents in all three communities thought that their community had been affected a great deal by the farm crisis. Only a few respondents felt that their community had not been affected at all. Significant differences were also found in the responses of residents in the various communities. As expected, the proportion of Community A residents (88 percent) who thought that their community had been affected a great deal by the farm crisis was higher than in either Community B (70 percent) or Community C (61 percent).

In an open-ended question respondents were also asked to list some of the ways that their community had been impacted by the farm crisis. In all three communities, residents were most likely to mention employment problems (no jobs available, people losing their jobs, being forced to migrate from the community, etc.) and negative effects on local businesses. Community A residents were the most likely to mention employment problems, while Community B residents were the most inclined to mention the problems experienced by the local businesses.

The final variable shown in Table 2 presents the results of a question that asked the respondents how many local businesses had closed as a result of the

the farm crisis. About one-third of the respondents in each community thought that five or more businesses had closed recently as a direct outgrowth of the crisis. However, Community C residents, followed by Community B residents were more likely to state that the number was two or less. Community A residents, on the other hand, were more likely to believe that over two businesses had closed in their community, suggesting that the residents of this community perceived the impacts of the farm crisis to be much more severe.

Table 2

Comparison of the Community and Business Effects of the Farm Crisis on the Local Community as Perceived by Community Residents (Percents)

Effect	Community A	Community B	Community C
Extent to which community has been effected by farm crisis*			
A great deal	88	70	61
Some	12	28	30
Not at all	0	2	9
Effects of the farm crisis that were mentioned*			
Employment down/people have to move	33	16	14
Local businesses negatively affected	43	59	53
Other	24	25	33
Number of businesses closed as a result of farm crisis*			
2 or less	29	32	42
3-4	37	35	22
5 or more	34	33	36

*Differences between the communities are statistically significant at the .05 level.

In sum, residents in all three study communities felt that their community had been affected a great deal by the farm crisis. Further, as expected, the residents of Community A were more likely than the residents of the other two communities to view their community as having been affected a great deal by the farm crisis. Community C residents were the least likely to perceive such extensive effects. In addition, Community A residents were the most likely to state that employment opportunities had been reduced by the farm crisis, and as a result, some people were having to move away. Community A residents were also the least likely to perceive that two or fewer local businesses had closed as a result of the farm crisis.

Perceptions of Individual Effects

In addition to their perceptions about the effects of the farm crisis on their community, we are also concerned about how the farm crisis is affecting the personal lives of nonfarm rural community residents. In Table 3, data are presented in which the residents of the three communities are compared on the perceived affects of the farm crisis on their personal lives. First, survey respondents were asked whether their personal lives had been affected a great deal, some, or not at all by the farm crisis. Overall, about one in five respondents said that their life had been affected a great deal by the farm crisis. In contrast, about one-third noted that they had not been affected at all by the farm crisis. As expected, a larger proportion of Community A residents (33 percent), compared to the residents of the other two communities (18 percent of Community B and 11 percent of Community C residents), stated that their lives had been affected a great deal by the farm crisis.

Survey respondents also were read a list of events that could occur as a result of the farm crisis, and asked whether these events had recently occurred in their lives or those in their immediate relatives, and whether the occurrence of such events was an outgrowth of the farm crisis. The percent by community who had experienced each event as a result of the farm crisis is shown in the bottom panel of Table 3. An examination of the data shows that of the eight items examined, differences among residents of the three communities were statistically significant on seven items. There were no differences between communities on the percent who were experiencing unusual marital or family stress as a result of the farm crisis (16 percent in each community). On the remaining seven items, Community A residents were the most likely to have experienced five of the events, namely, lost a farm, lost a business, lost a job, los a major possession, or suffered depression or other emotional problems. Community B residents were the most likely to have had a reduction of pay or benefits, or been divorced or separated. Overall, the farm crisis-related events most commonly experienced by the residents of the three study communities included having a reduction of pay or benefits (45 percent), losing a job (31 percent), and suffering from depression or other emotional problems (22 percent).

In sum, survey results reveal that the farm crisis had affected the personal lives of persons in rural agriculturally-dependent communities. Further, the residents of communities with greater economic dependence on agriculture were the most likely to have stated that their lives had been affected a great deal by the farm crisis. Although the evidence was not overwhelming, Community A residents were the most likely to have experienced a number of negative events in their own lives or the lives of their immediate relatives as a result of the farm crisis.

The Relative Effects of Personal and Area Characteristics on the Perceptions of Rural Community Residents

It could be argued that the variations found among the residents of the three communities relative to their perceptions about the impacts of the farm crisis could be a result of differences in the composition of the population in the communities, and not a result of the economic or farm-related conditions in the communities. To test for such effects, a multiple regression analysis was completed. Dummy variables were used to represent the communities and several personal characteristics of the respondents (age, education, and income). Two dependent variables were utilized in this analysis: (1) the respondents' perceptions of the overall effects of the farm crisis on the community; and (2) their perceptions of the overall effects of the farm crisis on their personal lives.

Table 3
Comparison of the Perceived Personal Effects of the Farm Crisis by Community (Percents)

Personal Effect	Community A	Community B	Community C
Extent to which personal life has been effected by the farm crisis*			
A great deal	33	18	11
Some	39	45	42
Not at all	28	37	47
Percent of respondents or immediate relatives who have recently experienced the following events as a result of the farm crisis			
Lost a farm*	11	5	6
Lost a business*	14	8	8
Lost a job*	34	25	34
Had a reduction of pay or benefits*	39	50	45
Lost a major possession*	12	7	7
Suffered depression or other emotional problems*	26	23	18
Experienced unusual marital or family stress	16	16	16
Been divorced or separated*	9	16	10

*Differences between the communities are statistically significant at the .05 level.

The results of this analysis are presented in Table 4. These data generally confirm the results of the earlier analysis. Even when controlling for the effects of the respondents' personal characteristics, the dummy variable representing Community A residents was the strongest variable in the analysis for both dependent variables. Age and education also were significantly related to the residents' perceptions of community effects. None of the individual variables were significantly related to perceptions of the personal effects of the farm crisis. Overall, this set of independent variables explained only a small proportion of the variation in the dependent variables. However, the fact that the community of residence was the strongest predictor variable suggests that the differences found among the communities, relative to their perceptions of the effects of the farm crisis, were real.

Table 4

Standardized Regression Coefficients and R-Square of Community of
Residence and Individual Variables on Perceptions of the
Effects of the Farm Crisis

| | Dependent Variables | |
Independent Variables	Effects on Community	Personal Effects
Dummy 1 (Community A)	.26*	.25*
Dummy 2 (Community B)	.06	.07
Respondent's Age	.13*	-.08
Respondent's Education	.15*	.05
Family Income	.04	.10
Model R²	.10*	.07*

*Statistically significant at the .05 level.

CONCLUSIONS

For more than 40 years, social scientists have been concerned with the influence that agricultural structure and changes therein have on rural communities. More recently, an extensive amount of research has been directed
toward understanding the causes and consequences of the financial crisis in
American agriculture. By utilizing the experiences of communities as they
respond to the farm crisis, it may be possible to improve our understanding
of the relationship between agriculture and the community.

In this study, a random sample of residents in three rural communities in
North and West Texas were interviewed to determine the perceived effects of
the farm crisis on their community and their own personal lives. It was found
that the farm crisis is having major impacts on the lives of many individuals
not directly involved in agricultural production. More than 60 percent of the
respondents in each of the three study communities reported that their community had been affected a great deal by the farm crisis. In addition, a substantial minority of the respondents reported that the farm crisis had caused
important personal effects in their own lives or those of close family members.

Also, it was found that the impacts of the farm crisis appear to be greatest
in communities that are more economically dependent on agriculture. On the
host of variables examined, it was found that the effects of the farm crisis were
greatest in Community A and least in Community C, with Community B being intermediate. This directly corresponds with the dependence of these communities on agriculture.

From this study, it tentatively can be concluded that the farm crisis is having important effects on rural communities and their residents. Further, relationships between agriculture and the community are greatest in areas that

are most economically dependent on agricultural production. This clearly suggests that rural communities with high dependence on agriculture are likely to have extensive needs for financial and personal counseling services not only for their agricultural producers, but for their nonfarm residents as well.

A great deal of additional research is needed on both the effects of the farm crisis and the relationship between agriculture and rural communities. Ideally, research of this nature would use a longitudinal framework so that the impacts could be traced over time. Obviously, the communities in the present study were different to begin with, and the variations that were found may be a result of these initial differences. Further, this study examined the respondents perceptions of the effects of the farm crisis. The extent to which perceptions represent reality is an important concern. Despite these problems, it is evident from this study that for many areas, the farm crisis is not merely a farm problem, but a crisis for rural society.

REFERENCES

Albrecht, Don E., Steve H. Murdock, Rita R. Hamm, and Kathy L. Schiflett. 1987a. *The Farm Crisis in Texas: Changes in the Financial Condition of Texas Farmers and Ranchers, 1985-86.* Department of Rural Sociology Technical Report 87-3. College Station: The Texas Agricultural Experiment Station.

_____. 1987b. *Farm Crisis: Impact on Producers and Rural Communities in Texas.* Department of Rural Sociology Technical Report 87-5. College Station: The Texas Agricultural Experiment Station.

Blundall, J. 1985. "Community and family: responding to immediate needs." Paper presented at the Governor's Conference on Agriculture in Transition: Impact upon the Family, the Community, and the Economy, Des Moines, Iowa.

Brooks, Nora L., Thomas A. Stucker and Jennifer A. Bailey. 1986. "Income and well-being of farmers and the farm financial crisis." *Rural Sociology* 51(4):391-405.

Bultena, Gordon, Paul Lasley and Jack Geller. 1986. "The farm crisis: patterns and impacts of financial distress among Iowa farm families." *Rural Sociology* 51(4):436-448.

Campbell, Rex R., William D. Heffernan and Jere L. Gilles. 1984. "Farm operator cycles and farm debt: an accident of timing." *The Rural Sociologist* 4(6):404-8.

Doeksen, Gerald A. 1987. "The agricultural crisis as it affects rural communities." *Journal of the Community Development Society* 18(1):78-88.

Eberts, Paul. 1979. "The changing structure of agriculture and its effects on community life in northeastern U.S. counties." Paper presented at the annual meeting of the Rural Sociological Society, Burlington, Vermont.

Flora, Jan L., Ivan Brown and Judith Lee Conby. 1977. "Impact of type of agriculture on class structure, social well-being, and inequities." Paper presented at the annual meeting of the Rural Sociological Society, Madison, Wisconsin.

Gilles, Jere L., Don Hirschi, Rex Campbell and William Heffernan. 1984. "Agricultural change and quality of life in three major land resource regions: a correlation analysis." Paper presented at the annual meeting of the Rural Sociological Society, College Station, Texas.

Ginder, Roger G., Kenneth E. Stone and Daniel Otto. 1985. "Impact of the farm financial crisis on agribusiness firms and rural communities." *American Journal of Agricultural Economics* 67(5):1184-90.

Goldschmidt, Walter. 1946. *Small Business and the Community: A Study in Central Valley of California on Effects of Scale of Farm Operation.* Report to the Special Committee to Study Problems of American Small Business, United States Senate, December 23.

_____. 1978. *As You Sow: Three Studies in the Social Consequences of Agribusiness.* Montclair, New Jersey: Allanheld, Osmun and Co.

Goodwin, H.L., Jr. and Lonnie L. Jones. 1986. "The importance of off-farm income in the United States." *The Rural Sociologist* 6(4):272-279.

Green, Gary P. 1985. "Large-scale farming and the quality of life in rural communities: further specification of the Goldschmidt hypothesis." *Rural Sociology* 50(2):262-274.

Hargrove, David S. 1986. "Mental health response to the farm foreclosure crisis." *The Rural Sociologist* 6(2):88-95.

Harris, Craig K. and Jess Gilbert. 1982. "Large-scale farming, rural income, and Goldschmidt's agrarian thesis." *Rural Sociology* 47(3):449-458.

Heffernan, William D. 1972. "Sociological dimensions of agricultural structure in the United States." *Sociologia Ruralis* 12(3/4):481-499.

Heffernan, William D. and Judith B. Heffernan. 1986. "Impact of the farm crisis on rural families and communities." *The Rural Sociologist* 6(3):160-170.

Heffernan, William D. and Paul Lasley. 1978. "Agricultural structure and interaction in the local community: a case study." *Rural Sociology* 43(3):348-361.

Jolly, Robert W. 1984. "Microeconomic characteristics of farm debt." *Financial Stress in Agriculture.* Proceedings of a workshop at the Kansas City Federal Reserve Bank, Kansas City, Mo.

Korsching, Peter F. and Judith Gildner (eds.). 1986. *Interdependencies of Agriculture and Rural Communities in the Twenty-first Century.* Conference Proceedings, Ames, Iowa: The North Central Regional Center for Rural Development.

La Rose, Bruce. 1973. "Arvin and Dinuba revisited: a new look at community structure and the effects of scale of operation." Pp. 4076-4083 in Select Committee on Small Business, U.S. Senate (ed.), *Role of Giant Corporations.* Hearings before the subcommittee on Monopoly of the Select Committee on Small Business, U.S. Senate. Washington, D.C.: U.S. Government Printing Office.

Leholm, Arlen G., F. Larry Leistritz, Brenda Ekstrom and Harvey G. Vreugdenhill. 1985. *Potential Secondary Effects of Farm Financial Stress in North Dakota.* Department of Agricultural Economics Report No. 199. Fargo: North Dakota State University.

Leistritz, F. Larry and Brenda L. Ekstrom. 1986. *Interdependencies of Agriculture and Rural Communities: An Annotated Bibliography.* New York: Garland Publishing, Inc.

Murdock, Steve H., Rita R. Hamm, Don E. Albrecht, John K. Thomas and Janelle Johnson. 1985. *The Farm Crisis in Texas: An Examination of the Characteristics of Farmers and Ranchers Under Fincial Stress in Texas.* Department of Rural Sociology Technical Report 85-2. College Station: The Texas Agricultural Experiment Station.

Murdock, Steve H., Don E. Albrecht, Rita R. Hamm, F. Larry Leistritz and Arlen G. Leholm. 1986. "The farm crisis in the Great Plains: implications for theory and policy development." *Rural Sociology* 51(4):406-435.

Murdock, Steve H., F. Larry Leistritz, Arlen G. Leholm, Rita R. Hamm and Don E. Albrecht. 1987. "Impacts of the farm crisis on a rural community." *Journal of the Community Development Society* 18(1):30-49.

Poole, Dennis L. 1981. "Farm scale, family life, and community participation. *Rural Sociology* 46:112-127.

Rossman, Michael P. and Frances J. Joslin. 1985. "Mental health assistance to farm crisis victims." Paper presented at the Annual Conference of the Iowa Council on Family Relations, Des Moines, Iowa.

Schotsch, Linda. 1985. "Who will farm in five years?" *Farm Journal* 109:13-15.

Small Farm Viability Project. 1977. *The Family Farm in California: Report of the Small Farm Viability Project.* Sacramento, California: Small Farm Viability Project.

Sonka, Steve T. 1979. "Consequences of farm structural change." Report prepared for the Project on a Research Agenda for Small Farms. Washington, D.C.: National Rural Center.

United States Department of Agriculture. 1985. *The Current Financial Condition of Farmers and Farm Lenders.* Economic Research Service, Agricultural Information Bulletin Number 490, Washington, D.C.: U.S. Department of Agriculture.

Walden, M.L. 1982. *Lessons Farmers Can Learn From Economic Hard Times.* AG-294, Raleigh, North Carolina: North Carolina State University.

14

Community Forces and Their Influence on Farm Structure

Lionel J. Beaulieu
Michael K. Miller
David Mulkey

The farm financial crisis of the 1980s has introduced severe hardships to rural communities dependent on agriculture for their economic vitality (Heffernan and Heffernan, 1986a; Mueller, 1986; Murdock et al., 1987). Its effects have been observed across a number of arenas. Agribusiness firms, as providers of important support services for the farm community, have suffered appreciable declines in their economic health (Hines et al., 1986; Tubbs, 1985), lending institutions have been rocked with increasing numbers of problem agricultural loans (Green et al., 1986; Melichar and Irwin, 1985; Milkove et al., 1986), and with a declining demand for goods and services, local retail establishments have witnessed a steady erosion in their volume of sales (Dillman, 1986; Ginder et al., 1985). As a result, the property tax base of many rural communities has been seriously strained, placing local government officials in a quandary regarding the maintenance of important public services (Green et al., 1986; Heffernan and Heffernan, 1986b). Recognizing the bond between the farm sector and the local community, a recent U.S. Senate Subcommittee report declared that the farm economic crisis, in combination with reduced federal and state aid, has placed many of the nation's rural communities under stress that is unmatched since the Great Depression (U.S. Senate, 1986).

However, the notion that the farm sector has important impacts on the local community is not an issue of recent vintage. Rather, since the early works of Goldschmidt (1947), much effort has been directed at exploring the influences of farm level characteristics (e.g., scale of farm operations) on the quality of life of rural communities (see Goss and Rodefeld, 1977; Green, 1985; Heffernan, 1981; Leistritz and Ekstrom, 1986; Skees and Swanson, 1988; Small Farm Viability Project, 1977). But, despite the well-developed body of literature on this subject, there is a paucity of information regarding the effects of community level forces on the farm sector (Buttel, 1983; Deaton, 1986; Swanson, 1982). Clearly, the absence of such information impedes efforts to identify the full range of local strategies available for enhancing the viability of the agricultural sector. Logic would dictate that efforts to assist the farm sector during this "crisis" period must move beyond "on farm" solutions. Consideration must be given to approaches that show sensitivity to the broader community context in which agriculture functions.

In this chapter, a framework is offered that provides a beginning point for systematically assessing the effects of key community changes on the local farm sector. In addition, empirical testing of selected aspects of the conceptual model is undertaken using secondary data on all counties in the South. Results are interpreted in terms of the model's utility in helping articulate the nature of the ties between the community and its agricultural sector. Finally, implications of our findings in the context of the current farm financial crisis are presented.

UNDERSTANDING COMMUNITY/FARM LINKAGES: A PROPOSED MODEL

Although fragmented, factors that influence the local agricultural sector have been given some treatment in the social science literature. For example, population change, economic development initiatives, land use management, and shifting values of local residents, have been singled out as elements impacting the farm community (see Breimyer, 1977; Deaton, 1986; Harper et al., 1980; Magleby and Gadsby, 1979; Penn, 1979). While a diversity of forces have been recognized, little has been done to systematically consider these forces within an integrated framework.

A conceptual model that incorporates key community forces and their possible consequences for the farm sector is presented in Figure 1. In this paradigm, detailed more fully by Beaulieu and Mulkey (1985), changes within the farm group are viewed as the end result of a set of interrelationships occurring within the community. The model suggests that the structure of the farm enterprise is influenced by three key elements of the local arena—a SOCIOECONOMIC COMPONENT that considers the sociodemographic and economic characteristics of the locality, a COMMUNITY VALUES COMPONENT that embodies the normative structure of the local population, and a LOCAL GOVERNMENT COMPONENT that reflects the usual taxing, spending, and regulatory activities of government. Changes in any of these components may be transmitted directly to the farm sector. These forces may also indirectly affect the welfare of local farmers by spurring changes in the price or availability of INPUTS that are vital to the farming community and by providing a wider range of non-farm employment alternatives for farm families. In this chapter, we explore the impact that local SOCIOECONOMIC and INPUTS factors have on the structure of local farms.[1]

For purposes of this chapter, the farm sector is assumed to consist of farmers or farm families which are atomistic, maximizing units producing commodities for sale in markets in competition with other producers of the same items. It is recognized that even in similar situations, different farms will not respond in like fashion (Patterson and Marshall, 1984). Nonetheless, the economic health of the farm relative to that of other farms producing the same products is a critical factor determining the nature and long-run viability of the farming enterprise.

How might farmers be affected by community changes? For one, such forces may influence the cost structure of farm operations in a particular community relative to farms producing similar products elsewhere, or community change may affect prices received by farmers for various commodities. Both can result in farm income changes. For instance, population expansion (which represents one aspect of the socioeconomic dimension of the community) may increase demand for locally produced agricultural products, and thus, contribute positively to farm income. On the other hand, such growth may intensify demand for land (a key farm input) and spur increases in the cost structure of the farm (since land prices are likely to accerelate under these conditions).

Community shifts may also influence farm family income by changing the opportunity costs of farm labor. Growth in the nonfarm economy of the community, for example, may generate more lucrative employment alternatives for farm family members. The subsequent reduction in family labor available to farm may prompt changes in the mix of commodities produced (perhaps to less labor intensive activities as posited by Deaton (1986) and Leistritz et al. (1982)), in the scale of operation (a change in farm size or a switch from full-time to part-time farming), or in the level of dependence on nonfamily labor resources.

In sum, the model argues that socioeconomic changes within the community may directly or indirectly influence the structure of the farm sector by affecting the comparative cost structure of the farm and/or the opportunity costs of farm labor. That is, local community forces may alter the price or availability of key inputs (such as land), prompt structural shifts in the scale of the farm operation (increases, decreases, or move to part-time), and/or alter the farm enterprise's reliance on labor resources (such as hired labor or

Figure 1

A Model of Community/Farm Sector Linkages

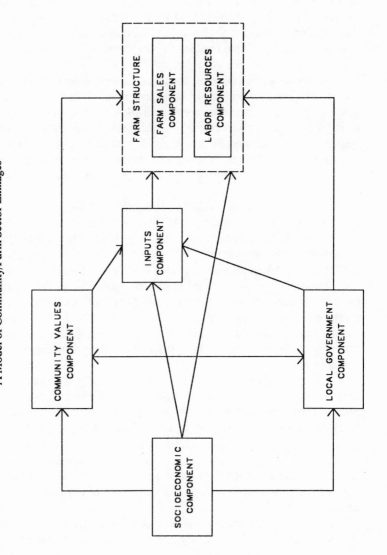

capital equipment). An important caveat, however, is that the exact nature of the impact will depend on the type of shift that is taking place, on the existing stock of community resources, and on the type of agriculture prevalent in the local area.[2]

Two specific questions serve to guide the empirical analysis undertaken in this chapter:

- Do shifts in the socioeconomic structure of a community result in direct effects on the agricultural sector, as reflected in the scale of operation and expenditures for labor resources?

- Do key inputs (such as the price and availability of land, or the availability of off-farm employment) mediate the impact of the socioeconomic structure of the community on the farm sector?

By addressing these questions, one can begin to develop a better understanding of the strength of the ties that exist between the community and its farm sector. In addition, the knowledge gained can serve as an important ingredient in delineating possible strategies for dealing with the financial crisis currently affecting many farmers in the Southern region of the United States.

AN OVERVIEW OF THE LITERATURE

There is evidence to support the notion that the farm sector is directly impacted by changes in the community's socioeconomic structure. For example, moderate increases in the number of small scale farm operators have been found to be influenced, in part, by growth in the local population (Harper et al., 1980). The numerical expansion of small farm enterprises is believed to be rooted in the intrinsic rewards that newcomers associate with farming (Coughenour and Gabbard, 1977) or in the simple desire that people have to work the land on a part-time basis (Nuckton et al., 1982; Ploch, 1978). Community growth can also stimulate increased consumer demand for goods and services, thereby benefiting farmers via the creation of more markets for their agricultural products (Shaffer et al., 1986a).

Socioeconomic forces also have profound effects on local labor markets. As businesses and industries locate in the area, their need for labor places them in direct competition with the agricultural sector (Penn, 1979). With higher wages as an inducement, nonfarm employers often succeed in attracting farm laborers to off-farm jobs (Freudenberg, 1982). To slow the flow of labor away from the farm, farmers are forced to increase the wages paid to farm workers (Deaton, 1986).

While direct linkages between the community's socioeconomic structure and its farm group are recognized, the former's ties to local inputs is where significant impacts on the farm sector are most likely to be felt. One need only begin with land to quickly demonstrate this point. The evidence shows that the demand for land accelerates in concert with local population growth and economic expansion (Healy, 1985; Wilson and Sullivan, 1985). To accommodate the demand for new homes, business establishments, highways, and recreational areas, land formerly dedicated to agricultural production often is transformed to these urban-type uses (Breimyer, 1977; Garkovich, 1982). As Lapping (1975) notes, much of the land that is converted represents prime agricultural land.

Complementing increased demands for land are higher land costs. Growth effectively changes the economic value of farmland and makes its use for nonfarm development activities more profitable (Blobaum, 1978; Evans, 1978). Agricultural lands located on the periphery of metropolitan locales are subjected to greater competition than those situated in more remote areas. Thus, prices are likely to be much higher for farmland that is directly in the path of urban expansion (Blobaum, 1978; Heaton, 1980; Thomas and Baker, 1976; Wilson and Sullivan, 1985).

The end result of high demand and value for land is burgeoning costs for the farm sector. For farmers wishing to purchase more land to expand production, the higher price of land serves to increase the cost of producing farm products, thereby reducing one's ability to compete effectively in the marketplace. Moreover, rising land values may increase taxes on property, placing added financial strains on farmers, especially those with marginal holdings (Garkovich, 1982). In many cases, spiraling land costs, coupled with increasing property taxes, make the sale of land for urban uses a more viable option for farmers (Evans, 1978; Prunty, 1979).

Changes in land costs and availability that emanate from shifts in the socioeconomic structure of the community also may affect farm scale. Under conditions of high demand and cost, investment by nonfarm people in agricultural lands generally intensifies. According to Wilson and Sullivan (1985:21), these investors include: "(1) developers who want the property for its commercial or residential value; (2) speculators who think land investment properties are favorable; and (3) people who use farm land as a hedge against inflation." In the short run, it is not uncommon for investors to establish small scale farm operations, delaying movement of farm lands to nonfarm uses until conditions are most favorable (Coughenour and Swanson, 1983; Flinn, 1982; Garkovich, 1982). Large farms also benefit in a climate of high demand and cost since their superior resources provide them with a competitive advantage (over smaller farm operators) in the purchase of additional land (Penn, 1979; Skees and Swanson, 1988).

Off-the-Farm Employment and Farm Viability

Expanded industrialization in a community serves to increase the number of off-farm options for farm families (Powers and Hobbs, 1985). In many respects, the outcomes are positive for the farming community. For one, off-farm employment increases the income of farm families, contributing to the continued viability of many farm enterprises (Buttel, 1983; Coughenour and Swanson, 1983; Deseran et al., 1984; Paarlberg, 1980; Shaffer et al., 1986b). In the case of small-scale farms, for example, the income realized from off-farm work actually subsidizes the costs of farming, and helps explain why small farms continue to persist even in times of sagging farm incomes (Heffernan et al., 1981; Pulver, 1986). Second, nonfarm income helps shelter many farm families from the economic downturns associated with agriculture, providing a more stable income for farm families (Brooks et al., 1986; Green et al., 1986). Finally, as Deaton notes (1986), off-farm employment opportunities actually serve to facilitate new entrants into agriculture on a part-time basis.

But there is little doubt that participation in off-farm work places constraints on the day-to-day operation of the farm (Carlin and Ghelfi, 1979). At issue is how family labor can be allocated to satisfy the requirements of both farm and nonfarm activities. Since off-farm work limits the amount of family labor that can be allocated to on-farm pursuits, farmers must compensate by changing the nature of the operation, by investing in farm machinery, or by expending resources to hire farm labor (Carlin and Ghelfi, 1979; Coughenour and Swanson, 1983; Johnson, 1985). However, as Skees and Swanson (1988) recently have shown, average expenditures for farm machinery and nonfamily labor actually decrease (rather than increase) as the proportion of farm operators with 100-plus days of off-farm employment increases. Thus, it appears that a lessening of one's scale of operation may be the ultimate result for those who are heavily dependent on off-farm work.

DATA AND METHODS

To determine the nature of the relationship among the components of the model being considered in this chapter, a series of variables were employed using county-level data from the Censuses of Population and Agriculture. All counties located in the Southern region of the United States were included in the study (i.e., counties in Alabama, Arkansas, Florida, Georgia, Kentucky, Louisiana, Mississippi, North Carolina, Oklahoma, South Carolina, Tennessee, and Virginia). Why county-level data and why the South? While our model does provide a framework for exploring impacts of community forces on agriculture, detailed secondary data on community as the unit of analysis are simply nonexistent. Given this restriction, county is employed as a proxy for community. This is done with the full realization that county-level data may very well mask important relationships among the components being examined.

The South provides a perfect laboratory for assessing the effects that shifts in the socioeconomic structure of a community have on the local farm sector. The pace of population growth in the South has outdistanced that of any other region of the country since the beginning of the 1970s. Growth in the labor force has accelerated at a quicker rate as well (Sullivan and Avery, 1987). In addition, the number of acres of agricultural lands converted to urban uses in the South has exceeded the amount in all other regions combined (Healy, 1985). Finally, Southern farmers' dependence on off-farm employment has grown more rapidly than in other areas of the United States during the past several years (Skees and Swanson, 1988).

Listed in Table 1 are the variables used to operationalize the four components of the model being explored in this chapter. The SOCIOECONOMIC COMPONENT includes six variables.[3] Three variables not addressed in the earlier literature review (change in the percent of the county's population that is black, 1970-80; change in the percent of families with incomes below poverty level, 1969-79; and change in the percent of the population 25 years of age or above with a college education, 1970-80), deserve comment at this point. These variables are introduced into the model as control variables. Evidence suggests that population and economic growth are more likely to take place in areas that have a smaller minority population, a more affluent populace, and a better educated workforce (Ford Foundation, 1986; Johnson, 1986; Rosenfeld et al., 1985). Thus, their inclusion in the model enhances the ability to more accurately measure the impact of growth and economic development on the farm sector.

The INPUTS COMPONENT of the model incorporates variables which reflect changes in the price and availability of farm land, as well as shifts in the dependence of Southern farmers on off-farm sources of employment. Farm structure is represented by two key dimensions : FARM SCALE and LABOR RESOURCES components. The former considers changes between 1974 and 1982 in farm size (as reflected in the value of gross farm sales), while the latter includes shifts (1974-82) in the value of farm capital equipment and expenditures for hired farm labor.[4] Both dimensions are identified by Wimberley (1986) as important indicators of agricultural structure.

The model outlined in Figure 1 was estimated as a block recursive system containing a total of eight equations. The INPUTS block included equations for change in off-farm employment, change in the value of land and buildings, and change in farmland acreage. The FARM SCALE block included equations for the change in the number of small, medium, and large farms. The third and final block, LABOR RESOURCES, included two equations, one for the change in the market value of machinery and equipment and one for the change in expenditures for hired labor. Variables included in each of the eight equations were those suggested by the literature as being important. The following section presents the findings for these equations.[5]

Table 1. Operational Measures of the Community/Farm Sector Linkages Model

Component/Variable Names	Description
SOCIOECONOMIC COMPONENT	
Total Population	Measured as the change in the county's total population between 1970 and 1980.
Civilian Labor Force 16 years+	Refers to the percentage shift that took place between 1970 and 1980 in the number of persons 16 years of age or older classified as being in the civilian labor force.
Pct. Black Population	Change in the percent of the county's population that is black, 1970-80.
Pct. Families in Poverty	This variable reflects the change in percent of families with incomes below the poverty level over the 1969 to 1979 time period.
Pct. College Graduates	Reflects the change in the percent of people 25 years of age or older who have completed a four-year college degree.
Metropolitan Code	This variable is a 17 category scale developed by Glenn Fuguitt that provides a measure of a county's degree of rurality, beginning with a value of "1" for core counties having more than 1 million population and ending with a value of "17" for nonmetropolitan, nonadjacent counties with largest size of place being under 2,500 persons.
INPUTS COMPONENT	
Off Farm Labor	Percent change in the number of farm operators having 100 days or more of off-farm employment between 1974 and 1982.
Land and Buildings	This measure reflects the percent change in the dollar value of farm land and buildings on a per acre basis as reported in the Census of Agriculture for 1974 and 1982.
Farm Land Area	Reflects the percent change in farm land, 1974-82.
FARM SCALE COMPONENT	
Small Farms	Percent change taking place in the number of small farms (those with gross farm sales of less than $40,000) between 1974 and 1982.
Medium Farms	Percent change in the number of middle-sized farms ($40,000 to $99,999 gross farm sales, 1974-82).
Large Farms	Percent change in the number of large-scale farm operations (gross farm sales of $100,000 or more) over the 1974 to 1982 time period.
LABOR RESOURCES COMPONENT	
Market Value of Machinery	This variable measures the percent change in the market value of farm machinery and equipment (in dollars) as reported in the 1974 and 1982 Censuses of Agriculture.
Hired Labor Cost	Refers to the present shift in expenditures (payroll dollars) for hired labor on the farm, 1974-82.

FINDINGS

As noted from the size of the R^2 values, the three input equations shown in Table 2-A had very poor model fits, ranging from .038 for change in farmland acreage, to .077 for change in off-farm employment. Looking specifically at the off-farm employment equation, it can be seen that only three variables were important predictors at the conventional significance level of $P=.05$. From the input sector, as the change in value of land and buildings increased, the change in the off-farm employment increased. The strongest positive relationship was $B=.231$ for change in the percent of families in poverty. Conversely, as the change in the percent black increased, the change in off-farm employment decreased ($B=-.096$). Interestingly, the indirect effects of change in percent black and change in percent in poverty were opposite their direct effects.

The results of the off-farm employment equation are not fully consistent with the literature. For example, contrary to expectation, economic growth (as measured by change in the civilian labor force) did not directly stimulate increases in off-farm employment, although moderate indirect effects were uncovered. Further, increases in the percent of families living in poverty was expected to temper economic growth in a community and thus, limit expansion of off-farm jobs for farmers. But, the family poverty variable was positively associated with shifts in off-farm employment.

On the other hand, as argued in the literature, change in the proportion of persons in the community who are black did tend to depress growth in the proportion of farmers with off-farm jobs. The suggestion is that areas with increasing black populations have been by-passed with regard to growth in off-the-farm work opportunities.

The change in the socioeconomic structure of the community accounted for .068 percent of the variance in the change in the value of farmland and buildings. In this case, the rate of change in the civilian labor force ($B=.136$) and being a more rural county ($B=.131$) resulted in increases in the rate of change in the value of farmland and buildings. Conversely, increased rates of change in the concentration of poverty families ($B=-.157$) and in the concentration of college graduates ($B=-.064$) were found to be associated with decreases in the rate of change in the value of agricultural land and buildings. Given the structure of the specified models, there were no indirect effects in this equation.

Again, some of the results appear to be at odds with the literature. Expansion in the civilian labor force did increase the value of farmland and buildings, as expected. However, the positive relationship between degree of rurality (labeled "metropolitan code") and change in the value of farmland and buildings did run counter to the literature. One possible explanation is that rural areas in the South did undergo major industrial and population growth during

Table 2-A
Structural Linkages Among the Farm Sector and the Community
(Standardized Coefficients in Parentheses)

	INPUTS COMPONENT								
	Δ Off Farm Labor			Δ Land and Buildings			Δ Farm Land Area		
	Total Effect	Direct Effect	Total Indirect Effect	Total Effect	Direct Effect	Total Indirect Effect	Total Effect	Direct Effect	Total Indirect Effect
SOCIOECONOMIC COMPONENT									
Δ Total Population	0.055	(0.020) 0.044	0.011	0.092	(0.040) 0.092	0.000	0.024	(0.038) 0.024	0.000
Δ Civilian Labor Force 16 yrs.+	0.761	(0.051) 0.560	0.201	1.604	(0.136) 1.604	0.000	-0.208	(-0.062) -0.203	0.005
Metropolitan Code	0.685	(0.037) 0.465	0.202	1.755	(0.131) 1.755	0.000	0.147	(0.041) 0.154	-0.007
Δ Pct Pop. Black	-1.425	(-0.096) -1.514	0.089	0.709	(0.042) 0.709	0.000	-0.526	(-0.111) -0.523	-0.003
Δ Pct Families in Poverty	1.205	(0.231) 1.326	-0.121	-0.964	(-0.157) -0.964	0.000	0.231	(0.133) 0.228	0.003
Δ Pct College Grad	0.248	(0.020) 0.435	-0.187	-1.497	(-0.064) -1.497	0.000	0.029	(0.004) 0.024	0.005
INPUTS COMPONENT									
Δ Off Farm Labor									
Δ Land and Buildings	0.125	(0.134) 0.125	0.000				-0.033	(-0.013) -0.003	0.000
Δ Farm Land Area									
FARM SCALE COMPONENT									
Δ Small Farms									
Δ Medium Farms									
Δ Large Farms									
LABOR RESOURCES COMPONENT									
Δ Market Value of Machinery									
Δ Hired Labor Cost									
R^2	0.077			0.068			0.038		

_____ Indicates Direct Effect is Statistically Significant at ($P <= 0.05$)

n = 1,264

the 1970s and farmland/buildings in these less urbanized locales may have increased in value as a consequence.

The impacts of the changing socioeconomic structure on changing farmland acreage were quite divergent from the impacts on the other two inputs. Specifically, an increasing rate of change in the civilian labor force decreased the rate of change in farmland acreage (B=-.062), as did the change in the concentration of the black population in the community (B=-.111). Consistent with the off-farm employment equation, the rate of change in the concentration of families in poverty increased the rate of change in farmland acreage (B=.133). Once again, the structure of the models resulted in virtually no indirect effects of the changing socioeconomic structure of the community on shifts in the percent of land dedicated to farming.

The important linkage discovered between change in the civilian labor force and shifts in farmland acreage supports the notion that economic expansion creates a greater demand for land, often resulting in the conversion of farmland for such nonfarm uses. Contrary to expectation, change in total population and degree of rurality (metropolitan code) of a county were insignificant forces with regard to farmland acreage changes.

Farm Scale Equations

The second endogenous block in the model consisted of three equations relating to farm scale (Table 2-B). In this instance, the ability of the specified models to explain variation in the change of the percentage of farms declined monotonically as one moved from small farms (R^2=.284) to medium-sized farms (R^2=.073) to large farms (R^2=.018). However, the nature of the empirically estimated relationships for the change in small and medium farms was very similar. In both instances, an increase in the rate of change of the three inputs (off-farm employment, value of land and buildings, and farmland acreage) resulted in increases in the rate of change of small and medium farms. In both cases, the change in the value of land and buildings had some minimal additional positive indirect effect. When examining the direct effects of the socioeconomic structure of the community, it is seen that only the degree of rurality (i.e., metropolitan code) had a statistically significant impact, but the impact was in opposite directions. The rate of change of small farms decreased as the area became more rural. Stated differently, proportional growth in the number of small farms was greater in more urbanized areas. With medium sized farms, the reverse was true. As the degree of rurality increased, the rate of change in medium-sized farms increased.

Contrary to the findings of Harper et al. (1980), population growth had no significant impact on small farm changes. What is clear is that the proportional growth of small-scale farms was closely tied to off-farm employment. As off-farm work among farmers grew, so did farms classified as small in

Table 2-B
Structural Linkages Among the Farm Sector and the Community
(Standardized Coefficients in Parentheses)

	FARM SCALE COMPONENT								
	Δ Small Farms			Δ Medium Farms			Δ Large Farms		
	Total Effect	Direct Effect	Total Indirect Effect	Total Effect	Direct Effect	Total Indirect Effect	Total Effect	Direct Effect	Total Indirect Effect
SOCIOECONOMIC COMPONENT		(0.278)			(0.032)			(0.003)	
Δ Total Population	0.276	0.259	0.017	0.167	0.115	0.012	0.060	0.027	0.033
Δ Civilian Labor Force 16 yrs.+	0.127	0.000	0.127	0.145	0.000	0.145	-0.347	0.000	-0.347
		(-0.253)			(0.056)			(0.088)	
Metropolitan Code	-1.170	-1.376	0.206	1.759	1.190	0.640	5.172	4.970	0.202
Δ Pct Pop. Black	-0.296	0.000	-0.296	-0.768	0.000	-0.768	-0.587	0.000	-0.587
Δ Pct Families in Poverty	0.185	0.000	0.185	0.345	0.000	0.345	0.166	0.000	0.166
Δ Pct College Grad	-0.021	0.000	-0.021	-0.150	0.000	-0.150	-0.037	0.000	-0.037
INPUTS COMPONENT		(0.327)			(0.109)			(-0.027)	
Δ Off Farm Labor	0.142	0.142	0.000	0.186	0.186	0.000	-0.120	-0.120	0.000
Δ Land and Buildings		(0.103)			(0.097)			(0.008)	
	0.059	0.042	0.017	0.173	0.154	0.019	0.014	0.034	-0.020
		(0.159)			(0.204)			(0.098)	
Δ Farm Land Area	0.233	0.233	0.000	1.166	1.166	0.000	1.489	1.489	0.000
FARM SCALE COMPONENT									
Δ Small Farms									
Δ Medium Farms									
Δ Large Farms									
LABOR RESOURCES COMPONENT									
Δ Market Value of Machinery									
Δ Hired Labor Cost									

R^2 0.284   0.073   0.018

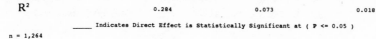 _____ Indicates Direct Effect is Statistically Significant at ($P <= 0.05$)

n = 1,264

scale. Off-farm employment had a less influential, but still significant, effect on changes in medium-sized farms. Both trends proved to be in concert with the literature.

In addition, change in the value of farmland and buildings, and change in farmland acreage, had positive effects on shifts in the number of small farms. It is possible that some of the individuals who established small farms during the 1974-82 period did so as a short-term strategy, with the longer-term goal being that of selling the land at a profit at some future point in time.

Given the data just presented, it is evident that the rate of change in the percent of small and medium-sized farms was affected most directly by changes in the input sector. However, if the columns of total indirect effects are examined, it becomes clear that the changing socioeconomic structure of the community produced some rather substantial indirect effects on change in farm scale, mediated through the inputs. The indirect effects of changes in black population (-.768—the only negative indirect effect), degree of rurality (.64), and change of percent of families in poverty (.345) for the medium-sized farm equation are particularly noteworthy. Change in the civilian labor force also had a positive indirect effect in both instances.

For the change in large farm equation, the results were very different. Only one input variable, change in acres in farms, had a statistically significant relationship (B = .098) with change in percent of large farms. The nature of the net relationship indicates that as the rate of change in farmland acres increased, the change in the percent of large farms increased. Similarly, only one dimension of the socioeconomic structure of the community had a direct impact on rate of change in large farms. Specifically, as the degree of rurality increased, the rate of change in large farms increased (b=4.97). As was true for both small and medium-sized farms, the change in the concentration of the black population, change in the civilian labor force, and change in the concentration of poverty families all had indirect impacts on change in large farms via their structural relationships with the input sector.

In summary, farm scale was directly impacted by the input sector in much the same fashion, but in varying magnitudes. Further, and potentially more important for the current analysis, the changing socioeconomic structure of the community exhibited virtually no direct effects on farm scale, but did have substantial indirect effects mediated by the structural relations specified among the input sector and the socioeconomic structure of the community.

Labor Resources Equations

The final endogenous block is a labor resource dimension that constitutes two equations, one for change in the market value of farm machinery and equipment, and one for change in expenditures for hired labor. As can be seen from the coefficients in Table 2-C, this dimension is primarily a function of

Table 2-C
Structural Linkages Among the Farm Sector and the Community
(Standardized Coefficients in Parentheses)

	LABOR RESOURCES COMPONENT					
	Δ Market Value of Machinery			Δ Hired Labor Cost		
	Total Effect	Direct Effect	Total Indirect Effect	Total Effect	Direct Effect	Total Indirect Effect
SOCIOECONOMIC COMPONENT						
Δ Total Population	0.162	0.000	0.162	0.126	0.000	0.126
Δ Civilian Labor Force 16 yrs.+	0.181	0.000	0.000	-1.049	(-0.068) -1.152	0.103
Metropolitan Code	0.157	0.000	0.157	0.388	0.000	0.388
Δ Pct Pop. Black	-0.720	0.000	-0.720	-0.176	0.000	-0.176
Δ Pct Families in Poverty	0.314	0.000	0.314	0.022	0.000	0.022
Δ Pct College Grad	-0.174	0.000	-0.174	-0.141	0.000	-0.141
INPUTS COMPONENT						
Δ Off Farm Labor	0.184	(0.135) 0.122	0.062	0.024	(-0.035) -0.054	0.078
Δ Land and Buildings	0.187	(0.172) 0.145	0.042	0.108	(0.040) 0.057	0.051
Δ Farm Land Area	1.098	(0.308) 0.934	0.164	0.412	0.000	0.412
FARM SCALE COMPONENT						
Δ Small Farms	0.408	(0.197) 0.408	0.000	0.303	(0.086) 0.303	0.000
Δ Medium Farms	0.034	(0.065) 0.034	0.000	0.221	(0.246) 0.221	0.000
Δ Large Farms	0.019	(0.095) 0.019	0.000	0.056	(0.165) 0.056	0.000
LABOR RESOURCES COMPONENT						
Δ Market Value of Machinery						
Δ Hired Labor Cost						

R^2 0.264   0.106

 Indicates Direct Effect is Statistically Significant at (P <= 0.05)

n = 1,264

the inputs and the scale of farming components, with the impacts of the so-cioeconomic structure of the community being indirect (with the one excep-tion of the impact of a changing civilian labor force on change in labor resources).

If the model coefficients for the change in market value of farm machinery and equipment are examined, it is seen that the multiple individual dimen-sions of inputs and farm scale all had positive signs. In short, ceterus para-bus, as the rate of change in any individual dimension increased, so did the rate of change in the market value of farm machinery and equipment. An examination of the standardized beta coefficients show that the input com-ponent was relatively more important than the farm scale component, with change in acres of land in farms being the strongest predictor (B=.308). As was true with the farm scale models, the socioeconomic structure of the com-munity impacted the changing market value of farm equipment and machinery indirectly through the mediating mechanisms of agricultural sector inputs and farm scale.

The findings provide important evidence that the value of farm machinery and equipment does increase in concert with percentage growth of farmers with 100+ days of off-farm work. In essence, it would appear that capital equipment purchases are used to compensate for the loss of labor to these off-farm pursuits. Moreover, positive shifts in small-scale farms do result in increases in the value of farm machinery and equipment, suggesting that small scale operators do depend on capital equipment to assist in farm production activities.

The final equation in the model for change in hired labor cost shows that the input dimension played no significant direct role in the explanation of change in hired labor expenditures, although change in the quantity of land in farms did have a positive indirect effect (.412) mediated by farm scale. Worthy of attention is the failure to uncover a significant relationship between change in off-farm employment and change in the cost of hired labor. Simply put, growth in off-farm work dependence did not increase farmers' expenditures for hired labor.

As was true with the market value equation, the farm scale dimension had significant direct effects on the change in hired labor expenses. Further, all direct effects of farm scale were positive, with a change in medium-sized farms being most important (B=.246), followed by a change in large farms, and fi-nally by a change in small farms. From the socioeconomic component, the contention that economic growth (i.e., change in the civilian labor force) would increase farmers' outlays for hired labor was not supported empirically in this study. In fact, the relationship was found to be negative.

Although there were several indirect effects of the socioeconomic structure of the community, the one that is most prominent is the degree of rurality variable. The nature of the indirect effect suggests that the rate of change in the expenditures for labor assistance increases as the area becomes more rural. This is also true in areas where the rate of change in population is more rapid. An increased rate of change in the concentration of blacks and the concentration of college graduates has a negative indirect effect on change in the monetary outlay for hired labor.

DISCUSSION AND CONCLUSIONS

It is instructive to return to the two critical questions raised earlier. Do shifts in the socioeconomic structure of the community result in direct impacts on the farm sector? And do key inputs mediate the impact of the socioeconomic structure of the community on the farm sector?

In attempting to respond to these questions, a complex set of linkages between the community and the farm sector in the Southern region was explored in this chapter. In general, socioeconomic forces appear to have limited direct effects on the two dimensions of farm structure (i.e., farm scale and labor resources) examined in this study. In fact, degree of rurality is the lone socioeconomic force with significant direct effects on changes in the numbers of small, medium, and large size farms. Similarly, the only direct influence on change in the expenditures for hired labor (one aspect of the labor resources component) comes from change in the number of persons in the civilian labor force. What is abundantly clear, however, is that socioeconomic factors have substantial indirect effects on the farm sector mediated by the structural relations among the input and socioeconomic components of the community.

Our findings offer some important insights on strategies for responding to the farm crisis in the South. One must remain mindful of the fact, however, that county is used as a proxy for community in this study. Therefore, it is plausible that our findings fail to fully capture the relationships among the components in our model since community-specific data are not available. In addition, it is not until the early stages of the 1980s that the farm financial crisis began to emerge as an issue of major importance in the region. Unfortunately, the data employed in our model do not extend beyond the year 1982. While our results do not embrace the dynamics of what has taken place in the South since 1982, they do serve as a valuable foundation for discerning what local strategies might hold promise for bringing about improved conditions for financially stressed farmers in the area.

With these caveats, we would suggest that the strength of the relationship between the community and its farm sector is primarily a function of farm scale of operation. That is, the viability of small-scale farming appears to be influenced significantly by factors within the local milieu (be it socioeconomic factors or inputs-related forces). In fact, the socioeconomic and inputs components of our model explain 28 percent of the variance in the proportional change in the number of small farms between 1974 and 1982. Our model is far less successful in explaining changes in medium-sized farms, and of virtually no help in understanding shifts in the number of large-scale farm operations. It would appear that the economic viability of these larger farm enterprises (especially those with gross farm sales of $100,000 or more) is shaped, in large part, by forces outside the local setting. Thus, efforts to deal with the farm financial dilemma must, by necessity, require the active involvement of different institutional levels. Local institutions can perform a major function in helping smaller scale farmers survive (i.e., through creation or expansion of local markets for farm products, increasing locally-based off-farm job opportunities), but are unlikely to gain much success in maintaining the economic health of larger farms. Addressing the economic stresses of these larger operators will require active involvement beyond the local arena, namely, by state and federal institutions since the very survival of these enterprises is so intimately tied to national and international conditions (i.e., federal monetary and trade policies, agricultural performance of Third World countries).

On a related theme, off-farm employment remains a critical ingredient in the persistence and growth of small farms in the South. Of particular interest is our finding that growth in small farm numbers is occurring in more urbanized areas. In some respects, this could reflect a desire among many small farmers to locate in areas where off-farm job opportunities are more readily available or accessible. Off-farm employment also proves important in explaining growth in the number of medium-sized farms. But, as our data reveal, growth in medium-sized farms is occurring in the more rural areas of the South. Sadly, the decade of the 1980s has seen the decline or demise of many manufacturing and mining firms in rural areas of the region, and as Hines and Petrulis (1986) have noted, it is these very industries that have been "of utmost importance to the economic health of farm households and the farm sector in general." Therefore, one essential strategy is to focus attention on the creation of off-farm job opportunities for middle-sized farm operators—in those localities that are more rural in nature, and in job areas that take full advantage of the talents and skills of these farmers/farm family members. This approach would appear sensible in light of the fact that much of the pinch associated with the farm financial crisis in the South is being felt by middle-sized farmers, and their capacity to survive will be partly dependent on how successful they (or family members) are in securing off-the-farm employment.

As our findings reveal, the opportunity costs of farm labor are such that many small and medium-sized farmers are being drawn to off-farm work. Also, growth in the number of small and medium-sized farms is being accompanied by changes in the value of farm machinery/equipment and expenditures for hired labor. These sets of interrelationships suggest a need for those organizations who provide valuable assistance to the farm sector (i.e., Cooperative Extension Service, state departments of agriculture) to closely monitor how these additional expenses may be affecting the small and medium-sized farmers' costs structure. It is possible that by compensating for the loss of family farm labor via the purchase of capital equipment and/or expansion of hired labor, farmers are effectively reducing their ability to compete in the marketplace. With educational programming and technical expertise, these agencies can provide valuable assistance to those farmers who are trying to balance their on-farm activities with the demands associated with their off-farm employment.

Finally, we feel that it is important to move beyond the parochial view that the survival of the farm sector is likely to be realized through on-farm solutions (i.e., improved farm management, shift to alternative agricultural commodities). At least for small scale farmers and, to some extent, medium-sized farmers, this narrow view likely will prove catastrophic. To enhance the economic viability of these farm operations, the broader community within which these farms operate must be introduced into the formula.

NOTES

[1]The decision to limit our analysis to the SOCIOECONOMIC and INPUT components of our model was based upon the fact that operational measures for these dimensions could be readily secured from published secondary data sources. Pertinent information associated with the COMMUNITY VALUES and LOCAL GOVERNMENT components would have, by necessity, required the use of more first hand data gathering techniques.

[2]It is recognized that the proposed model does not fully capture the variety of interrelationships which might exist between the community and its agricultural sector. This chapter should be viewed as an important first step in the systematic assessment of some of these community/agricultural linkages.

[3]The metropolitan code variable included in the SOCIOECONOMIC COMPONENT dimension represents a 17 category "degree of rurality" scale that was developed by Glenn Fuguitt. The categories are as follows:

   1 = Core counties more than 1 million
   2 = Fringe counties more than 1 million
   3 = Core of SMSA's 750,000 to 999,999
   4 = Fringe of SMSA's 750,000 to 999,999
   5 = Core of SMSA's 500,000 to 749,999
   6 = Fringe of SMSA's 500,000 to 749,999
   7 = Core of SMSA's 250,000 to 499,999
   8 = Fringe of SMSA's 250,000 to 499,999
   9 = Core of SMSA's 100,000 to 249,999
  10 = Fringe of SMSA's 100,000 to 249,999
  11 = SMSA's of 99,999 or less
  12 = Nonmet, adjacent counties size largest place 10,000+
  13 = Nonmet, adjacent counties size largest place 2,500 to 9,999
  14 = Nonmet, adjacent counties size largest place less than 2,500
  15 = Nonmet, nonadjacent counties size largest place 10,000+
  16 = Nonmet, nonadjacent counties size largest place 2,500 to 9,999
  17 = Nonmet, nonadjacent counties size largest place less than 2,500

230 LIONEL J. BEAULIEU, MICHAEL K. MILLER AND DAVID MULKEY

[4]If individual farm-level data were available at the two points in time (1974 and 1982), it would be desirable to adjust the gross farm sales data to constant dollars. However, the data from the Census of Agriculture are available only as proportions in broad classes of farm sales in any given year. As a result, it becomes impossible to deflate the 1982 gross farm sales to constant 1973 dollar terms in a way that preserves the comparability of the sales categories in any meaningful form. Because of this data limitation, the farm sales data employed in the current study are expressed as differences in nominal dollars.

[5]The analysis of change is central to the current effort. We realize that there are any number of ways a model can be specified to explicitly examine change. We have chosen to estimate a set of first difference equations, i.e., $\Delta Y = \beta_1 \Delta X + \epsilon$. It should be realized that linear difference equations involving ΔY as dependent variables are mathematically equivalent to those involving only static scores at the two time points. The interested reader should consult Kessler and Greenburg (1981) and Liker et al. (1985) for discussions of practical and theoretical considerations that suggest the use of one specification over another. Liker et al. look explicitly at the advantage of using first difference models.

REFERENCES

Beaulieu, Lionel J. and W. David Mulkey. 1986. "An assessment of community forces and agricultural change." Pp. 267-299 in Joseph J. Molnar (ed.), *Agricultural Change: Consequences for Southern Farms and Rural Communities*. Boulder, Colorado: Westview Press.

Blobaum, Roger, 1978. "The loss of agricultural land." Pp. 389-402 in R. D. Rodefeld, J. Flora, D. Voth, I Fujimoto, and J. Converse (eds.), *Change in Rural America*. Saint Louis: The C. V. Mosby Company.

Brooks, Nora L., Thomas A. Strucker, and Jennifer A. Bailey. 1986. "Income and well-being of farmers and the farm financial crisis." *Rural Sociology* 51 (Winter): 391-405.

Buttel, Frederick H. 1983. "Farm structure and rural development." Pp. 103-124 in David E. Brewster, Wayne D. Rasmussen, and Garth Youngberg (eds.), *Farms in Transition*. Ames, Iowa: The Iowa State University Press.

Carlin, Thomas and Linda Ghelfi. 1979. "Off-farm employment and the farm sector." Pp. 270-273 in *Structure Issues of American Agriculture*. Agricultural Economic Report 438. Washington, D.C.: U.S. Department of Agriculture.

Coughenour, C. Milton and Anne V. Gabbard. 1977. "Part-time farmers in Kentucky in the early 1970s: The development of dual careers." Paper RS-54. Lexington, Kentucky: Department of Sociology, Agricultural Experiment Station.

Coughenour, C. Milton and Louis Swanson. 1983. "Work statuses and occupations of men and women in farm families and the structure of farms." *Rural Sociology* 48 (Spring):23-43.

Deseran, Forrest A., William W. Falk, and Pamela Jenkins. 1984. "Determinants of earnings of farm families in the U.S." *Rural Sociology* 49 (Summer):210-228.

Dillman, Don A. 1986. "Social issues impacting agriculture and rural areas as we approach the 21st century." Pp. 19-31 in *New Dimensions in Rural Policy: Building Upon our Heritage*. Studies prepared for the use of the Subcommittee on Agriculture and Transportation of the Joint Economic Committee, Congress of the United States. Washington, D.C.: U.S. Government Printing Office (June 5).

Evans, John V. 1978. "Agriculture and growth management." *State Government* (Winter):160-161.

Flinn, William L. 1982. "Communities and their relationships to agrarian values." Pp. 19-32 in William P. Browne and Don F. Hadwiger (eds.), *Rural Policy Problems: Changing Dimensions*. Lexington, MA: Lexington Books.

Freudenburg, William. 1982. "The impacts of rapid growth on the social and personal well-being of local community residents." Pp. 137-170 in Bruce Weber and Robert Howell (eds.), *Coping with Rapid Growth in Rural Communities*. Boulder, Colorado: Westview Press.

Garkovich, Lorraine. 1982. "Land use planning as a response to rapid population growth and community change." *Rural Sociology* 47 (1):47-67.

Ginder, Roger G., Kenneth F. Stone, and Daniel Otto. 1985. "Impact of the farm financial crisis on agribusiness firms and rural communities." *American Journal of Agricultural Economics* 67 (December): 1184-1190.

Goldschmidt, Walter. 1947. *As You Sow.* Glencoe, Ill.: Free Press.

Goss, Kevin F. and Richard D. Rodefeld. 1977. "Farming and place population change in Michigan, 1930-1970." Paper presented at the Annual Meeting of the Rural Sociological Society. Madison, Wisconsin (August).

Green, Gary P. 1985. "Large-scale farming and the quality of life in rural communities: further specification of the Goldschmidt hypothesis." *Rural Sociology* 50 (Summer):262-274.

Harper, Emily B., Frederick C. Fliegel and J. C. Van Es. 1980. "Growing numbers of small farms in the North Central States." *Rural Sociology* 45 (Spring):608-619.

Healy, Robert G. 1985. "How much urban impact on the South's farm and forest lands?" *Rural Development Perspectives* 2(October): 27-30.

Heaton, Tim B. 1980. "Metropolitan influence on United States farmland use and capital intensity." *Rural Sociology* 45 (Fall): 501-508.

Heffernan, William D. 1981. "The structure of agriculture and quality of life in rural communities." Pp. 337-346 in D. A. Dillman and D. J. Hobbs (eds.), *Rural Sociology: Research Issues for the 1980s.* Boulder, Colorado: Westview Press.

Heffernan, William D., Gary Green, R. Paul Lasley, and Michael F. Nolan. 1981. "Part-time farming and the rural community." *Rural Sociology* 46 (Summer):245-262.

Hines, Fred and Mindy F. Petrulis. 1986. "An overview of the Southern nonmetro economy: An historical and current view with emphasis on Southern agriculture." *Proceedings of the Emerging Issues in the Rural Economy of the South Conference.* Mississippi State: Southern Rural Development Center (April).

Johnson, Kenny. 1986. "The Southern stake in rural development." *Rural Flight/Urban Might: Economics Development Challenges for the 1980s.* The 1986 Commission on the Future of the South; Cross-cutting Issue Report No. 3. Research Triangle Park, N.C.: The Southern Growth Policies Board.

Johnson, Thomas G. 1985. "Off-farm employment of small farm operators: A strategy for survival." Pp. 105-118 in Thomas T. Williams (ed.), *Strategy for Survival of Small Farmers....International Implications.* Tuskegee Institute: Human Resources Development Center.

Kessler, Ronald C. and David F. Greenburg. 1981. *Linear Panel Analysis: Models of Quantitative Change.* New York: Academic Press.

Lapping, Mark B. 1975. "Symposium: Agriculture and urbanization." *Journal of the American Institute of Planners* 4 (November):369-370.

Leistritz, Larry, Steve Murdock, and Arlen Leholm. 1982. "Local economic changes associated with rapid growth." Pp. 25-61 in Bruce Weber and Robert Howell (eds.), *Coping with Rapid Growth in Rural Communities.* Boulder, Colorado: Westview Press.

Leistritz, F. Larry and Brenda L. Ekstrom. 1986. *Interdependencies of Agriculture and Rural Communities: An Annotated Bibliography.* New York: Garland Publishing, Inc.

Liker, Jeffrey K., Sue Augustyniak, and Greg J. Duncan. 1985. "Panel data and models of change: A comparison of first difference and conventional two-wave models." *Social Science Research,* 14:80-101.

MDC, Inc. 1986. *Shadows in the Sunbelt: Developing the Rural South in an Era of Economic Change.* A Report of the MDC Panel on Rural Economic Development (May).

Magleby, Richard and Dwight Gadsby. 1979. "Environmental regulations: Impacts on farm structure." Pp. 195-200 in *Structure Issues of American Agriculture.* Agricultural Economic Report 438. Washington, D.C.: USDA-ERS.

Melichar, Emanuel and George D. Irwin. 1985. "Condition of rural financial intermediaries." *American Journal of Agricultural Economics* 67 (December): 1178-1183.

Milkove, Daniel L., Patrick J. Sullivan, and James J. Mikesell. 1986. "Deteriorating farm finances affect rural banks and communities." *Rural Development Perspectives* 2 (June): 18-22.

Nuckton, Carole Frank, Refugio I. Rochin, and Douglas Gwynn. 1982. "Farm size and rural community welfare: An interdisciplinary approach." *Rural Sociology* 47 (Spring):33-46.

Paarlberg, Don. 1980. *Farm and Food Policy: Issues of the 1980s.* Lincoln: University of Nebraska Press.

Patterson, Mitchell, Jr. and J. Paxton Marshall. 1984. "Policy alternatives to reduce barriers affecting access to resources for small farms in rural areas." *Increasing Understanding of Public Problems and Policies—1984,* Oak Brook, Illinois: Farm Foundation.

Penn, J. B. 1979. "The structure of agriculture: An overview of the issue." Pp. 2-23 in *Structure Issues of American Agriculture.* Agricultural Economic Report 438. Washington, D.C.: USDA-ESCS.

Ploch, Louis. 1978. "The reversal in migration patterns—some rural development consequences." *Rural Sociology* 43 (Summer):296-302.

Powers, Ronald C. and Daryl J. Hobbs. 1985. "Changing relationships between farm and community." *Ag Policy Update.* Iowa State University, Ames (November).

Prunty, Merle. 1979. "Agricultural lands: A Southern perspective." *Proceedings of the Agricultural Lands Study Workshop.* Mississippi State: Southern Rural Development Center.

Pulver, Glen C. 1986. "Economic growth in rural America." Pp. 491-508 in *New Dimensions in Rural Policy: Building Upon Our Heritage.* Studies prepared for the use of the Subcommittee on Agriculture and Transportation of the Joint Economic Committee, Congress of the United States. Washington, D.C.: U.S. Government Printing Office (June 5).

Rosenfeld, Stuart A., Edward Bergman, and Sarah Rubin. 1985. *After the Factories: Changing Employment Patterns in the Rural South.* Research Triangle Park, North Carolina: Southern Growth Policies Board (December).

Shaffer, Ron, Priscilla Salant, and William Saupe. 1986a. "Rural economics and farming: A synergistic link." Pp. 55-72 in Peter F. Korsching and Judith Gildner (eds.), *Interdependencies of Agriculture and Rural Communities in the 21st Century: The North Central Region.* Ames, Iowa: The North Central Regional Center for Rural Development.

_____. 1986b. "Understanding the synergistic link between communities and farming." Pp. 308-321. *New Dimensions in Rural Policy: Building Upon Our Heritage.* Studies prepared for the use of the Subcommittee on Agriculture and Transportation of the Joint Economic Committee, Congress of the United States. Washington, D.C.: U.S. Government Printing Office (June 5).

Skees, Jerry R. and Louis E. Swanson. 1988. "Public policy for farm structure and rural well-being in the South." In Louis E. Swanson (ed.), *Agriculture and Community Change in the U.S.: The Congressional Research Reports.* Boulder, Colorado: Westview Press (forthcoming).

Small Farm Viability Project. 1977. *The Family Farm in California.* Report to the State of California, Sacramento.

Sullivan, Gene D. and David Avery. 1987. "Structural change in the Southeastern economy since 1960." Paper presented at the Annual Meeting of the Southern Rural Sociological Association. Nashville, Tennessee (February).

Swanson, Louis E., Jr. 1982. "Farm and trade center transition in an industrial society: Pennsylvania, 1930-1960." Unpublished dissertation. University Park: The Pennsylvania State University.

Wilson, Gene and Gene Sullivan. 1985. "Farmland price behavior: A study in diversity." *Economic Review,* Federal Reserve Bank of Atlanta (April):20-26.

Wimberley, Ronald C. 1986. "America's three agricultures." Pp. 192-221 in *New Dimensions in Rural Policy: Building Upon Our Heritage.* Studies prepared for the use of the Subcommittee on Agriculture and Transportation of the Joint Economic Committee, Congress of the United States. Washington, D.C.: U.S. Government Printing Office (June 5).

U.S. Bureau of Census. 1970. *U.S. Census of Population: General Social and Economic Characteristics Final Report - United States.*

_____. 1970. *U.S. Census of Population: Number of Inhabitants Final Report - United States.*

_____. 1974. *Census of Agriculture - United States, Summary and States Data.* Vol. 1, Part 51.

_____. 1980. *U.S. Census of Population: General Social and Economic Characteristics Final Report - United States.*

_____. 1980. *U.S. Census of Population: Number of Inhabitants Final Report - United States.*

_____. 1982. *Census of Agriculture - United States, Summary and States Data.* Vol. 1, Part 51.

U.S. Senate. 1986. *Governing the Heartland: Can Rural Communities Survive the Farm Crisis?* Report prepared by the Subcommittee on Intergovernmental Relations of the Committee on Governmental Affairs, United States Senate (May).

PART THREE

Agriculture and Rural Development Policies: Past Reflections, Future Directions

15

Reflections on Agricultural Policies and Their Consequences for the South

Patricia A. Duffy
Ronald D. Knutson

Since the 1930s when federal farm policy legislation was first developed, a variety of different federal programs for agriculture have been implemented. These programs have traditionally been tied to the production of specific commodities and have been centered around some combination of price supports, direct subsidies, and supply management. There is no clear consensus about how these programs have affected either producers or consumers over the long run, but there appears to be growing dissatisfaction with the current farm policies among both groups. Judging the ultimate effect of the farm programs is complicated by the important regional differences in the agricultural sector. Different crops are grown in different areas, and other aspects of agricultural structure vary considerably as well.

This chapter will provide a discussion of the effects of agricultural policy on resource use and agricultural structure, with emphasis on how these policies have affected the South. A discussion of policy options for the future will also be provided. Another important concern relates to the political realities of policy formulation. Southern politicians have long been recognized for their control over major agricultural legislation. It would be a major oversight not to evaluate the potential for the South continuing to control the policymaking environment.

BRIEF HISTORY OF THE FARM PROGRAMS

Understanding how farm programs have affected the South requires familiarity with the history of the farm programs. Accordingly, an overview of the farm programs is provided. Greater detail about specific programs can be found in Cochrane and Ryan (1976) or Rasmussen and Baker (1979).

Formal farm programs were first developed in the 1930s in response to the agricultural depression of that time. Commodities covered by farm bills include feed and food grains, dairy products, cotton, peanuts, and tobacco.

From the 1930s to the late 1960s, farm programs generally were characterized by high fixed price supports and rigid supply controls that kept commodity production from shifting from one region to another. The price support levels were generally based on a parity price formula that tied price and cost ratios to their 1910-1914 base. This formula pricing largely ignored regional differences in cost structure, changes in the cost structure over time, and the effects of technology on yields and incomes.

High price supports interfered with international marketing and led to an accumulation of stocks in government storage. "Demand enhancement" programs such as export subsidies and domestic and international food giveaways were developed to address the storage build-up.

Supply control programs were developed partly to address the stock accumulation problem and partly as a means of raising producers' revenues. Demand for agricultural commodities was believed to be inelastic, meaning that a small decrease in quantity would result in a relatively large increase in price, thus increasing producers' gross revenues.

The early supply control programs granted the right to produce only to those who had a history of growing the particular commodity. Producers approved the mandatory controls in a referendum in which only producers of the commodity in question were allowed to vote. The voters believed the rigid supply control system would prevent new entrants from bidding down prices and would limit existing producers in such a way as to benefit all. The long-term consequences of rigid supply controls were not considered to be important.

The "Southern commodities" (cotton, rice, peanuts, and tobacco) were all subject to rigid supply controls during the 1950s and 1960s. There have been major changes in the cotton and rice program, but tobacco production continues to be rigidly controlled. Peanut production outside the farm program, although no longer expressly forbidden, is generally unprofitable.

The tobacco program was established by the Agricultural Adjustment Act of 1938 and has remained in effect, with occasional minor modifications, ever since. The program involves a national quota and a price support subject to approval of two-thirds of the producers in a referendum. Burley and flue-cured tobacco quotas have been in effect since 1934 with quota determination tied to total stocks. Provisions for intracounty rental and transfer of quotas began in 1961 for flue-cured and in 1971 for burley. Because transfer or lease outside of the county has been forbidden, tobacco production has not shifted since the onset of the programs.

Until the 1981 farm bill, the peanut program involved acreage allotments that strictly limited production. Although the supply provisions have been relaxed to allow planting under contract outside the program, peanut production remains highly controlled. Support prices are two-tiered with a poundage quota limiting the quantity eligible for the higher support rate. Because the nonquota loan rate is generally less than half the quota support rate, production patterns probably will remain unchanged.

Cotton allotments were first announced in 1934 and the program continued, with some interruptions, until 1977. For all practical purposes, however, the allotments were abandoned in 1970 when mandatory marketing quotas were replaced by a voluntary set-aside program. Although the allotments were adjusted several times to allow some movement of cotton production, it was not until the 1970s that cotton production was allowed to be determined by economic efficiency. Removal of the allotments resulted in a general westward trend of production. California, in particular, benefited from the removal of the old allotments. From 1970 to 1979, California acreage planted in cotton rose from 666,000 acres to 1.65 million acres, while acreage in most southeastern states fell.

A switch from rigid to flexible supply control provisions was not the only change in the cotton program that occurred during the 1970s. Support prices were reduced dramatically and a direct subsidy payment to farmers was used to support income. The deficiency payments allowed farm income to be supported without interfering with international marketing.

Like the cotton program, the wheat and feed grain programs also were changed in the 1970s by the substitution of direct payments, lower support prices, and flexible supply control for high fixed support prices and rigid acreage control. In the 1985 farm bill, price supports for grains and cotton were once again materially reduced to the point where direct payments currently make up from 30 to 70 percent of farmers' receipts for farm program commodities.

From 1953 to 1973, the rice program was characterized by restrictive acreage allotments and marketing quotas. From 1973 to 1981, the allotments did not restrict plantings but were used to allocate and limit deficiency payments. Like cotton, rice production had shifted over time, particularly in the direction of Mississippi. By 1981, the allotments no longer reflected planting patterns. As a result, during the 1981 farm bill deliberations, political pressure resulted in the discontinuation of the allotments.

Although the direct payments eliminated the market interference of the old high support prices, the subsidy programs were not at first popular with the public because of cases in which individuals received more than $1,000,000 from the government. This led to the development of a $50,000 payment limitation per individual. Legal organization is often used, however, to avoid the payment limit (Taylor, 1987).

Supply control programs for cotton and grain are now characterized by voluntary participation, but farm program subsidies are offered only to those producers who comply with supply reduction. Economic incentives to participate in the farm program can be so strong that supply control is, in effect, mandatory. Supply control under the new farm programs has generally taken one of four forms: (a) set-aside, (b) acreage limitation, (c) paid diversion, and (d) conservation reserve. The last two are generally optional even to program participants.

A set-aside program is less effective than a quota or allotment in reducing production. Producers set aside less productive land and thus production does not fall proportionately to the acres set aside. Another concern with the set-aside program is that variable factors of production are not limited. This leads to a distortion in productive efficiency as variable inputs are substituted for land in production of the commodity (Floyd, 1965). Of course, this is also a problem with acreage allotments.

The acreage limitation (or acreage reduction) programs of the 1980s are less flexible than the set-aside programs. Under these programs, producers have an acreage "base" in program commodities. Under the 1981 farm bill, the base was generally the average of acres planted or considered planted for the past two years. The 1985 farm bill specifies a five year average, considerably reducing producers' ability to expand base acreage in a particular commodity. When an acreage reduction is announced, producers are limited to planting only a certain portion of their base acreage in a commodity if they wish to participate in the farm program. Because the acreage reduction programs, like set-aside programs, cause land to be idled, they result in the same resource allocation problems as the set-aside program.

Although the set-aside and acreage reduction programs in the 1985 farm bill are not as restrictive as the old mandatory supply control provisions, they may be as effective in locking production into specific regions. Given the current economic climate in agriculture, farm program benefits often comprise a significant portion of cash receipts for a commodity. Thus, as a practical reality, farmers are required to participate in the program.

In spite of commodity-specific supply control provisions, chronic surpluses have characterized much of the history of the farm program. Incentives for increased production in an environment of reduced income risk, combined with technologically driven yield increases, have more than offset the acreage reductions. To remove excess production over the long run, another policy tool, long-term land retirement, was developed. The Soil Bank program, established by the Agricultural Act of 1956, was the first major land retirement program. Under this program, farmers were paid to divert some or all of their cropland to soil-conserving uses under long-term contracts. By July of 1960, a total of 26.8 million acres in the U.S. were under contract. This amount steadily declined until the last land left the reserve in 1972. In the South, much of the conservation reserve land was converted to forestry use.

In developing the 1985 farm bill, farmers joined forces with conservationists to mandate a new long-term land retirement program. Under the new conservation reserve program, 45 million acres will be removed from production by 1991 in return for government payments. Because the idled land can be planted in trees, the conservation reserve program can be an attractive alternative to producers in wooded areas of the country, particularly the South.

For the last fifty years, agricultural policies have had a tremendous influence on resource allocation in the farm sector. Programs have provided price or subsidization incentives for the production of certain commodities while at the same time attempting to limit production through acreage reduction provisions or land retirement programs. Because of farm programs, production of some commodities such as tobacco and peanuts has been essentially "locked in" to certain regions. It is not surprising that many economists believe agricultural policies cause serious distortions in resource use (Rausser and Farrell, 1985).

FARM PROGRAMS AND THE SOUTH

To put the importance of farm programs in the South into perspective, it is important to understand what percentage of Southern agricultural receipts are from the farm program commodities. In this chapter, fourteen states are defined as the "South" and then further classified into four regions. The Appalachian region consists of Virginia, West Virginia, Kentucky, Tennessee and North Carolina. The Southeast consists of Florida, Georgia, South Carolina, and Alabama. Mississippi, Arkansas, and Louisiana comprise the Delta states, while Oklahoma and Texas comprise the Southern Plains.

For the South as a whole, 41 percent of cash receipts are from farm program commodities (Table 1). This is in line with the national average of 46 percent. However, farm program dependence varies widely in different regions of the South. In the Delta, 54 percent of cash receipts come from farm program commodities compared with less than 33 percent in the Southeast.

Although these figures do not indicate any unusual Southern dependence on farm program commodities, a strong case can be made that the "Southern" commodities carry significantly higher subsidies. An index of reliance on farm programs which relates the target or other support price to a market determined price ranges from over 3 for peanuts to 0.90 for soybeans. Southern crops generally have the highest indices (Table 2).

Land use patterns are also important in determining the effects of farm programs. Nationally, 33 percent of farmland is harvested cropland, 4 percent

Table 1. Cash Receipts from Commodities, 1985 (Percent)

Commodity	U.S.	South	Appalachia	Southeast	Delta	Southern Plains
Grains	19.7	11.1	9.5	3.8	15.2	19.0
Cotton	2.7	5.5	1.3	2.1	13.5	8.7
Tobacco	1.9	5.8	20.6	2.3	*	*
Soybeans	7.6	5.9	7.4	3.4	18.1[1]	.6
Peanuts	.7	2.3	1.7	4.8	*	1.3
Sugar	1.1	.5	*	.3	1.8	.4
Dairy	12.8	10.2	10.5	15.8	5.2	5.9
Total Farm Program Commodities	46.5	41.3	51.0	32.5	54.3	35.9
Livestock & Poultry	35.7	42.3	40.8	33.2	43.2	54.1
Horticultural Products	14.6	13.3	7.5	27.0	2.5	7.8
Hay	1.6	.8	.5	.3	.4	1.9
Other	1.6	2.4	.1	7.0	.1	3.7

* Not Reported.

[1]Figure may include a small amount of other oil seeds.

Source: *Economic Indicators of the Farm Sector*, 1985. *State Financial Summary.*

is woodland, and 53 percent is pasture (Table 3). Although the South as a whole does not diverge greatly from these averages, the different regions of the South exhibit different patterns. Unpastured woodland comprises over 20 percent of the acreage in the Appalachian region and over 17 percent of the acreage in the Southeast. In the Delta, nearly 50 percent of farmland is in harvested acres. The Southern Plains region has a high percentage of land in pasture (nearly 75 percent) and only 1 percent of land in woods.

With the important exception of dairy, most of the program provisions have primarily affected crop production. Of the four Southern regions, the Delta, with its unusually high proportion of cropland, has the greatest potential to be affected by farm programs. Conversely, programs that promote conservation usage may be most favorable to farmers in wooded areas. Appalachia and the Southeast are both much higher than the national average in this respect.

Table 2. Reliance on Government Programs for Price and Income Protection (1985/86)

Commodity	Market Price	Support	Ratio of Support to Market
Soybeans	5.05	4.56	0.90
Cotton	46.1	81.0	1.75
Tobacco	1.19	1.54	1.29
Wheat	2.29	4.38	1.91
Rice	6.62	11.90	1.80
Corn	1.55	3.03	1.95
Sorghum	1.40	2.88	1.34
Peanuts	7.50	28.80	3.84
Sugar	6.05	20.95	3.46

Table 3. Land use by Percent of Farmland, 1982

Region	Harvested Cropland	Woodland	Pasture
U.S.	33.1	4.4	53.4
South	26.9	7.8	57.8
Applachia	34.8	20.5	35.3
Southeast	32.1	17.2	42.1
Delta	49.4	10.8	30.7
Southern Plains	18.2	1.0	74.5

Source: *1982 Census of Agriculture.*

The overall effect of farm programs on the South also depends on the structure of Southern agriculture. In turn, farm programs can provide strong incentives for structural change. During most of the past fifty years, however, structural considerations have had at best a minor role in the development of agricultural policies. Instead, the major focus of the farm bills has been on price and income enhancement and stabilization. Recently, however, concern about the dwindling number of farms and the "industrialization" of agriculture has caused structure to emerge as an issue of importance. Understanding structure is important in understanding both the problems to be addressed by policies and the effects these policies might have.

Table 4. Farm Size Distribution 1982—Percent of Farms
by Sales Receipts

Region	Less than $10,000	$10,000 -39,000	$40,000 -99,999	$100,000 -249,999	$250,000 or more
U.S.	49.0	22.7	14.9	9.6	3.9
South	63.5	19.6	8.3	5.8	2.9
Appalachia	63.8	22.2	7.7	4.5	1.8
Southeast	62.5	16.7	8.7	7.5	4.6
Delta	63.1	14.5	8.7	8.8	4.7
Southern Plains	63.8	20.3	8.5	4.9	2.4

Source: *1982 Census of Agriculture.*

Agricultural structure encompasses a number of farm characteristics including size, organization, land tenure, and debt structure. The South is distinguished from other regions of the country in having a greater percentage of small, part-time farms. In Table 4, the percentages of farms in different size categories are presented for the U.S., the South in general, and also for the four different regions of the South. More Southern farms fall into the smallest size categories than do U.S. farms overall. In the United States, slightly less than half of all farms are in the smallest sales category (less than $10,000 annual sales) while in the South 63 percent of farms are in this category.

In an often cited study by Lin et al. (1981) it was found that a disproportionately high amount of farm program benefits accrue to large farms. These findings might seem to indicate that farm programs will encourage the growth and survival of the largest farms while placing the smaller farms at an increasingly disadvantaged position, thereby providing a powerful force for structural change in the South.

Because farm program benefits have almost always been tied to production in some way, it is not surprising that Lin et al. (1981) found that most farm program benefits are paid to large farms that produce more. It is instructive, however, to examine the pattern of dependence on farm program commodities by farm size as a somewhat different conclusion regarding farm programs and farm size emerges.

Using 1982 census data, Tweeten (1986) calculated cash receipts from different commodities for different sized farms. Nationally, farms with less than $10,000 in sales earned 31 percent of cash receipts from farm program commodities. On the largest farms (over $500,000 in sales), farm program commodities accounted for only 21 percent of cash receipts. The mid-sized farms, particularly those with $40,000-$99,999 in cash receipts, were the most heavily reliant on farm program commodities. Farms in the $40,000-$99,999 sales group received over 63 percent of cash receipts from farm program commodities. Farm programs therefore appear to be relatively more important to the medium-sized farms rather than the largest farms. Smith et al. (1984) found that termination of commodity programs would have the most adverse effect on farmers in the medium-size range.

It is difficult, if not impossible, to assess the net affect of past government programs on farm size distribution in the South. However, it is fairly clear that an abrupt cessation of the farm programs would have a devastating affect on medium-sized crop farms. The South, more than other regions of the country, is already characterized by an abundance of very small farms. Loss of farms in the medium-sized groups would result in an even more "bi-modal" distribution of agriculture.

Because many of the small Southern farms are part-time operations, Southern farmers are less reliant on farming for all of their income. Nationally, 55 percent of producers view agriculture as their principal occupation, while 39 percent list it as their only occupation (Table 5). In the South, these figures fall to 45 percent and 33 percent, respectively, reflecting the larger percentage of small farms. Unfortunately, the decline in rural manufacturing industries is reducing off-farm employment opportunities in many areas. Operators of small, part-time farms may benefit more from rural development strategies than from agricultural policy. Off-farm job opportunities, education, and training may thus be more important in the rural South than in other areas of the country.

Table 5. Percent of Operators who are Full Time Farmers, 1982

Region	Principal Occupation	Only Occupation
U.S.	55.1	38.5
South	45.2	33.0
Appalachia	46.7	33.7
Southeast	42.9	33.2
Delta	47.0	35.3
Southern Plains	43.8	30.9

Source: *1982 Census of Agriculture.*

POLICY OPTIONS FOR THE FUTURE

Although only a small percentage of the population in the rural South is directly employed in agricultural production, a continued decline in the agricultural sector will have serious consequences for the rural South. Reduced agricultural income and the consequent decline in land values can seriously reduce the tax base in rural communities. The reduced tax base in turn makes it more difficult for the community to maintain or develop services that might attract industry. Agricultural decline also leads to a decline in businesses that are agriculturally related. Hence, the future direction of agricultural policy should be of considerable concern to the rural South.

But, predicting future farm policy is a risky business. One of the popular topics among agricultural economists during the 1960s involved explaining how, because of reapportionment, decline in farm numbers, and changes in leadership of the Congress, agriculture was losing its influence (Talbot and Hadwiger, 1968). In the 1970s, Paarlberg (1975) stated that the agricultural establishment had lost control of the agricultural policy agenda. In the 1980 presidential campaign, candidate Reagan's agricultural platform involved decisive efforts to remove government from agriculture. Yet, since 1981, the governmental expenditures on farm programs have twice approached or exceeded $30 billion. Given this record of prediction and events, it would be foolhardy to suggest the farm programs are doomed.

Since there is a history of only a few major policy changes (policies tend to evolve rather than change), the best predictive tool is probably past policy. This would suggest a continuation of a relatively high level of farm program expenditures and direct payments to farmers, but there are those who contend that current programs cost too much. Reducing program costs, however, requires either a material lowering of income support to farmers or a sharp diversion of policy in the direction of high price supports and mandatory production controls.

Instead of predicting future policies, the strategy here is to present an analysis of policy alternatives. The basis for the analysis is a recently completed Texas A&M study of policy options for modifying the 1985 farm bill (Knutson et al., 1987). In the study, macroeconomic simulation and farm-level simulation were used to evaluate the probable outcomes of various policy alternatives. Several possibilities for the next few years are discussed briefly. Simulation results are summarized in Table 6.

Table 6. Summary Results of Analysis of Alternatives for the 1985 Farm Bill

Program Impact	Policy Option		
	Continue 1985 Farm Bill	25% Target Price Cut	Harkin Bill
Annual Average Net Cash Income ($ bil.)	6.8	(1.4)	29.7
Annual Average Government Cost ($ bil.)	12.9	4.9	13.2
1990 Ending Commodity Stocks (bil. bu.)	5.0	4.4	6.0
Probability of 5% Return on Initial Equity			
1360 Acre Texas High Plains Cotton Farm (%)	4	0	94
3300 Acre Texas High Plains Cotton Farm (%)	90	8	98

Source: Knutson et al., 1987.

Continuation of the 1985 Farm Bill

The 1985 farm bill is certainly not going to solve all the problems of Southern farmers. Assuming continued high federal budget deficits and moderate money supply growth, the Texas A&M study projects a relative stabilization of net farm income at about the current level and continued decline of farmland values. At the farm level, a 3,300 acre Texas cotton farm has a 90 percent chance of earning a 5 percent return on beginning equity over the remaining three years of the 1985 farm bill. Moderate size farms do considerably worse. A 1,360 acre Texas High Plains cotton farm, for example, would have only a 4 percent chance of earning a 5 percent return.

Livestock and poultry producers do relatively better than crop producers under the 1985 farm bill because relatively high target prices and low support prices mean low feed costs. Low market prices, brought about by weak export markets for grain, are unlikely to rise significantly in the short run because of the relatively high levels of government stocks.

Lower Target Price

The option studied for lowered target prices involved a 25 percent reduction in 1988 continued through 1991, a somewhat smaller reduction than the administration's proposed 30 percent cut spread over three years. The results of a 25 percent reduction in target price on the Southern crop producers could only be classified as devastating. Net cash farm income to crop producers declines from an estimated $6.8 billion under continuation of the 1985 farm bill to a negative $1.4 billion. The probability of a Texas program crop farm earning a 5 percent return on initial equity falls to less than 10 percent. This policy would lead to further reductions in land values and in greater loss of tax base in the rural communities. The target price reduction would, of course, reduce government stocks and expenditures on the farm program.

Mandatory Production Controls

There is a growing movement within agriculture for a return to strict production controls linked to high support prices. The much discussed Harkin bill is the current legislative front for this movement. The Harkin bill proposes supports set at 70 percent of parity, approximately double the current level. To avoid the normal export reduction consequences, Harkin would either establish an export cartel or subsidize exports to maintain U.S. market shares. Since an export cartel has little chance of working, export subsidies would be extensive and the cost would probably equal or exceed current program costs.

With an inelastic domestic demand for farm products and high levels of export subsidies, the Harkin measures would result in increased farm income. Under a 70 percent parity price support, the probability of earning a 5 percent return increases to nearly 100 percent, regardless of farm size.

Although the Harkin bill may appear desirable because of its effect on farm income, there are several problems with the bill. Questions arise as to whether the government could prevent subsidized exports from reentering the United States. This problem is the most serious in the cotton industry where the domestic textile industry could be very adversely affected by increased imports of textiles. The Harkin bill would also have adverse short-run consequences for the livestock and poultry industries where grains are an input. Eventually, higher support prices would be translated into higher consumer prices, particularly for meat and poultry. Finally, as noted above, government costs would probably not fall under the Harkin bill.

THE SOUTH AS A POLICY FORCE

The future direction of agricultural policy will have a large effect on Southern farms. Policy is not developed in a void, however, and the South may play an important role in shaping future farm policy. The South has a fascinating record of dominance of the agriculture committees in both the Senate and the House, as well as the House Appropriations Committee. On the House side, the Committee on Agriculture has been chaired by Southern Democrats almost without interruption. Representative Cooley (D, NC) was chair from the 1940s until 1966 when Representative Poage (D, TX) became chair. After a short hiatus when Foley (D, WA) was chair, de la Garza (D, TX) returned control of the committee to the South. On the Senate side, Chair Talmadge (D, GA) was preceded by Chair Ellender (D, LA). When the Democrats lost control of the Senate, Representative Helms (R, NC) took the chair. With the Senate reverting to Democratic control, Northern Senator Patrick Leahy (D, VT) assumed the chair. The importance of this change in leadership on the Senate side remains to be seen.

Southern political influence in agriculture is not confined to the agricultural committees. Analysts of the political power of agriculture have observed Southern control of other important committees and even of leadership of the Congress. A classic example is the "permanent secretary of agriculture," House Appropriations Committee Chair Jamie Whitten (D, MS), and his predecessor Representative Mayhon (D, TX). Southern control of Congress was particularly strong during the long tenure of Sam Rayburn (D, TX) as Speaker of the House, which coincided with Lyndon Johnson's (D, TX) prominence in the Senate.

Evidence of a history of Southern control of agriculture exists not only in the Congressional roles, but also in the past farm bills where Southern commodities have long been covered by favorable farm programs. An important question for the future of Southern agriculture is: will the South continue to shape farm programs of the future?

A continuation of Southern control of agricultural policy is indicated by the current composition and leadership of the agriculture and appropriations committees. On the House Committee on Agriculture, 14 of 26 Democrats are from the South, but only 3 of 17 Republicans. In addition to the chair, the next two ranking Democrats are from the South—Jones (NC) and Jones (TN). Brown (CA) is the third ranking Democrat, followed by two more Southerners—Rose (NC) and English (OK). As long as Democrats remain in the majority in the House, the South probably will retain control of the Committee on Agriculture for many years to come. On the Republican side, however, the highest ranking Southerner, Hopkins (KY), is only fifth in seniority.

In the 1986 shift in majority control of the Senate, the South lost control of the Senate Committee on Agriculture, Nutrition, and Forestry. Currently, 4 of 10 Democrats on the Committee are from the South and 3 of 8 Republicans. Although the South clearly does not control the Senate Agriculture Committee, there is still a substantial block of Southern political power.

The South is in control of both appropriations committees with Representative Whitten (D, MS) and Senator Stennis (D, MS) chairs of their respective committees. Aside from these powerful chairs, a strong case can not be made for Southern control in the future.

Overall leadership of the House and Senate is also an important indicator of who controls the Congressional agenda. Southern dominance was considerably more evident in the past than it is currently. Representative Wright's (D, TX) new position as Speaker of the House is a significant gain for the South. On the Senate side, Stennis (D, MS) and Byrd (D, WV) are in leadership positions.

It seems fair to conclude that in the future, the South will need to work harder to secure legislation favoring its agriculture. The link between Northern and Southern agriculture will need to be strengthened. Building bridges for commodities such as soybeans and wheat will become increasingly important. Southern agriculture also needs to develop stronger ties with the West. California, in particular, has become a prominent political force in agriculture. The state has three high-ranking Democrats (Brown, Panetta, and Coelho) and one Republican (Heiger) on the House Committee on Agriculture. In addition, Senator Wilson of California serves on the Senate Agriculture Committee. With common commodity interests in cotton, rice, sugar, fruits, and vegetables, strong political ties between the South and West should develop easily.

SUMMARY

This chapter has examined the history and impact of federal policies on agriculture in the South. In general, Southern commodities have received a high degree of protection under the various farm bills probably due to the pervasive influence of Southern politicians in formulating agriculture policy. Because tree planting is an attractive alternative use of land, farmers in the eastern South also have probably benefited from land retirement programs such as the Soil Bank and the new conservation reserve.

The old farm program agenda, and to a lesser extent more recent legislation, locked production of certain highly profitable commodities into specific Southern regions, creating economic distortions that have harmed some areas of the South and benefited others. By limiting acreage, policies may also have resulted in sub-optimal production strategies.

Southern farms, particularly in Appalachia and the Southeast, tend to be smaller than the national average and rely to a large extent on off-farm income. Although policy and stucture are linked to a considerable degree, contradictory incentives are often present in the farm bills that make the overall structural impact difficult to evaluate.

Politics will continue to be an important future dimension of Southern agriculture because farm programs are critical to the agricultural adjustment process, but the specific future of farm policy is very difficult to predict. Free market policies depend on growth in international trade which, in turn depends on favorable global economic conditions such as success in the Multilateral Trade Negotiations (MTN), reduced developing country debt, and reduced international tension. The necessity of reducing government expenditures on farm programs is often stated, but an equally strong case can be made that $30 billion is the new norm in farm program spending. The issues at the heart of future farm legislation are: (1) producers' preferences for high support prices linked to rigid supply control versus their willingness to make adjustments to less government support, and (2) the willingness of the American public to accept higher food prices as a consequence of a change in policy.

In a time when it can be argued that the South has lost some of its past control over agricultural policymaking, more attention should be given to the politics of agriculture as well as to agricultural policies.

REFERENCES

Cochrane, Willard W. and Mary E. Ryan. 1976. *American Farm Policy 1948-1973*. Minneapolis, Minnesota: University of Minnesota Press.

Floyd, John E. 1965. "The effects of farm price supports on the returns to labor and land in agriculture." *Journal of Political Economics* 73(No. 2):148-158.

Knutson, Ronald D., Edward G. Smith, James W. Richardson, John B. Penson, Jr., Dean W. Hughes, Mechel S. Paggi, Robert D. Yonkers, and Dean T. Chen. 1987. *Policy Alternatives for Modifying the 1985 Farm Bill*. College Station, Texas: Texas Agricultural Experiment Station, Bulletin B-1561.

Lin, William, James Johnson, and Linda Calvin. 1978. *Farm Commodity Programs: Who Participates and Who Benefits?* United States Department of Agriculture, Economic Research Service, Report No. 474. Washington, D.C.: U.S. Government Printing Office.

Paarlberg, Phillip P. 1975. "The farm policy agenda." *Increasing Understanding of Public Problems and Policies*. Farm Foundation, pp. 95-103.

Rasmussen, Wayne D. and Gladys L. Baker. 1979. *Price-Support and Adjustment Programs from 1933 through 1978: A Short History*. United States Department of Agriculture, Economics, Statistics, and Cooperatives Service. Agricultural Information Bulletin No. 424. Washington, D.C.: U.S. Government Printing Office.

Rausser, Gordon C. and Kenneth R. Farrell. 1985. *Alternative Agricultural and Food Policies and the 1985 Farm Bill*. Chapter 1, Gordon C. Rausser and Kenneth R. Farrell, ed. University of California: Giannini Foundation of Agricultural Economics.

Smith, Edward G., James W. Richardson and Ronald D. Knutson. 1984. "Cost and pecuniary economies in cotton production and marketing." College Station, Texas: Texas Agricultural Experiment Station, D-1475.

Talbot, Ross B. and Don F. Hadwiger. 1968. *The Policy Process in American Agriculture*. San Francisco, California: Chandler Publishing Co.

Taylor, Marcia A. 1987. "USDA wants to plug payment loopholes." *Farm Journal*. 3(No. 7):17.

Tweeten, Luther. 1986. "Impact of domestic policy on comparative advantage of agriculture in the South." *Southern Journal of Agricultural Economics* 18 (No. 1):67-74.

16

Development Strategies in the Rural South: Issues and Alternatives

David Mulkey
Mark S. Henry

It now seems clear that the early 1980s brought fundamental changes to rural America (Beaulieu, 1987; Drabenstott et al., 1986; Henry et al., 1986; Rosenfeld et al., 1985). Farm foreclosures, bank and business failures, financially stressed state/local governments, and other examples of economic decline reached epidemic proportions in many parts of the nation. As a result, concern for rural problems is widespread, and a variety of policy options are being considered at all levels of government. Providing a focus for that debate in the rural South is the major objective in this chapter.

During the decades of the 60s and 70s, rural areas were successful from a development point of view. In the South, a combination of factors—low taxes, low wages, a favorable business climate, investments in infrastructure, etc.—made the region attractive to industry. As a result, population and employment gains were significant both in absolute terms and relative to the nation as a whole (Cornell and McLindon, 1986; Mulkey, 1984; Southern Growth Policies Board, 1985). However, as noted, the fortunes of rural areas have changed dramatically in recent years. For the first time in more than 20 years, rural residents failed to make real economic gains relative to their urban counterparts (Henry et al., 1986). Rural areas in the South were particularly hard-hit by a combination of problems in agricultural and natural resource industries and a loss of manufacturing jobs.

More importantly, both national and regional studies conclude that current rural problems are not temporary, cyclical phenomena. Rural areas are undergoing a fundamental restructuring due to international forces, the shift within the United States to a service-based economy, deregulation of financial, transportation, and communications industries, and shifts in traditional agriculture towards larger numbers of small part-time farms and small numbers of large farms. The rural income problem is pictured as more of a long-term structural issue involving variables such as education, public infrastructure, job skills, and institutional change (Drabenstott et al., 1986; Henry et al., 1986; Rosenfeld et al., 1985). With particular regard to the South, Rosenfeld et al. (1985: xiv) conclude:

> *The evidence compiled suggests that long-term restructuring of the region's economy is indeed occurring, resulting in shifts in jobs from nonmetro to metro areas, in shifts among industrial sectors from manufacturing to services, and in shifts within manufacturing from traditional to emerging industries.*

This chapter argues that the underlying economic forces noted above provide the backdrop within which future development strategies for the rural South must be considered. Just as the changes facing rural areas are structural and fundamental in nature, so are the policy choices.

With the fundamental nature of the policy choices in mind, following sections offer a brief overview of change in the rural South using county-level data. Comparisons are made for metropolitan and nonmetropolitan counties in the South and for nonmetropolitan counties by source of income. Final sections of the paper then examine the policy alternatives in more detail.

THE RURAL SOUTH

The South's Rural Counties

How do the South's rural counties compare to their metropolitan counterparts and to rural areas in other parts of the nation? To answer this question, county-level data are used, and nonmetropolitan counties are assumed to constitute the rural South. Classification of nonmetropolitan counties is taken from the national study of rural counties by Henry et al. (1986). The definition of nonmetropolitan as rural is consistent with the framework developed by Bender et. al. (1985), and nonmetropolitan status is based on 1974 Office of Management and Budget designations. This choice of data and county classifications allows comparison between data presented here and the earlier study of rural counties in the nation.

Tables 1 and 2, respectively, present data on population and income for 1,304 counties in the South[1] and for the 3,067 counties in the nation. Of the Southern counties, 1,050 are classified as nonmetropolitan (rural) with a 1984 population of 26.7 million people. Together, nonmetropolitan counties in the South account for 37.5 percent of the region's population and for 30.9 percent of the region's income. Nationally, 2,441 counties are nonmetropolitan, containing 27.7 percent of the nation's population and accounting for 22.3 percent of total income. The 13 Southern states are more rural in character than is the nation as a whole, and the region contains approximately 41 percent of the nation's rural population.

Tables 1 and 2 also present population and income data for groups of nonmetropolitan counties in the South and the nation, respectively, classified by primary source of income. The most significant feature is the importance of manufacturing-dependent counties in the rural areas of the nation and in the rural South. Historically, there has been a tendency by the Department of Agriculture to view rural development policy as synonomous with agricultural policies and programs (Henry et al., 1986; Rasmussen, 1986). However, data in Tables 1 and 2 provide little justification for considering these as such. Nationally, manufacturing-dependent rural counties account for approximately 36 percent of rural population and income, compared to approximately 11 percent of population and income for the 602 agricultural-dependent counties. Differences are even greater in the South. The region contains more than one-half of the nation's manufacturing-dependent, nonmetropolitan counties, and these counties represent 40 percent of the region's nonmetropolitan population and income. In comparison, agricultural-dependent counties in the South contain 9 percent of the region's nonmetropolitan population and provide 8.4 percent of total income.

The dominant role of manufacturing in the rural areas of the South is even more marked in selected Southern states. Table 3 presents data similar to that in Tables 1 and 2 for an eight-state region of the central South (Arkansas, Alabama, Mississippi, Georgia, Kentucky, North Carolina, South Carolina, and Tennessee). In each of these states, the ratio of manufacturing employment to total employment exceeds the national average (Bureau of the Census, 1986). The eight-state region contains 276 of the South's 342 manufacturing-dependent counties. Collectively, the manufacturing-dependent counties represent more than 50 percent of the income and population in the selected states.

Retirement-dependent and trade-dependent counties are the next largest groupings among Southern counties, followed by those dependent on government activity. Together, these three groups account for fewer counties and a lower percentage of population and income than do the manufacturing-dependent counties in the Southern states. However, each group represents a larger percentage of the South's rural population and income than do the agricultural-dependent counties. In the eight selected states, counties dependent on retirement, government, and trade are less dominant than in the nonmetropolitan South as a whole.

Table 1. Population, Personal Income, and Per Capital Income—
Southern Metropolitan and Nonmetropolitan Counties, 1984

Type of County	Number of Counties	Population	%Total	Personal Income ($1,000s)	Percent of Total Counties	Per Capita Income
All Counties	1,304	71,394,847	100.0	820,830,976	100.0	11,497
Metropolitan	254	44,654,049	62.5	567,594,003	69.1	12,711
Nonmetropolitan	1,050	26,740,798	37.5	253,236,973	30.9	9,470
Manufacturing	342	10,830,150	40.5	103,101,774	40.7	9,520
Mining	80	1,698,344	6.4	16,299,480	6.4	9,597
Agriculture	188	2,394,628	9.0	21,195,380	8.4	8,851
Retirement	113	3,514,985	13.1	36,201,944	14.3	10,299
Government	87	2,791,368	10.4	25,841,432	10.2	9,258
Mix	68	1,165,169	4.4	10,125,150	4.0	8,690
Trade	131	3,566,376	13.3	34,830,993	13.8	9,766
Other	41	799,778	2.9	5,640,820	2.2	7,234

Table 2. Population, Personal Income, and Employment—
U.S. Metropolitan and Nonmetropolitan Counties, 1984

Type of County	Number	Population		Personal Income	
		(1000s)	%Total	(Billions $)	%Total
All Counties	3,067	232,882	100.0	2,971.52	100.0
Metropolitan	626	168,302	72.3	2,309.58	77.7
Nonmetropolitan	2,441	64,580	27.7	661.94	22.3
Manufacturing	618	23,401	36.2	240.76	36.4
Mining	176	3,918	6.1	38.01	5.7
Agriculture	602	7,407	11.5	77.57	11.7
Retirement	222	7,316	11.3	76.97	11.6
Government	239	8,329	12.9	84.26	12.7
Mix	128	1,896	2.9	17.75	2.7
Trade	370	10,571	16.4	110.75	16.7
Other	86	1,742	2.7	15.87	2.4

Table 3. Population, Personal Income, and Per Capita Income—
Metropolitan and Nonmetropolitan Counties, Selected States, 1984

Type of County	Number	Population (1000s)	%Total	Personal Income ($ 1000s)	%Total
All Counties	744	32,679	100.0	340,098,482	100.0
Metropolitan	125	16,030	49.1	189,503,484	55.7
Nonmetropolitan	619	16,649	50.9	150,594,998	44.3
Manufacturing	276	8,953	53.8	84,368,319	56.0
Mining	27	678	4.1	5,508,311	3.7
Agriculture	107	1,409	8.5	11,289,810	7.5
Retirement	35	1,169	7.0	10,798,735	7.2
Government	37	1,322	7.9	12,305,070	8.2
Mix	45	839	5.0	7,060,991	4.7
Trade	57	1,693	10.2	15,068,733	10.0
Other	35	587	3.5	4,195,029	2.8

States Include: Arkansas, Mississippi, Alabama, Georgia, South Carolina, North Carolina, Tennessee and Kentucky

In short, as Henry et al. (1986) note, the nation's rural areas are more diverse than is commonly recognized, and they are heavily dependent on manufacturing. In comparison, manufacturing is of greater importance to the economic base of the rural South. Further, the central South is more rural in character than the South as a whole, and manufacturing plays an even larger role in its economic base.

Metropolitan/Nonmetropolitan Comparisons

How have nonmetropolitan counties in the South fared relative to their metropolitan counterparts? Table 4 presents average annual rates of growth for real income, population, and per capita income for nonmetropolitan counties in the South for selected time periods between 1965 and 1984. Table 5 provides nonmetropolitan/metropolitan comparisons for per capita income over the same period. Data in Tables 4 and 5 are presented according to the groupings of counties based on income used in the previous tables.

With respect to per capita income, the periods 1965-69 and 1969-73 were years in which many nonmetropolitan counties in the South made significant economic gains relative to their metropolitan counterparts. Over the 1965-1969 period, only the trade-dependent counties failed to achieve growth rates in per capita income exceeding that of Southern metropolitan counties. During the 1969-73 period, all groupings of rural counties achieved per capita income gains exceeding those in metropolitan counties. However, relative growth rates in per capita income between nonmetropolitan and metropolitan counties were drastically different over the 1973-79 and 1979-84 periods compared to earlier time periods. Both metropolitan and nonmetropolitan growth rates for per capita income were less in the two later periods than over the earlier years, and fewer types of nonmetropolitan county groupings exceeded metropolitan growth rates. The retirement-dependent counties are the only counties in the nonmetropolitan South which consistently achieved higher rates of growth in per capita income than regional metropolitan counties. Even for these counties, however, growth rates were slower over the more recent periods.

For real income at the county level (total income deflated by the Consumer Price Index) results are similar to those for per capita incomes. Greater gains were achieved in earlier years (1969-1973) than in later years (1973-1984) by all types of counties in the South. However, due to higher rates of population growth in the metropolitan South, nonmetropolitan counties failed to make consistent gains in total income relative to the metropolitan counties. Only the group of retirement-dependent nonmetropolitan counties exhibited consistently strong growth in real income relative to metropolitan counties. As will be noted later, the retirement counties were the only group of nonmetropolitan counties in the South with population growth rates which exceeded those of metropolitan counties.

Table 4. Southern Region—Average Annual Rate of Growth by Selected Time Periods (Percent)

Year & Category	Manufacturing	Mining	Agriculture	Retirement	Government	Mix	Trade	Other	Metropolitan
Real Income									
65-69	6.5	5	4.7	6.3	6.6	8.3	4.2	4.3	8.9
69-73	5.9	7.2	8.3	8.9	5.4	6.4	6.1	6.6	5.7
73-79	2.7	5	1.4	5.5	2.7	2.9	3.3	3.1	3.6
79-84	1.8	0.4	0.9	4.5	2.9	1.5	1.4	0.6	3.3
Population									
65-69	1.2	-0.1	-1	1	1.2	1.5	-0.2	-1	3.7
69-73	1.6	1.2	0.7	4	1.4	1.5	0.9	0.4	2.5
73-79	1.4	1.9	1	3.3	1.9	1.6	1.1	1	2.1
79-84	0.9	1.2	0.9	3.1	1.6	0.9	1.1	0.5	2.1
Per Capita Income									
65-69	5.3	5.2	5.8	5.3	5.3	6.6	4.4	5.3	4.9
69-73	4.3	5.9	7.6	4.8	3.9	4.8	5.2	6.2	3.2
73-79	1.3	3.1	0.4	2.1	0.8	1.2	2.1	2.1	1.4
79-84	1	-0.8	0	1.4	1.3	0.6	0.3	0.1	1.1

Table 5. Ratio Southern Nonmetropolitan Personal Income to Southern Metropolitan Personal Income

Year	Manufac-turing	Mining	Agri-culture	Retire-ment	Govern-ment	Mix	Trade	Other
1959	66.6	66.1	60.6	67.0	68.4	57.4	69.0	44.7
1962	69.9	68.1	63.9	69.3	70.4	60.3	70.9	47.8
1965	72.3	67.4	64.9	71.3	71.6	63.4	72.7	50.9
1966	73.6	67.2	65.6	71.7	73.7	64.4	72.4	51.5
1967	73.7	69.1	65.8	72.4	74.8	64.1	73.3	53.1
1968	74.3	69.7	65.6	73.7	73.7	64.9	73.3	52.9
1969	73.3	68.0	67.0	72.2	72.7	67.4	71.1	51.6
1970	73.5	71.8	69.8	73.7	73.9	66.9	72.4	54.2
1971	73.8	70.8	69.1	74.4	73.5	66.0	72.3	55.3
1972	74.8	71.3	70.0	74.8	73.7	67.2	72.9	55.4
1973	76.4	75.4	78.8	76.8	74.8	71.5	76.7	57.9
1974	75.8	80.6	75.8	76.6	75.0	68.9	76.5	58.5
1975	74.9	82.2	73.2	76.3	73.7	70.5	76.6	56.5
1976	76.0	81.1	72.5	76.7	73.5	70.2	77.8	57.5
1977	75.3	82.4	71.8	76.8	72.6	68.6	78.0	56.5
1978	76.3	79.8	72.7	79.8	72.7	70.9	78.4	59.1
1979	75.5	83.2	73.9	79.9	72.3	70.5	80.0	60.0
1980	73.9	81.8	67.9	79.8	71.3	67.6	78.2	57.1
1981	73.6	83.5	69.8	80.8	71.7	68.4	79.9	57.2
1982	73.4	83.0	69.8	81.2	72.6	68.3	80.2	57.8
1983	74.2	76.2	68.0	80.9	73.0	67.1	77.2	56.9
1984	74.9	75.5	69.6	81.0	72.8	68.4	76.8	56.9

Growth rates aside, however, none of the Southern nonmetropolitan counties has achieved the income levels of their metropolitan counterparts. For all groupings of nonmetropolitan counties, per capita incomes as a percentage of metropolitan incomes were higher in 1984 than in 1965. However, all groups have experienced declines or lower rates of increase over the more recent years. Further, in absolute terms, no group of nonmetropolitan counties in 1984 had average per capita incomes exceeding much more than 80 percent of average per capita incomes for metropolitan counties in the South (Table 5).

Mining- and agricultural-dependent counties experienced more income variability relative to metropolitan averages over the 1965-1984 period. For these counties, per capita income levels in 1984 were significantly lower relative to metropolitan areas than they were over the latter one-half of the 1970s. Again, retirement-dependent nonmetropolitan counties have been consistently strong performers in terms of increasing per capita incomes over time relative to their metropolitan counterparts.

The position of the nonmetropolitan counties in the South relative to their urban counterparts with respect to population is different than is the case for income. Further, the metropolitan-nonmetropolitan comparison of population growth rates in the South is different than similar comparisons for other regions of the country (Beale and Fuguitt, 1986; Rosenfeld et al., 1985). Nonmetropolitan counties in the South grew faster in terms of population during the 1970s than in earlier periods, however, metropolitan counties grew even faster (Table 4). Between 1969 and 1984, only the retirement-dependent nonmetropolitan counties in the South grew faster than metropolitan counties. Again, the retirement-dependent counties are notably different from the other nonmetropolitan counties in the South.

Regional-National Comparisons

Table 6 provides a comparison between nonmetropolitan counties in the South and their national counterparts. For each grouping of counties in the South, Table 6 presents the ratio of per capita income to the same category of counties in the nation. Most of the county groupings in 1984 had per capita incomes exceeding 90 percent of that for the same group in the nation. Exceptions were agricultural-dependent counties (84.5 percent) and counties dependent on a mix of economic factors (83.7 percent). The mining-dependent and retirement-dependent counties in the South had per capita incomes closer to that of the national groups than did other county groups.

In summary, nonmetropolitan counties in the South remain behind metropolitan counties in the region and behind their national counterparts. The South is more rural in character than is the nation as a whole and contains 41 percent of the nation's rural population. The eight states of the central South alone contain over 16 million people who reside in nonmetropolitan counties. This

Table 6. Ratios of Southern Nonmetropolitan Average Per Capital Income to U.S. Averages by Type of County

Year	Manufac-turing	Mining	Agri-culture	Retire-ment	Govern-ment	Mix	Trade	Metro-politan
1959	79.4	88.0	80.2	82.6	82.2	69.2	85.7	81.3
1962	80.4	88.4	77.1	83.5	81.4	68.6	84.2	80.1
1965	81.8	89.3	75.4	86.1	84.3	71.4	85.4	81.6
1966	82.6	90.1	76.2	87.2	86.5	72.7	85.5	82.2
1967	83.8	92.4	79.1	88.3	87.9	74.7	87.3	83.5
1968	84.8	94.0	79.7	89.4	87.1	75.6	87.6	84.3
1969	85.4	92.8	79.8	89.4	88.4	78.6	86.6	85.7
1970	86.5	94.6	82.3	90.5	89.4	79.2	87.5	86.8
1971	86.8	93.6	81.6	90.5	88.7	77.7	87.3	87.4
1972	90.5	92.8	79.9	91.4	89.2	78.1	87.5	88.2
1973	88.1	94.5	76.9	92.1	89.3	78.1	87.2	89.0
1974	88.7	96.6	80.3	93.1	90.3	78.3	88.9	89.6
1975	88.7	96.6	79.1	92.7	89.4	81.7	88.8	89.9
1976	89.5	95.7	84.7	93.3	89.7	80.8	91.5	90.1
1977	89.2	97.4	83.7	93.5	90.1	80.2	92.0	90.4
1978	90.0	96.0	83.2	94.3	89.4	81.8	91.8	90.8
1979	89.7	97.1	83.4	94.7	89.5	82.0	92.9	91.1
1980	90.5	96.8	83.4	96.0	89.6	80.7	93.7	91.9
1981	91.3	98.7	82.1	97.6	90.5	82.1	95.1	93.3
1982	92.1	99.9	85.8	98.5	91.3	83.8	95.4	93.6
1983	92.8	98.4	87.9	97.8	91.4	82.8	94.5	93.0
1984	92.5	98.9	84.5	97.9	91.5	83.7	93.2	92.6

represents 62 percent of the region's nonmetropolitan population and 26 percent of that of the nation. In short, a large part of the nation's rural problem is the rural South.

DEVELOPMENT STRATEGIES: ISSUES AND ALTERNATIVES

A Policy Perspective

Where does the rural South go from here? Rosenfeld et al. (1985) note that the rural South is poorly positioned to benefit from the shift in the nation towards a service economy with an emphasis on markets, highly educated and skilled workers, and urban amenities. Relative to the nation, the rural South, especially in the eight states of the central South, is more dependent on manufacturing employment. Further, much of the manufacturing employment in the rural South is concentrated in lower skilled, lower wage industry, contributing to a persistent North-South earnings gap and making the rural South particularly vulnerable to a loss of manufacturing jobs to foreign competition. Also, the loss of Southern manufacturing jobs has further exacerbated agricultural problems due to the small, part-time nature of Southern agriculture relative to other areas of the nation and the greater dependence on off-farm income (Hansen, 1979; Rosenfeld et al., 1985; Taylor and Gwartney-Gibbs, 1985)

Conclusions by Henry et al. (1986) and Drabenstott et al. (1986) regarding fundamental change in rural America seem to be amplified for the rural South. Further, the policy choices which they pose for rural areas nationally seem to be particularly appropriate for the rural South. Choices must be made between "rural development" policies designed to reverse the effects of underlying economic forces, and "rural transition" policies intended to facilitate the movement of people and resources out of rural areas. Alternatively, some combination of development and transition policies may be chosen. Some segments of the rural economy and some rural places would be identified for development while others would be the focus of transition policies.

Issues and Alternatives

The choice between rural development and rural transition policies will not be an easy one. The decision to adopt rural transition policies will place rural communities and state-federal policymakers in the position of supporting programs designed to assist people in leaving rural areas, further contributing to the decline of many rural communities. Yet, policymakers may have little choice in the immediate future. Traditional policy efforts to recruit industry or stimulate agricultural incomes are not likely to promote widespread economic growth immediately, and in the short run, there appear to be few alternatives. Rural transition policies seem imperative. Programs to increase job skills and worker mobility (job training, relocation assistance, temporary income supplements, etc.) may offer relatively high short-run payoffs.

Over the longer run, the choice between rural development and rural transition policies is no less difficult. An attempt to develop all areas of the rural South is not likely to succeed due to a lack of resources and due to the strength of the underlying forces shaping the current situation. On the other hand, attempts to focus only on transition policies may overlook rural areas with considerable growth potential.

The solution may lie in the choice of a combination of programs designed to accomplish both rural development and rural transition simultaneously (Drabenstott et al., 1986). Programs would encourage transition in those segments of the rural economy that are declining and in those rural areas with little prospect for future development. Other programs would be aimed at encouraging growing segments of the rural economy and encouraging the development of rural areas with high prospects for future development. Both transition and development policies could be designed to meet the needs of particular areas.

The combination approach would still require difficult choices between rural communities and between segments of the rural economy, but it offers more realistic chances for success. To be sure, such an approach ensures only the success of some rural areas and may worsen the situation for many communities. However, if efforts are made to develop all rural areas, scarce resources may be diffused to such an extent that the success of no rural area is assured. The result could be a continuation of unemployment and underemployment problems. With this in mind, the following sections address some components of a rural development-rural transition approach.

HUMAN CAPITAL DEVELOPMENT

Regardless of the choice between rural development programs and rural transition programs, it seems clear that the future of the South is dependent on improved educational systems and a sustained commitment to the improvement of the region's human capital. The importance of education is stressed by the Southern Growth Policies Board. They note that the key to jobs in the future is investment in new and different types of infrastructure and that a quality education system is a key component of such investment (Southern Growth Policies Board, 1985). The 1986 Commission on the Future of the South outlined ten regional objectives for the upcoming six year period, and five relate directly to education (Southern Growth Policies Board, 1986). Commission member Tschinkel notes, "Improving education is the overwhelming imperative in developing the adaptable work force that will boost our competitiveness for the kinds of jobs that will lead to better living standards" (Federal Reserve Bank of Atlanta, 1987). In short, the economic future of the South depends on significant improvements in education and human capital.

However, for the rural policymaker, particularly at the local level, education may pose a dilemma. Education programs in rural communities may serve as a force for development or for transition, depending on the particular community. For the community with growth potential, improved educational systems will enhance the attractiveness of the community for development. Yet, at the same time, the development of a more highly educated, skilled labor force may simply reinforce the fundamental structural changes which are contributing to the growth of metropolitan areas at the expense of rural communities. That is, successful education programs may only serve to facilitate the movement of people out of the rural areas by increasing their ability to compete for higher paying jobs in urban centers. Successful development depends on a commitment to education, but education programs alone will not solve the problems of declining rural communities.

This latter point provides a justification for a strong state and federal role in providing quality education to rural residents. To the extent that education programs are perceived to facilitate the movement of people out of local communities, local support for such programs may be reduced. This is especially true when increased expenditures for education come at the expense of investments in physical infrastructure. The latter are more visible in the short run and do make the community more attractive for potential development, while education programs provide long run benefits and may simply assist people in leaving in the short run.

REGIONAL PLANNING

From the standpoint of both the development and transition objectives, there seem to be opportunities for rural areas through increased regional planning efforts. Such efforts would involve several counties or rural communities and would focus on establishing closer ties between stressed rural areas and existing growth centers in both rural and urban areas. Vigorous economic growth continues in the retirement- and government-dependent counties of the rural South. Some manufacturing and farming areas (especially livestock regions) are also doing well. Further, most metro counties in the South continue to grow faster than their national counterparts in terms of real income and population. The challenge for rural policymakers is how to link up with these growth areas to maintain the viability of rural communities.

One proposal for increasing regional linkages focuses on improved transportation services (Johnson, 1986). It is suggested that improved transportation services be established to provide the means for moving unemployed workers in declining areas to new employment opportunities. As a transition policy tool, transportation investment might serve to maintain the viability of rural residential and commercial activities for communities facing the loss of basic employment opportunities in their community.

Along similar lines, transportation system improvements can also serve as useful development tools. Examples are provided by the current efforts of several Southern states to improve their state highway networks (Bergman, 1986). Improved and expanded highway networks can allow for increased worker commuting by improving rural residents' accessibility to employment centers. Further, expanded highway systems reduce the isolation of rural communities and enhance their attraction as sites for the location of new manufacturing, warehousing and trade activities. Politically, transportation investment is attractive as a visible effort to do something to improve the plight of stagnating areas.

The key to the success of efforts such as those mentioned here is the targeting of investment to areas where it will be most beneficial for alleviating rural stagnation. This is a research area that has been neglected but holds great promise for guiding the use of public investment for rural development. Both the identification of growth areas and guidelines as to the best type of investments to facilitate development represent important research needs.

Transportation has been suggested as one area for investment, but equally rewarding opportunities may exist in areas such as communications or capital formation. For example, new efforts aimed at stimulating local development through seed capital subsidies with a focus on smaller business development seem warranted. As Till (1987) notes, the managerial and financial resources that come with new branch plants are often missing in rural areas. The key policy issue for successful "home-grown" development is how to provide these resources in rural areas of the South (see Miller, 1987 for a cautionary note on the role that small business growth has played in nonmetro areas). Again, some type of coordinated regional approach, involving several counties keyed around a particular growth center or growing segment of the economy in such a center, seems more likely to succeed.

CONCLUDING COMMENTS

In this chapter we have argued, based on evidence presented here and elsewhere, that rural areas of the South are undergoing fundamental structural change due to underlying national and international forces operating beyond the control of regional policymakers. In the face of these changes, we further argue for a combination of rural development and rural transition programs consistent with existing market forces as opposed to development-oriented policies designed to overcome and reverse current trends in the rural South.

Within the combination strategy proposed, the longer-run policy goal remains the enhancement of the human capital base in the rural South. Better education and training is critical to the future of rural areas and to the South in general. However, investment in education is a long-run development

effort and will not solve the problem of rural communities in the immediate
future. The combination approach proposed would concentrate on an effort
to strengthen rural linkages to Southern growth centers in the interim.

REFERENCES

Beale, Calvin L. and Glenn V. Fuguitt. 1986 "Metropolitan and nonmetropolitan population growth
    in the United States since 1980." Pp. 46-62 in *New Dimensions in Rural Policy: Building Upon
    Our Heritage*. Washington, D.C.: Joint Economic Committee, Congress of the United States.
Beaulieu, Lionel J. 1987. "The rural South in crisis: New challenges for rural development." Presiden-
    tial Address presented at the Annual Meeting of the Southern Rural Sociological Association,
    Nashville.
Beaulieu, Lionel J. and David Mulkey. 1986. "An assessment of community forces and agricultural
    change." Pp. 267-300 in Joseph J. Molnar (ed.), *Agricultural Change: Consequences for Southern
    Farms and Rural Communities*. Westview Press.
Bender, Lloyd D., Bernal L. Green, Thomas F. Hady, John A. Kuehn, Marlys K. Nelson, Leon B.
    Perkinson, and Peggy J. Ross. 1985. *The Diverse Social and Economic Structure of Nonmetropoli-
    tan America*. Washington, D.C.: U. S. Department of Agriculture, Rural Development Research
    Report 49.
Bergman, Edward. 1986. "Urban and rural considerations in Southern development." Pp. 7-12 in *Rural
    Flight/Urban Might: Economic Development Challenges for the 1990's*. Raleigh: Southern Growth
    Policies Board.
Bureau of the Census. 1986. *Statistical Abstract of the United States. Washington, D.C.: U.S. Govern-
    ment Printing Office*.
Cornell, W. Glenn and A. Kelly McLindon. 1986. "The seven states of the Southeast." *Business and
    Economic Review*, College of Business Administration, University of South Carolina, 33(1): 3-7.
Drabenstott, Mark, Mark Henry, and Lynn Gibson. 1986. "The rural economic policy choice." *Eco-
    nomic Review*, Federal Reserve Bank of Kansas City (January) 41-58.
Federal Reserve Bank of Atlanta. 1987. *Southeastern Economic Insight* 7(1).
Hansen, Niles. 1979. "The new international division of labor and manufacturing decentralization in
    the United States." *The Review of Regional Studies*. 9(1): 1-11.
Henry, Mark, Mark Drabenstott, and Lynn Gibson. 1986. "A changing rural America." *Economic
    Review*, Federal Reserve Bank of Kansas City (July/August) 23-41.
Johnson, Kenny. 1986. "The Southern stake in rural development." Pp. 13-20 in *Rural Flight/Urban
    Might: Economic Development Challenges for the 1990's*. Raleigh: Southern Growth Policies Board.
Miller, James P. 1987. *Recent Contributions of Small Businesses and Corporations to Rural Job Cre-
    ation*. Washington, D. C.: U. S. Department of Agriculture, Staff Report AGES861212, (February).
Mulkey, David. 1984. "Changing socio-economic conditions and the need for new development poli-
    cies in the South." *Review of Regional Studies* 12(3): 3-12.
Rasmussen, Wayne D. 1986. "Agricultural and rural policy: A historical note." Pp. 32-38 in *New Dimen-
    sions in Rural Policy: Building Upon Our Heritage*. Washington, D.C.: Joint Economic Com-
    mittee, Congress of the United States.
Rosenfeld, Stuart A., Edward Bergman, and Sarah Rubin. 1985. *After the Factories: Changing Em-
    ployment Patterns in the Rural South*. Research Triangle Park, North Carolina: Southern Growth
    Policies Board.
Southern Growth Policies Board. 1985. "The new infrastructure: Creating a climate for growth." *SGPB
    Alert*, Research Triangle Park, North Carolina (June).
_____. 1986. *Halfway Home and a Long Way to Go*. Research Triangle Park, North Carolina.
Taylor, Patricia A. and Patricia A. Gwartney-Gibbs. 1985. "Economic segmentation, inequality, and
    the North-South earnings gap." *Review of Regional Studies* 15(2): 43-53.
Till, Thomas E. 1987. "The shadows in the sunbelt report: Has the wave of factory jobs ended in
    the nonmetropolitan South?" Presented at the Annual Meeting of the Southern Regional Science
    Association, Atlanta.

17

Economic Development in the Rural South: An Uneven Past—An Uncertain Future

Thomas A. Lyson

During the decade of the 1970s, the occupational and industrial fabric of the rural South underwent a profound transformation. Full-time employment in agriculture and farming dropped precipitously as the tenant/sharecropper system of production finally dissolved and as many family farmers found it necessary to find off-farm jobs to supplement their farm earnings. At the same time, the textile and apparel industries, while still major bulwarks of the Southern nonfarm economy, especially in rural areas, saw their employment begin to decline as more and more mills found it impossible to compete against factories in the Third World.

Supplanting the decline in agricultural and textile employment was a tremendous influx of new jobs across the industrial spectrum. In the region's quest for new jobs, however, the major metropolitan centers of the South clearly outpaced the remainder of the region. Not only did these places add more jobs during the 1970s than rural areas, but they attracted more "good" jobs—those offering high wages, lucrative fringe benefits and high prestige. As has been noted elsewhere (Falk and Lyson, forthcoming), part of the reason why the South was able to improve its socioeconomic standing vis-a-vis the rest of the country in recent years was due to the boom that took place in the region's large metropolitan centers.

Rural areas of the South also saw employment levels rise during the 1970s. But, the types of jobs created in these places were more likely to be low wage, low skill and relatively low prestige positions. Branch plant expansion was a dominant engine behind the growth in employment in the rural South during the 1970s. Between 1959 and 1977, for instance, over 1.1 million new manufacturing jobs were created in rural areas.

Despite the impressive expansion of employment in the rural South in the 1970s, at the beginning of the 1980s, nonmetropolitan areas of the sunbelt found themselves in very vulnerable economic positions. Many of the manufacturing industries that have moved South to escape the high wage, unionized areas of the North were now by-passing the sunbelt and shifting their production directly to Third World Countries (where wages were even lower and the workers even less organized than in the rural South). Unemployment rates in many nonmetropolitan counties rose to double digit levels during the last recession and in many instances have yet to return to prerecession levels. And poverty levels rose to the extent that there were more people living in poverty in the mid 1980s than there were in 1970 (MDC Inc., 1986; Rosenfeld et al., 1985).

To understand how the urban South was able to make great strides in closing the economic gap with the rest of the country and yet leave a rural underclass behind in its wake, it is important to look at the sets of policies and programs that have guided development efforts in the region. Without going into great detail here, it can simply be noted that over the past 25 years the primary concern of state and local development officials in the South has been with creating as many jobs as possible. Whether these jobs were white collar or blue collar, high wage or low wage, dead-end or on a promotion track was overshadowed by the overwhelming desire to report job numbers (Falk and Lyson, forthcoming).

De facto industrial policies implicitly rest upon the notion that economic development is a contest that pits one locality against another. The "prize" in this contest is a new industry or firm and the jobs it brings with it. To enter into this game, communities must arm themselves with an arsenal of business incentives. Much like a high stakes poker game, one community's incentives are bid against another community's incentives in an effort to "win" a new employer. In this game, however, there may be no real winners. Obviously, states and towns that invest in incentives of one sort or another and fail to stimulate new economic growth are losers. But, localities that get carried away in their efforts to lure new businesses and sweeten the pot too much, may find that they have bartered away their ability to improve the lot of the most disadvantaged people in the region. Rural communties, because they have fewer "chips" to offer prospective employers, are certainly placed in a structurally disadvantaged position in this game (Lyson and Falk, 1986).

The limitations of the de facto industrial policy approach that has guided economic development in the rural South was neatly summarized by Stuart

A. Rosenfeld, Director of Research and Programs for the Southern Growth Policies Board (1983) when he noted:

> ....*rural communities, which have been primed for 1960s style growth, with waste disposal systems, roads, industrial parks, and vocational-technical centers, now find themselves facing a new 1980s style growth. Just as they began to catch up, the ground rules have changed. A skilled workforce, strong schools, and extensive communications links have been added to the list of factors needed to sustain growth.*

In the near term, at least, the economic prospects for the rural South do not appear promising.

POLICY ALTERNATIVES

In light of the current economic crisis facing the rural South, it is useful to explore various policy scenarios that could be adopted to guide future economic development activities in the region. Below, I sketch out three policy alternatives. Each suggests a very different role for federal, state and local governments, private businesses, labor organizations and local citizens themselves in shaping future employment opportunities in the region. I offer these alternatives not as absolute blueprints for change, but rather in hopes that they will stimulate discussion about the direction future economic development strategies will take in the coming years.

The Case for Continuing Down the De Facto Industrial Policy Path

Despite numerous and varied criticisms of the de facto industrial policy approach (Cobb, 1982; Falk and Lyson, forthcoming), there are several compelling reasons why this approach might remain the primary vehicle for rural economic development in the South. First, state and local industrial development initiatives have proven very effective in creating employment opportunities in a region that historically has had little to offer potential employers but cheap land and labor. Second, every Southern state and many local governmental entities have a well-established administrative and legislative apparatus to support and justify the wide variety of ad hoc development measures. Third, even though the competition among localities for new industry has intensified considerably in recent years, most local officials and industrial recruiters believe that they can continue to attract new businesses to their area. And fourth, neither the current administration in Washington, nor Congress appears willing to act on any comprehensive and unified national industrial policy at this time. In other words, the de facto approach to rural economic development in the South becomes the "only game in town."

The role of the federal government in such a rural development strategy would be to simply "get out of the way" of state and local officials as they pursue their quest for jobs. John Block, Ronald Reagan's first secretary of agriculture, recently articulated this position. In submitting the 1983 rural development policy report, "Better Country: A Strategy for Rural Development in the 1980s," he wrote:

> *The fundamental premise of this strategy is that local and state governments have the right—and should have the authority—to decide how public resources should be spent in rural America. The federal role becomes one of support rather than direction, and the agenda for action is set primarily by rural citizens themselves* (Office of Rural Development Policy, 1984:1).

If the rural South continues to rely on state and local initiatives to guide economic development, it is important to recognize and acknowledge the shortcomings of this approach. First, the effectiveness of many business incentives in luring new enterprises to a particular area is diminishing as more and more state and local governments match each others' incentive packages. Speaking to this issue, Ralph Nader's Public Interest Research Group recently noted with respect to one especially ubiquitous business incentive: "When 47 states make industrial development bond financing available to industries, this device obviously loses its positive force as an attraction to any given state" (Jacobs, 1979:8-9).

Second, there remains a general disagreement over which, if any, particular business incentive or package of incentives is most advantageous in attracting jobs to rural areas. Instead, many policymakers have come to the conclusion that not one but a package of factors including low labor costs, tax abatements, subsidized vocational training and a generally positive attitude toward business is necessary to coax private industry to invest in the rural South (Cobb, 1982). What this means, of course, is that rural communities must offer comprehensive packages of giveaways, many of which may not be needed, but whose cost must still be borne by local residents.

Third, as the competition for new employers increases, state and local governments are being forced to offer ever more lucrative incentives to a diminishing number of footloose industries. It is the observation of many that in their efforts to attract and keep industry through tax abatements and other giveaways, states and counties have locked themselves into a race to the bottom in which all stand to lose (Harrison and Kanter, 1978). And it is a race in which rural areas in the South are the least able to compete.

Lastly, as the pressure builds on already economically vulnerable rural areas in the South to enhance their incentive packages in hopes of attracting new businesses, the costs associated with these various programs and activities will be borne by those least able to shoulder them. And to the extent that a local area is "sold" to a prospective employer as a place where labor costs are low and the workforce unorganized, the opportunity for rural workers to improve their economic position is seriously compromised.

Toward a National Industrial Policy for Rural America

In recent years, support for a national industrial policy that would direct economic development activities in both rural and urban places has been heard from policymakers, financiers, academicians and politicians. During the 1984 campaign for president, for example, every Democratic contender for the nomination embraced some sort of national industrial policy and even President Reagan created a Presidential Commission on Industrial Competitiveness that embraced the logic, if not the rhetoric, of a national industrial policy. And it appears that some type of national economic development policy will be a cornerstone of the 1988 Democratic platform and perhaps the Republican platform as well.

While the details differ among various industrial policy proponents, virtually all of them recognize that the federal government has an important and positive role to play in maintaining and strengthening the economy. In its simplist form, a national industrial policy with relevance to the rural South would call on the federal government to adopt a set of trade, loan, regulatory, and other policies to channel private capital toward firms that can achieve competitive leadership in domestic and world markets (Reich, 1982; Rohatyn, 1981). At the same time, the federal government would provide support and/or establish guidelines for states to follow with respect to human resource development, infrastructure improvements, small business development and the like.

For the rural South, forging a national industrial policy means coordinating and complementing activities at the national, state and local levels to achieve an equitable distribution of employment opportunities across the country. It means implementing programs to encourage the existing industrial base in the South to remain and grow, helping new firms to get started and recruiting high growth industries that not only match the skills of the local labor force but help to upgrade those skills.

Several industrial policy agendas, many organized around the role states can play, have already been put forth by various groups and individuals concerned with economic development in the rural South. The Southern Growth Policies Board, for instance, believes that human resource development is central to the health of the rural economy and that improved education is one key to rural economic growth. In addition to upgrading the quality of the instruction in rural schools, other important areas to target include increasing adult literacy rates and providing older workers in declining industries with the prerequisites for retraining (Rosenfeld, 1983).

The Southern Growth Policies Board also recommends that rural communities should restructure their vocational education programs. They believe that the narrow skills training currently taught in most vocational education programs leaves young people unprepared to change jobs if the skills they acquired become obsolete or if their employer leaves the area. They propose instituting a type of "generic" vocational training that emphasizes basic industrial skills and behaviors related to independence, responsibility and entrepreneurship. These skills could then be combined with on-the-job training or an apprenticeship program where the more technical and industry specific skills would be acquired (Rosenfeld, 1983).

The Southern Growth Policies Board and others also see the need to nurture the creation and development of new and small businesses in rural areas. They base this recomendation on the fact that over 80 percent of all new jobs in recent years have been created in establishments with less than 50 employees. Small service businesses, specialty manufacturing and crafts, agribusiness and tourism can all play an important role in the future economic growth and development of the rural South. To assist these ventures, small business incubator facilities are necessary. An incubator facility is a building or set of buildings which provide space and support services such as office equipment, clerical help, and legal and technical assistance to fledgling entrepreneurs (Southern Rural Development Center, 1984).

Another component of a national industrial policy with relevance to the rural South is the assurance of venture or risk capital to small businesses which are just getting started. Risk capital could be generated through a variety of ways including subsidized government loans, state-federal matching funds, or direct federal grants to states. Further, risk capital and incubator facilities could be targeted to businesses that would employ particularly disadvantaged groups in the local labor market (Rosenfeld, 1983).

Finally, a national industrial policy would take into consideration and deal with the job problems faced by various diadvantaged segments of the labor force. Previous research has shown that the interests of minorities and women have not been well served by the de facto industrial policies of the past (Falk and Lyson, forthcoming). In the rural South, blacks and women are frequently relegated to the least desirable positions in the workforce. And recent figures from the Census Bureau indicate that the numbers of women and minorities falling below the poverty line have increased dramatically since 1980.

Industrial policy must target for special attention those areas of the South where the most disadvantaged groups of workers are concentrated (e.g., the Black Belt and Appalachian counties). In these places, preferential hiring agreements between new or expanding employers and the local community are needed. The goal of these hiring agreements would be to match job opportunities with disadvantaged workers. At the same time, efforts must be directed toward bringing more "good" jobs to rural areas. Low skill, dead-end positions that offer only the minimum wage do relatively little to improve the economic status of workers in the rural South. Instead, attention should be directed toward upgrading the skill level of the rural labor force and enhancing job opportunities in the rural labor markets of the region (Bradshaw and Blakely, 1982).

In summary, in contrast to the de facto industrial policies that have shaped economic growth and development in the South over the past several decades, a national industrial policy categorically rejects the uncoordinated and ultimately self-defeating strategies of luring industries with low taxes, low wages and minimal public services. As the U.S. Commission on Civil Rights recently reported, to the extent that tax abatements, guaranteed loans, subsidized vocational training and other forms of public assistance affect the decision of a company to locate in a particular county, their net effect is often merely to shift jobs from one place to another rather than to create any new employment opportunities. And if these subsidies do not affect location decisions, they are tantamount to public subsidies of private businesses paid for at the expense of foregone public services (Squires, 1981). It is the rural counties of the South, which are already hard pressed and forced to compete with other more affluent areas in the quest for jobs by matching (or bettering) their benefits and subsidies, that suffer the most.

Democratic Economic Planning: A Distant Goal

A third policy alternative for economic development in the rural South involves moving beyond the type of national industrial policy that was discussed above. Rather than aiming toward creating an environment conducive for private investment for what is hoped will be socially beneficial as well as profitable business activity, democratic economic planning directly questions the implicit assumption that a market based allocation of all goods and services best serves the social and economic interests of the nation in general, and the rural South in particular. In addressing solutions to the current rural crisis in the South, democratic economic planners would begin by raising a set of fundamental questions about whose interests are being served by current economic development policies. Who reaps the benefits from the various incentives and subsidies that are offered to private corporations? Who pays for these programs? And who decides what types of industries and jobs should be subsidized?

Answers to these questions then lead to additional questions about the locus of control of investment decisions in the rural South; the geographical distribution of employment opportunities; and the extent to which socially useful goods and services are being adequately produced by private industry. In its boldest form, the goals of economic democracy include a rising standard of living for working people; an adequate supply of socially useful goods and services, whether or not they can be made at a profit; a more hospitable, less authoritarian and safer work environment; and an increased participation by workers in the day-to-day running of the economy (Bluestone and Harrison, 1982).

A specific agenda that translates these goals to rural areas of the South has not been proposed. As Bluestone and Harrison (1982:244) note in this regard:

> *At this point....any sketch of radical industrial policy can (and should) be extremely tentative. Even the most tentative discussion, if it is to be anything more than a purely academic exercise, would have to presume that a broad-based political movement will emerge during the 1980s and 1990s in response to both the destabilization of communities by hypermobile capital and the attempts by the Right to dismantle the social wage in support of the long-term profit requirements of that capital.*

Despite this caution, Bluestone and Harrison proceed to identify a set of policy tools including public subsidy, public ownership and worker control, that could be used to address the current rural crisis in the South. First, they note that, at any time, there will be a range of new products that can be profitably produced and marketed by private industry once technical and/or financial economies of scale are reached. To achieve these economies of scale may require an initial public subsidy. Electricity cogeneration and biological and biochemical research apparatus are two examples given (Bluestone and Harrison, 1982:245). Currently, the American economy is rift with many of these so-called public-private partnerships. However, under existing policies, subsidies are provided to private industry with "no strings attached."

Under a democratic planning agenda, the benefits of these public subsidies could be more equitably distributed by instituting planning agreements between government and private corporations. A planning agreement is simply an arrangement whereby a firm that receives a public subsidy of some sort is required to meet certain criteria such as locating a plant in an economically depressed area such as the rural South, adhering to specific affirmative action guidelines, and meeting other conditions that lead to greater public control over economic development decisions (Holland, 1978).

Second, Bluestone and Harrison call for the development of public enterprises at all levels of government to meet the needs for goods and services that private enterprises cannot or will not produce. A list of these needs in the rural South might include better health care facilities and delivery systems, improved mass transportation, publicly supported and licensed day care facilities and appropriate technology to enhance the productivity and profitability of small farms (Bluestone and Harrison, 1982).

In practical terms, Community Development Corporations (CDCs) are one way to meet these needs. Very simply, CDCs are organized efforts on the part of local citizens to develop community-wide responses to local social and economic problems. CDCs often provide a variety of other services to an area. Funding can come from a variety of sources including foundations, labor organizations, private industry and government (Squires, 1981).

A third item on the economic democracy agenda deals with industries and businesses whose economic livelihood is threatened because their product can be produced more cheaply elsewhere. This issue has special relevance to the rural South where many textile and electronics firms are finding it difficult to compete with Third World countries. To address this problem, democratic economic planners call for programs to assist employees in purchasing potentially profitable plants that might otherwise be closed. A considerable body of evidence suggests that many branch plants of large corporations targeted for closing can be operated locally at a profit. Some establishments, for example, are being closed not because they are unprofitable, but because the rate of return is below some arbitrary corporate mandate. Other plants are closed because of high corporate overhead that could be considerably reduced if the enterprise was uncoupled from the corporation. And, there is at least some evidence that businesses that are employee owned and managed are often more efficient, productive and profitable. Producers who would allow employees to purchase potentially profitable businesses would serve a dual purpose. They would save jobs and they would allow local areas to gain some control over their economic destinies (Bluestone and Harrison, 1982; Munger, 1986; Rosenfeld, 1983).

Because of its radical departure from existing policies, democratic economic planning has received far less attention from policymakers and government officials than either de facto industrial policy or even a national industrial policy. Nevertheless, a small, but growing body of literature in this area has already begun to outline a democratic economic development strategy for the United States (Bowles and Gintis, 1986; Bowles et al., 1983; Carnoy and Shearer, 1980). There are at least three underlying tenets which distinguish democratic economic planning from de facto industrial policy and national industrial policy. First, it places primary emphasis on meeting public or social needs directly rather than as the indirect result of policies aimed at maximizing return to private investments. Second, democratic economic planning encourages broader, more democratic, and hence more accountable control of economic resources and decision making. And third, it is directed at achieving a more equitable distribution of the benefits of economic growth not only among men and women and various racial/ethnic groups, but also among rural and urban areas of the country.

AN UNEVEN PAST—AN UNCERTAIN FUTURE

In the short run, at least, economic development in the rural South will be guided by the de facto industrial policies discussed above. Communities will continue to vie with one another for new manufacturing enterprises. The de facto policies worked best in the rural South during the 1960s and 1970s when manufacturing firms were seeking to move at least some of their operations out of the high wage and heavily unionized labor markets in the North. While not every area of the rural South was able to attract new businesses during this era (e.g., the Black Belt was virtually by-passed by the migrating firms), many places did "capture" a manufacturing plant of one sort or another.

Today, as the recent report, *Shadows in the Sunbelt*, noted the "buffalo hunt" is over (MDC, 1986). The rate of branch plant expansion has slowed considerably in the 1980s and the rural South has neither the infrastructure nor the human capital necessary to sustain any significant indigenous industrial development. To date, no coherent or unified development strategy has been put into place to deal with this new reality.

The rural South faces a very uncertain future. Areas like the Black Belt that were unable to attract industry during the heyday of Southern economic growth remain mired in the backwaters of the nation's economy. With little to offer prospective employers other than a low wage, non-union workforce and with a dwindling pool of potential employers seeking to set-up shop in the rural South, the Black Belt faces a precarious future indeed. At the same time, those rural localities that attracted outside industry during the 1960s and 1970s are now seeing their gains being slowly eroded as these plants shut down in the face of Third World competition. And with nothing to replace this industry pool, these places also face dubious economic prospects in the years ahead.

The economic development challenge to the rural South in the coming years is obvious. How can the South best create jobs that will further integrate the region into the economic mainstream of the nation? Past de facto industrial policies have taken the rural South about as far as they can. The time has come to begin to dismantle the de facto programs that currently exist and replace them with a more coordinated development effort. Such a strategy can only enhance the economic opportunities and standard of living for people living in the rural South. Until such actions are begun, however, the rural South will remain the nation's number one economic problem and trapped in a game of increasingly cut-throat competition for new industry in which it has little chance of winning.

REFERENCES

Bluestone, Barry, and Bennett Harrison. 1982. *The Deindustrialization of America*. New York: Basic Books.

Bowles, Samuel, and Herbert Gintis. 1986. *Democracy and Capitalism*. New York: Basic Books.

Bowles, Samuel, David M. Gordon, and Thomas E. Weiskopf. 1983. *Beyond the Wasteland*. New York: Anchor Books.

Bradshaw, Ted K., and Edward J. Blakely. 1982. *New challenges and opportunities for rural development*. Institute for Governmental Studies, University of California, Berkeley.

Carnoy, Martin, and Derek Shearer. 1980. *Economic Democracy: The Challenge of the 1980's*. White Plains, New York: M.E. Sharpe, Inc.

Cobb, James C. 1982. *The Selling of the South*. Baton Rouge, Louisiana: Lousiana State University Press.

Falk, William W., and Thomas A. Lyson. Forthcoming. *High Tech, Low Tech, No Tech: Recent Occupational and Industrial Changes in the South*. Albany, New York: SUNY-Albany Press.

Harrison, Bennett, and Sandra Kanter. 1978. "The political economy of states' job-creation business incentives." *AIP Journal*, October:424-435.

Holland, Stuart. 1978. *Beyond Capitalist Planning*. New York: St. Martin's Press.

Jacobs, Jerry. 1979. *Bidding for business: Corporate auctions and the 50 disunited states*. Washington, D.C.: Public Interest Research Group.

Lyson, Thomas A., and William W. Falk. 1986. "Two sides to the sunbelt: Economic development in the rural and urban South." Pp. 158-165 in D. Jahr, J. Johnson and R. Wimberley (editors), *New Dimensions in Rural Policy: Building Upon Our Heritage*. Joint Economic Committee of the U.S. Congress, Washington, D.C.

MDC Inc. 1986. *Shadows in the Sunbelt: Developing the Rural South in an Era of Economic Change*. A Report of the MDC Panel on Rural Economic Development (May).

Munger, Guy. 1986. "Hope in jobs hunt: Worker-owned firms." *Raleigh News and Observor*, June 8, pp. 1D and 5D.

Office of Rural Development Policy. 1984. *Rural Development and the American Farm*. U.S. Department of Agriculture, Washington, D.C.: U.S. Government Printing Office.

Reich, Robert. 1982. "Making industrial policy." *Foreign Affairs*, 60(4):852-881.

Rohatyn, Felix. 1981. "Reconstructing America." *New York Review of Books*, February 5.

Rosenfeld, Stuart A. 1983. "Prospects for economic growth in the rural South." *SGPB Alert*, Research Triangle Park, North Carolina, p.4.

Rosenfeld, Stuart A., Edward Bergman, and Sarah Rubin. 1985. *After the Factories: Changing Employment Patterns in the Rural South*. Research Triangle Park, North Carolina: Southern Growth Policies Board.

Squires, Gregory D. 1981. *Shutdown: Economic Dislocation and Equal Opportunity*. U.S. Commission on Civil Rights, Washington, D.C.: U.S. Government Printing Office.

Southern Rural Development Center. 1984. "North Carolina offers grants to start small businesses." *SRDC Capsules*, November 30.

18

State Rural Development Policies: An Emerging Government Initiative

Judith C. Hackett

The farm crisis reached the top of the legislative agenda in most states during the 1980s. In the country with the richest farmland in the world, farmers have gone broke, banks are failing at a rate unequaled since the Depression, agricultural businesses are floundering and small communities are on shaky economic ground. Other rural businesses and industries such as oil, gas, mining and manufacturing have experienced similar economic downturns.

Rather than depending exclusively on the nation's capital, farmers and rural communities have turned to their statehouses in search for assistance. Demands for new state-level farm and rural development programs represent a significant change in focus by farm groups and rural citizens. Traditionally, programs of this nature have been run almost exclusively by the federal government, with state functions limited to regulation, inspection and grant administration. Why are states now becoming more involved in this area, one that is heavily influenced by policies and programs over which states have little control? This chapter attempts to provide a framework for understanding state agricultural and rural policy development.

INTERGOVERNMENTAL CHANGES

Our intergovernmental system of governance in the United States is based upon a partnership among national, state and local governments. Landmark statutes at the national level have been adopted in education, rural electrification, community development and health care since the early 1930s resulting in more than 200 federal grant programs. Accompanying these initiatives have been mounting grant outlays—for example, $7 billion in 1960, $24 billion in 1970, and $91.5 billion in 1980 (Council of State Governments 1986b). Despite the increased income, some state and local officials have objected to the duplication, complexity and intrusiveness of categorical programs. In 1980, the Reagan administration made a large-scale reduction in federal aid a major goal of its domestic policy. Since the defense budget and "social safety net" programs were exempt, most cuts came from grant-in-aid and general government operations. While Congress resisted major grant cuts or elimination of traditional aid programs, the administration was able to preserve much of its program.

Since the beginning of the 1980s, a major enhancement in the quality of state and local governments has occurred. State and local officials have achieved a new level of professionalism. Some states with robust economies have been able to replace some of the lost federal funding. The scope of innovative state activities in areas from criminal justice to health cost control have been impressive and their aid to local governments has risen steadily.

In this era of "New Federalism," concern that the states would be unable or unwilling to handle their responsibilities has proved unwarranted. The Office of Management and Budget (1986:16), in its fiscal year 1987 management report, noted:

- 68 percent of the states surveyed reported less time and effort devoted to filing federal applications and meeting reporting requirements.

- 33 percent reported they were able to make more effective use of their own state personnel.

- Most states indicated their need for technical assistance had diminished in areas affected by block grants.

They concluded that Federalism works, and works quite well, and that the States and localities are ready and able to assume more program responsibility.

SOUTHERN STATE GOVERNMENTS

Other authors, many of whom have contributed to this volume, have documented the demographic and socioeconomic characteristics which distinguish Southern states from the rest of the nation. However, in order to discuss the evolution of state government rural policy and programs, an understanding of southern states' structure is basic.

Structure

All state governments have a structure that is very similar to the federal government; that is, an executive, legislative and judicial branch system. New policy and program initiatives can be introduced by either the executive or the legislative branch, but concurrence from both is generally needed to establish major new policies or programs.

A simplistic view of state government would lead one to believe that the governor is a strong corporate chief executive officer, solely responsible for all state government policies and programs. This is seldom the case. Particularly in the South, the legislatures and legislators have great influence on policymaking. This is due, in part, to the dispersion of executive branch authority among a large number of agencies. In Southern states, because of their great number of statewide elected offices, governors share both the authority and responsibility for new policy.

Just five of the fifty states elect only the governor (and running mate) in a statewide race (Council of State Governments, 1986c). In these instances, all of the state's top offices are filled by gubernatorial appointees similar to the presidential appointment process nationally. Most states are not like the federal government, and many key executive branch offices are held by elected rather than appointed officials. Secretaries of state, attorneys general, and treasurers are elected by the public in the majority of the states.

Nowhere are voters more likely to directly select state officials than in the Southern states. To illustrate this point, an organizational chart for the state of Alabama is presented as a typical Southern state. Note that there are nine executive branch offices filled through statewide election.

Citizens of almost every Southern state, ranging from Texas to West Virginia, choose the head of their department of agriculture in statewide elections. In contrast, only two non-Southern states (Iowa and North Dakota) elect their chief agriculture executive. Voters in Southern states are also more likely to directly elect the treasurer, auditor, and insurance commissioner than those in any other part of the country.

Effect of Structure on Policy Development

The tendency for Southern voters to have an initimate role in the selection of state agency heads has implications for new policy development. When citizens have many avenues for input, many leaders become involved in new state initiatives. This leads to competition for resources, and may also lead to confusion about responsibility for implementing new programs.

In the past, most states did not directly address rural problems. Most departments of agriculture carried out functions which were regulatory or administrative in nature, primarily at the direction of the U.S. Department of Agriculture. State agriculture programs were a function of geographical convenience rather than a result of deliberate policy decisions.

Midwestern states have tended to define rural problems as agricultural problems, and the South has done so as well. Southern states, however, have had their rural economies tied to resource-based industry, and the economic declines in coal, oil and gas, manufacturing and textiles have caused policymakers to define the problems and solutions much more broadly. As a result, state departments responsible for job retraining, industrial development, public works, and human services all have had a part to play in rural programming in the South.

STATE GOVERNMENT POLICY DEVELOPMENT

The primary purpose of government is to address problems of fairness (equity) or access (efficiency) experienced by citizens. If market forces do not treat citizens equally or fairly, governments may consider a number of program or policy options. In agriculture and rural development, most federal, state and local government alternatives fall into one of three major categories: crisis intervention, innovation, and prevention.

Figure 1. Government's Approach to Rural Development

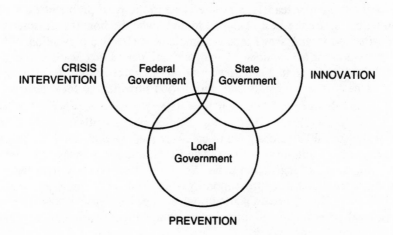

Crisis Intervention

Crisis intervention is the most costly type of government program and is seldom used by states. It occurs when we need quick results and highly visible solutions to problems with high costs to society. These are the measures taken when there is blood on the battlefield. They are usually best handled by the federal government due to its bigger budget and superior revenue-raising ability.

National rural crisis intervention has not occurred during the 1980s, probably because the economic problems have different regional consequences and do not lend themselves to national solutions. However, there have been several state crisis intervention programs in the agriculture and rural development field. Hay sent from the Midwestern and Eastern states, while not expensive, was a highly visible solution to an emergency. State farm credit assistance and mandatory mediation on farm foreclosures are two crisis intervention strategies which have been frequently used in the Midwestern states. When states intervene in a crisis, they seldom invest significant financial resources.

Prevention

Prevention is the least costly, most long-term government policy and its programs are educational and planning-oriented. Since prevention policies are developed long before a problem becomes severe, they are the most difficult to establish in situations where elected officials only serve two or four year terms. Obviously, substantive results usually take longer to realize than in a single or two term period of office.

Local community leaders, who are close to the rural problems on a continuing basis, are the best equipped to undertake the honest assessments of strengths and weaknesses needed to implement effective prevention. While it is common for academicians to call for national or state leaders to undertake long-range planning and prevention, these government officials usually can act best as coordinators and information providers to local leaders.

However, there are a few examples of state prevention programs. The New York Legislative Commission on Rural Resources, established in 1982, was the first state initiative designed to carefully analyze problems, identify solutions, and institute new policies. The Commission continues to introduce new programs and legislation today. Southern states recently have had two notable examples of rural prevention: North Carolina's Commission on Jobs, and Florida's Task Force on Agriculture. Both projects have involved leaders from local government and the business community, assuring a longer term focus to the recommendations.

Innovation

States are the middlemen in the intergovernmental community, and most of their agriculture and rural development policy initiatives fall into the category of innovation. States programs most readily encourage change, seek new ways to address old problems, and depend on a good system for gathering, assimilating, and distributing information. Typical of state approaches are:

- Seed money for new crops/businesses/marketing,
- Coordination among state agencies in problem solving,
- Publicizing and organizing available services,
- Incentives for new rural business development,
- Collecting, packaging, and redistributing information,
- Experimenting with new technologies.

These initiatives usually require legislation, appropriations or executive orders to be implemented. Also they usually require leadership of a highly visible policymaker from the executive or legislative branch of state government.

STATE INITIATIVES IN RURAL DEVELOPMENT

A growing need for state assistance to small and rural communities has reached the top of both legislative and executive branch agendas in Southern states. Declines in the value of agricultural land have eroded the tax base of many rural areas, and the loss of revenue sharing has created a situation in which many small communities are unable to provide basic services to their citizens. People who moved to the country in the 1970s and the 1980s seeking an improved quality of life and lower taxes are more likely to move than pay for needed improvements. The rural poor, who still make up a significant part of Southern rural populations, cannot finance these services.

Defining the Problem

Agriculture has been viewed by state leaders as an important and vital industry that assures Americans high-quality, affordable, nutritious diets. Agriculture is now an industry in transition. Much like the automobile or steel industries, advances in technology, increased foreign competition, high interest rates, and the strength of the dollar have created a surplus of goods and weakened prices. A nation of farmers at its founding, the United States now finds less than three percent of its population living or working on farms. More than a million American farm families now depend on off-farm, rural small businesses for a large part of their annual income.

Recognizing that the economic survival of many American farm families hinges on the nonfarm rural economy, state policymakers have placed considerable emphasis on improving the profitability of agriculture. They do not choose to focus only on improving the non-agricultural economy, but look first at ways to help farmers, particularly family farmers. However, the health of the agricultural sector and that of rural communities are inextricably intertwined. According to a 1985 report prepared by the Economic Research Service, 29 percent of all rural counties are dependent on farming, and are located primarily in Midwestern states, with smaller concentrations found in the Delta region of the South and the upper-tier region of the West (Bender et al., 1985).

Addressing the Problem

In a 1986 survey conducted by the Center for Agriculture and Rural Development, 34 different types of state programs were identified, many of which only emerged during the past few years. Results of this survey of governors, departments of agriculture, economic development, and community affairs are presented for the Southern region in Table 1. The array of state-managed programs now available is impressive, although many are familiar to economic development professionals.

States have usually developed four types of programs:

- Agriculture-related Development
- Transition Assistance
- Rural Business Assistance
- Rural Community Assistance

Three state agencies are emerging as the principal actors in state rural development policy formulation, and program development: agriculture, economic development, and community/local affairs. Each agency identifies ways that their present staff, budget and legislation can be used to help the rural areas of their state.

State rural development policies are also being formulated and carried out by other units of state government, particularly to meet the needs of citizens and communities undergoing change. These changes, or transitions, are being eased through programs of state departments of education, health, employment and training, transportation and environmental protection.

Most Southern states have stepped up their assistance to farmers and agribusiness, through their departments of agriculture. The elected leaders of these agencies have been particularly aggressive in their new marketing initiatives. In many cases, they have worked in cooperation with the governor, lieutenant governor, and legislature.

In Mississippi, the legislature recently passed a comprehensive piece of legislation providing financial assistance, counseling and a loan fund for alternative agricultural enterprises. Perhaps no single state official has received as much attention as Texas' Commissioner of Agriculture Jim Hightower, whose aggressive

Table 1. State Rural Economic Development Programs (The Council of State Governments—Southern States)

	AL	AR	FL	GA	KY	LA	MD	MS	NC	OK	SC	TN	TX	VA	WV
I. Agricultural-Related Development															
A. Agricultural Export Development		•	•	•		•		•				•	•	•	•
B. Attracting Value-Added Business		•	•	•								•		•	
C. Beginning Farmer Program	•				•	•						•			
D. Biotechnology and Technology Transfer			•	•	•	•			•			•		•	
E. Crop Diversification												•			
F. Marketing Agricultural Products	•		•	•		•		•			•	•	•	•	
G. Other							•								
II. Transition Tools															
H. Task Force or Commission	•		•	•	•	•	•	•			•	•		•	
I. Assessing Competitive Advantages															
J. Farmer and Agribusiness Financial Prog.	•	•	•	•	•							•		•	
K. Farmer Retraining and Counseling		•	•	•										•	
L. Other								•							
III. Rural Business Assistance															
M. Economic Development (Comprehensive)	•		•	•		•	•	•	•		•	•	•	•	
N. Entrepreneurship and Business Incubators					•						•		•	•	
O. Job Creation and Training	•	•		•										•	
P. Location of New Industry and Business	•														
Q. Marketing and Exports															
R. Plant and Military Base Closing															
S. Procurement Assistance															
T. Retention and Expansion of Existing Business	•			•	•	•	•	•	•	•	•	•	•	•	
U. Small Business Assistance	•			•	•	•		•	•	•	•	•	•	•	
V. Rural Enterprise Zones					•	•				•					
W. Tax Incentives for Private Investment	•		•	•	•	•	•	•	•	•	•	•	•	•	
X. Technology Transfer														•	
Y. Other															
IV. Rural Community Assistance															
Z. Culture and Arts	•			•			•				•		•	•	
AA. Financial (Block grants, etc.)	•	•	•	•	•	•	•	•	•	•	•	•	•	•	•
BB. Housing															
CC. Infrastructure	•	•	•	•	•	•	•		•	•			•	•	
DD. Land Use															
EE. Parks and Recreation	•	•	•	•		•	•		•				•	•	
FF. Quality of Life															
GG. Tourism	•	•		•		•		•	•	•	•	•	•	•	
HH. Other															

This chart is based upon a recent 50-state survey conducted by the Center for Agriculture and Rural Development.

Information about the programs has been entered into the Center's Rural Economic Development Database. Programs are entered upon identification.

Information about programs or the database is available from the Center for Agriculture and The Council of State Government, P.O. Box 11910, Iron Works Pike, Lexington, KY 40578 (606/252-2291) May 28,1987 promotion of farmers' markets, agricultural fairs, alternative crops, international trade and export development has set a standard for promotion and assistance for farmers and farm-related businesses by state.

The agricultural business sector is now receiving new attention from economic development specialists in the South. For example, the Arkansas Industrial Development Commission employs an agriculture specialist to work specifically with agribusiness. Florida passed an Agricultural Economic Development Policy Act in 1987, an effort designed to identify all state programs which can help agriculture. Most agriculturally-dependent states have placed special emphasis on state programs to stimulate international trade, expand production of value-added products and develop specialty markets. The phenomenal success of the catfish industry in Mississippi, like the wine industry in California, is nurtured by responsive state programs, research dollars and technical assistance.

During the period from 1984 to 1986 most state innovation was demonstrated in legislation providing credit assistance to farmers. These laws are similar to state laws that were passed in the Depression of the 1930s. Today, many state leaders are involving farm groups, agribusiness, other private sector leaders and universities. They are addressing agricultural problems as economic problems, and are developing appropriate solutions for industries in transition.

The lieutenant governor of North Carolina, for instance, recently completed a major study as chairman of the Commission on Jobs. The Commission recommended that the state create a Rural Economic Development Center. Its purpose would be to coordinate the activities of all public and private entities involved in the rural economy and to provide seed capital for research and development activities designed to create jobs in rural communities.

Programs for rural business assistance and rural community assistance, noted in Table 1 are not, in most cases, new initiatives. They are programs which are particularly important or effective in rural areas, for which states increasingly are targeting funds or assistance to small communities. The demand for new job creation programs will continue to grow, and states with significant rural populations have innovative economic development strategies that support small, existing businesses. At least four states in the Northeast and Midwest have established procurement assistance programs to help companies located in rural areas compete successfully for federal contracts. While this has not been a focus in the South, we may see it in the future. Business programs, tax credits, retraining programs, and retention and expansion programs are in place in almost every Southern state. The bidding wars and raids on Northern industrial plants have caused a very competitive environment among states. Industrial recruitment will never be eliminated, but greater regional cooperation can be expected as state policymakers realize that they are competing mainly with foreign countries rather than neighboring states.

A PROPOSED STATE STRATEGY

The coming years will find many new initiatives proposed by legislative branch leaders as a result of their interim study activities. In 1986, 20 states developed new agriculture initiatives on farm credit, agricultural business sector economic development, and rural community job development (Council of State Governments, 1986a). Tennessee and Kentucky, for example, pursued alternatives to tobacco; Washington, Montana, and Louisiana undertook comprehensive assessments of agricultural development opportunities; Arkansas considered establishing an agriculture commissioner; and Rhode Island studied farmland preservation. Given the myriad of alternatives, where should states focus?

The First Six Steps

If improvement in the health of the agricultural community is to be realized, state elected leaders must place emphasis on agriculture-related development. Within the structure of each own state's government, programs should be implemented to encourage innovation among farmers and agribusiness.

Taking a strategic approach to rural economic development, states must initiate programs which maximize their strengths but minimize their weaknesses in both the agricultural and the non-agricultural business sectors. Figure 2 illustrates the basic programs which all states should consider.

Figure 2. Components of a State Rural Economic Development Strategy

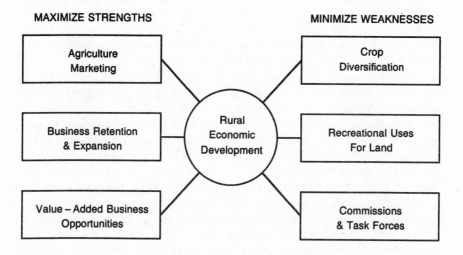

The top two programs are agricultural marketing and crop diversification, both aimed directly at the farmer. While most states have had marketing programs for a number of years, they must now become more aggressive and innovative in matching farmers with buyers. Increased funds for state programs, training and information to farmers, organization of producer groups, and improved sales strategies may all be necessary. Crop diversification programs, on the other hand, provide encouragement and incentives for farmers to grow products to meet the demands of new markets. Rather than producing wheat for export to Russia, a farmer could grow blueberries for sale to the local food market.

State-sponsored marketing programs are being developed across the country to serve farmers who have not traditionally benefited from the current marketing system. States as diverse as New Jersey and Indiana actively promote produce grown in-state, encourage the development of farmers' markets, promote crop diversification, and seek new markets for farm products. According to a survey conducted by Nebraska's Task Force on Agricultural Finance and Rural Development, roughly half of the 50 states are considering export financing initiatives to help small firms. Minnesota's Trade Office, for example, promotes the state's products both domestically and internationally.

States also must earmark assistance for agribusiness enterprises, particularly those that increase the value added to crops grown in state. This is the third step in state agriculture and rural development programs. Both Illinois and Iowa provide loans to help new agri-processing enterprises. Minnesota recently enacted an agricultural loan guarantee program to help facilities that produce a marketable product from renewable agricultural crops, livestock, wood, wastes, and residues. The Texas Agricultural Development Act provides for the creation of quasi-public corporations at the county level to finance producer processing operations. West Virginia has undertaken an ambitious effort to attract new wood processing and manufacturing operation to the state. These programs are all aspects of value-added business opportunities, identified in Figure 2 as a program to maximize strengths.

The fourth step is for states to establish business retention and expansion programs. Economic development agency strategies, as well as those of local development organizations, will become better targeted when state policymakers turn their attention to existing businesses. Retention and expansion programs promote rural economic development through the growth and survival of local firms. States with active programs in 1986 included Ohio, Kentucky, Louisiana, New Jersey, Wisconsin, and Michigan. States' rural areas have a better chance of successfully achieving growth when they help existing firms.

Recreational uses for land is the fifth component of a state rural economic development strategy. Its purpose is to identify income-generating possibilities for land which had previously been used for farming. These programs may fall within the responsibility of state tourism or natural resource agencies, including state parks and resorts, amusement centers, forest management, hunting, fishing and activities which support other recreational activities. The income generated from recreational uses of land can be a supplement for farm family income, and may actually provide a new source of jobs for rural communities.

Finally, commissions and task forces are the most basic step in creating future state strategies. It is critical for state leaders to have a thorough understanding of the problems and needs in their own state before adopting new laws or appropriating funds for programs which work elsewhere. In order to be most effective, these Commissions should include representatives of local governments, rural businesses, farmers, agribusiness and the educational community. Their tasks should be to identify: (1) characteristics of the state's rural areas and citizens, (2) problems and opportunities presented by the economy and job prospects, and (3) solutions appropriate statewide, to rural communities, and to rural people. It would then fall on the shoulders of elected officials to take the solutions generated and craft them into new policies and programs.

THE FUTURE

A number of trends and issues will influence the future of state rural economic development policies: citizens' growing demand for public services and programs, declining or unpredictable federal support, more state and local innovation, an aging and more mobile population, increased urban growth (particularly in the South and West), change and disruption from new technologies, and the increasing importance of the international economy.

The effectiveness of state agriculture and rural development programs and policies will depend on the collective influence of these factors, as well as on the success of policy crafters and implementors. How will we know if the states have contributed to the solution of the farm and rural crisis? When we lose fewer farmers than predicted in USDA studies, when farm incomes increase, when rural communities stop disappearing and banks stop closing, then state policymakers may well make the claim that their policies have been successful.

REFERENCES

Bender, Lloyd D., Bernal L. Green, Thomas F. Hady, John A. Kuehn, Marlys K. Nelson, Leon B. Perkinson and Peggy J. Ross. 1985. *The Diverse Social and Economic Structure of Nonmetropolitan America*. Agriculture and Rural Economics Division, Economic Research Service, U. S. Department of Agriculture. Rural Development Research Report No. 49.

Council of State Governments. 1986a. "State Legislative Interim Studies - 1986." Lexington, Kentucky (August).

_____. 1986b. "State Federal Relations." *State of States*. Lexington, Kentucky.

_____. 1986c. *The Book of the States*. Lexington, Kentucky.

Office of Management and Budget. 1986. *Management of the U. S. Government: Fiscal Year 1987*. Executive Office of the President. Washington, D.C.: U. S. Government Printing Office.

PART FOUR

Opportunities for the Vitalization of the Rural South

19

Traditional and Non-traditional Opportunities and Alternatives for Local Economic Development

Gary P. Green
Kevin T. McNamara

The current economic uncertainty in the rural South has sparked considerable debate about appropriate strategies for the future development and stability of rural areas (MDC, Inc., 1986; Southern Growth Policies Board, 1986). Recent analyses suggest that strategies employed by rural communities to promote economic development in the 1970s will be less effective in the 1980s because of a number of exogenous factors affecting the rural economy. The purpose of this chapter is twofold. First, we discuss various development strategies and their potential for stimulating future rural development. We then focus on new institutional arrangements that can be utilized to improve local development opportunities by increasing access to debt and equity capital, and fostering ownership structures to help maintain manufacturing facilities. These strategies can improve a community's ability to sustain or expand its economy in the short run. Improving access to debt and equity capital also can complement long run strategies to stimulate economic growth through human capital investment and development of entreprenuers.

Both traditional and nontraditional strategies for local development need to consider the conceptual basis for rural development and the factors affecting the local economies in the rural South. In addition, these strategies can benefit from the cooperation between local and state governments.

Rasmussen (1985) summarizes the major rural development objectives of federal programs from the 1908 Country Life Commission through the 1982 establishment of the National Advisory Council on Rural Development. The general objectives of the programs are consistent with Deavers' (1980) definition of rural development policy as

> *deliberate action by federal, state, and local governments and private institutions and individuals to achieve three goals: (a) improved rural income levels and employment opportunities; (b) improved access by rural residents to adequate housing and essential community facilities and services; and (c) responsible use of rural resources and the rural environment to preserve the quality of rural life.*

A key element in achieving these goals is stimulating local economic development to provide rural residents with employment opportunities and to generate local government revenues as a basis for providing "a publicly-prescribed minimum level of services" for rural people.[1]

Adelman's (1975) argument for a balance between growth and equity provides the conceptual basis for a reexamination of rural development policy in the South. Although Southern states are leading the nation in population and industrial growth (Saporta, 1987), the distribution of the growth is not even. The contrast between the relatively high growth metropolitan areas of the South and the social and fiscal stress of rural communities arising from adjustments in both the agricultural and manufacturing sectors, calls attention to the need for policymakers to address employment and service access disparity issues, even at some expense to rapid urban growth.

Castle and Goldstein (1984), Deavers and Brown (1984), and Bender et al. (1985) each examine the variation in the social and economic structures of nonmetropolitan counties in the United States. These studies clearly show the diversity of these rural community structures both between and within states and regions.[2] Policies to promote rural development should recognize variation across rural communities and focus on developing strategies that build on the strengths of specific localities. Rural development activities must be formulated on sound economic concepts and built on local comparative advantages.

FACTORS AFFECTING THE ECONOMY OF THE RURAL SOUTH

The rural economy is in a period of serious adjustment. Major trends have been identified that are shaping the future of the American economy (Deaton and Weber, 1985; Johnson, 1986). Several factors are of particular importance to the rural South because of their implications for rural development.

First, financial deregulation is contributing to centralization of the American banking system. It appears that deregulation has reduced access to credit for both the agricultural and nonagricultural sectors of rural communities as banks' investment decisions are shifted from locally owned community banks to the main offices of state and regional banks (Green, 1984; Markley, 1984). Continued centralization of financial markets threatens to further reduce rural access to markets for both equity and debt capital with serious implications for future rural development.

Second, cyclical economic forces, driven by both international events and technological change, continue to have a major impact on rural communities. Rural economies are experiencing the impact of a manufacturing cycle that has seen the migration of the traditional rural manufacturing base (textiles, apparel, shoe) to cheap labor Third World countries. Some firms have stayed, but have become capital-intensive to remain competitive. So, whether firms migrate or intensify capital investments, the net result is fewer rural manufacturing jobs.

Third, "New Federalism" is decentralizing the federal system in terms of both fiscal authority and control. Many rural communities, especially those experiencing declines in population and income (Broder and McNamara, 1987), are facing severe fiscal pressure as they adjust to lower federal transfers (Reeder, 1985). Rural leaders are caught between demands for increased service levels and declines in revenues.

Fourth, the crisis in agriculture extends economic uncertainty far beyond the farm gate. In particular, it has the potential of eroding the tax base and the economy of many rural communities (Lawson, 1986). The approximately one hundred farming-dependent Southeastern counties face the most serious problems as income declines and depressed land values threaten to erode the tax base of rural communities (McNamara et al., 1987).

Fifth, demographic changes are occurring across the rural South that are drastically altering the age, income, and labor structure of rural communities. While the 1970s witnessed a rural population turnaround that continued into the 1980s, rural areas have experienced a disproportionate rise in population age as well as poverty (Deavers and Brown, 1984). This offers both opportunity and challenges to rural communities. Transfer payments to those 55 years and older now account for 14 percent of rural income nationally (Smith et al., 1985). Retirement income accounts for 10 percent of total disposable income in the Southeast (Carter, 1983). As Summers and Hirschl (1985) point out, the income and human capital resources of this "older" population offers unique rural development opportunities.

STRATEGIES FOR ECONOMIC DEVELOPMENT

Economic development strategies have been grouped into five general categories: industrial recruitment, industry expansion and retention, new business formation, capturing local dollars, and increasing state and federal transfers (Pulver, 1979). Each of these general strategies (not necessarily mutually exclusive) offers growth potential for local economies through export expansion, import substitution, or increased productivity. The key for successful rural economic development is the identification of strategies that provide the greatest potential returns to the community from some combination of these three sources of growth. Each of the strategies is discussed below to identify factors that suggest appropriate alternatives for various types of rural communities.

Industrial Recruitment

Industrial recruitment long has been the foundation of economic development in the South. It produces growth directly through export expansion and indirectly through import substitution. Recent studies suggest that recruitment will no longer be a viable option for Southern economic development as industrial migration patterns change (MDC, Inc., 1986; Southern Growth Policies Board, 1986). Evidence, however, suggests that recruitment does offer growth potential for at least some Southern communities. Six Southern states (Florida, Georgia, Kentucky, Mississippi, North Carolina, and Virginia) rank among the top 10 states in the United States in new industry and expanded industry growth (Saporta, 1987). The 926 new and expanded industries in these states clearly offer development potential.

Analysis of the 599 new industry locations announced in Georgia during the 1980-1985 period provides insight into the spatial distribution of the new firms. The firms accounted for a projected employment increase of almost 40,000 jobs. The spatial distribution of these new firms indicates that 69 percent of the firms located in a Metropolitan Statistical Area (MSA) or in nonmetropolitan counties adjacent to the Atlanta MSA (McNamara, 1987). With a few notable exceptions, the slowed "stampede" of new industry to Georgia is directed toward metropolitan counties. Rural counties on the urban fringe can compete for new industry. As Rosenfeld et al. (1986) imply, however, the low-skilled labor force and physical infrastructure of more remote rural communities no longer attracts new jobs and industry.

Expansion and Retention

Expansion and retention of existing industry is a development strategy that combines increased productivity and export expansion. The concept was used in the Northeast to stave off further economic decline after the textile industry moved out. Retention and expansion programs have been successful in Illinois, Michigan, and Ohio as those states continue to cope with changes in their heavy manufacturing industries (auto, steel, tire, etc.). More recently, Southern states have developed industry retention and expansion efforts to secure their economic base. Employment growth rates suggest this strategy is more appropriate for urban areas than rural ones. Data for the Southeastern region from 1977 to 1982 indicate that metropolitan areas accounted for 80 percent of employment growth in the South, while these areas accounted for only 68 percent of the population (Rosenfeld et al., 1985). If innovative capital access and management structures were developed, rural industry that is currently closing because of competition from domestic and foreign markets could obtain the capital to modernize their facilities or transfer ownership to individuals that could maintain the facility profitably as part of the community's economic base.

Economic structure, industry characteristics, infrastructure, physical location, and labor quality are among community attributes that influence firm performance (Deaton and Smith, 1981). Of course, the size and structure of the local economy are the limiting factors with expansion and retention as an economic development strategy. Communities with a small basic sector or a large number of firms in a declining sector (textiles, shoes, wood processing) face little opportunity through a retention and expansion strategy. Retention and expansion programs, like industry recruitment, offer little rural development potential for many communities in the rural South.

New Business Development

New business development is an economic development strategy that has become increasingly important in the South as communities that lack the physical, social, and human capital infrastructure to attract and/or retain manufacturing industry look for ways to stimulate economic development. This strategy utilizes combinations of local initiative, human and financial capital, and natural resources to promote economic development.

Early "new business" formation efforts occurred as states and communities began to realize the potential for economic expansion through the development and marketing of recreational and vacation facilities. Orlando, Florida and Williamsburg, Virginia are two areas that have experienced tremendous economic growth by marketing tourism and recreation. Helen, Georgia has achieved the same success on a smaller scale by marketing its rural, mountainous location as a vacation spot for Georgia's metropolitan population. Hundreds of communities throughout the South have capitalized on some local attribute (river, lake, mountain, weather) to stimulate economic growth through tourism and recreation.

New business formation also can focus on local entreprenuers. Two recent Georgia examples make the point. The first is the Cabbage-Patch doll manufacturing industry that grew out of a North Georgia hobby. Through management and marketing, a young Georgian entrepreneur's idea has had a tremendous impact on his community's economic health. Another example of entrepreneurs' success is from Miller County, a depressed agricultural community in South Georgia. Four women pooled $400 each to begin the mayhaw jelly industry. The women have developed a specialty jelly product from a local swamp fruit. In three years the business has grown to three full-time employees and 40 part-time workers during fruit season. The price of mayhaws has increased from $1 to $5 a bushel. The four mayhaw entrepreneurs have had a measurable impact on their county's depressed economy; first, by stimulating the economic activity; and second, by changing community perception about local growth potential.

Capturing Local Dollars

Increasing the number of times that dollars are spent in a community adds to the employment and income of a community. This is often referred to as reducing economic leakages. Recognizing the importance of spending to the viability of the local commercial sector, many communities have developed programs to encourage local spending, capturing a large share of local peoples' expenditures. This is a form of import substitution.

The structure and size of the rural retail sector has changed considerably as transportation links have reduced urban-rural transportation costs. The results have been a general decline in the rural retail share that is unlikely to reverse (Scott and Johnson, 1976). However, opportunities to increase local retail sales exist. The Rocky Mountain Institute, for instance, has developed an intensive community based program in a small Colorado town to systematically identify import substitution opportunities, as well as other economic development strategies. Under this program, a community coordinator surveys local business and industry to identify goods and services that can be locally produced to substitute for imported goods.

In conjunction with import substitution efforts, communities are beginning to recognize the importance of nonmanufacturing industry development (service and retail firms) as a means of export expansion. Service industries—firms that sell goods or services as opposed to producing something—have been a growth area for the export base of many communities accounting for up to 85 percent of sales for some sectors (Smith, 1984). Improved telecommunication linkages increase the potential growth for rural communities with a strong human capital base through expansion of service industries.

Increasing Federal and State Transfers

Many local governments have been successful in reacquiring dollars taxed away by broader governmental units. Planning district commission staff have provided immeasurable assistance in these efforts, especially for rural county governments that do not have the human resources for grant writing. A major thrust of this assistance has been directed at building the physical infrastructure (roads, water, sewer, etc.) communities need to sustain their economies. While "New Federalism" has altered opportunities for grantsmen, local governments still are competing for dollars in social services for groups like the elderly and handicapped and for various types of physical infrastructure such as roads, parks, water, and sewer. In a period of declining federal transfers to state and local government and increasing competition for new economic activities, attracting state and federal transfers is critical for rural development efforts.

NONTRADITIONAL ALTERNATIVES FOR STIMULATING ECONOMIC GROWTH

The previous section reviewed a variety of strategies for promoting rural development. Industrial recruitment, the basis for economic development in the rural South, will be less effective as a strategy for rural development in the future. The alternative strategies reviewed do offer a realistic base for rural development in many rural communities. The success of these nonrecruitment strategies, however, is based on the existence of traditional community institutions for human and financial capital to provide the basis for sustained economic growth. Communities must develop new institutions and identify new strategies for supporting the growth of their economic bases. In this section, we discuss the need for alternative methods of generating economic growth involving nontraditional institutional structures to provide the support to successfully pursue traditional economic development objectives. In particular, we focus on two general factors influencing growth: access to financial capital, and patterns of firm ownership and organizational structure. First, we evaluate alternative means of providing credit and their potential in rural communities. Second, we consider alternative forms of ownership within firms as a means of promoting rural development.

The changing social and economic structure of rural America (Castle and Goldstein, 1984; Deavers and Brown, 1984), the decentralization of the federal system, and deregulation of financial markets have combined to create new barriers for rural development. The barriers are especially severe for communities that are isolated from metropolitan financial and labor markets and urban transportation systems. These communities must examine local rural development potentials that build on local resources and create new institutions to provide the support needed for successful development.

The increasing importance of small firms in the expansion of the economy and creation of new employment (Birch, 1979; Coffey and Polese, 1985; Rosenfeld et al., 1985; Shaffer, 1982) has put rural communities with low-skill, low-wage labor at a disadvantage in attempts to stimulate economic development. Bruno and Tyebjel (1982) identify venture capital availability, technically skilled labor force, market access, support services, and transportation facilities as critical factors for small business and entrepreneurship development. Communities that are lacking in one or more of these attributes must develop new institutional arrangements to support rural development efforts and to overcome or compensate for missing attributes. Two broad areas in which institutional innovations are being, or have been, utilized to promote or facilitate rural development are in financial markets and ownership structures.

Finance and Capital Markets

Two critical factors influencing development in the rural South have been access to and cost of credit. The South was relatively slow to integrate into national capital markets. This lack of integration was facilitated by the monopolistic control of commercial banks by the planter class. Changes in the institutional structure of capital markets and the spatial structure of production have led to the South's integration into national capital markets. New developments are once again restructuring rural capital markets in the region. The discussion below examines structural and regulatory changes that are influencing capital flows in the region today.

Banking Deregulation. Capital markets in the United States are undergoing a fundamental restructuring which should have significant consequences for the performance of financial institutions. Banking deregulation, which began with the Depository Institutions and Deregulation and Monetary Control Act of 1980 (DIDMCA) and the Garn-St. Germain Depository Institution Act of 1982, is responsible for much of the structural change in the commercial banking industry. These regulatory changes focus on three basic issues. First, by removing the ceiling on interest rates (Regulation Q), deregulation removed limits on the amount of interest banks may pay to depositors. Second, regulatory changes have increased significantly the range of services that financial insititutions can provide. For example, financial institutions will be able to underwrite stocks and to offer mutual funds in the future. Third, the geographical limits on banking activities are being eliminated. In certain cases, banks have been allowed to acquire troubled banks across state lines. Regional banking systems, which permit banks in one state to acquire a bank in another state if the reverse is also permitted, have been established in several regions. In addition, several states have already passed interstate banking laws, which permit out-of-state banks to acquire any of their financial institutions.

These recent changes have significant consequences for the structure and performance of capital markets in rural areas. Deregulation will most likely increase the stress on small, rural banks (Milkove et al., 1986). Deregulation may also directly influence the performance of financial institutions in the South. First, the elimination of Regulation Q has increased volatility within the financial system. As credit is tied more closely to national and international markets, banks are forced to pass higher costs on to borrowers or take greater risks in their large loans. Second, the weakening of geographical restrictions encourages mergers and more formal lending policies. Hughes et al. (1986) estimate that by 1990 there will be about one-third fewer banks than there are today. Finally, deregulation of the services and activities of financial institutions may change the traditional emphasis of commercial banks on the provision of loans, particularly certain types of loans. If these new services and activities compete (profit-wise) with loans, banks may chose to reduce the capital available for loans and increase the capital available for more profitable activities.

Regional interstate banking, the precursor to nationwide interstate banking, is contributing to the changing structure of capital markets in the region. Among the major super-regionals are SunTrust Banks, Inc. and Citizens and Southern Corp. of Atlanta; NCNB and First Union of Charlotte, N.C.; and Barnett Banks of Florida, Inc. of Jacksonville, Fla.; and First Wachovia Corp. of Atlanta and Winston Salem, N.C. First Union has been one of the most aggressive banks in the region, acquiring 17 banks, while tripling its assets to $26.8 billion in the past two years (*Business Week*, 1987). The South is moving toward a dualistic structure of banking with a large number of small, rural banks and a few super-regional banks with branches across the region.

The Development of a Credit Gap. Recent changes in the structure of capital markets may further restrict access to credit in rural communities. Commercial banks are structured in a manner that encourages "safe and sound" lending. The primary source of funds for banks comes from deposits which places a great deal of importance on maintaining public confidence in the safety and soundness of banks. Commercial banks focus on lending which is basically low risk and provides a low return.

Another segment of the finance industry, venture capital partnerships, is geared toward the opposite end of the market—high risk, high return loans. Venture capitalists must provide equity financing to firms that will guarantee a 40 to 50 percent annualized rate of return. This high rate of return is necessary because after deducting losses and overhead, an annualized rate of return of 20 percent must be guaranteed to investors. Venture capital firms generally prefer to make loans in urban areas, where they can more closely monitor their borrowers.

The structure of commercial banks and venture capital partnerships produces a significant credit gap between the low risk, low return loans, and the high risk, high return financing of venture capitalists. One strategy for channeling capital to borrowers who fall into this credit gap is for the state to either directly provide loans to borrowers or for the state to guarantee loans, encouraging commercial banks to make loans to higher risk customers. Regulatory constraints and the tendency for commercial banks to make low risk loans even if guaranteed by the state, however, have failed to solve these problems. Alternative credit institutions must be developed to address these problems. The discussion below briefly examines alternative institutional arrangements for meeting capital needs in rural communities.

Business and Industrial Development Corporations (BIDCOs). One mechanism for directing capital to borrowers who have difficulty in obtaining loans from commercial banks and venture capitalists is a Business and Industrial Development Corporation (BIDCO). BIDCOs use an approach referred to as a "risk return initiative." Developed in the early 1970s, BIDCOs are structured to meet the financial needs of companies (particularly small businesses) that fall into this credit gap. Two different means of channeling credit to small businesses are used by BIDCOs.

First, BIDCOs can make Small Business Association (SBA) loans and sell the guaranteed portion of these loans on the secondary market. By selling these loans, it is possible to leverage capital up to 10 to 1. BIDCOs are able to achieve an interest rate spread that provides them with a method of leveraging their own equity while maintaining a favorable return to investors.

Second, BIDCOs can borrow from private sources and make non-SBA loans. For example, a BIDCO can make subordinate loans with equity features. A BIDCO could make a 10 percent loan with warrants to purchase stock. The 10 percent loans make financing affordable to small businesses that would not otherwise be able to afford financing. If the company is successful, it could mean as much as a 20 percent total return on investments. Such a plan accomplishes several objectives: (1) it increases the accessibility of financing to small businesses while being sensitive to their cash flow problems; (2) it compensates the BIDCO for its risk and provides equity for more loans; and (3) it provides investors with a return that is comparable to that of venture capitalists.

Capital Access Programs. Capital Access Programs are based on much different principles than the traditional type of insurance or guarantee program. Capital Access Programs are based on a portfolio or pooling concept. An example of this program is the Loan Loss Reserve Program developed by the Michigan Strategic Fund. Under this program, a special reserve is established for banks participating in the program to cover loan losses. The reserve is established through matched payments made by the borrower and the bank. Borrowers and the bank must make a contribution between 1.5 percent and 3.5 percent. This means that the contribution to the reserve will be between 6 percent and 14 percent of the loan. The advantage of this program is that banks are partially protected against loan losses. If a bank makes a portfolio of loans under the program, it will have approximately 10 percent of the total amount of their portfolio in the reserve fund. As a result, the full amount of the total reserve is available to cover any loan losses under the program. The program also encourages commercial banks to be more aggressive.

Community Reinvestment Act. The preceding section suggested that commercial banks in the United States are structured in a manner that encourages "safe and sound" lending. As a result, bank lending focuses primarily on low risk, low return businesses. We are not arguing, however, that commercial banks cannot take more risk in their lending practices. In particular, many banks could, and should, provide more loans and services in black and low-income communities and to small—especially minority—businesses. Structural factors influencing lending and banking consolidation often encourage commercial banks to seek more profitable, and less risky, loans.

Many community organizations have found the Community Reinvestment Act of 1977 (CRA) to be an effective tool for challenging the lending practices of commercial banks and forcing them to be more concerned with issues of local economic development. The CRA (along with the Home Mortgage Disclosure Act) was passed to prevent lenders from "redlining" loans and services to neighborhoods on the basis of race or economic class of the population. Lenders are required to provide data on loans to the local community. These data are reviewed by federal regulators before a merger is approved and are available for public scrutiny. As a result, community organizations and coalitions have challenged several bank mergers and obtained agreements with banks to provide an additional $3.7 billion for home mortgages, small business, and other loans to minority and low-income groups. These CRA challenges have taken place primarily in urban, rather than rural areas.

The Association of Community Organizations for Reform Now (ACORN) has been particularly effective in negotiating with commerical banks to make more investments in local communities. In Phoenix, where interstate banking laws have resulted in the proposed acquisition of nine of the state's ten largest banks by New York, California, or money-center institutions, ACORN has successfully negotiated a program for housing development. In St. Louis and New Orleans, ACORN won a series of negotiations with major banks. These negotiations are important because they establish a baseline for other commercial banks in the region. More recently, challenges have been made of major banks in Georgia and North Carolina. By establishing programs for housing development and loans to minority businesses, a precedent is established for other banks in the region.

CRA challenges have produced 15 reinvestment agreements in the Southeast. There are two different models under which these agreements have been negotiated (Carras, 1986). The first model involves a community organization adopting an adversarial relationship with a commercial bank, particularly those banks that are in the process of acquiring other banks. An agreement is made which specifies future lending obligations to specific projects (e.g., housing projects, minority businesses, etc.). A second model involves a negotiation between banks and a statewide organization (such as a legal services program) in a nonadversarial atmosphere. Usually these agreements do not specify the amounts to be reinvested in the community. The latter approach would appear to have the greatest potential for rural areas in the South that lack community based organizations.

Employee/Community Ownership

The loss of manufacturing jobs in the United States over the past decade has been extensively documented (Bluestone and Harrison, 1982). The problems of the manufacturing sector have been attributed to a combination of factors, such as the high cost of labor, lack of productivity, too many governmental regulations, and high taxes (Bowles et al., 1984). There is a growing consensus that the underlying factor making these changes relevant is the growing competitiveness of the world market. Therefore, the issue is not really the lack of profitability of U.S. manufacturing, but the surplus profits that can be realized in developing countries.

The textile and apparel industries in the rural South have experienced severe economic pressures from these changes in the world market over the past decade. Both the apparel and textile industries experienced significant declines during the recession of the early 1980s. The apparel industry has recovered from many of these losses, but employment in textile mills is down by 16 percent from its peak in 1973. During the past decade, the Southeast has lost approximately 250,000 jobs in these industries.

One proposal for averting plant closings is the development of employee/community-owned firms (Stern et al., 1979). The literature suggests that employee/community firms have several advantages compared to regular capitalist firms (Rosen, 1985). Studies have found these firms to have higher profits and a greater productivity growth rate (Conte and Tannenbaum, 1980; Marsh and McAllister, 1981). They also generate more jobs than conventionally owned firms (Rosen and Klein, 1981). Approximately 8,000 firms and 7 to 8 percent of the workforce are involved in shared ownership in the United States.

The key advantage of employee/community-owned firms is that they may be able to operate even when other firms choose to close because of higher rates of return to capital overseas. Employee ownership also creates a transition in which the base of the community's economy is owned by outside or corporate interests to direct local ownership and control.

Employee/community ownership has been used in a small number of cases over the past decade to avert a plant shutdown. Rosen (1985) estimates that 60 to 65 companies have been acquired by employees in the past 10 years in response to a potential plant closing. Of these cases, four of these plants have closed and two are in Chapter 11. Rosen concludes that these 60 to 65 acquisitions saved about 50,000 jobs. Although this is only a small fraction of the total number of jobs that have been lost to deindustrialization, employee/community ownership is one option that should be considered by employees and communities.[3]

One of the major obstacles to employee/community ownership is the capital required to purchase the firm. Several strategies have been used to finance acquisitions by workers and communities. The most simple type of financial arrangement is direct purchase by workers or communities. However, the size and capital intensity of modern capitalist firms makes this increasingly problematic. An alternative method of financing employee/community acquisitions is through trust-based ownership. Rosen (1985) indicates that this method is based on the establishement of a trust to hold worker/community ownership. This method insures that employees will share ownership of the firm on a relatively equitable basis.

One type of trust-based ownership limits ownership of the firm to workers (referred to as the worker cooperative approach). Another type of ownership is based on the Employee Stock Ownership Plan (ESOP). Under an ESOP, a trust fund is established to purchase stock in the company to allocate stock to full-time employees. Typically, a worker gradually gains rights to the stock in their account. After a specified time period, workers can require the company to purchase their stock at fair market value.

Employee/community ownership has several benefits. First, employee/community ownership establishes a better link between the long-term needs of the community and the interests of the firm's shareholders. The pressures for short-term profits are avoided by this alternative. Second, employee/community ownership is a step toward democratizing our economy. This is particularly important for the rural South where economic development is so dependent upon a reduction of inequality.

CONCLUSIONS

The South has entered a new era of economic development. Over the past two decades the South, particularly rural areas, experienced rapid economic and population growth. Much of the economic growth resulted from successful efforts to attract new industries that employed low-skilled, low-wage labor. The growing internationalization of the economy, however, has made this strategy less effective in many rural areas.

In this chapter, we argue that although there are a wide range of strategies to promote rural development, communities must create new institutional arrangements to provide the underpinnings for a strong economic development program. New industry recruitment will continue to be effective for a limited number of communities, primarily ones that are on the urban fringe and have access to urban human capital, financial markets, and transportation systems. Alternative strategies (e.g., expansion and retention, new business development, capturing local dollars, and increasing federal and state transfer payments), in most cases, will provide benefits to a wider range of rural communities than traditional attempts to encourage new industry. These strategies, which build on the existing strengths of communities and current institutional structures, offer realistic development potential.

Many of the barriers facing rural communities in the South are associated with the existing institutional structure. Historical forces, such as rural poverty and an unequal distribution of income, make local economic development problematic for the 1980s. Alternative institutional arrangements for providing debt and equity capital and for plant ownership may have a positive effect on development in the region. These alternatives address the equity issues that are so important in the rural South. But, other institutional changes will be required if rural communities in the South are to grow and develop.

NOTES

[1]This phase was used by Deaton to emphasize both public involvement in determining minimum services levels and the potential for changes in the minimum standard over time.

[2]An article by Beers and Hembree, "A Tale of Two Cities," (*The Nation*, March 21, 1987) suggests a need to address the balance of growth within metropolitan statistical areas as well.

[3]One problem that many employees and communities face in the rural South is that employee wages are extremely low. As a result, employees are unable to make wage concessions to facilitate a buyout.

REFERENCES

Adelman, Irma. 1975. "Development economics—a reassessment of goals." *American Economic Review*, 65(2):302-309.

Bender, Lloyd D., Bernal L. Green, Thomas F. Hody, John A. Kuehn, Marlys K. Nelson, Leon B. Perkinson, and Peggy J. Ross. 1985. *The Diverse Social and Economic Structure of Nonmetropolitan America*. Rural Development Research Report Number 49, Economic Research Service, United States Department of Agriculture, Washington, D.C.

Birch, D. L. 1979. *The Job Generation Process*. Cambridge, MA: MIT Program on Neighborhood and Regional Change.

Bluestone, Barry, and Bennett Harrison. 1982. *The Deindustrialization of America*. New York: Basic Books.

Bowles, Samuel, David M. Gordon, and Thomas E. Weiskopf. 1984. *Beyond the Wasteland*. Garden City: Anchor Press.

Broder, Josef M., and Kevin T. McNamara. 1987. *Local Government Activities Under Separate Population Growths*. University of Georgia Experiment Stations Research Report 518.

Bruno, A. V., and T. T. Tyebjel. 1982. "The environment of entrepreneurship." In C. A. Kent, Donald L. Sexton, and K. H. Vesper (eds.) *Encyclopedia of Entrepreneurship*. Englewood Cliffs, N.J.: Prentice-Hall.

Carras, John. 1986. "Getting your money's worth." *Southern Exposure* XIV (56): 79-82.

Carter, Charlie. 1983. "Economic influences of retirees on selected southeastern communities." *Economic Review* (June):30-43.

Castle, Emery N., and Mark Goldstein. *Income, Poverty, Natural Resources, and Public Policies: Conceptual and Research Issues*. Part II, Rural Development, Poverty, and Natural Resources Workshop, Resources for the Future, Washington, D.C.

Coffey, W. J., and M. Polese. 1985. "Local development: Conceptual bases and policy implications." *Regional Studies* 19:85-93.

Conte, Michael, and Arnold Tannenbaum. 1980. *Employee Ownership*. Ann Arbor: University of Michigan Survey Research Center.

Deaton, Brady J. 1983. "Rural development as a land-use policy." *Proceedings of a Conference on Land-Renewable Resources: Institution and Use*. Department of Agricultural Economics, Virginia Polytechnic Institute and State University, Blacksburg.

Deaton, Brady J. Thomas G. Johnson, Berkwood M. Farmer, and Patricia A. Schwartz. 1985. *Rural Virginia Development Foundation: The Making of an Institution*. Publication 302-002, Virginia Cooperative Extension Service, Blacksburg, Virginia.

Deaton, Brady J., and Eldon D. Smith. 1980-1981. "Developing an industrial site strategy for your community." *Municipal Management: A Journal* 3:87-95.

Deaton, Brady J., and Bruce A. Weber. 1985. "Economics of rural areas." Paper presented at American Agricultural Economics Association Conference on Agriculture and Rural Areas Approaching the 21st Century, Ames, Iowa.

Deavers, Kenneth L. 1980. "Social science contributions to rural development policy in the 1980's." *American Journal of Agricultural Economics* 62(5):10-21.

Deavers, Kenneth L., and David L. Brown. 1984. *Sociodemographic and economic changes in rural America*. Part I, Rural Development, Poverty and Natural Resources Workshop, Resources for the Future, Washington, D.C.

Green, Gary P. 1984. "Credit and agriculture: Some consequences of the centralization of the banking system." *Rural Sociology* 49(4):568-579.

"How 'Fash Eddie' is pulling first union out ahead." *Business Week* March 23, 1987.

Hughes, Dean W., Stephen C. Gabriel, Peter J. Barry, and Michael D. Boehlje. 1986. *Financing the Agricultural Sector*. Boulder, Colorado: Westview Press.

Johnson, Thomas G. 1986. "Changing employment patterns in the rural and urban South." Paper presented at the 44th Professional Agricultural Workers Conference, Tuskegee, Alabama.

Lawson, Michael. 1986. "The impact of the farm recession on local governments." *Intergovernmental Perspectives* (Summer) 17-23.

Markley, Deborah M. 1984. "The impact of institutional change in the financial services industry on capital markets in rural Virginia." *American Journal of Agricultural Economics* 66(5):686-693.

Marsh, Thomas, and Dale McAllister. 1981. "ESOPs tables." *Journal of Corporation Law* 6 (Spring):613-617.

McNamara, Kevin T., Rusty Brooks, and Millard Blakey. 1987. "Local government revenues by source and public expenditures: Implications for a fifteen-county area of southwest Georgia." Paper presented at the Southern Rural Sociological Association meetings, Nashville, Tennessee.

McNamara, Kevin T. 1987. "New manufacturing industry locations in Georgia, 1980-85: A look at urban rural distribution." *Georgia Business and Economic Conditions*.

MDC, Inc. 1986. *Shadows in the Sunbelt: Developing the Rural South in an Era of Economic Change*. A Report of the MDC Panel on Rural Economic Development (May).

Milkove, Daniel, Patrick J. Sullivan, and James J. Mikesell. 1986. "Deteriorating farm finances affect rural banks and communities." *Rural Development Perspectives* 2 (June):18-22.

Pulver, Glen C. 1979. "A theoretical framework for the analysis of community economic development options." In Gene F. Summers and Arne Selvik (editors), *Nonmetropolitan Industrial Growth and Community Change*. Lexington, MA: Lexington Books.

Rasmussen, Wayne D. 1985. "90 years of rural development programs." *Rural Development Perspectives* 2(June):2-9.

Reeder, Richard J. 1985. *Rural Governments: Raising Revenues and Feeling the Pressure*. Rural Development Research Report No. 51, Economic Research Service, U.S. Department of Agriculture, Washington, DC.

Rosen, Corey. 1985. "Financing employee ownership." In Warner Woodworth, Christopher Meek, William Foote Whyte (editors), *Industrial Democracy*. Beverly Hills: Sage Publications.

Rosen, Corey, and Katherine Klein. 1981. "Job creating performance of employee owned companies." *Monthly Labor Review* 106 (August):15-19.

Rosenfeld, Stuart A., Edward M. Bergman, and Sarah Rubin. 1985. *After the Factories: Changing Employment Patterns in the Rural South*. Research Triangle Park, North Carolina: Southern Growth Policies Board.

Saporta, Maria. 1987. "Florida, Georgia lead region in new industry." *Atlanta Constitution*, February 26, 1987.

Scott, John T., and James D. Johnson. 1976. *The Effect of Town Size and Location on Retail Sales*. North Central Regional Center for Rural Development, University of Iowa, Ames, Iowa.

Shaffer, Ron. 1982. *Economic Development Trends*. Community Economics No. 69, Department of Agricultural Economics, University of Wisconsin.

Smith, Gary W., David B. Willis, and Bruce A. Weber. 1985. *The Changing Structure and Importance of Transfer Payments in the Economics of Washington and Oregon*. Department of Agricultural Economics, Oregon State University.

Smith, Stephen M. 1984. "Export orientation of nonmanufacturing business in nonmetropolitan communities." *American Journal of Agricultural Economics* 66(2):145-155.

Southern Growth Policies Board. 1986. *Halfway Home and A Long Way to Go: The Report of the 1986 Commission on the Future of the South*. Research Triangle Park, North Carolina.

Stern, Robert, K. Haydn Wood, and Tove Helland Hammer. 1979. *Employee Ownership in Plant Shutdowns*. Kalamazoo, MI: W.E. Upjohn Institute for Employment Research.

Summers, Gene F. and Thomas A. Hirschl. 1985. "Capturing cash transfer payments and community economic development." *Journal of the Community Development Society* 16(2):121-132.

20

Educational Reform and Regional Development

Brady J. Deaton
Anne S. Deaton

Education reform is a critical building block for the "vitalization" of the rural South. The process of vitalization for the South requires that Southern leadership undertake purposeful action drawing on the resource base of the the region and nation. The human resource base of the South must be prepared to cope with a global economy which generates greater economic uncertainty for rural communities while imposing severe adjustments on their citizens, businesses, and public sectors.

International flows of capital and commodities shift the competitive edge among countries, resulting in sudden new investments in one place while plants close in another. Within the U.S. South, textile plants and sewing factories have closed in many rural areas and moved their operations to foreign countries. Similarly, agricultural adjustments due to international competition have disrupted input and output markets. The greater risk to public and private investments growing out of these conditions is not offset by as high a level of traditional, countercyclical, federal transfer program benefits associated with unemployment, welfare, educational and job training programs. While increasingly resilient and skilled human resources are needed to absorb the necessary adjustments to economic change, social and economic trends appear to be moving in the opposite direction. Guiding this process and generating new resources through creative management of incentives is the challenge to the leadership of the South.

The Problem Context

Human resource development is receiving renewed attention in the South today as its role in the region's economic future is reassessed. The resurgence of interest in this area has come not from regional economists (although they have long recognized the importance of human resources), but from Southern leaders themselves who are impatient with the unmet needs in education and training, health care, and social services that have too frequently been eclipsed in the build-up of the region's infrastructure (e.g., highways, industrial parks, airports, and water and sewage systems). In a 1986 Commission on the Future of the South report (Southern Growth Policies Board, 1987:10), Southern leaders focused on education deficits in the following observation:

> *Raising levels of education, which is certainly one of the strongest public goals in the South today, will not reach fruition without looking beyond the doors of the public schools and acting on those conditions that impede the acquisition of knowledge. By expanding human resource development beyond its traditional educational framework, the Committee acknowledges the connection between education and training and the other facets which affect the quality of the region's human resources.*

The purpose of this chapter is to identify and discuss four "conditions" which the authors believe demand innovative responses not only "beyond the doors of the public school" but *behind* them as well. These conditions are: (1) fiscal structure, (2) illiteracy, (3) linkages between schools and the community, and (4) access to lifelong education. Deficits in these conditions impede human resource development and, in turn, regional economic growth in the South. We address these conditions first by briefly listing the "demand" factors that call for educational reform, and second by discussing, in greater depth, a "supply side" perspective of institutional change that is posited and used to analyze the previously listed four conditions.

DEMAND-SIDE PERSPECTIVE ON EDUCATIONAL REFORM

Disparities in income, public services, poverty, infant mortality, and illiteracy between the South and other regions of the nation continue two decades after Johnson's Great Society and War on Poverty were established to abolish them. Moreover, disparities between rural and urban areas in the South itself widened during the 1970s and still threaten to worsen in the future. The severity of these deficits is underscored by their occurring at a time when improved communication systems, high mobility of capital and labor, and rapid technological change in the work place mandate an adaptable, skilled, and knowledgeable labor force. In his book, *Future Shock,* Toffler (1970:35) asserted that "the individual must become infinitely more adaptable and capable than before" because of the quickening pace of social change which Figure 1 dramatically illustrates. This figure compares the time span of social change with the increased years of individual longevity. The contrast between the past and present clearly reflects Toffler's concern. Historically, an individual's life span was much shorter than major eras of social change until perhaps the past century. Now in the 20th century, a single life span encompasses several periods of rapid social change making essential the need for access to continuing education throughout one's life.

One major area of social change has been in the workplace due to the reverberations of a knowledge explosion, computers and other technological innovations, and both job creation and job obsolescence—all of which comprise factors of the demand side for educational reform. The waning of the influence of labor unions and the penetration of foreign-owned manufacturing firms in the region can also be expected to produce new patterns of worker-management relationships which must be understood to be mutually beneficial.

Figure 1. The Relationships of the Time-Span of Social Change to Individual Life-Span

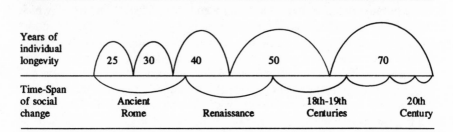

Malcolm Knowles. 1980. *The Modern Practice of Adult Education.* Chicago: Follett Publishing Co., Chapter 1.

Yet, despite these developments which are integrally related to the expansion of the economy and quality of life in the South, our schools remain underfunded—or worse, unimaginative—in their efforts to design and implement innovative programs in the basic areas of language arts, math, science, and in the critically important area of career and vocational education (which ought to have a strong experiential component). The 1986 Commission on the Future of the South called attention to many shortcomings in the educational system and made explicit recommendations for change. Other authors (Rosenfeld, 1985; Sher, 1987) have called our attention to exemplary cases of innovative alternatives to traditional programs in secondary education which deserve attention and replication. While some innovative examples of educational reform can be cited, the question remains of how best to stimulate and guide change in a systematic and more comprehensive fashion by effectively tapping the incentive structures that govern our educational institutions. To identify and understand these levels of change that can lead to reform and innovation, we must understand the societal web within which the educational system at all levels is bound up. The next section on the "supply-side" perspective of human resource development presents a model of institutional change that is useful for this purpose.

SUPPLY-SIDE PERSPECTIVE OF HUMAN RESOURCE DEVELOPMENT

At the outset of this chapter, it was noted that Southern leaders have taken the initiative in calling the nation's attention to the current human resource development need in the region. This effort deserves complementary attention from economists through their application of appropriate theoretical models that can help regional and community leaders understand the problem and pinpoint areas requiring intervention in order to bring about the desired change. It is also important to recognize the interrelatedness of various facets of institutional change so that public policy can be more effectively guided by research-based knowledge. We have chosen to use a modified version of the Ruttan-Hayami (1983) interpretation of institutional change to illustrate important interrelationships among the four conditions or "constraints" on educational reform identified above (Figure 2).

Figure 2. Components of Institutional Change with Spatial and Dynamic Dimensions

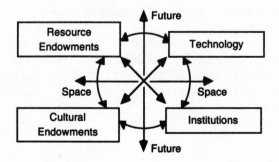

In this sense, the model provides a basis for interpreting the supply side components of education; that is, the decisions governing the structure, content, and delivery of education. The model does not ignore the basic precepts of cost-reducing, supply shifting factors which are common aspects of economic analysis. Rather, the role of economies of scale, technological change, and reduced factor prices are implicitly incorporated into the model. Institutional innovation is treated endogenously. A cause-effect framework is established within which cost-reducing factors can be understood and interpreted.

In order to effectively apply this model to educational reform, explicit time and space dimensions are introduced into the model. First, placing the Ruttan-Hayami model in a *temporal* context is essential for interepreting human resource investments whose objectives go well beyond narrow economic criteria. Only in this sense can change across generations be interpreted. For education is the current generation's means for shaping its own future image. Subsequently, educational systems must adapt to changes in a society's value structure while pursuing more cost-effective ways of achieving their goals. Significant educational changes have also been stimulated by federal initiatives designed to achieve equal opportunity, national security objectives including strengthened citizenship for democracy, and for meeting critical scientific needs of the nation. The public at all levels responds to fundamental concerns such as these.

The second expansion of the Ruttan-Hayami model involves the spatial dimensions. The spatial dimension encompasses the effects of regional economic adjustments, providing a framework for interpreting interregional and even international capital and labor flows. Of particular concern is the relationship of human resource development to reduced inequality of earnings and to enhanced regional economic growth. The tax base of local jurisdictions is altered by inter-regional factor flows, and the fiscal capacity to undertake educational reforms is determined by this spatial dimension.

Assessment of Factors Impeding Educational Reform

Each of the four conditions identified earlier as potential impediments or facilitators for economic development in the South can be interpreted within this pattern model of institutional change. They correspond to respective components of the model of institutional change posited above and can be classified as follows:

CONDITION	CORRESPONDING COMPONENT OF MODEL
1. Changing fiscal conditions	Institutional
2. Illiteracy	Resource endowment
3. Linkages with community	Technology
4. Access to lifelong education over the lifespan	Cultural Endowment

As the model reveals, interactions among the components are pervasive. Human resource development in a formal sense grows out of a process of interaction among an individual's personal traits, peer group influences, family, church, community, school, and work environment. The relative influence of the direct inputs of each sub-system varies over time in the process of human capital accumulation. Figure 3 illustrates this concept. Each of the four conditions above interacts with each component of the model and helps shape the society's ability and willingness to undertake educational reform. Each condition will now be discussed in the context of the pattern model.

CHANGING FISCAL STRUCTURE: IDENTIFYING SOURCES OF INSTITUTIONAL REFORM

The recent philosophical shift away from federal responsibilities for education, basic human services, and various public services raises a number of issues that many once believed were already settled aspects of the political value structure and economy, particularly in areas of health care, welfare, education, wastewater treatment, and environmental protection. In a very fundamental sense, the basic values and rules of our institutional framework are undergoing change. Decisions in the voting booth and in the courtroom are both reflecting and quickening these changes. Prior to this shift, pervasive externalities associated with education and social concern for the poor resulted in such safety nets as food stamps and other welfare programs representing widely accepted public goods of society. Nevertheless, the values and regulations of society are continually being reexamined, and the New Federalism provides an excellent opportunity to reassess the balance of public vs. private service provision and, among publicly provided services, to determine the proper mix of local, state, and federal support.

Economists bring to this reassessment a significant body of thought that addresses issues of supply and demand of public services and that purports to provide measures of economies of scale, price and income elasticities, rates of technological changes, externalities, and the local response to changes in state and federal financing behavior. Unfortunately, there has been little

310

Figure 3: Human Capital Accumulation Process, Source: Deaton and McNamara (1984)

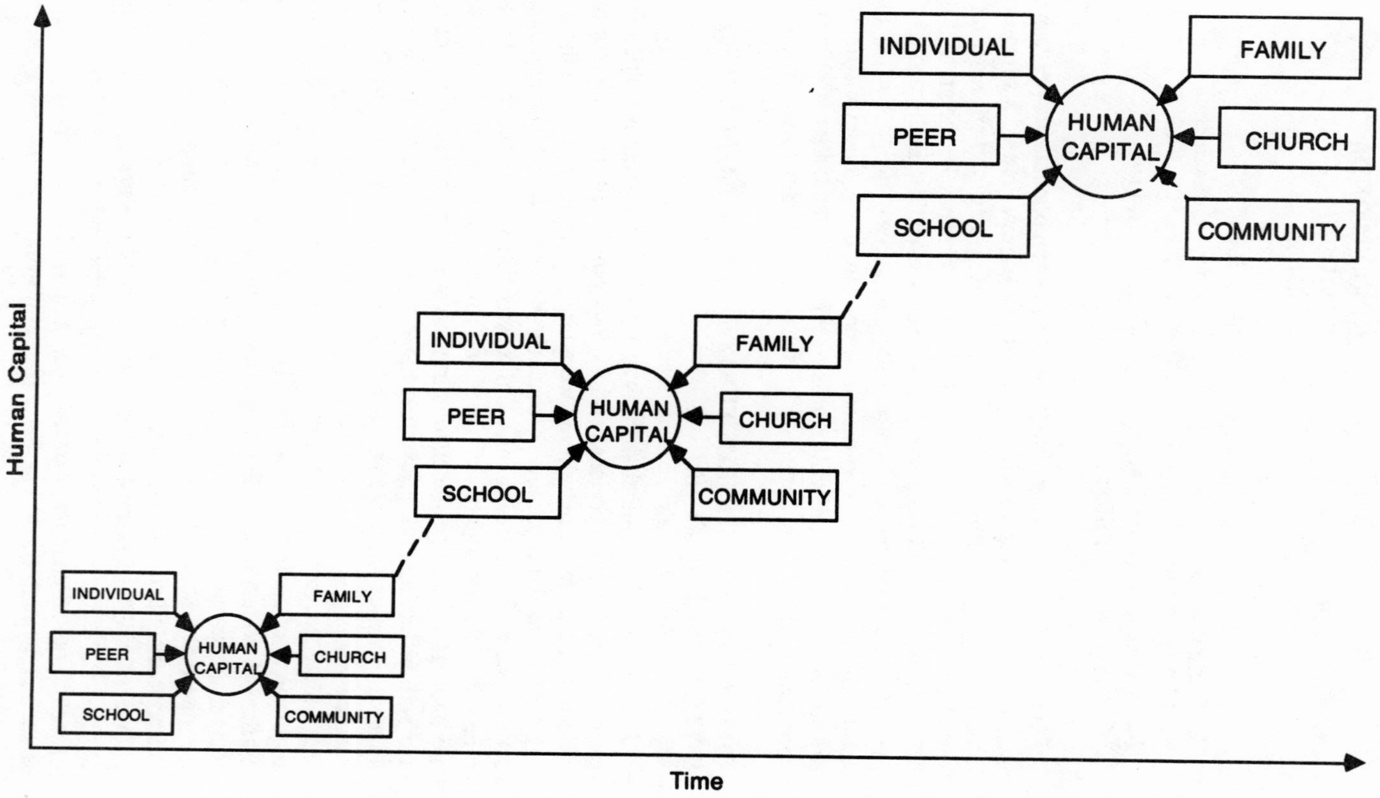

attention paid to this body of knowledge, and few economists are willing to state a clear position on the strength of these well-established concepts.

The dearth of valid input-output analyses of our contemporary educational system, as well as analyses of supply and demand associated with its sub-systems (private, public, and proprietary), reduces the public's perception of the social significance of the field of economics. For example, a recent court case revealed, on the one hand, society's concern for social justice relative to education, and, on the other hand, its low esteem for the role economic analysis could play in directing educational resources to mitigate problems at the local level. This particular case also calls attention to the role of social and cultural values as interpreted by the judiciary in shaping the relative dimensions of federal, state, and local affairs—a major aspect of the institutional design of society.

The case referred to is *Hobson* vs. *Hansen* (Clune, 1972) which dealt with differences in per-pupil expenditures as an aspect of racial discrimination in the public school system of Washington, D.C. The defendants in the case presented economic evidence which purported to demonstrate that resource allocation decisions based on economies of size were not discriminatory but rather rational allocations which had led to reduced expenditures for the school system with no inherent reduction in quality of education. The court was not persuaded. It rejected the economic evidence provided by the defendants because "the theoretical and statistical assumptions and guesses involved in this procedure disqualify it as proof" (Clune, 1972: 280). As Clune (1972: 279) stated, "We cannot observe anything about how output changes with other factors because we cannot measure educational output satisfactorily or control for the influence of factors 'other than size' ".

In terms of the model, the nested microeconomic relationships governing lower cost supply of education through economies of scale could not be established in the minds of the court even if they existed. This was because racial discrimination, an aspect of our cultural endowment, was an overriding concern that was preeminent in the court's decision of *Hobson* vs. *Hansen*. However, more appropriate economic evidence may have altered the court's decision. On the other hand, concern about tilting economic support in favor of groups suffering from historical discrimination may have won out in any event. The narrow economic criterion is often insufficient for assessing the realization of broader social and philosophical concerns.

The impact of the New Federalism on both the quality of education and on equitable access to education across the life span is a critical issue which economists should address. By design, under the New Federalism, the federal government has reduced its role in education while states have attempted to pick up the brunt of the burden. Nevertheless, broader social values will continue to significantly shape the extent of local discretion over educational funding and administration as the above court case reveals. In any event, the local government financial contribution to public education is still more than half of the total, but the state share has been increasing. Interstate competition for new jobs that arise from the location of manufacturing plants, including direct foreign investment, is one important incentive for the states' willingness to pick up the slack caused by dwindling federal funds. But this willingness faces finite resources for which there is fierce competition. Local jurisdictions will have to become more resourceful in order to retain improvements in educational curriculum and delivery that have been made and to continue to innovate.

Many significant institutional innovations in the delivery of publicly provided elementary and secondary educational services occur as a result of court decisions at both state and federal levels which alter the public conception of the financing, organization, and administration of public education. The most fundamental changes in recent years resulted from landmark legal challenges to the form of organization and financing of public education. These include the famous 1954 Civil Rights case, *Brown* vs. *the Board of Education*, and others, including *Serrano* vs. *Priest*, and *Rodriguez* vs. *San Antonio Independent School District*. These cases reflected both society's depths of concern and basic values held toward education. The following brief discussion of the deliberations in the two latter cases reveals the philosophical dimensions of this most vital public service and demonstrates how these philosophical underpinnings affect the process of institutional reform.

Public education as an institution is influenced by cultural endowments which represent a dynamic source of doctrine and shared values. Essentially the court ruled in *Serrano* vs. *Priest* that state funding schemes based on local property taxes resulted in discrimination against the poor and, in doing so, violated the equal protection clause of the Fourteenth Amendment. This conclusion led to a new era in educational finance, and recognized education as a fundamental interest of the state.

The precedent that *Serrano* vs. *Priest* set for the direction of subsequent court decisions in similar cases was altered with the Rodriguez decision in 1973 (U. S. Supreme Court, 1973), thereby ending a four-year period of major evolution in educational finance reform. In the *Rodriguez* case, the Supreme Court was unwilling to invoke the Fourteenth Amendment to require equal school expenditures among jurisdictions and left the issue principally in the hands of the states (Howard, 1986). Nevertheless, the impact of these and other related cases led state legislatures to move away from dependence on the local property tax and to identify new sources of revenue for school finance. Subsequent court action raised public attention about the need for reform of public school financing.

The nation's court system continues to be the scene of serious debate over whether a socially specified level and quality of education is an inherent right or simply the means to equal opportunity. While the latter interpretation has held sway, the implications for social justice may not be so different. The emphasis on equality of access to the fruits of society remains strong and must be addressed when considering state and federal support of education. West Virginia's recent statement of intent to provide "high quality educational standards...[to] all public school students on an equal educational opportunity basis" (West Virginia Senate, 1984: 39) is further evidence of the strength of the equality issue. The concern places stringent limits on the extent to which the nation's educational system will be relegated to state and local decisionmakers.

ILLITERACY IN THE SOUTH—AN INCENTIVE FOR REFORM

"Illiteracy is like a cancer. It's unseen and hidden, yet it's just eating away at the underbelly of the state—socially and economically" (former Governor Bob Scott as quoted in Southern Growth Policies Board report, 1986:20).

The Committee on Human Resource Development of the Commission on the Future of the South concluded that functional illiteracy may be "the most pressing issue in the region, and the major impediment to retraining efforts" (Southern Growth Policies Board, 1986: 20). They found that functional illiteracy was higher in the South than in other regions and much higher in the rural South and among blacks. As a proxy measure for these rates of functional illiteracy, Figure 4 is provided from the Committee's Report. Clearly, a seriously weaker human resource endowment for rural areas and for the South impedes regional economic growth and, more importantly, robs society of its dignity and self-esteem.

Clearly, it matters where we draw the line on the definition of illiteracy, and we realize that functional illiterates by many standards may be successfully competing in the labor market and making important contributions to their community. Nevertheless, the illiteracy levels in the South even by conservative measures represent a limited human resource base and a serious threat to the current fiscal structure of the South, particularly in rural areas. Since functional illiterates earn around 44 percent less than those with a high school education, they invest less in homes and in productive sectors of the economy. Also, functional illiterates are less likely to stimulate learning in their children. Consequently, the resource base is even further eroded for subsequent generations.

Ruttan and Hayami (1983) argue that one important condition for institutional change is when the benefits of new income streams that accrue as a result of the institutional change exceed the costs of implementing the change. Illiteracy imposes such severe costs on both the public and private sectors of the economy that significant benefits would broadly accrue from programs

314

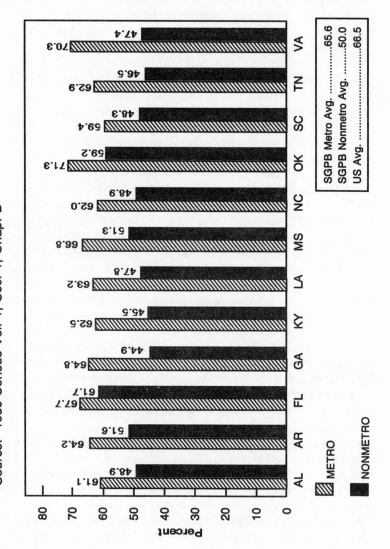

Figure 4: Population 25 And Over Who Are High School Graduates (1980)
Source: 1980 Census Vol. 1, Sec. 1, Chap. D

to reduce illiteracy. These benefits will be realized in diverse public and private income streams, such as reduced unemployment, improved health and public safety. The public good components would appear to be sufficient to justify rather significant public investments. *USA Today* reports, for example, that the annual cost of illiteracy has been estimated at $6 billion in welfare and unemployment benefits. This excludes the costs of incarcerating three quarters of a million offenders whose crimes may be related to their inability to function in society, partly due to illiteracy.

In Kentucky, the Department of Labor estimates that 80 percent of the state's unemployed cannot be retrained for new jobs because they lack basic skills, including the ability to read and write (Southern Growth Policies Board, 1986: 21). Kentucky's problems are not unique. Functional illiteracy is consistently associated with high drop-out rates throughout the region.

In Virginia, research has shown that low levels of educational attainment and high drop-out rates also impede the development of a number of other important indicators of regional life quality, including the ability to attract new industrial jobs (Kraybill et al., 1987; McNamara, 1986). The metro regions of the South rank almost the same as the nation in the proportion of the population 25 and over who are high school graduates (65.6 and 66.5, respectively). But, the nonmetro areas of the South lag considerably behind the metro areas in the proportion of high school graduates in the adult population as revealed in Figure 4. The nonmetro regions lag 15 percent behind, a much greater gap than exists in other regions of the United States. This is not an optimistic picture for the rural South. It may suggest that many areas will continue to lag behind the rest of the state and nation in terms of education and in the potential for new job creation. These low levels of educational achievement lead to low earnings, less capital investments that generate taxable property and, consequently, lower educational achievements in the future.

A broader view of the resources component of the model is no more heartening. Local governments and their local property tax base remain the backbone of local school finance, but many rural communities face a deteriorating local tax base relative to urban communities. Neither does illiteracy promote a cultural atmosphere that nourishes learning nor stimulate future academic excellence and informed citizens. Unfortunately, the literature shows that insufficient public resources are directed at adult literacy programs. Without the numerous, but again insufficient, number of volunteer literacy programs, the problem would be catastrophic.

A national study released in 1986, *Technology and Structural Unemployment: Reemploying Displaced Adults* (Office of Technology Assessment, 1986), indicates that up to 20 percent of the participants tested in displaced worker projects have shown deficiencies in basic education skills; some of these workers require intensive remedial education before they can benefit from vocational skills courses.

The report also targets community colleges as educational institutions which are in a unique position to respond to the needs of undereducated workers. This report states that educational institutions may need to make changes in program design, curricula, logistics and outreach to attract some older workers. Community colleges are credited with the institutional flexibility to adapt to the working adult's needs. Similar thinking led to the Committee of Human Resource Development's (Southern Growth Policies Board, 1986:24) recommendation that the number of functionally illiterate adults be reduced by half within six years by assigning responsibility and allocating appropriate resources to the state community college system. In a very real sense, however, these are mop-up strategies. They will require significant financial resources and, at least in the short run, will do nothing to reduce the continued outpouring of functional illiterates and undertrained workers from primary and secondary schools. A more fundamental perspective and strategy that attacks the roots of these educational deficiencies will be necessary.

LINKAGES WITH COMMUNITY: TAPPING AVAILABLE TECHNOLOGY

Innovative human resource development programs have drawn on the broader resources of private firms, other educational institutions, and volunteer groups. The closing of the Ford Milpitas assembly plant in California led to a community response which exemplifies how socioeconomic constraints can produce new cooperative approaches to human resource development. Prior to closing and for sixteen months thereafter, the plant provided personalized counseling, testing of every worker who wanted remedial education or skills training, and local job search assistance. Approximately 1,997 workers were served at a cost of $2,000 to $3,600 each. This cost was funded by the cooperative efforts of the state of California, Jobs Training Partnership Act (JTPA), Title III, and a union fund. Additionally, this linkage of volunteer literacy groups offered services through local public libraries, public television and radio, and adult education programs. Different units charged with educational responsibilities represent both a social and often a physical technology that adds a new dimension to knowledge acquisition (Figure 5).

Figure 5. Linkages with Communities.

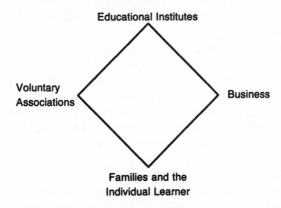

New and different linkages and new coalitions have also developed in response to anticipated reductions in federal expenditures for primary and secondary education. Among the more prominent responses to recent reductions in educational budgets, the following examples reported by the Education Commission of the States (1981; 1982) are notable:

• Tight budgets and a shrivelling economy have forced many school districts to look to their communities as a source of funding for school programs. Many of these depend on independent, nonprofit, community-based organizations that raise and allocate money for school programs.

• In Iowa, concern over tuition tax credit proposals brought together a new group of education and civic organizations.

• A new law in New York defines substitute teachers as public employees if they have "reasonable assurance of continuing employment" with a school district "sufficient to disqualify the substitute teacher from receiving unemployment insurance benefits."

• A new source of revenue for local school districts was proposed in 1982 in the form of a one cent sales tax in order to move away from dependence on property taxes and to minimize the effects of wealth differentials.

The supply-curve for institutional innovations depends on the incremental costs of mobilizing the economic and political resources needed to design new institutions (Ruttan and Hayami, 1983). Needed institutional change will be realized more quickly if the supply curve is more elastic (i.e., a greater change in the institution results from a given change in the level of costs) and/or can

be shifted to the right in economic terms. Local and state leaders can play
a critical role in bringing about such conditions by linking the educational
system into the broader community in ways that enhance the learning experience.
Recent students reveal some fascinating examples of such educational innovations and represent one of the notes of optimism about the future potential
in education.

Contemporary examples of significant modifications to traditional educational approaches have been identified by the Southern Growth Policies Board.
Attention is called to a few of the many examples cited in its reports which
focus on eliminating educational deficiencies in the school curricula which
draw on the broader resource base of the community.

Exemplary High Schools

Rosenfeld (1985) cited three Southern schools in rural or nonmetropolitan
communities that exemplify some of the more innovative examples of effective linkages between schools and the broader community:

- The Hartwell County High School in northeastern Georgia joined the community to help revitalize the local economy. The school system has created
  a School-Based Enterprise (SBE) that provides experiential learning for
  students in existing or new job opportunities. Students are afforded business experience in planning, finance, management, and marketing in such
  enterprises as a retail store selling local cottage industry goods, operating
  the Hartwell Railway Company as a tourist excursion train, and converting
  an old warehouse into a community theater.

- The Byng High School in Oklahoma was essentially built by students themselves with the support and cooperation of local construction companies
  and trade unions. Cooperation between school administrators, vocational
  educators, and community leaders is apparent in all educational matters.
  Through part-time work opportunities and through emphasis on both academic and vocational education, the school takes advantage of both its small
  size and its relative isolation. The school prepares students well for immediate employment and serves itself as an attraction to new businesses.

- Shelbyville High School in Tennessee joined with the town's largest employer, the American Can Company, to develop programs and marshall
  resources that brought the school and community into an effective economic development partnership. Their "Service Plus" program enables
  teachers to serve as consultants to community public service organizations
  and public agencies while being paid by a foundation created through a
  public/private partnership. Evaluations cited by Rosenfeld reveal that this

program has improved the quality of life of the community, but has not resulted in improved educational programs. In the long run, the community hopes that higher quality teachers will be attracted into the community.

Other Southern schools have attempted to comprehensively reassess their curricula in view of current and future demands of a global economy. A few of these will be cited, drawing on another excellent analysis by Rosenfeld (1984).

The North Carolina School of Science and Mathematics, a residential school for high school juniors and seniors, is explicitly viewed as one means for achieving the long-term economic development plan of North Carolina. State leaders recognized that the quality of primary and secondary education was a major impediment to continued economic growth in the state. Companies in the Research Triangle assisted the state efforts by bringing professionals and technicians from the private sector into the schools. A rigorous curriculum was developed that includes:

- six semesters of science
- four semesters of English
- four semesters of foreign languages
- two semesters of history

Students must also demonstrate computer proficiency, complete a year of community service, and two years of work service through mentorships for one half day per week that are undertaken in coordination with such prominent entities as:

- Dental Research Center of the University of North Carolina
- Data General
- Burroughs Wellcome
- Duke Medical Center
- Research Triangle Institute
- EPA

A progressive, global perspective on curriculum is exemplified by North Fulton High School in Atlanta which offers a course of study in international business. This program prepares youth to participate in an international economy and deals with issues inherent in the growing integration of the South into a global economy. The curriculum is designed to match international education programs afforded youth in urban centers of other industrialized countries. The curriculum includes:

- English, math, science
- Four years of foreign languages and geography
- International economics
- Intercultural communications
- International art, music, and dance
- International seminars and cultural events
- Foreign exchange programs
- Global issues, comparative politics

The Atlanta school has developed hands-on experience through internships with international businesses. For example, an import/export business was established with a Jamaican sister school in Montego Bay.

The above examples of rural and urban innovation recognize the need for linking schools with the vast resources of their communities. Also, curriculum revisions that reflect the emergence of new technology, such as computer-assisted learning, foreign language instruction, and the interrelatedness of the global community, are almost certainly bellwethers of things to come. These approaches expand the level of available resources for education at relatively low cost and incorporate dynamic, synergistic aspects of community economic development.

LIMITED ACCESS TO LIFELONG EDUCATION

The perception that education is principally the domain of the young is a rapidly changing aspect of this nation's cultural endowment. A combination of socioeconomic factors point to the increasing necessity to have viable access to work-related education (WRE) over an individual's working career. For example:

- Between January, 1979 and January, 1984, 11.5 million workers lost jobs due to plant closing or relocation and the abolition of positions or work shifts (Office of Technology Assessment, 1986).

- High tech manufacturing sectors are unlikely to rescue many workers displaced from traditional manufacturing sectors. While these sectors have created jobs faster than the economy as a whole, the employment base of these industries is small, the number of jobs created is modest (Office of Technology Assessment, 1986).

- There has been an improvement in the physical health of the older population at a time when advanced technology has greatly reduced the physical stress associated with many jobs. When this factor is combined with the recent end to mandatory retirement, and the emergence of innovative job schedules (e.g., flexi-time, time-sharing), it can reasonably be anticipated that increased interest in delayed retirement will result (Best, 1979; Deaton, 1987).

This combination holds dire consequences for the nation's economic productivity and for the quality of life of many families. Consequently, it appears reasonable to suggest the following:

• WRE for the workers may be one of the most cost-effective means by which government and private industry can enhance national economic productivity.

• The region that first successfully addresses both of the above factors may gain a significant competitive edge over other regions.

• Older workers represent a cost-effective addition to a locality in terms of total social costs and benefits.

• Age discrimination must be attacked for its legal and moral deficiencies and for its serious, negative economic repercussions.

Plans to train and encourage the employment of older workers were priority items at the 1981 White House Conference on Aging. Subsequent recommendations by 1981 delegates called for the development and delivery of career and vocational education programs to prepare older adults to reenter the labor force. Similarly, the National Institute on Aging (1982) has called for parallel research goals for increasing the productivity of older adults as an essential research need for the 1980s and beyond.

The new Jobs Training Partnership Act (JTPA) was signed into law in 1982. Unlike its predecessor, the Comprehensive Employment Training Act (CETA), the JTPA utilizes federal funds for job training costs (rather than for paying the salaries and wages of the workers being trained, as was done under CETA), emphasizes job expansion in the private sector (versus emphasis solely on subsidized jobs in community service) and increases the responsibilities of state and local governments in coordinating JTPA activities in cooperation with private enterprise. The Senior Community Service Employment Act, which also is funded by Title V, operates in tandem with JTPA to stimulate the creation of jobs for disadvantaged adults (Coombs-Fiske and Lordeman, 1984). These legislative actions have significantly increased WRE opportunities for low-income older adults, but there is still need for improving conditions for the general older adult population relative to WRE. The National Council on Aging (1984) reported that while $738 million was appropriated in 1984 for vocational education, no monies were allocated to meet the needs of older Americans.

The public response to the training needs of older workers has already advanced at an unsteady pace, while age discrimination in the private sector appears rampant (Deaton, 1987). As Ruttan and Hayami (1983) have noted, institutional change must yield sufficient benefits to political entrepreneurs to justify the risks they take to bring about the changes. The growing numbers of elderly also certainly will provide adequate political support to bring about the new conditions in the workplace that provide equitable opportunities for older workers.

CONCLUSIONS

Continuing reform and adjustment in the educational institutions of the South will be essential to strengthening the region's economic position. Southern rural communities appear to face even more serious problems than the region as a whole. In general, the picture for the rural South is quite bleak. On the other hand, cultural values that favor equality of economic opportunity provide a basis for continued federal involvement to promote educational reform. At the same time, the South's leadership is increasingly acting on the knowledge that enhanced economic growth and international competitiveness of the region's business and industry requires a renewed and sustained commitment to human resource development.

This chapter argues that an understanding of the institutional mechanisms that can lead to an improved educational system is enhanced by a consideration of the four basic components of the pattern model illustrated in Figure 2. Interaction among these components over geographic space and time provides a further perspective for determining the extent of improvement that can be achieved. Given the current set of resource limitations in the South, improvement will occur at a much slower pace than desired by most citizens and leaders. Such serious problems as functional illiteracy impede institutional change because of feedback loops that continue to reduce the cultural emphasis placed on educational reform. Leadership in the South must recognize the subtleties inherent in the interactions in the pattern model and seek more refined information to guide public decisions regarding education.

The following suggestions appear to follow from the preceding discussion:

- **Think international**—New demands are being placed on the South's human resource base as the region becomes more exposed to global capital, product and labor markets. An improved endowment of human capital is the most effective source of economic security for the region's rural communities and their citizens.

- **Link education into the community**—Business, government, and voluntary associations provide a vast store of innovative experience and expertise that can help revitalize public education at all levels. These relationships represent important social technologies that can enhance access to diverse information, education, and career opportunities.

- **Promote experiential learning**—Linkages into the community provide a basis for developing internships in many fields while simultaneously establishing two-way flows of information that enhance learning by all parties involved. Primary and secondary students can gain invaluable, and otherwise inaccessible, practical experience in business start-ups, finance, and in understanding entrepreneurship.

- **Increase WRE opportunities—especially for older workers**—Older adults represent a relatively untapped store of knowledge and experience whose talents may be able to reverse the economic decline of many communities. Cultural perceptions of older workers in particular, and their role in society will have to change as their economic and social potential is recognized. They are eager, capable, and quite willing to undertake innovative jobs, new learning experiences, and flexible work schedules. These will be important aspects of the future international economy of the South. Their contribution to intergenerational transmission of wisdom and values should not be underestimated or undervalued.

- **Engender community involvement and support of educational reform**—Broad involvement helps fulfill several important objectives including greater understanding of the potential and the limitations of a given institutional framework. The ideals of a democracy are both the means and the ends of public education in the United States. Cultural endowments and institutions of society play significant roles in either encouraging or impairing educational reform. The process of institutional innovation can be enhanced and effectively guided by an active community which recognizes explicitly that its future lies in its own hands.

Educational investments help shape our "conception of justice, the general form of a just society, and the ideal of the person consistent with it" (Rawls, 1971: 261). School finance is restricted by local resource endowments, existing technology, and current institutional arrangements. Our conceptions of justice and the ideals toward which we seek to remold society are not so restricted. They depend on our visions of the possible. It is toward this vision that the South must turn as we look to educational reform as a foundation for the region's future development.

REFERENCES

Best, F. 1979. "The future of retirement and lifetime distribution of work." *Aging and Work* 2 (3): 173-180.
Clune, W. H., III. 1972. "Law and economics in *Hobson* vs. *Hansen*: An Introductory Note." *Journal of Human Resources*. 275-282.
Coombs-Fiske, S. and A. Lordeman. 1984. "State units launch employment initiatives." *Aging*. (February-March): 18-21.
Deaton, Anne S. 1987. "Work-Related Education Among Older Adults: Case Studies of Selected Older Women in an Urban Area." Unpublished Ed.D. dissertation, Department of Adult and Continuing Education, Virginia Polytechnic Institute and State University, Blacksburg, Virginia.
Deaton, Brady J. 1983. "New institutional arrangements for supplying local public services under New Federalism with special reference to education." *American Journal of Agricultural Economics*. 65 (December): 1124-1130.
Deaton, Brady J. and Kevin T. McNamara. 1984. *Education in a Changing Environment: Impact of Population and Economic Change on the Demand and Cost of Public Education in Rural America*. Mississippi State, MS: Southern Rural Development Center (February).
Education Commission of the States. 1981 and 1982. *Working Papers in Education Finance*. Denver, Colorado.
Howard, A. E. Dick. 1986. "The Renaissance of State Constitutional Law," University of Virginia, *Institute of Government Newsletter*, September, 1986.
Kraybill, David, T. G. Johnson, and B. J. Deaton. 1987. *Quality of Life in the Appalachian Coal Fields*, Department of Agricultural Economics, Virginia Polytechnic Institute and State University, 1987.
Knowles, Malcolm. 1980. *The Modern Practice of Adult Education*. Chicago: Follett Publishing Co., Chapter 1.
McNamara, Kevin T. 1986. "A Theoretical Model for Education Production and an Empirical Test of the Relative Importance of School and Nonschool Inputs." Unpublished Ph.D. Dissertation, Virginia Polytechnic Institute and State University, (July).
National Council on Aging. 1984. "Employment opportunity before and after age 65." *Perspectives on Aging*. (March-April): 26-31.
National Institute on Aging. 1982. *A National Plan for Research Aging*. National Institute of Health Publication No. 82-2453. Washington, D.C.: U.S. Government Printing Office.
Office of Technology Assessment. 1986. *Technology and Structural Unemployment: Reemploying Displaced Adults* (GPO No. 052-003-01020-8). Washington, D.C.: U.S. Government Printing Office.
Rawls, J. *A Theory of Justice*. Cambridge, MA: Harvard University Press.
Rosenfeld, Stuart. 1984. "Exemplary High Schools: Enriched Educational Programs for the South's Economic Future." *Foresight*. Southern Growth Policies Board (September).
_____. 1985. "The High School in a Rural Economy," *Foresight*. Southern Growth Policies Board, Vol. 3, No. 2, (Summer).
Ruttan, V.W., and Y. Hayami. 1983. "Toward a Theory of Induced Institutional Innovation." Unpublished paper. Department of Agriculture and Applied Economics, University of Minnesota.
Sher, Jonathan P. (editor). 1977. "Education in rural America: A reassessment of Conventional Wisdom." Boulder, Colorado: Westview Press.
Southern Growth Policies Board. 1986. *The Report of the Committee on Human Resource Development*. Commission on the Future of the South. Research Triangle Park, North Carolina.
Toffler, Alvin. 1970. *Future Shock*. New York, NY: Random House.
USA Today. 1986. As quoted in AACE *Newsletter*, "Gannett and *USA Today* Join to Promote Literacy Funding, Washington, D.C., American Association for Adult and Continuing Education, (October).
U.S. Supreme Court. 1973. 441: U.S. 1, (March 21).
West Virginia Senate. 1984. Senate Bill No. 131. Passed March 10. Charleston, West Virginia.

21

Entrepreneurship as a Community Development Strategy for the Rural South

J. Norman Reid

Rural America cannot live off the creativity of urban areas without paying a severe economic penalty. Entrepreneurship is critical to the maintenance of a healthy rural economy. (Pulver, 1987: 5)

Entrepreneurship—the creation of new products, processes, and organizations in the economy—is the mechanism by which economic innovation occurs and is the vehicle for creating economic growth. While there are numerous reasons to believe that rural economies will always lag behind urban areas, the recent record of rural business creation, a surrogate for entrepreneurial innovation, suggests that rural areas can share in growth through entrepreneurship. Economic development strategies that rely on entrepreneurship appear to offer not only a chance for improved local employment and incomes, but also a type of growth that responds well to broader community interests. Research evidence suggests that communities can stimulate enterprise development through community action. The strategy of local development through entrepreneurship appears to hold promise for the South, though several important obstacles—especially lagging educational quality—will have to be overcome.

In government as in society, fashions come and go. It is as certain that buzz-words will change from one administration to the next as that hemlines will rise and fall. We only need to recall the debates about PPBS and ZBB[1] of just a few years ago to see that this is so.

"Entrepreneurship" is the latest rage.[2] In recent months, numerous articles, books, conferences, television programs, and even presidential statements have defined, described, counted, evaluated, and extolled the virtues of entrepreneurship. Interest in the subject, which follows an international trend toward market-oriented economic policies, is worldwide (Organization for Economic Cooperation and Development, 1986: 28-34).

The rising attention paid to entrepreneurship has been accompanied by growth in the number of new businesses. Some have come to regard entrepreneurship as a means for restoring the "competitiveness" of the American economy. And many organizations throughout the country—both public and private—are looking for ways to use these individual initiatives to strengthen local economies. Rural developers are among them.

Will this current passion for entrepreneurship turn out to be more than a passing fad? It is important to realistically assess entrepreneurship as a rural economic development strategy. What is an "entrepreneur" and how does entrepreneurship contribute to community development? Is it realistic to expect entrepreneurial growth to be a major creator of jobs in rural America? What community factors affect the chances for successful enterprise development? Is there a useful role for governments and public service organizations in encouraging it? Will the benefits of entrepreneurial strategies outweigh their costs? And how does the rural South compare with the rest of the country in its chances for growth through entrepreneurship?

Despite the mountains that have been written about entrepreneurship, our understanding of it, especially its applicability to rural areas, is not good. That understanding will only come by asking the right questions. Identifying some of them is the objective of this chapter.

A MATTER OF DEFINITIONS

The term "entrepreneur" is one of the most misunderstood in the English language, perhaps because the word is not English at all, but French. Current mythology associates entrepreneurship with high technology ventures—especially in the electronics industry—and conjures up visions of Boston's Route 128, or California's Silicon Valley. But thinking about entrepreneurs only as high tech tinkerers is misleading. While not inaccurate (there are entrepreneurs in high tech ventures), this popular view is too limited and the type of economic activity it suggests is likely to be irrelevant for many places, especially in rural areas.

Our misunderstanding of the term has its roots in the original French: entrepreneur refers to both business managers, who combine and organize the factors of production in traditional ways for established purposes, or adventurers, who strike out in entirely new directions. The classical definition (Schumpeter, 1961) emphasizes the role of the entrepreneur as an innovator and the agent for change within the economy. Economic innovation can come in several ways:

- by introducing a new or different quality of good;
- by changing the method of producing it;
- by developing new markets for it;
- by exploiting a new source of raw materials; or
- by changing the organization of the industry (Malecki, 1986).

Economic growth leading to the improvement of income occurs mainly through these innovations, which contribute new, better, or less costly goods and services (Drucker, 1985).

A point of frequent confusion is the popular belief that entrepreneurs are born, not made. While it is true that successful entrepreneurs often share certain personal and attitudinal characteristics, most observers now regard many aspects of entrepreneurship as teachable. The wide variety of persons who have succeeded in business suggests that many people with good ideas and some management skills have a good chance, with hard work, of succeeding (Friedman, 1987; Shapero, 1984: 28). This point is critical for community developers. If entrepreneurship skills were hereditary, there would be little opportunity for community developers to foster economic growth through enterprise development.

In this chapter, entrepreneurship is defined as the creation of new, independent business (i.e., not branches, franchises, or subsidiaries). This definition is used a a matter of convenience: it can be measured using available data. But it is important not to lose sight of the fact that not all innovations are introduced by new businesses, and that not all new businesses embody innovations.

ENTREPRENEURSHIP AS A SOURCE OF RURAL JOBS

Interest in entrepreneurship centers on its potential contribution to the performance of rural economies. This contribution comes in several ways. Births and deaths of firms are a principal means by which the economy adjusts to changing market conditions, substituting new ventures for firms whose inefficiency or unresponsive product lines make them noncompetitive. A lively rate of firm births and deaths may signify greater capacity in a local economy to respond to changing economic conditions. Entrepreneurship can also lead to strengthened human capital by educating the citizenry and stimulating further new business ventures. And it can be argued that a strong base of locally-controlled enterprises makes up a more socially desirable economic structure than one dominated by firms controlled from the outside. But entrepreneurship's most apparent contribution is the creation of new jobs and the generation of additional income as new firms start and existing ones grow. Let us look first at the record of job creation by new firms in rural areas.

Some observers, among them the noted management analyst Peter Drucker, have argued that the American economy is experiencing a boom in entrepreneurship (1985: 7-11). Miller's (1987) analysis of job creation between 1976 and 1980 supports the argument. Miller examined new independent[3] firms as a surrogate measure of entrepreneurship and found that employment in these firms grew at a much faster net rate (82 percent) than existing firms (including corporate affiliates, branches, franchises, or subsidiaries), which grew only 9 percent.

Miller found similar trends in both nonmetropolitan and metropolitan areas.[4] The overall rate of job growth was slightly higher (17 percent) in nonmetro than in metro counties (15 percent); a somewhat smaller proportion of new jobs was created by new independent firms in nonmetro counties (44 percent) than in metro counties (47 percent). These small differences suggest that nonmetro economies were able, in the 1976–1980 period at least, to keep up with urban areas in spawning new enterprises.

The picture for the 1980–1984 period is much different (Table 1). The overall rate of job growth in the economy, as measured by Dun & Bradstreet (D&B) data, was less than 5 percent, reflecting the recession and slow recovery that occurred during the period.[5] The most rapid job growth occurred among branches, franchises, and subsidiaries (10 percent), while independent firms grew less than half as fast; headquarters establishments suffered a net job loss of 6 percent. Still, new independent firms contributed nearly half (46 percent) of national job growth, nearly as much as from the expansion of existing headquarters, branches, franchises, and subsidiaries (48 percent).

These national figures mask major differences in the performance of the metropolitan and nonmetropolitan economies. While the D&B data show metro employment growth of almost 6 percent between 1980 and 1984, it declined by half a percent in nonmetro areas. Metro areas benefited from a 9 percent expansion of existing branch plants and from net births of independent firms, especially those with fewer than 20 employees, which grew at the same rate. Nonmetro areas grew the most from branch plant expansion (3 percent) and births of larger independent firms (2 percent), but their gains were nearly offset by job losses as branch plants closed or moved elsewhere. Both metro and nonmetro areas lost jobs in headquarters plants.

Table 1. Sources of employment change in the South and the U.S., 1980-84.

Item and firm type	South			U.S.		
	Metro	Non-metro	Total	Metro	Non-metro	US
	Percentages					
Percentage change in total						
employment	8.5	0.6	6.6	5.6	-0.6	4.5
Independent firms	9.7	2.3	7.8	5.2	1.2	4.5
Less than 20 employees	13.6	1.2	10.0	8.8	-0.4	6.6
20 employees or more	6.5	3.5	5.8	2.5	3.2	2.6
Headquarters establishments	-6.6	-4.2	-6.2	-6.5	-5.3	-6.4
Branches, subsidiaries	13.9	0.1	10.2	11.9	-1.4	9.5
Employment change from						
net of firm births less deaths	6.3	-1.3	4.4	3.3	-1.3	2.5
Independent firms	9.1	1.5	7.1	5.7	1.1	4.8
Less than 20 employees	13.5	1.2	9.9	8.8	0.1	6.7
20 employees or more	5.6	1.8	4.7	3.3	2.2	3.1
Headquarters establishments	-0.3	-1.0	-0.4	-0.8	-1.7	-0.9
Branches, subsidiaries	6.1	-4.2	3.4	2.8	-4.0	1.5
Employment change from						
net of expansion less con-						
traction, existing firms	2.3	1.9	2.2	2.3	0.7	2.0
Independent firms	0.6	0.8	0.7	-0.4	0.1	-0.3
Less than 20 employees	0.2	0.0	0.1	0.0	-0.6	-0.1
20 employees or more	0.9	1.8	1.1	-0.8	1.0	-0.5
Headquarters establishments	-6.4	-3.2	-5.8	-5.7	-3.6	-5.5
Branches, subsidiaries	7.7	4.2	6.8	9.2	2.6	7.9
Employment change from						
net births as percent of ab-						
solute total employment						
change	73.2	-216.2	66.6	59.2	-215.5	55.5
Independent firms	44.3	108.2	45.8	42.8	87.5	46.0
Less than 20 employees	29.6	46.4	29.9	28.9	5.4	29.7
20 employees or more	14.8	61.9	15.8	13.9	82.1	16.2
Headquarters establishments	-0.6	-18.0	-1.0	-2.7	-34.7	-3.6
Branches, subsidiaries	29.4	-306.4	21.8	19.1	-268.3	13.1
Employment change from net						
expansion as percent of abso-						
lute total employment change	26.8	316.2	33.4	40.8	115.5	44.5
Independent firms	2.8	61.4	4.2	-3.3	11.0	-3.1
Less than 20 employees	0.4	-0.8	0.4	0.1	-24.8	-0.5
20 employees or more	2.5	62.2	3.8	-3.4	35.8	-2.6
Headquarters establishments	-13.1	-58.0	-14.1	-19.4	-71.5	-21.6
Branches, subsidiaries	37.0	312.8	43.3	63.4	176.1	69.2

Source: Computed from extract from Dun & Bradstreet's USEEM file.

Employment growth in the South, according to the D&B data, occurred at a faster rate (7 percent) than in the U.S. as a whole. While job growth was concentrated in metro areas, the nonmetro South registered a small gain. The metro South had a 14 percent growth from the birth of small independent firms, higher than any other region. It also gained from the expansion of existing branch plants (8 percent) and the creation of new ones (6 percent). The strongest nonmetro growth was from expansion of existing branches (4 percent) and larger independent firms (2 percent). New independent firm births in the nonmetro South were a third higher than the national nonmetro rate, probably on the strength of the economies of the region's urban areas, but they were still less than one sixth of the rate for the metro South.

What conclusions should we draw about new firms as potential job creators in nonmetro areas? Independent firm births accounted for 46 percent of the net new jobs in the U.S. during 1980–1984, but 87 percent of the nonmetro growth. In the South, new independent firms contributed 44 percent of net new jobs in metro areas, similar to the U.S. average, but in nonmetro areas they accounted for all of the net job growth and offset 8 percent of the jobs lost among other firms as well!

Nonetheless, far more jobs were created by existing branch plants in nonmetro areas, which produced new jobs totaling more than one and a half times the net job growth rate nationally, and three times that rate in the nonmetro South. Had job creation from expansions not been offset by a high rate of job losses from branch plant deaths[6], the relative contribution of new firms would have been much smaller. This performance underscores the importance of local entrepreneurship efforts in an environment in which branch plant performance was as volatile as it appears to have been in rural areas generally, and the rural South in particular, in the early eighties. Thus, new enterprise development should be considered as a potential source of new jobs by rural developers.[7]

DO RURAL COMMUNITIES HAVE AN EQUAL CHANCE TO BENEFIT FROM ENTREPRENEURSHIP?

There are good reasons for believing that entrepreneurship may produce less real economic innovation in rural areas than in urban settings (Jacobs, 1984: 39). Because they are already centers of economic activity, urban areas have certain advantages that rural areas characteristically lack. Urban areas have diversified labor markets, which means that new businesses are more likely to find local employees with needed skills. Urban economies also benefit from established networks of firms servicing other businesses that, taken together, make up a supportive economic fabric that allows new firms to concentrate on their innovations, rather than spread their efforts across all aspects of the business operation (Miller and Bluestone, 1987; Quevit, 1986). Most urban areas are large enough to provide ready markets for specialized products, which reduces operating costs and permits firms to adopt "niche" strategies (Drucker, 1985). The close proximity of urban firms to each other and their markets makes it easier for them to follow and respond to market developments, thus increasing their chances for profitability and growth. And most urban areas benefit from more highly developed systems of public infrastructure which, acting as inputs to business production, helps them produce at lower cost.

An important question for rural areas, which have traditionally depended on nearby raw materials, is whether entrepreneurship, or for that matter any economic development strategy, can hope to produce the sort of economic health that urban areas have achieved. The simple answer is no. The advantages of agglomeration enjoyed by urban areas are not only responsible for their economic success, but they are, in effect, the principal features that define and distinguish urban economies from rural (Jacobs, 1984).

But if it is unrealistic to expect rural areas to demonstrate the same innovative capacity as cities, are the prospects for entrepreneurial growth similar for all rural places? And if not, which places seem most likely to benefit from the strategy? One of the most important lessons of recent years is that while rural economies are typically specialized, these specialties vary from one locale to another; it is easy to fall into overly simplistic generalizations about rural economies (Bender et al., 1985). Thus, the development potential of rural areas is best considered on a case-by-case basis.

A key question is the extent to which entrepreneurial behavior is driven by the general economic climate, especially macroeconomic conditions, versus non-economic community features or characteristics of the entrepreneurs themselves. Research to date suggests that characteristics of the community's environment, such as the levels of knowledge and skill within the local labor force, the quality of communications and information flows, the level of vitality in the small business sector, and the current pattern of self employment, have important effects on rates of entrepreneurship (Hobbs, 1986; 1987; Malecki, 1986: 9-13).

Instability in a community's economic and organizational environment also appears to create a climate in which enterprise formation increases as new opportunities become available, though it may be less important than is sometimes supposed. A recent study of firm startups in Minnesota and Pennsylvania found that the effects of stress in the local economy may differ depending on the market orientation of the firm. Business startups among firms serving mainly local markets were more rapid in regions with high unemployment rates, suggesting that economic necessity is a more important explanation for these firms. However, startup rates among firms oriented to export outside the region were higher in regions with greater educational attainment among the population, suggesting that for these firms perceived opportunity is a more powerful motivating factor (Reynolds 1986: 18-23).

These differences in context probably limit the value of entrepreneurship strategies in some communities. One writer, summarizing research on entrepreneurship in Britain and The Netherlands, concluded that entrepreneurship is likely to be strategically perverse, that there is "a strong tendency for entrepreneurship to be strongest precisely in those regions which need it least, suggesting that to rely on new and small firms will not eliminate regional economic differentials" (Malecki, 1986: 11). Regional differences in local ability to benefit from entrepreneurship arise not only from variations in human resources and community organization but also from differences in financial resources, without which enterprise development is difficult, though not impossible. (Fitzgerald and Meyer, 1986) Because entrepreneurship will work less well in some communities than in others, developers need to consider these factors carefully before encouraging communities to invest too many of their resources in enterprise development programs.

But within the limits imposed by a community's human and financial resource base, it is clear that positive action can lead to increased levels of entrepreneurial behavior. Community organization, institutions, and leadership appear to be especially important in providing both a supportive climate for entrepreneurship, and in some cases the spark that unleashes creative potential in the economic sphere of community life (Gatewood et al., 1984). Watkins (1987: 25) finds "emerging evidence that regional entrepreneurial vitality is closely linked to the quality of institutional relationships which exist between both private and public institutions, and among private sector firms themselves."

In summary, then, differences in entrepreneurial activity levels, possibly major ones, should be expected from one community to another, and perhaps from one region to another. The aggregate level of economic activity appears to have important effects on the levels of enterprise formation, though perhaps not as much as previously believed. Non-economic community characteristics are also important in stimulating entrepreneurial behavior, and in the end, they may be the most important factors. Above all, the chances for entrepreneurship are not solely determined by given community features, but can be enhanced or diminished by the actions of community members themselves. This point is critical, since it is the basis on which programs to stimulate and support entrepreneurship rest.

SOME IMPLICATIONS OF CHOOSING AN ENTREPRENEURSHIP STRATEGY OF COMMUNITY DEVELOPMENT

A number of recent reports and conferences have suggested a new strategy of community economic development that focuses on developing the internal capacities and strengths of a local economy, rather than trying to attract new employers from the outside. Variously called local development, endogenous regional growth, or community self-development, it has specific implications for rural communities and the ways they seek to achieve development (Coffey and Polese, 1984).

Fundamentally, a self-development strategy calls on communities to identify their comparative economic advantages and undervalued local resources and to initiate locally-controlled ventures that increase the amount of value added by the local economy (Organization for Economic Cooperation and Development, 1986: 29-32). Self-development strategies draw on entrepreneurship strategies for the creation of new, usually small, local enterprises. But self-development strategies are broader than entrepreneurship, and include energizing community organizations and leadership where they exist or creating them where they do not (Organization for Economic Cooperation and Development, 1986: 76-77).

The antithesis of self-development is the strategy of encouraging growth by attracting external investment (Vaughan et al., 1984: 42-46). The typical example is the recruitment of outside corporations, often by offering them an assortment of inducements such as tax abatements, financing and site development to locate a plant in the community (Hamilton et al., 1985). Retention and expansion strategies that focus on existing firms within the community fall somewhere between these two extremes, depending on whether the firms are locally or externally owned.

Several advantages are claimed for self-development. Because it encourages the creation of locally owned and operated firms, it strives to put economic decisions in the hands of local managers, for whom the welfare of the total community—not simply the firm's balance sheet—is likely to be important. Locally owned firms may be more likely to return benefits in such forms as greater community service, consideration of community values in scheduling, siting, and other decisions, and a commitment to stay in the community in the face of short-term financial disadvantages to the firm. Locally controlled firms are thus less likely to be footloose (Hobbs, 1986: 2). They are more likely to contribute to the enhancement of local entrepreneurial capacity and help build vitality in the local economy (Pulver, 1987). While they cannot insulate the community's economy from changing macroeconomic conditions, they can at least make their responses to those changes with the community's perspective in mind.

The literature suggests that a strong base of independent businesses adds vitality to the industrial ecology of an area and can buffer a local economy against the loss of some of its industries (Jacobs, 1984: 97). To the extent that an economic base is diversified, it is more likely to avoid major economic shocks due to shifts in macroeconomic conditions (Killian and Hady, 1987). And because the birth and death of firms is the principal mechanism by which a free economy adjusts to changing conditions, a vital base of small businesses—and a community climate that supports them—may constitute a capacity for economic adjustment that allows a community to adapt more easily to whatever changes befall it. It also creates an economic climate attractive to larger firms that might wish to settle in the community. And it can have positive social effects, leading to a socially responsible corporate citizenship with a sense of commitment to the community and a citizenry better trained in business methods (Coffey and Polese, 1984; Malecki, 1986: 10; Pulver, 1987; Watkins and Allen, 1987: 3).

An entrepreneurial strategy can offer these benefits because it attempts to build on the human capital in a community, rather than taking advantage of the low costs of labor and land historically available in many rural communities (Wilkinson, 1986: 11). Relying on cheap labor costs, in particular, creates a special vulnerability for rural communities. Industries that are sufficiently sensitive to labor costs to choose rural locations are just as likely to substitute capital for labor or move elsewhere (e.g., overseas) when it becomes profitable to do so (Jacobs, 1984). Communities that wish to make permanent enhancements to their economic base and thus avoid the threat of rapid job loss will do better to encourage developments that rely on unique characteristics of the area—special skills in the labor force, for example, or specializations in products—that cannot be readily duplicated in other locations. (Coffey and Polese, 1984).

Rural communities can develop comparative advantages that are not principally price advantages; doing so permits them to avoid reliance on minimum wage labor and to escape the disadvantage of high costs of transporting goods and services to market. Drucker (1985: 233-242) describes several entrepreneurial strategies for developing products that meet specialized needs (niches) and for which price is not a principal factor affecting sales. For example, an unemployed woman living in rural Fairview, Utah, developed a small business producing chocolate candies in her kitchen, which in less than one year grew to more than 25 part-time employees. The success of her business was due to the innovativeness of her products—tailored to distinctive markets, such as candies in the form of business cards for favors at convention banquets—which allowed her to overcome price disadvantages from the distance between her chosen place of residence and the markets she serves. While distance from markets will continue to limit the access of rural entrepreneurs to urban markets, such niche strategies nonetheless offer the potential for rural communities to overcome disadvantages of location.

In many ways, community self-development is much more difficult to accomplish than a traditional business recruitment strategy. It requires a vision of what a community can be, based on a search, perhaps an agonizing one, to find new strengths the community can develop as comparative economic advantages. Such introspection requires leadership that many communities lack and implies a self-examination that many may be unwilling to undergo. And it requires a long-term perspective on community development that offers no quick fix to pressing needs for improved jobs and income. But it is a strategy that can be implemented by community members themselves, through their

Figure 1. How local communities can promote entrepreneurship.

Many positive steps can be taken by local communities in their own behalf. The following illustrate the possibilities:

1. Develop a community climate hospitable to new businesses
   a. Explain entrepreneurship as an alternative to business recruitment and build a supportive opinion climate
   b. Publicize success stories and make "how to" information widely available
   c. Stimulate community spirit through communitywide activities, such as a festival or a community improvement campaign
   d. Give public recognition to business leaders who can provide useful role models for potential entrepreneurs
   e. Find ways to reward risk-takers and remove the penalties associated with risk-taking
   f. Remove barriers to new business startups, such as by simplifying administrative requirements for new firms, relaxing regulations where possible, and establishing one-stop permit procedures
   g. Build working relationships with outside organizations, such as university and extension service officials who can help the community develop and carry out an entrepreneurship strategy

2. Redirect resources toward entrepreneurship strategies
   a. Encourage community organizations to participate in business development programs
   b. Develop school curricula that teach business skills
   c. Establish school-based enterprise development programs
   d. Invite university and other experts to help identify the community's comparative economic advantages and underused resources
   e. Hold community discussions to identify possible new ventures
   f. Create a forum for successful business owners to share their ideas and skills with those just starting out
   g. Ask existing businesses to help identify community features that inhibit business startups, and act on these suggestions
   h. Scrutinize carefully any proposal to recruit firms from the outside, making sure the community understands the costs, as well as the benefits, of this approach to development

3. Assist individual business startups
   a. Appoint a coordinator to help new businesses get started, and to apply for state and federal government aids
   b. Establish an incubator to support new businesses
   c. Make sure that local entrepreneurs know about the information and advice they can get from organizations like the extension service and their state small business development center
   d. Encourage local banks to make "one more high risk loan"
   e. Pool the savings of community residents by creating a local venture capital fund or encouraging financial institutions to do so
   f. Construct needed infrastructure or assist with site development, if cost effective
   g. Use local tax dollars for business loans or equity financing, if permitted by law

own actions using resources available within the community and often with relatively little expenditure of funds (Figure 1) (Ryan, 1987).

Community support for self-development programs may be hard to obtain. Residents sometimes oppose assistance to their neighbors, perhaps out of jealousy (Bernier and McKemey, 1987). Entrepreneurial strategies sometimes generate community conflicts (Gatewood et al. 1984; Reid, 1987). And political leaders may be less willing to support development strategies that take longer than their term of office and produce undramatic and incremental results when they succeed.

Ryan (1987) argues that rural communities may be more successful in promoting development if they approach the task on a regional basis, by cooperating in programs and through sharing of services and facilities. Regional specialization in products could be added to his list. Even though it is unrealistic to hope that any rural region can become self-sufficient in all areas (otherwise it would not be rural), any region may capture some of the benefits of agglomeration by specializing in a narrow range of products. Many rural areas, for example, specialize in tourism related to the area's history or natural features, others in handicrafts that draw on their ethnic heritage. There is no a priori reason why this principle of specialization could not be extended to other types of industry. As an illustration, it has been proposed that the Finger Lakes region of New York state develop a ceramics industry that draws on the research facilities at Cornell and Alfred Universities, as well as the Corning Glass works that have long operated in the area. Such an industry could include a mix of products at the cutting edge of technological development, as well as lower tech, labor-intensive art and crafts. The chief drawback is that any attempt at economic specialization leaves a region vulnerable if an economic downturn hits its principal industry. In addition, implementing such a strategy would have to overcome the natural tendency of individual communities to resist cooperation and "go it alone;" the record of success in such cooperative ventures is not encouraging.

High rates of business closures among small firms have led some observers to the conclusion that small business development as a strategy is highly risky. But there is evidence that an entrepreneurship approach is at least as likely to produce results as traditional business recruitment strategies, characterized by one recent report as a "buffalo hunt," that pit tens of thousands of rural communities against each other in the search for an estimated 1,200–1,300 new plant openings announced each year (MDC, 1986: 11; Jacobs, 1984: 102-103).

It is impossible to come to an unambiguous conclusion about entrepreneurship as an economic development strategy. While entrepreneurship can be startlingly successful in some communities, it will not succeed in all. For some places, especially those lacking in human capital and community leadership, external investments may still provide the best hope for new jobs. But the potential for community development implicit in the entrepreneurship strategy argues that community developers should include it in their bag of tools (Ryan, 1987). No matter how much the phrase "entrepreneurship" may smack of faddism, there is something fundamentally sound about getting people to think seriously and creatively about the economic opportunities that they, and their communities, may wish to exploit.

PROSPECTS FOR ENTREPRENEURIAL GROWTH IN THE SOUTH

Self-development is not a strategy that will find easy application in the South, if past experience is a good guide. The South, more than any other region, is characterized by absentee ownership of its businesses (Jacobs, 1984). In 1980, for example, 27 percent of the nonmetro South's businesses were headquartered outside the region, compared with 21 percent nationally (Figure 2). This difference, which holds for all industry groupings, is especially large for manufacturing and for finance, insurance, and real estate. The proportion of absentee-owned businesses is largest in the East South Central (32 percent) and South Atlantic (27 percent) census divisions, but remains above the U.S. nonmetro average in the West South Central division (22 percent) as well.

An assessment of the chances that entrepreneurship strategies can help the rural South must take account of several major obstacles to economic progress in the region. First and most important is the appalling state of human resources in the region. In both the average number of years of school completed and the number of years of college completed, the rural South falls far behind all other regions of the country (Swanson and Butler, 1987). Truly innovative entrepreneurial ventures are fed by the intelligent analysis of opportunities and resources by the potential innovator. And community self-development efforts require thoughtful consideration of community assets, liabilities, and aspirations. Formal education creates neither intelligence nor thoughtfulness, of course, but it can unleash them in constructive ways. While some Southern states have recently launched efforts to make significant long-term improvements in educational quality, the overall record of performance nonetheless remains depressingly poor. School dropout rates are alarmingly high in some areas of the South (Swanson and Butler, 1987). And in spending per pupil for elementary and secondary education, the 12 Southern states that participate in the Southern Growth Policies Board rank in the lower half of the 50 states and nine are among the bottom 10 (Southern Growth Policies Board, 1986b). Until these conditions have been corrected, human resources are likely to put a brake on entrepreneurial growth in the region.

Second, community activeness has been shown to be important in the success of some kinds of development efforts (Lloyd and Wilkinson, 1985). But cultural and political traditions in the South have favored an elitist model of

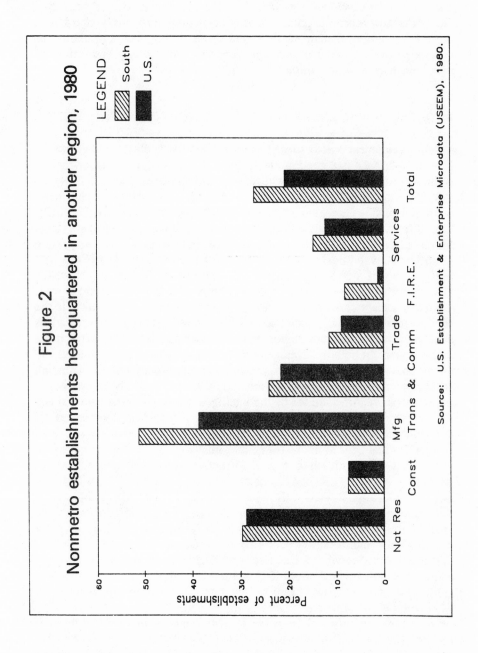

Figure 2

Nonmetro establishments headquartered in another region, 1980

Source: U.S. Establishment & Enterprise Microdata (USEEM). 1980.

community decisionmaking, rather than a participative model. While lack of community support does not prevent individuals from initiating new ventures, these efforts must succeed on their own. In communities with lower levels of participation, the chances that new ventures will be launched are reduced, as are their prospects of succeeding once started.

Third, the rural South's large black population, which has comparatively little business experience, presents a special developmental challenge. Research has shown that new entrepreneurs tend to have had significant exposure to other entrepreneurs—often a family member or close friend. Such entrepreneurial experience leads to additional attempts at enterprise formation. Without special attention to help blacks participate more fully in enterprise development, this large population group might not share in the benefits of development, and the overall rate of economic growth in the rural South might be retarded as well.

Finally, the South's business climate may not be appropriate for an entrepreneurially generated burst of economic growth. A recently released report challenges the conventional view that the South is the most hospitable region for new economic enterprises[10] (Corporation for Enterprise Development, 1987). That study analyzed 78 potential determinants of current and future growth in four general categories: economic performance, including income and job growth and quality of life; business vitality, especially the competitiveness of existing businesses and the ability to spawn new ones; economic capacity, including human and physical capital; and policy strength, the effectiveness of state and local governance and regulation, as well as tax policy. As a group, the 16 Southern states rated just over a D average overall, with the highest rating coming for business vitality and the lowest for economic performance. Nine states were graded D or less. While seven were performing at the B or C level, no Southern state was rated A overall. The national average was much higher. Contrary to the conventional view about business climate, which places most emphasis on business cost factors such as wage levels, tax levels, and the prevalence of unionization in an area, the Corporation for Enterprise Development's analysis argues for states to consider their total environment, especially the human resource climate, in making themselves attractive for business growth and development. If the CED's assessment is correct, Southern states have much work to do.

But these factors should not be overemphasized; the rural South has important strengths as well. First, the strong performance of Southern metropolitan areas undoubtedly has important spillover benefits for surrounding nonmetro areas. As business in urban centers booms and in-migrants settle into new jobs, opportunities are created to provide new goods and services to both. It is reasonable to think that some of the benefits from urban growth can spill over to rural residents, especially in communities close to metropolitan areas. In fact, it is very likely that the above average rates of enterprise formation in the nonmetro South during 1980–84 were due in large part to the rapid metro economic growth that occurred in this period.

Second, the fact that the large black population has had little experience at entrepreneurship need not be unduly discouraging. Research has shown that nobody who is willing to cultivate a new idea and take a risk is automatically shut out from taking advantage of this strategy (Friedman, 1987; Hoy, 1987). Given attention to the particular educational and technical assistance needs of blacks, there is no reason why the poor past record of participation in the economy by blacks need be seen as an immutable constraint on future economic growth.

Finally, it is apparent that stimulating enterprise formation is an area in which public action can help. Policy measures can lead to observable improvements in the prospects for growth through entrepreneurship. Many of the features of the region's business climate that are likely to discourage enterprise development are amenable to change by state government actions, for example. Among the alternatives are, enhancing the educational system, strengthening community leadership and organization and using it to promote economic self-development, and developing creative ways for financing local development efforts (Hobbs, 1987; Popovich and Buss, 1987: 37-41; Ryan, 1987; Vaughan et al., 1984: 67-113).

CONCLUSION

Entrepreneurship should not be regarded as a panacea for all the rural South's economic problems. It is not a magic bullet that will insulate rural economies from macroeconomic trends or improve the performance of lagging industries. It is a synonym for innovativeness and hard work.

But neither is entrepreneurship a phenomenon that must necessarily pass rural areas by. While they face inevitable disadvantages in competing with the stronger economies of urban areas, rural areas have considerable strengths of their own that they can and should exploit.

In the final analysis, entrepreneurship presents rural areas with an opportunity and a challenge. The opportunity is for rural communities to reshape their economies in ways of their own choosing. The challenge to community and regional leaders in the South is to perceive this opportunity and to seize it.

NOTES

¹The puzzled looks these terms evoked from my junior colleagues qualifies them for the list of things that distinguish those of us who are older than we think from others who must surely be wet behind the ears. PPBS refers to the integrated planning, programming, and budgeting systems introduced first into the Department of Defense in the early 1960s and later advocated for more general application

as a means for controlling policymaking through the budgetary process. ZBB stands for zero-base budgeting, which had similar motivations but was more clearly focused on the problem of runaway spending.

[2]"Latest" does not have to imply "new." Entrepreneurship also was popular in the late 1940s and again in the late 1960s. Dare we suggest that there is a natural cycle to these things?

[3]New firms are defined here as those less than 5 years old in 1980. Independent firms are those not a branch, franchise, or subsidiary of a parent company.

[4]Metropolitan areas are defined here as the 725 counties in a Metropolitan Statistical Area (MSA) as designated by the Office of Management and Budget. The remaining 2,416 are nonmetropolitan.

[5]The Dun & Bradstreet data have been criticized for incompletely representing some sectors, especially services, and smaller firms. These criticisms are discussed in Miller, 1979. Also, because of the way the data are collected, they do not include all firms and there are differences between industries in the percentage of firms reported. This causes employment totals reported by D&B to differ from those obtained from other sources. The most appropriate use of the D&B data, therefore, is to investigate the composition of employment changes, rather than their size.

[6]A variety of interpretations for net branch plant deaths are possible; these include business failures, voluntary closings, relocations to other sites, or the merger and absorption of the branch into another firm.

[7]It should be understood that even if no net new jobs resulted from new enterprise formation, it would be incorrect to conclude that entrepreneurship has no positive effects on the economy (Vaughan et al., 1984: 1). Births and deaths of firms are the principal adjustment mechanism by which new ideas are introduced to the economy and outdated ones weeded out. Thus, even if births and deaths were exactly balanced, the economy might still, had, the process of restructuring, be better positioned from a net competitive standpoint.

In addition, job creation by independent firms may be understated since not all deaths of independent firms reported by the Dun & Bradstreet data file resulted in a real loss of jobs. In some cases, such as when an independent firm is absorbed into an existing larger firm, perhaps as a new branch establishment, the transaction may be reported as the death of an independent firm and the expansion of an existing firm (or the birth of a new branch plant). It is impossible to trace these organizational changes with available data.

[8]This point can be easily overstated. Numerous examples can be cited of company towns in which local owners profited by exploiting local workers through monopoly power. For example, see Caudill (1963).

[9]The more conventional perspective on state business climates is given by Alexander Grant & Company, 1985.

REFERENCES

Alexander Grant & Company. 1985. *General Manufacturing Climates of the Forty-Eight Contiguous States of America*. Chicago: Alexander Grant & Company.

Bender, Lloyd D., Bernal L. Green, Thomas F. Hady, John A. Kuehn, Marlys K. Nelson, Leon B. Perkinson, and Peggy J. Ross. 1985. *The Diverse Social and Economic Structure of Nonmetropolitan America*. Washington: U.S. Department of Agriculture, Rural Development Report No. 49.

Bernier, Robert E., and Dale R. McKemey. 1987. "Entrepreneurial excavating: A case study in rural business development." *Proceedings of the National Symposium on Rural Entrepreneurship*. Mississippi State, Mississippi: Southern Rural Development Center: pp 46-56.

Caudill, Harry M. 1963. *Night Comes to the Cumberlands: A Biography of a Depressed Area*. Boston: Little, Brown and Company.

Coffey, William J., and Mario Polese. 1984. "The concept of local development: A stages model of endogenous regional growth." *Papers of the Regional Science Association* 55: 1-12.

Corporation for Enterprise Development. 1987. *Making the Grade: Development Report Card for the States*. Washington: Corporation for Enterprise Development.

Drucker, Peter. 1985. *Innovation and Entrepreneurship: Practice and Principles*. New York: Harper & Row, Publishers.

Fitzgerald, Joan, and Peter B. Meyer. 1986. "Recognizing constraints to local economic development." *Journal of the Community Development Society of America* 17 (No. 2): 115-126.

Friedman, Robert E. 1987. "The role of entrepreneurship in rural development." *Proceedings of the National Symposium on Rural Entrepreneurship.* Mississippi State, Mississippi: Southern Rural Development Center: pp. 1-6.

Gatewood, Elizabeth, Frank Hoy, and Charles Spindler. 1984. "Functionalist vs. conflict theories: Entrepreneurship disrupts the power structure in a small southern community." In John A. Hornaday, Fred Tarpley, Jr., Jeffrey A. Timmons, and Karl H. Vesper (editors), *Frontiers of Entrepreneurship Research.* Wellesley, Mass.: Babson College Center for Entrepreneurship Studies.

Hamilton, William, Larry Ledebur, and Deborah Matz. 1985. *Industrial Incentives: Public Promotion of Private Enterprise.* Washington, D.C.: Aslan Press.

Hobbs, Daryl. 1987. "Enterprise development: Is it a viable goal for rural communities?" *Proceedings of the National Symposium on Rural Entrepreneurship.* Mississippi State, Mississippi: Southern Rural Development Center: pp. 83-93.

Hobbs, Daryl. 1986. "Entrepreneurship as a development strategy for rural communities." *Outlook '87: Proceedings of the Annual Agricultural Outlook Conference.* Washington, D.C.: U.S. Department of Agriculture: 475-87.

Jacobs, Jane. 1984. *Cities and the Wealth of Nations: Principles of Economic Life.* New York: Vintage Books.

Killian, Molly Sizer, and Thomas F. Hady. 1987. "The economic performance of rural labor markets." In *Rural Economic Development in the 1980s: Preparing for the Future.* Washington, D.C.: U.S. Department of Agriculture, ERS Staff Report No. AGES870724, chap. 8.

Lloyd, Robert C., and Kenneth P. Wilkinson. 1985. "Community factors in rural manufacturing development," *Rural Sociology,* 50: 27-37.

Malecki, Edward J. 1986. "Entrepreneurship and regional development: A preliminary assessment of the issues." Paper presented at the North America Meetings of the Regional Science Association, Columbus, Ohio.

MDC, Inc. 1986. *Shadows in the Sunbelt: Developing the Rural South in an Era of Economic Change.* Chapel Hill, N.C.: MDC, Inc.

Miller, James P. 1987. *Recent Contributions of Small Businesses and Corporations to Rural Job Creation.* Washington, D.C.: U.S. Department of Agriculture, ERS Staff Report AGES861212.

Miller, James P. 1979. *Research with Dun and Bradstreet data.* Washington, D.C.: U.S. Department of Agriculture, Economic Research Service, EDD Working Paper No. 7903 (March).

Miller, James P., and Herman Bluestone. 1987. "Prospects for service sector employment growth in nonmetro America," In *Rural Economic Development in the 1980s: Preparing for the Future.* Washington, D.C.: U.S. Department of Agriculture, ERS Staff Report No. AGES870724, chap. 6.

Organization for Economic Cooperation and Development. 1986. *Rural Public Management.* Paris: Organization for Economic Cooperation and Development.

Popovich, Mark G., and Terry F. Buss. 1987. *Rural Enterprise Development: An Iowa Case Study.* Washington, D.C.: Council of State Policy and Planning Agencies.

Pulver, Glen C. 1987. "Fitting entrepreneurship into community development strategies." *Proceedings of the National Symposium on Rural Entrepreneurship.* Mississippi State, Mississippi: Southern Rural Development Center: pp. 93-101.

Quevit, Michel. 1986. *Le Pari de l'Industrialisation Rurale: La Capacite d'Entreprendre dans les Regions Rurales des Pays Industrialises.* Lausanne, Switzerland: Editions Regionales Europeennes S.A.

Reid, J. Norman. 1987. "Commercial business development strategies: Views of program administrators." *Proceedings of the National Symposium on Rural Entrepreneurship.* Mississippi State, Mississippi: Southern Rural Development Center: pp. 77-79.

Reynolds, Paul. 1986. "Organizational births: Founder characteristics, contextual features, and the emergence of new firms." Unpublished paper.

Ryan, Vernon D. 1987. "The significance of community development to rural economic development initiatives." In *Rural Economic Development in the 1980s: Preparing for the Future.* Washington, D.C.: U.S. Department of Agriculture, ERS Staff Report No. AGES870724, chap. 16.

Schumpeter, Joseph A. 1951a. "The creative response in economic history," *Journal of Economic History* 7 (November 1947): 149-159. Reprinted in Richard V. Clemence (ed.), *Essays on Economic Topics of J.A. Schumpeter.* Port Washington, N.Y.: Kennikat Press: 216-226.

_____. 1951b. "Economic theory and entrepreneurial history." *Change and the Entrepreneur.* Cambridge, Mass.: Harvard Univ. Press: 63-84. Reprinted in Richard V. Clemence (ed.), *Essays on Economic Topics of J.A. Schumpeter.* Port Washington, N.Y.: Kennikat Press: 248-266.

_____. 1961. *The Theory of Economic Development*. New York: Oxford University Press.

Shapero, Albert. 1984. "The entrepreneurial event." In Calvin A.Kent (ed.), *The Environment for Entrepreneurship*. Lexington, Mass.: Lexington Books: pp. 21-40.

Southern Growth Policies Board. 1986a. *Profile of the South*. Research Triangle Park, N.C.: Southern Growth Policies Board.

_____. 1986b. *The Report of the Committee on Human Resource Development*. 1986 Commission on the Future of the South. Research Triangle Park, N.C.: Southern Growth Policies Board.

Swanson, Linda L., and Margaret A. Butler. 1987. "Human resource base of rural economies." In *Rural Economic Development in the 1980s: Preparing for the Future*. Washington, D.C.: U.S. Department of Agriculture, ERS Staff Report No. AGES870724, chap 7.

U.S. Small Business Administration. 1986. *The State of Small Business: A Report of the President Transmitted to the Congress, 1986*. Washington, D.C. : U.S. Government Printing Office.

Vaughan, Roger J., Robert Pollard, and Barbara Dyer. 1984. *The Wealth of States: Policies for a Dynamic Economy*. Washington, D.C.: Council of State Policy and Planning Agencies.

22

Alternative Enterprises for Strengthening Southern Agriculture

Emerson M. Babb
Burl F. Long

The search for alternatives to bolster incomes of farmers and rural residents has been an ongoing process for many decades. Studies conducted in the 1930s were addressing many of the same issues of low income, rural poverty, farm financial stress and the search for income-producing alternatives for rural people that are receiving so much attention today. Nevertheless, the current financial stress in agriculture and rural communities has generated an intense search for farm and non-farm alternative enterprises.

While the interest is high, much of the information presented has been in the popular press and has lacked the scientific basis necessary for informed decisionmaking. More detailed analyses and research findings are beginning to appear as public and private agencies respond to the demand for information. For example, in a previous paper, we analyze factors influencing the adjustment to alternative enterprises in the South such as production environment, comparative advantage, labor availability, technology, agricultural policy, risks, and economic development (Babb and Long, 1987). In this chapter, our focus is on providing information that can be useful to agencies advising farmers about the transition to alternative enterprises. It examines the potential market for these products and services, obstacles to success, and activities which can help reduce these obstacles. As used in this chapter, "alternative enterprises" refers to a mix of products and services that involve nonconventional crops and animals, access to various uses of land and water, and integrated farm and off-farm activities.

MARKET POTENTIAL

Those interested in alternative enterprises have very little information regarding the size of the market for products and services. How much can be sold and at what prices? It may be possible to grow in the South many of the 20,000 known edible plants,but how many can be sold profitably? A major source of risk for those considering the transition to alternative enterprises relates to market size. Projections of market potential for alternative products are thus important, even though they may be very imprecise, because they force people to recognize that there are limits to market size. The hazards of market projections are all too obvious. How do you project sales of a product that has never been consumed in the South?

During the next 20 years, the demand for alternative products and services will significantly expand. More affluent consumers and larger numbers of persons from varied ethnic and cultural backgrounds will expand the consumption of new and exotic foods. Many families will purchase new foods to add variety to meals and to enhance status among peers. As medical research and technology raise the health consciousness of consumers, consumption of food considered nutritious, low in calories, free of chemical and pharmaceutical additives, and low in substances associated with heart and circulatory problems, will expand (Havlicek, 1986).

Persons in the rural South should benefit from changes in consumer behavior such as increased purchases of fruits and vegetables, exotic foods and ornamental plants (Hamm, 1985), as well as greater uses of services such as farm-based recreation and integrated off-farm activities. For much of the South, there are large numbers of consumers nearby and the pace of population growth is expected to remain relatively high. The South has relatively high proportions of retirees and persons visiting the area for vacation and recreation. The number of persons splitting their residence between the South and some other area of the country has been growing. The population has become increasingly diversified with respect to race, ethnic and cultural background. Not only are these trends likely to persist, but they will continue to provide potential niches for products and services. Market development should be focused on markets in the South, but the opportunities to sell alternative products to other regions or even in the export market need to be analyzed. Proximity to customers is a requisite to success in some, but not all, alternative enterprises.

Studies which have projected the consumption of fruits and vegetables provide the best available guidelines for alternative food product consumption
(Blaylock and Smallwood, 1986; Capps, 1986; Estes, 1985; Hamm, 1985;
Smallwood and Blaylock, 1984). Consumption of all vegetables has increased
about three percent per year, but consumption of some vegetables such as broccoli and cauliflower have been spectacular, increasing 10 to 15 percent per
year. Blaylock and Smallwood (1986) suggest that consumption of fruits and
vegetables in the U.S. may increase in the range of 1.5 to 1.8 percent per year
over the next 20 years. These changes in consumption are related to population growth, changes in demographics and higher incomes. While population
is projected to increase nationally by 0.9 percent per year thru the year 2000,
it is expected to increase by 1.6 percent per year in the South Atlantic states
(Bureau of Census, 1987: 14). Food expenditures for fruits and vegetables in
households with persons 45 years of age and older are substantially higher
than in households with younger persons.The growing number of older persons in much of the South should have the effect of further expanding the market for alternative food products in this area. Given these favorable factors,
an increase in consumption for all fruits and vegetables in the South may
approximate 2.5 percent per year.

Production of fruits and vegetables in the South will likely increase at a
rate greater than the expansion of consumption. In recent years, growth in
production of vegetables has been greater in states which are not traditional
producers (Hamm, 1985). An emphasis on fresh fruits and vegetables would
increase the share of production in the South, and raise the market potential
to an increase of perhaps 4.0 percent per year (2.5 percent increase in consumption plus 1.5 percent additional increase in production). Increases in
production of more than 1.5 percent per year above the increase in consumption will become progressively more difficult to market, as this would involve taking sales outlets from competing states. In this analysis, the assumption
is made that imports from other countries will not change substantially. Imports are a relatively small part of the fresh market, but they have been growing. Further, other countries may have comparative advantage for some
alternative products which are native to them.

Some of the alternative food products may compete only indirectly with traditional fruits and vegetables. The growth in consumption of these alternative
products will probably be greater than the 2.5 percent per year figure earlier
used for all fruits and vegetables in the South. Growth will be more rapid
because these products will be novel and start from a small base. Further,
many of these products will respond well to good marketing strategies. There
will be some superstars which will more than offset the duds. For these reasons, an annual increase of 5 percent in market potential for alternative food
products in the South may be possible (4.0 percent increase in production plus
1.0 percent addition for higher growth rate of newer, alternative products). The

effectiveness of market development could easily result in the actual increase varying by the full amount of the 5 percent growth approximation.

For the South, growth of alternative enterprises related to services is likely to be greater than growth of alternative enterprises producing food. The factors contributing to growth of alternative food products will be important, especially population growth, more retirees, and more visitors. Alternative services such as access to recreation (fishing, hunting, camping, hiking), farm and dude ranch vacations, vacation homesites, sale of products at roadside markets, and pick-your-own operations are based on buyers having time available for the pursuit of these activities. The South seems especially well positioned to capitalize on demands generated by time available for leisure and recreation. The income elasticities of alternative food products are probably high, and those for services are likely still higher. While growth in demand for services in the South will be influenced by the strength of the economy and income gains, it could easily exceed 5 percent per year. This high rate of growth is partly due to the small base of services in rural areas. Recreational services are now concentrated in urban centers.

Growth of some services may be affected by the extent to which various other services are concentrated in one place. The joint efforts of local organizations and firms may combine to attract a large number of customers with varied interests. On the other hand, it may be wise for some communities to differentiate the product in terms of isolation, back to nature, and the like.

The growth in market potential for alternative food products and services in the South is promising. Unfortunately, the shift to these enterprises will not solve the farm problem in the South or for the rest of the country. This should not discourage efforts to promote alternative enterprises and to enhance the chances of success for those who shift from traditional enterprises. The problem with conventional enterprises is excess productive capacity. Withdrawal of resources from conventional enterprises to produce alternative products and services obviously will reduce the problem in conventional agriculture, but the effects of this withdrawal are likely to be swamped by technological developments and increases in productive capacity in the rest of the world. Fruits and vegetables are now produced on some six million acres of land in the U.S. If the market potential for alternative products and services were to expand at 5 percent per year for the next 20 years, and imports were to remain constant, land requirements would be only about 12 million acres. In contrast, about 330 million acres in the U.S. are currently devoted to conventional crops, excluding fruits and vegetables. An additional 660 million acres are used for pasture.The withdrawal of capital and labor from conventional enterprises would probably have little effect on output of these enterprises. The reason that production of alternative products and services deserves attention is not that this will solve the farm problem, but because it has the potential to improve the welfare of many persons and the quality of life of rural communities where they live. Those concerned with assisting in the transition to alternative enterprises need to be guided by principles and strategies relevant to economic development rather than to the solution of the crisis in agriculture.

OBSTACLES

While many who shift to alternative enterprises will be successful in improving net returns, there will be many cases where returns are reduced. In some instances, the shift will result in business failure. A large proportion of business failures are for small firms. In 1985, 24 percent of the firms that failed had liabilities of less than $25,000 and 71 percent had liabilities of less than $1,000,000 (Economic Analysis Department, 1986). Failures tend to be most prevalent in new businesses. In 1985, 39 percent of the failing firms had been in business three years or less and 55 percent had been in business five or less years. During the 1950-85 period, between 85 and 90 percent of the failures were caused by lack of experience in a line of business, lack of managerial experience, and incompetence. The probability of business failure is higher for small firms, newer firms, those which lack experience in their line of business, and those with inexperienced or incompetent management. Given this pattern of business failure, those considering a shift to alternative enterprises and persons advising farmers should proceed with caution.

Some of the obstacles to success in alternative enterprises may be reduced by actions of the land-grant system, state departments of agriculture, community agencies, nonprofit organizations and private firms (Table 1). There are large incentives for these groups to provide assistance to increase the percentage of firms that successfully make the transition to alternative enterprises.

Table 1.
Obstacles to Success in Alternative Enterprises and Organizations
Best Suited to Reduce Obstacles.

Obstacle	Provider of Assistance
Information	State Universities and Departments of Agriculture, USDA
Entrepreneurship	Individual
Human Capital	State and Local Agencies
Market Coordination	Agribusiness Firms
Infrastructure	State Agencies and Agribusiness Firms
Venture Capital	Agribusiness Firms and Individuals

Firms that succeed in improving their performance by shifting to alternative enterprises can effectively enhance employment in the rural South, strengthen the economy in their area, and contribute to the maintenance of the community infrastructure. Failure among firms that shift not only can adversely affects persons in the firms, but also the community in which they are located.

Information

One reason for the higher risk of shifting to alternative enterprises is the lack of good information. Information about production practices, marketing alternatives, net returns, and size of market varies from poor to nonexistent. The information bases developed by public and private organizations for conventional enterprises are not transferrable or useful in understanding the production and marketing of new alternatives. Major investments in the production of relevant information are needed for the realization of the potential in alternative enterprises. Enterprise-specific costs and returns data, management practices, marketing alternatives, and market potential information will be needed. For many alternatives, the identification of market segments, market windows, and market niches will be critical.

It has been suggested that producers in other countries know more about our food trends and eating habits than do those in U.S. agriculture (Meeks, 1986b). If true, this does not bode well for success in alternative enterprises since many of the food imports involve the products of these enterprises. Many alternative enterprises originated in other countries and were produced for the diets of ethnic groups which consume the product in the U.S. This suggests a need to develop information about consumption in other countries where the potential for sales for some products may be as great or greater than in the U.S. It may be easier to export food products which are already in the diet than to export our surplus agricultural products which are not grown or consumed in the traditional diet of the importing country.

Entrepreneurship

Entrepreneurship is probably the most important ingredient to success with alternative enterprises. The role of entrepreneurs is to assess trends and conditions which give rise to future opportunities and to assume the risk required to obtain the rewards presented by these opportunities. The entrepreneur will be searching for opportunities to develop the best utilization of those resources that he or she commands. Each family may possess some unique resources which make it particularly suited to engage in various farm/non-farm activities. These resources may be the product of both farm and non-farm experiences and relate to functions such as production, finance and merchandising.

Government payments which currently constitute a large portion of farm income, are not likely to be extended to alternative enterprises, and other forms of financial assistance from federal and state governments will be limited (Conway, 1986). Thus, those involved with alternative enterprises will be more dependent on their own skills and creativity in finding market niches and in developing markets for their products. They cannot rely on government as a market to absorb excessive production or to establish programs which have the effect of reducing output if production expands beyond what can be sold at prices which recover costs. A different mindset will be required for success with alternative enterprises. Farmers have long claimed that poor performance in agriculture was largely the result of defects in marketing and have called for emphasis on marketing research and education. There is some validity to this claim in the case of conventional enterprises, and even more so for alternatives. Alternative enterprises will flourish or disappear depending on the success in creating markets for these products and services and in designing effective marketing strategies.

Human Capital

Managerial problems are a major cause of business failure. They can equally reduce performance of those involved with either conventional or alternative enterprises. The managerial skills required for conventional enterprises may not be adequate or transferable to the production and marketing of alternative enterprises, which may include nonfarming enterprises. Many alternative enterprises will test management skills in marketing to a much greater extent than has been the case for conventional enterprises. For enterprises that involve selling to customers or other contacts with customers, new skills will need to be developed. The manager may need to be a good salesperson, promoter, developer, communicator, production manager, marketing manager and financial manager all wrapped up in one person. Services may be an important component of the output from alternative enterprises, maybe the only component. For example, the sale of access to recreation, the sale of products at roadside markets, and even pick-your-own operations, involve selling services in varying degrees. The concept of selling services rather than physical commodities may pose a barrier to entry to those with experience in conventional enterprises. There may be more skills in common for success among a variety of alternatives involving the sale of services than between those for conventional enterprises and any alternative enterprise.

Conventional enterprises are supported by a large number of persons in agribusinesses who have specialized skills and knowledge regarding such things as credit, risk management, transportation, storage, tax management, marketing outlets, grades and standards, and financial management. Much of this human capital may not be directly transferable to alternative enterprises. The diversity and smaller total volume of alternative enterprises will place limits on the investments which can be justified to develop appropriate human capital. For example, consider the number of experts on wheat futures who are available to assist farmers. How many such experts could we have for broccoli? The demands for human capital development related to alternative enterprises will be large. Public and private organizations will need to analyze the allocation of their limited resources to these many new demands and to the maintenance of human capital to support conventional enterprises.

Coordination

There are many channels through which the products and services of alternative enterprises can be sold, such as traditional wholesale distributors and brokers, farmers' markets, retail outlets operated at the farm (roadside stands and access to recreation) and in town (food specialty stores, home delivery routes), direct selling to food retailers and marketing cooperatives. These channels are not as well developed for alternative products and services and there may be little coordination between producers and others in the system. In some cases, the farmer may perform the coordination function. For example, minimal coordination with others is required for producing vegetables to be sold at a roadside stand or to operate a pay fishing pond. Where the product or service is not sold directly to the final consumer, considerable coordination may be required. This would be especially true for products to be sold in regional, national or international markets where processing facilities, warehousing, transportation and financing might be needed. There are considerable efficiencies to be gained through performing market development on a joint, coordinated basis, even where farmers sell direct to final consumers and coordinate all other functions.

Various types of contracting or cooperative marketing might provide vehicles for coordination. Farmers seldom know how increased production of alternative products will affect prices or how much the market can absorb. Without coordination of production and marketing, flows of product to geographic markets during different time periods would likely be inefficient. Small changes in quantity could produce volatile prices.

Infrastructure

The spatial pattern of alternative enterprises will vary. Some products and services will be sold in local markets and depend on the proximity to urban consumers. For farmers not close to urban centers, location will thus be an impediment to success in these enterprises. For other enterprises, development of an appropriate infrastructure for production and marketing will influence location. Production and marketing of many alternative enterprises may develop in locational matrixes which are most favorably situated relative to industrial-urban centers (Schultz, 1953).

Much of the existing processing and storage facilities may not accommodate alternative commodities. New investments, especially for commodities requiring processing, could be large. Those with investments in existing infrastructure will be reluctant to make new investments that would make existing facilities obsolete or reduce utilization of capacity.

Venture Capital

The capital needs for production and marketing of alternative products and services will be significant given that access to some of the traditional sources of agricultural credit will be limited. New enterprises are usually viewed as high risk by lenders. Production and marketing information is extremely limited; thus, traditional agricultural lenders will find it difficult to judge the expected profitability of these new enterprises. This lack of information will create uncertainty for the potential lender and likely make financing more difficult and expensive. Also, it is likely that many of the producers of alternative enterprises will not have the experience or knowledge of sources of finance which is found among many conventional producers.

Given the inherent risk and uncertainty associated with new types of agricultural operations, producers may have to rely more heavily on sources of venture or equity capital. Such forms of financing are common for new business ventures or new technologies in other sectors of the economy, but they have not been widely used in most of conventional agriculture. New sources of venture capital will need to be identified and cultivated, but many producers will not be familiar with the sources or methods involved.

REDUCING OBSTACLES

Public and private organizations can do much to increase the chances of success for those involved in alternative enterprises. Their resources are limited, however. They must, therefore, determine those areas for which they have comparative advantage. The following discussion attempts to provide some indication of what organizations at different levels are now doing to assist those producing alternative products and services and where they might be most effective in providing assistance.

National Government

The U.S. Department of Agriculture (USDA) established an Office of Small Scale Agriculture to monitor current developments, disseminate information and bring together groups with common interests. The Federal Extension Service could provide a valuable service by coordinating the development of information pieces which could be used by states. Funds could be allocated for research grants to analyze various problems associated with alternative enterprises. Agencies within USDA could also conduct research, especially on problems of national scope (such as demand projections). The Agricultural Cooperative Service could examine the feasibility of marketing alternative products cooperatively, as well as the role cooperatives could play in the coordination of production and marketing. At present, agricultural credit programs are available to producers of alternative commodities.

While it is not likely, USDA could administer programs such as those which now apply to conventional commodities. If such programs were extended to alternative commodities, they would have to be accepted with caution. Programs such as the price support programs have not been overwhelmed by success and they may prove impractical for dealing with commodities produced in small volumes and traded on thin markets. The resultant consequences of an agricultural program that provides incentives to produce 50,000 acres more wheat than will clear the market at a desired price, are mild compared to one that increases the production of ginseng by 50,000 acres.

Federal agencies such as the Small Business Administration may be effective in providing technical assistance and loans, especially to firms that may be processing and marketing the output of a group of producers of alternative products. Groups in the USDA, Commerce Department, and State Department may assist firms that seek to export products by providing information needed to gain access to foreign markets and by helping with market development. In sum, federal agencies should primarily be involved in reducing the information obstacle.

State Government

State governments are probably more active than federal agencies in providing assistance to producers of alternative products and services, a fact that may reflect comparative advantage. Research, education, and information are important products of the land-grant university in each state. Greater emphasis on the production and marketing of alternative commodities at these and other state colleges and universities could do much to mitigate information and human capital obstacles.

In response to conditions of stress in agriculture, almost half of the states have initiated some type of farm credit program (Gardner, 1986). These programs are not directly related to assistance with alternative enterprises and consist of linked deposits (10 states), low interest loans (10 states), loan guarantees (7 states), interest buy downs (6 states), interest deferrals (4 states), and bond programs to provide tax exempt financing for beginning farmers (17 states).

States in the South are much less involved with these credit programs (Meeks, 1986b:15). States also have initiated programs to relieve agricultural stress, such as referral and counseling services, job search and retraining assistance, and education programs on financial management (Chicoine and McDowell, 1987). If states provide financial assistance for expanding alternative enterprises, these funds might be more effective if used to improve the infrastructure, e.g., low cost loans to construct or remodel marketing and processing facilities. There are numerous other state activities which can assist those in alternative enterprises (Meeks, 1986b). Perhaps the most predominant activity is operation of farmers' markets. These can provide sales outlets for many alternative products, but the mere fact that there is a physical facility called a market does not insure that alternative products will move at any price. Imagine someone unexpectedly bringing 200 pounds of edible snails to a farmers' market for sale.

Some states have product promotion boards. Since market development is one of the most important keys to success for alternative products, states may be able to provide valuable assistance by reorienting some of their development efforts. Many states have export offices to assist those who seek to expand the exports of products produced in the state. If these offices focus on niches for products in export markets, as does the one in Minnesota, they may be more useful in expanding sales of alternative products.

States publish newsletters and information sheets which provide names and locations of pick-your-own operations, roadside markets, new uses of agricultural products and the like. These publications and other media could be used to promote alternative products, some of which may be completely new to consumers. Consumers need to know about the existence of the product and how it can be used.

Given the number of retirees living in the South and the number of visitors to the area, the sale of access to recreation may have more potential in the rural South than in many other parts of the U.S. State agencies responsible for promoting tourism might place greater emphasis on publicizing information about rural recreation opportunities to potential users (Meeks, 1986a). Landowner liability for injuries to others is the major obstacle to expansion of rural recreation enterprises. States may be able to provide some relief in the form of limits on liability.

Several states have committees or task forces which are assessing the potential of alternative enterprises. These groups will undoubtedly recommend additional state functions to expand alternative enterprises and to improve their viability. While states have been involved in reducing those constraints previously described (except entrepreneurship), they probably have a comparative advantage in working on obstacles relating to information, human capital, and infrastructure deficiencies. This is where they have the most experience and have been most effective in the past.

Local

County and community organizations are close to the action and more directly realize the consequences associated with successes and failures of those in alternative enterprises. Unfortunately, the financial resources available to localities for strengthening alternative enterprises are limited. But, they can provide counsel and advice on a more personal and immediate basis than can State agencies. Thus, their comparative advantage is in reducing obstacles related to human capital. They can also disseminate information developed at the state or federal level.

Local governments make decisions about taxes and expenditures of funds collected, including development and maintenance of infrastructure, which can influence the viability of alternative enterprises. Use-value tax assessments and tax credits may make some alternatives more feasible, especially those related to recreation. Local governments can make and enforce many regulations which relate to property rights, and such activities can encourage or discourage the establishment of some alternative enterprises.

There are many instances of concentrations of alternative enterprises in a community. This may reflect substantial economies for concentrating such enterprises at one location, such as sharing common technical expertise, purchasing inputs collectively, achieving aggregate levels of volume which attract buyers, being identified by quality standards or name recognition (Vidalia onions), providing a variety of products and services in one area that makes a trip worthwhile, and developing a pool of people with specialized skills. Where concentrations of enterprises have occurred, leadership on the part of one or more persons in local government, nonprofit organization, or business have served as the driving force behind that development. Communities need to audit and evaluate their unique attributes which might give rise to comparative advantage and economies of concentration at a location. The rewards for leadership and creativity may be greater at the local level than at state and federal levels.

Agribusiness

For conventional commodities, agribusiness firms (including cooperatives) have had the major responsibility for solving problems related to market coordination, market development, facilities, and venture capital. This will continue to be the case for alternative products and services.

For most agribusinesses, alternative products represent uncharted waters. They will be learning together with farmers who do business with them. They will need to spend more time with farmers for such things as planning production than would be the case for conventional commodities. Mechanisms for coordination, such as contracting, will have to be developed and these may be quite different for individual commodities. Risk of business failure for these agribusinesses will increase, but it may be reduced if alternative products constitute an added line of business in combination with more conventional products. Firms will require greater profit incentives to make investments which have higher risks.

Agribusiness firms will have the major role in market development. They can obtain help from state and federal agencies, but they will bear most of the responsibility for implementation. Since much of the success in alternative products depends on market development, agribusiness performance of this function will greatly influence the size of the market for these products.

Individuals

Development of entrepreneurship and evaluation of one's entrepreneurial spirit are prime responsibilities of individuals contemplating a shift to alternative enterprises. Those individuals also provide some of the venture capital.

State agencies and others can provide training to improve various managerial skills, but they cannot train good entrepreneurs. The often heard phrase "entrepreneurial spirit" conveys a sense of what is involved. Those persons who are troubled by dealing with the unfamiliar, who feel threatened by problems, who do not feel a challenge in organizing people, money and facilities to achieve some objective, and who do not sleep well at night if they are in risky situations, would be well advised to leave the production and marketing of such things as shiitake mushrooms and alligator tails to others.

SUMMARY

Many of the alternative products embody attributes which satisfy other than physiological needs. Annual increases in production of alternative products in the South are expected to average about five percent and income from services should increase even more. The withdrawal of resources from conventional enterprises to produce alternative products and services will do little to reduce productive capacity in conventional agriculture, especially with increases in production from technological developments.

Obstacles to success with alternative enterprises are varied. The most important obstacles are related to information, entrepreneurship, human capital, market coordination, infrastructure, and venture capital. Effective roles for public and private organizations to reduce impediments should be explored. They should be guided by principles and strategies relevant to economic development rather than to the solution of the farm problem.

REFERENCES

Babb, Emerson M. and Burl F. Long. 1987. "The role of alternative agricultural enterprises in a changing agricultural economy." *Southern Journal of Agricultural Economics* 19:forthcoming.

Blaylock, James R., and David M. Smallwood. 1986. *U.S. Demand for Food: Household Expenditures, Demographics, and Projections*. Washington, D.C.: U.S. Department of Agriculture, Technical Bulletin 1713.

Bureau of the Census. 1987. *Statistical Abstract of the United States, 1986.* Washington, D.C.: Department of Commerce.

Capps, Oral. 1986. "Changes in domestic demand for food: Impacts on Southern agriculture." *Southern Journal of Agricultural Economics*, 8:25-36.

Chicoine, David L., and George R. McDowell. 1987. "State policies to help farm people adjust." In *Increasing Understanding of Public Problems and Policies*. Chicago: Farm Foundation.

Conway, Carol. 1986. "The state role in agricultural trade promotion." *Southern International Perspectives*, Southern Growth Policies Board, (Spring).

Economic Analysis Department. 1986. *Business Failure Record*. New York: Dunn and Bradstreet.

Estes, Edmund A. 1985. "Alternative cash crops: How big is the market." In *Proceedings of Analyzing the Potential for Alternative Fruit and Vegetable Crop Production Seminar*. Raleigh, North Carolina: North Carolina Agricultural Experiment Station.

Gardner, Richard L. 1986. "The state role in addressing farm financial problems." Paper presented at the Annual Meeting of the American Agricultural Economics Association, Reno, Nevada.

Hamm, Shannon R. 1985. "Profile: Consumption and production of the U.S. vegetable industry." In *Proceedings of Analyzing the Potential for Alternative Fruit and Vegetable Crop Production Seminar*. Raleigh, North Carolina: North Carolina Agricultural Experiment Station.

Havlicek, Joseph. 1986. "Megatrends affecting agriculture: Implications for agricultural economics." *American Journal of Agricultural Economics*, 68:1053-1064.

Meeks, Gordon. 1986a. "Potential private revenue and public benefits from alternative agriculture." In *State Legislative Report* 11(4). Denver, Colorado: National Conference of State Legislatures.

_____. 1986b. *The State of Agriculture: Some Observations*. Denver, Colorado: National Conference of State Legislatures.

Schultz, Theodore W. 1953. *The Economic Organization of Agriculture*. New York: McGraw-Hill Book Company.

Smallwood, David M. and James R. Blaylock. 1984. *Household Expenditures for Fruits, Vegetables, and Potatoes*. Washington, D.C.: U.S. Department of Agriculture, Technical Bulletin 1690.

23

Charting a Course for the Rural South

William F. Winter

The rural South in which I grew up and where my roots go back through several generations remains a region of incredible paradoxes. It is a place where great pride is taken in family and personal relationships. Yet, it is also the place where live the greatest number of underdeveloped and undereducated human beings in the nation. It is a region that combines an abundance of all of the basic natural resources—productive land, energy, water and timber— that should make it the country's richest area. The fact is that it is the poorest. It is the section that has most fiercely resisted change. But it is the region that in recent years has been most drastically affected by change.

This is the place where a short decade ago the leading economic indicators were pointed upward. Profitable cotton, tobacco and soybean production brought new prosperity to Southern farms. There was unprecedented demand for oil and gas and coal, as world energy prices skyrocketed. The steady hum of thousands of sewing machines attested to the productivity and stability of the myriad manufacturing plants scattered across the countryside. Poverty had dropped from thirty-five percent of the population to eighteen percent in the preceding ten years (Southern Growth Policies Board, 1986b). And to top it all off, a native son of rural Georgia was ensconced in the White House. What could be finer than to be in Carolina—or any where else in the South—in such heady, halcyon days? This was the Sunbelt, and the rural South, after a hundred years of deprivation, was coming into its own.

Now, less than a decade later, clouds appear over the region, or at least over most of its rural areas. They are not the angry black thunderheads that we have seen in the past, but smaller scattered patches of cloud that nevertheless cast long shadows across the face of the land. For a time they were not noticed in the glare from the bright lights of the urban shopping centers, but they have recently become very real to that considerable number of Southerners whose manufacturing jobs have gone to Taiwan or Singapore or Latin America or for those miners and oil field workers who are devastated by the depression in the coal fields and the oil patch, or for those farmers, large and small, who have become the unsuspecting victims of their own productivity, along with federal monetary and trade policies that have served to diminish their markets overseas.

At the same time that all of the dislocations arising from manufacturing, agriculture, and energy have been creating havoc in the rural areas, federal support has been ebbing for economic development and social programs. Since 1981, state and local governments in the South have lost more than $20 billion as a result of federal budget reductions (MDC, Inc., 1986). These cuts have fallen disproportionately harder on the rural areas, many of which lack the fiscal capacity to maintain basic physical infrastructure needs, not to mention essential human services.

What is the result of these developments and policies? Put very plainly, it means that the poor areas are getting poorer and the rich areas are getting richer. This is another way of saying that the rural areas of the South are getting poorer.

Without some bold new approaches, the ultimate effect of all this will, of course, be an accelerated migration from the rural areas to the cities. But unlike the 1940s and 1950s, this migration will not be to the cities of the North and East, but instead to the cities of the South. Problems brought about by urban sprawl and uncontrolled population growth will be repeated in Southern cities at the same time that the population base necessary to maintain a strong rural society gradually disappears from the South.

In adjusting to these realities, it is obvious that new long-range strategies must be applied if the rural South is finally to shake loose from its old social and economic chains. Governor Bill Clinton, the dynamic young Governor of Arkansas, perhaps said it best when, in setting up the 1986 Commission on the Future of the South (a group charged with examining the region's condition) observed that we are "halfway home and a long way to go." What he was referring to was the fact that in spite of the economic progress of the last four decades, millions of rural Southerners remain locked in ignorance, poverty and unemployment. And while the per capita income of the entire region has eased up to 88 percent of the national average, rural per capita income remains static at about 75 percent, and in a number of areas has dropped to below what it was ten years ago. The number of Southerners below the poverty level has increased by 2.5 million during the 1980s (Southern Growth Policies Board, 1986b), and unemployment in many rural counties is triple that in the metro areas.

COMBATING FUNCTIONAL ILLITERACY

The difference between now and a decade ago is that even as federal economic policy and overall economic patterns have changed, the nature of the job market has changed even more drastically. Then, even many of the higher-paying jobs in manufacturing, not to mention the readily available minimum wage positions, did not require more than a grade school education. Now most of the run-of-the-mill service jobs call for skills much more advanced than before. This is really the heart of the problem. Handicapped by decades of educational neglect, one in four rural Southerners above the age of twenty-five is functionally illiterate, and in spite of considerable progress recently in improving educational quality, the region graduates fewer high school students, spends less per elementary and secondary pupil, and has an eighth-grade drop-out average twice that of the rest of the country (Southern Growth Policies Board, 1986a).

Our immediate task, then is to rescue these Southerners who have been left behind. Central to this must be an immediate and massive commitment to the reduction and ultimate elimination of adult illiteracy. Since we know that functional illiterates, even when they can find jobs, earn 44 percent less than high school graduates, it is just plain good economic sense to invest more than the $100 per adult that we are now spending on literacy programs. If even one-half of the functional illiterates in the South earned as much as a high school graduate earns, it could result in an additional $17 billion in personal income in the region (Southern Growth Policies Board, 1983).

Simultaneously we must make sure that we have produced our last generation of functional illiterates. That means that the present secondary and elementary education reforms must not leave anybody out. It also means more than improving education per se, for there is involved here a task as challenging as the school reform movement itself. The stark truth is that educational improvement will not automatically come to those who need it most unless at the same time we attack the fundamental problems that result in low educational achievement in the first place.

Here we are confronted with the crux of the dilemma. The rural areas with the most limited resources, are the places afflicted with the most pervasive problems—substandard health care and nutrition, teenage pregnancies, inadequate housing, and structural unemployment. This is where we finally have to acknowledge that those disadvantaged children of today will become the non-productive welfare-dependent adults of tomorrow and that unless we do something about it now, we shall create, perhaps irreversibly, a permanent underclass with overtones of unrest and violence that are unworthy of our heritage. With more at-risk families than the rest of the nation, the South must now make the additional investments in child care, parenting, family planning, remedial education and job training that will finally break the generational cycles of poverty and dependency that still affect so many of its citizens.

ENTREPRENEURIAL SPIRIT AND ECONOMIC DEVELOPMENT

There is yet another change that calls for new strategies for the rural South. Since the end of World War II, the region has benefited from a flood of branch plants from the North and East attracted by lower wages and lower operating costs. More than one million manufacturing jobs were created in the nonmetro areas of the South in the 50s, 60s and early 70s. Now, like the old buffalo hunts of the Western Plains, this hunt is just about over, too. No longer can we look to Northern industry to bail us out, nor should we. What should occupy us now is bringing Southern business initiative and entrepreneurship to the fore. Combining the creativity of its institutions of higher learning, including its well-developed systems of community colleges, with the homegrown business acumen of the likes of Arkansas's Sam Walton or Mississippi's Warren Hood, the rural South must now develop more of its own business and industry. This will in many cases involve the creation of new products, new services, new markets and—what may well be most important in a global economy—a new competitiveness.

What we are really talking about is the capacity to respond and adapt to change—a capacity that is based on the entrepreneurial spirit. And we must remember that in devising an economic development strategy, there are no absolute guarantees or foolproof formulas for success.

There are, however, conditions that greatly affect success in a given community. Community economic development almost always depends on the existence of local indigenous entrepreneurs—businessmen and women who have a stake in the community and who are not just passing through on the way to make a fast buck and then go somewhere else.

A local newspaper editor in the Midwest city of Kokomo, Indiana wrote that when the plants there began to close in the early 80s, "We went from being a locally owned place to being a big company place and never gave it a thought. We didn't even worry that the most important businessmen in town were suddenly guys who were waiting to move up the [corporate] ladder."

The communities that will have the soundest prospects for growth in the future will be those where a strong local entrepreneurial spirit prevails—

where relatively small, diverse locally owned businesses continue to thrive and do well. This spirit is often stimulated by negative forces. The hard times in some of the traditional industries may encourage more people to pursue their own creative business ideas and become self-employed.

The access of small businesses to capital, thus, will be more important than ever—not just in the creation of such enterprises, but in enabling established businesses to adapt to new technological and competitive circumstances. There must be progressive and resourceful financial institutions that recognize a responsibility to provide incentives and guidance to ambitious and creative but frequently unsophisticated and struggling ventures. Studies of how business start-ups are financed in this country indicate that for more than 60 percent of these, initial capital is provided by entrepreneurs themselves, by family members, or by friends. Too many rural communities in the past have been dominated by local banks committed to an ultra-conservative lending policy that insured the maintenance of the status quo. We must increase the availability in the rural areas of venture capital in order to create the new enterprises that are essential to community growth.

A number of initiatives to accomplish this are being established in several states. Arkansas, for instance, has launched a rural development bank, with initial funding made available by the Rockefeller Foundation, the Ford Foundation and other similar groups to help create new businesses in the rural areas. North Carolina has just formed the Rural Economic Development Corporation with funding from state as well as private sources. Other states have designed similar programs in recognition of both the distress and the opportunity in the rural areas.

While the number of traditional manufacturing plants locating in rural areas will undoubtedly suffer a continuing decline in future years, for those industries that do locate or remain, modernization and automation will create jobs that are more secure, more productive and better paying. A small labor force still will have the capacity to generate more spendable income. Again, the emphasis will be on increased skills and a better trained work force.

In the agricultural sector, the production of the old staple crops will give way in many situations to the raising of specialty crops with emphasis on high product quality and professional marketing. The transfer and application of technology by the schools of agriculture and the Cooperative Extension Service have already resulted in the development of many new food and fiber products. Last year, for example, Mississippi farmers earned an income of over $200 million from 220 million pounds of catfish raised on 75,000 acres—all from a crop little more than ten years in development.

A major source of new economic development lies in the areas of tourism, recreation and retirement services. Thousands of Southerners who left the farms thirty and forty years ago are now coming back to their roots and bringing with them a retirement income that provides new purchasing power in the small communities to which they return. The lower living costs and relatively simple, benign lifestyle of the rural South will serve increasingly as a base of population growth for many areas. The Ozarks of northern Arkansas and the scenic mountains of the Carolinas, Georgia, Tennessee, and Virginia are attracting both retirees and tourists in unprecedented numbers. The almost unlimited outdoor recreational opportunities afforded in the rural South are now being regarded as commercially viable resources that can contribute substantially to a community's economic base.

Many community colleges now form a unique nucleus for job creation in the areas in which they are located. In Mississippi, for example, almost all of the twenty or more campuses are in municipalities of fewer than 3,000. As such, they form an area network of adult education and retraining opportunities and an economically stabilizing force in the communities where they are located. They represent an under-utilized and under-recognized economic development force in many areas of the rural South.

Another unlikely and underestimated potential force for rural development in the future lies in the advances that have been made in telecommunications. Now the most remote hamlet has access to instant contact with the outside world via satellites and the other sophisticated facilities that permit, for example, one of the nation's most widely followed investor services to originate in rural North Georgia. Those same advances in technology enable the National Geographic Magazine to be published in its entirety in a small city in rural Northeast Mississippi. More and more there is the opportunity for the creation of compatible combinations of technological innovation with the amenities of small-town living in ways that will be increasingly attractive to many Americans weary with the traffic jams and street crime of the big cities.

THE NEED FOR VISIONARY LEADERS

In suggesting a course for the rural South, there are two additional things that need to be said. The first is that we must understand that those forces that determine national economic policy can overshadow and cancel out the best-laid strategies and decisions made at the local level. Federal fiscal policy, the deficit (and its impact on interest rates), inflation, defense spending, domestic assistance programs, farm policy, deregulation, migration, and foreign trade policies all singly and interrelatedly will have a critical impact on the future of the nonmetropolitan South. This is why those of us committed to the interests of rural communities must mobilize to influence policy at the national level that will be mindful of the precarious economic balance that exists in these areas. National policies that are not sensitive to the region's special needs can wind up creating an irreversible decline for many Southern nonmetropolitan communities in spite of all that may be attempted at the state and local level.

Still, the difference for many communities will lie in the quality of local leadership. Too often we have permitted the least creative and the least visionary to make the strategic decisions. We have fallen behind in many cases because we have relied on the "good ole boys" on the one hand or the "I've got it made" defenders of the status quo on the other. In either case, there has usually been the motivation of "what's in it for me." It is my observation that those communities which are doing the best are those which are led by bright, creative, unselfish business and political leaders who understand the realities of the world around them and who are willing to make bold and innovative choices. If that leadership does not automatically emerge in a community, strategies should be developed to identify and develop a more progressive cadre of leadership through organized training programs such as now exist in several states.

CONCLUSION

The rural South, having turned away from the old, bad days of racial segregation and political isolation, must now devote its full attention to recognizing and attacking its remaining social and economic problems. With a new generation of able and nationally respected state political leaders who have, in most Southern states, demonstrated a rare combination of idealism with a can-do ability to get things accomplished, the region, after more than a century of outside exploitation and inside bumbling, has the capacity and I believe the will to put it all together. In preserving an economically viable rural South, we shall serve not only the interests of those who live there, but in the final analysis we shall be serving the interests of the nation as well. For what is more important to our future national well-being than the maintenance of that historic cultural and social balance between a vibrant rural and urban life that is a basic and fundamental strength of the American experience?

REFERENCES

MDC, Inc. 1986. *Shadows in the Sunbelt: Developing the Rural South in an Era of Economic Change.* A Report of the MDC Panel on Rural Economic Development (May).
Southern Growth Policies Board. 1986a. *A Profile of the South.* Research Triangle Park, North Carolina.
_____. 1986b. *Equity: The Critical Link in Southern Economic Development.* Research Triangle Park, North Carolina.
_____. 1983. *Economic Survival Skills: The Aim of Adult Basic Education.* Research Triangle Park, North Carolina.

24

Improvements in The Rural South: They Won't Come Easy

Lyle P. Schertz

There is a consensus among authors of chapters in this book that (1) educational opportunities in the rural South are inadequate, (2) these inadequacies have been a brake on rural development, and (3) improvements in education are critical to substantial improvements in the rural South in the future.

The consensus of these authors is part of a larger consensus among governors, selected federal officials, and most importantly voters. The 1986 Commission on the Future of the South reminds us that growth relies more on intellect and access to an educated populace than on roads and proximity to markets. Secretary Bennett points to inadequacies of educational achievements throughout our country. And in spite of protestations by many educational leaders, he continues to garner political support for his themes. While Secretary Bennett has been unwilling to confront the need for larger funding of education, his ideas capture the imagination and the endorsement of voters—parents and others alike. The Secretary understands the aspirations of parents and children for better education.

It is difficult, however, to explain why education is receiving special attention at this particular time. Other leaders have, in the past, recognized the importance of education and parents have always aspired for better opportunities for their families. At least part of the explanation may relate to a better understanding of the very information included in this book. Educational achievements in the rural South (and in some other communities of our nation as well) are low. These condidions hamper economic development and are associated with poverty. In addition, the internationalization of our markets and the frequent comparisons by the press to the Japanese create a teachable moment that has eluded us in the past.

Regardless of the reasons for the current attention to education, it is important to recognize that it provides a unique opportunity to incorporate education—elementary, secondary, and adult—as an emphasis in rural development efforts.

The recognition of the critical role of education in rural development confronts the USDA/land grant system with critical choices. While the system has emphasized adult education, it has not dealt directly with illiteracy—an area of great need in rural America. In addition, neither the USDA nor colleges of agriculture have been closely linked to efforts to improve elementary and secondary education. To do so now would require major adjustments. However, not to do so runs the chance that other efforts on rural development will be stifled.

Social scientists have recognized over many years the importance of education. However, opportunities to seriously relate social science work to programs that gave top priority to elementary and secondary education and skill training have eluded these professions. Regardless of the response of the USDA/land grant system as a whole to the educational needs of rural America, social scientists may now have an opportunity to relate their disciplines to education and skill training. And the important question is, are social scientists—their institutions and individually—ready?

WE MAY NOT BE READY

A substantial effort to improve education in the South could benefit from inputs from many of the institutions represented by authors of chapters in this book. In fact, the effective support by such institutions may be essential if educational improvements are to be achieved in the rural South.

Specifically, it is important to ask if the USDA/land grant system is ready for an emphasis on education. Most of the institutions represented by authors in this book are in that system. It is that system that I know best, however inadequately. Other institutions are important, too. But I must look to others to contribute their insights about the potential role of these other institutions.

Is the USDA/land grant system ready? This system has emphasized farm products. Rural people have been considered but they have not been the centerpiece of the USDA/land grant system. Because of this system and how it spends its resources, there is more known about corn, cotton, and cattle—how to produce them and how to market them—than is known about ways to educate rural children, their farm and non-farm job opportunities, the costs of acquiring technical skills, and the costs associated with finding and changing employment.

If, in fact, education becomes the cornerstone of rural development, this system will be challenged to change. The response will disclose if the USDA/ land grant system is one of the people and for the people, including those disadvantaged Americans now living in rural areas of the United States.

FEDS ARE SUPPOSE TO HELP

There is a conceptual rationale for federal assistance for education. Educational expenditures change the income earning power of individuals. In our mobile and dynamic economy, the realization of incomes commensurate with education often requires moving to another community. The higher incomes are bid into higher prices for property. The adopted communities tax these higher values and use the proceeds locally even though they are traceable to the investments made in education in earlier years in faraway communities. And the federal and state governments largely preempt the collection of income taxes.

At the same time, inadequate education means wasting resources. Poorly educated people are not able to hold jobs that produce services and products people want. And in some cases, these poorly educated people have a claim on federal expenditures for farm programs, food stamps, and unemployment compensation.

Thus, there are spillover effects. Inadequate education in communities means higher federal expenditures in coping with the effects. On the other hand, better education can mean more products, services, and higher income streams in future years that can raise the nation's standard of living and competitiveness. These externalities are the basic reasons why it is good business for the federal government to assist education.

Opponents of greater federal aid for education appeal to tradition which has emphasized local financial responsibility for elementary and secondary education. But these appeals gloss over how changes in transportation and communication technologies contribute to greater mobility of people. In turn, the benefits of education accrue to communities and industries located far away from the community that paid for the education. Thus, the benefits of education accrue to the nation as a whole. In addition, the internationalization of markets means that the economic fortunes of people and communities are increasingly tied to fiscal, monetary, and military policy.

Further, the land grant system, the GI Bill, and vocational agricultural training demonstrate that in particular circumstances the involvement of the federal government in education has led to programs that have had a lasting positive effect on society.

USDA'S LEAD ROLE

The USDA has lead responsibility for rural development among federal agencies. But, while education has been recognized as important to rural development, neither the USDA nor the land grant universities have undertaken or directly supported action programs targeted on literacy and basic improvements in elementary and secondary education. Admittedly, attention to adult retraining has been greater, but it has been limited, especially in comparison to the need among rural people.

Thus, the current attention to education also raises a dilemma for the USDA/land grant system. On the one hand, the USDA/land grant system could conclude that it should not actively support improvements in education. That would mean that the critical input to rural development as seen by authors in this book, either would be provided by others, or would be left undone. And, if left undone, the effectiveness of other rural development efforts (such as credit for community facilities) would be seriously jeopardized.

Alternatively, the USDA/land grant system may decide to give emphasis, through resources and leadership, to educational improvements of rural America. This emphasis would contribute to improvements in elementary and secondary education and it would enhance the potential payoffs from related efforts to improve the welfare of rural people. At the same time, it would require many activities not previously common to the USDA/land grant system. And, in many cases, these activities would involve rural people not now part of the clientele groups of the system.

I visualize four possible roles for the USDA/land grant system: funding (discussed in a later section of this chapter); adult education, including a focus on literacy; job market information; and social science research and extension focused on the household, community, and regional economic and cultural benefits and costs associated with education.

Adult Education.

Most everyone agrees that adult education is an appropriate role for the system. A wide range of education is involved —recipes, conservation plans, production methods, marketing advice, and more—for those who can read and write. If it is appropriate to "extend" recipes, isn't it also reasonable for the same system to help people learn how to read them?

Effective development of rural communities requires not only correction of the adult illiteracy problem but also the training of adults in skills needed in local, as well as more distant labor markets. These efforts would benefit the individual families. In addition they would facilitate the movement of people out of farming and in turn increase returns for those who remain in farming.

Job Information

USDA regularly produces statistics. The emphasis is on commodities—acres, yields, production, marketings, stocks, exports, and prices. In contrast, if a rural resident—any place in this country—wanted to consider alternative employment to farming, or unskilled employment in a small rural town, where would he/she go for information? Such a person would want to at least know wage levels in various locations for people with different skills. The individual would be interested in the supply/demand balance in these locations for different skills, the costs of acquiring such skills, and the costs of transferring from one location to another.

Difficult tasks? Of course. But it is important to remember that as a society we regularly spend resources so that farmers can ascertain not only prices for corn in different markets, but prices for different grades of corn, as well as the weekly, if not daily, movements of the commodity. Further, the USDA/ land grant system expends large amounts of resources attempting to anticipate commodity supply, demand, and price conditions for the future. Should less be done for rural human resources than is done for commodities?

The Role of Social Scientists

While an emphasis on education would have implications for most components of the USDA/land grant system, they are perhaps greatest for social scientists. These implications hold even if the USDA/land grant system opts not to embrace educational improvements. Social scientists can serve a pivotal role in making education a cornerstone of rural development in the near term and in garnering a sustained resource commitment to such an orientation.

What is being done by social scientists to support such a thrust? To ask the question is to answer it. Not much. Or at least not enough. How do we respond to a governor or a secretary of agriculture who asks what difference would it make if $5 billion of commodity support money were used for education and skill training instead? For whom? Do we know? Are we trying to address the question? How large would a program have to be and for how many years to realize a 10 percentage points drop in illiteracy in the rural South?

In thinking about the potential of a political consensus and sustaining support of programs reflecting this consensus, I am impressed with the importance of information in a democratic country with a free press. That is why social scientists are pivotal in a rural development educational focus. Three thrusts for social science research and extension are of great importance:

Quantification of relationships. There is a critical set of relationships that need investigating. For example, how does education affect economic development—job creation and incomes in rural communities? Chapters in this book are important steps in developing adequate answers. More needs doing.

Measurement of educational achievements. Sustained implementation of any program requires monitoring important target variables. This is particularly important for programs that must be sustained over many years if they are to be effective. Ineffective program provisions will need to be exposed and changed. New provisions will similarly need monitoring. In order to do this, it is important to measure quality of educational achievements, as well as the usual quantity variable—number of years of schooling completed.

Measurement of underemployment. Measuring underemployment of human resources in rural America is important to a major assault on educational inadequacies. A significant part of this country's human resources could be contributing services and products to society. This would not only raise the standard of living of these individuals, but that of the rest of us. This, of course, is the basic economic rationale for an emphasis on education in rural America.

In terms of potential program interest and sustained support, the measurement of underemployment is akin to the comparison of per family income of farmers to that of nonfarm families. The charting of these income comparisons initiated in the Bureau of Agricultural Economics many years ago (and continued until recently by the Economic Research Service), symbolized the purpose of farm commodity programs and the need to transfer incomes from urban to farm people.

Similarly, the regular announcement of the number of unemployed auto workers symbolizes the goal of full employment of industrial workers. It helps focus attention and helps renew commitments to creating jobs in urban areas. At least it did in earlier years.

The measurement of underemployment is difficult. To do it effectively on a monthly basis by counties, or at least major substate regions, will necessitate substantial resources. But such information is critical if public support for improved education is to be mobilized and subsequently sustained.

IT WON'T BE EASY

These kinds of information and the quantification of relationships will require a great deal of effort. On the one hand, an emphasis on education is a very big umbrella that probably would permit most social scientists to continue whatever they want to do. However, a policy emphasis on education would also imply making the work relevant to education. In some cases, because of the limited availability of resources, a policy emphasis on education would require a redirection of our effort.

Overall, it would not be business as usual. There would be more resources for information and analysis, but there would be continued pressure to produce timely and relevant material useful in deciding how to use program resources more wisely so that literacy is enhanced, skills upgraded, and people find productive activities that provide satisfactory incomes.

AVOIDING COMMUNITY IN SPACE SYNDROME

Making education the cornerstone of rural development efforts has significant implications for how society thinks about rural development, as well as how more traditional programs are implemented. In particular, there are implications for the concept of "community" as used in a spatial context. Many rural development programs embrace, either explicitly or implicitly, the notion that all communities should be saved. Such an emphasis leads to organizing programs whereby all communities are entitled to money in behalf of rural development. Emphasis on fire protection, sewage treatment, medical care facilities, modernizing main street, and credit for such programs are the consequences of this kind of orientation.

The outcome of such an orientation is that all communities share in rural development resources. But in the end, there are inadequate resources where it counts. This emphasis on community and space reflects the reality that no one, whether they be an educator, program administrator, or elected official, has the wisdom or the courage to say which communities "deserve" to live and thrive and which ones should be allowed to die.

But we all know that changes in communication and transportation technologies, and the vicissitudes of markets (especially due to their internationalization), make it uneconomic to sustain some communities. The effects of these technological and market forces will, in many cases, overwhelm whatever government programs can do. Simply put, some communities will die—slowly, but certainly.

Note how an emphasis on education changes the perspective about community. Education and skill training changes the income earning power of people. These individuals search for better income earning opportunities. Firms search for individuals with better skills and training. The outcome is a mix of people moving to available jobs—urban and rural—and business investments in old and in new communities—urban and rural. Entrepreneurial activities occur in all communities by individuals, public officials, and industrial managers as they search for ways to optimize their situations in response to changes in technology, the internationalization of markets, and their own wealth, education, and skills. These entrepreneurial activities, of course, include closing some plants, keeping others open, building still others, and people moving. An emphasis on education leads to changes in the dynamics of communities. Some die, some remain static, others grow as a result of many different decisions by countless individuals. Federal government decisions that subsidize sewer systems become relatively less important. The emphasis on education essentially says, give individuals the skills and mental capacity to operate effectively in our society, let these individuals optimize with respect to their employment and where they want to live, and let them make decisions as to where investments should be made. In turn, adjustments with respect to number, size, and location of communities, in say the year 2010, will reflect the multitude of decisions made by these individuals.

A PRACTICAL REASON FOR USDA INVOLVEMENT

The obvious question is "where would financial resources come from for an emphasis on elementary and secondary education in rural America?" Several facts are relevant to the answer. USDA has the lead responsibility for rural development in the federal government. People increasingly recognize the important role of elementary and secondary education yet, these are generally considered the responsibility of local and state governments. The outlook for local revenues in rural areas is discouraging since farm land values have declined substantially and federal revenue sharing has eroded. Primary federal responsibility for education is with the Department of Education. And, the federal deficit is overwhelmingly large.

A major consideration is the availability of increased resources for elementary and secondary education, as well as adult training. The increases will be sufficient only if the public understands what authors of this book have written—education in the rural South is inadequate, its improvement is critical to rural development, and these conditions adversely affect the nation as a whole.

The social scientists in the system have a special responsibility to develop useful information on the importance of education, as argued earlier. But in addition, department heads, deans, faculty, USDA officials, and the press have special responsibilities to see that rural people understand current educational conditions and what can be done, with what effects.

Financial resources may be inadequate unless responsibility for changing these conditions is shared with a federal department that feels an allegiance to rural people and has the potential flexibility to shift funds among programs.

In this context, it is useful to recall the significant increases in the funding of food stamp programs. During the 1970s, funds were shifted from traditional farm programs to food stamp programs. Ardent supporters of food stamp programs wanted the program transferred from the USDA to HEW, as did several Departmental officials. However, the fact that the program was kept in the Department of Agriculture, I am satisfied, made it possible for the food stamp program to be larger in the 1970s than it would have been if it had been transferred. The White House could more easily force reallocation of funds within the Department than to first collect program savings from USDA and then re-allocate them to HEW for food stamps. There are limits to the number of decisions that can be made at the White House and management time available to see that the decisions are implemented is scarce.

This line of thinking raises the question of "availability" of the commodity program funds for other government programs in or out of the Department. Again, one cannot be sure. However, two possibilities exist. Both have low probabilities. One is a turnaround in the commodity markets. The second is a decoupling of support for farmers from production. Both possibilities could free up some funds for other purposes or reduction of the budget deficit.

Increases in commodity market prices would lead to lower deficiency payments since these payments are tied directly to differences between market prices and the target prices. If reactions to individual large commodity program payments make decoupling a reality, it may be that departmental officials and related congressional committees will be looking for ways to broaden their clientele groups. Effective emphasis on education for rural development is one possible alternative.

Government-held farm commodities could be used to finance education in rural America. At the present time, government farm commodity stocks are used to compensate farmers for participating in USDA programs. Farmers receive generic commodity certificates for their participation. The certificates are negotiable. The person receiving them can exchange them for USDA held commodities which can, in turn, be sold in the market, or the certificates can be sold to others who, in turn, can exchange the certificates for USDA commodities. Similarly, if education improvement were deemed as important as supporting farm income, generic commodity certificates could be issued to institutions contributing to education of rural Americans.

SILENT REVOLUTIONS

It is important that leaders who support an emphasis on education understand the fundamentals of what they embrace. This kind of understanding facilitates clear thinking in setting goals and measuring progress.

In this context, remember that upgrading the education system of the rural South and other rural areas of our nation involves changing the distribution of real wealth in America and thus, the distribution of related income flows. Investment in human capital means higher wages and incomes for those who obtain better education and improved skills. It should not necessarily mean, however, lower incomes for others. However, in some extreme cases it may.

Now, I do not suggest that social scientists concentrating on information related to education wear revolutionary fatigues or wave revolutionary flags. But I do suggest that everyone keep in mind the fundamentals—education involves changing the distribution of wealth—human capital in this case—and related income flows. An emphasis on education essentially says that some people have inadequate opportunities for education. Their incomes are inadequate because their education is deficient. And, there ought to be public programs—local, state, and/or federal—to facilitate changes in these conditions.

The full, but silent, understanding of the revolutionary nature of these kinds of changes may sound strange to many. But they would not be to those who visualized the creation of the USDA/land grant system. Those revolutionaries also perceived a disadvantaged group—farmers. They also embraced education as a way to change the economic lot of farmers. Educational opportunities were to reach the most disadvantaged through the creation of the department of agriculture and the creation of land grant universities in every state.

Many people owe much to the system that these silent revolutionaries created. Now, over 100 years later, we are saying that educational achievements in important parts of rural America do not measure up to the challenges ahead. If we are serious about rural development, the education systems must change. Are we, social scientists and others, ready?

Index